Wolfgang Menzel

Germany from the earliest period

Vol. 1

Wolfgang Menzel

Germany from the earliest period
Vol. 1

ISBN/EAN: 9783337724351

Printed in Europe, USA, Canada, Australia, Japan

Cover: Foto ©ninafisch / pixelio.de

More available books at **www.hansebooks.com**

GERMANY

FROM THE

EARLIEST PERIOD

BY

WOLFGANG MENZEL

TRANSLATED FROM THE FOURTH GERMAN EDITION
By MRS. GEORGE HORROCKS

WITH A SUPPLEMENTARY CHAPTER OF RECENT EVENTS
By EDGAR SALTUS

VOLUME I

NEW YORK
PETER FENELON COLLIER
MDCCCXCIX

LIST OF ILLUSTRATIONS

GERMANY

VOL. I.

Frontispiece—Capture of Frederick the Handsome at Muehlberg .
Nuremberg . . . .
Cologne . . . .

THE HISTORY OF GERMANY

FIRST PERIOD

HEATHEN ANTIQUITY

PART I

ORIGIN AND MANNERS OF THE ANCIENT GERMANS

I. *The Primitive Forests of Germany*

BEFORE Germany was peopled, the country appears to have been almost entirely covered with primitive forests. When the Romans, not long before the birth of Christ, became acquainted with these regions, they already contained a numerous population, although at that period but little of the ancient forests seems to have been cleared away; according to their account, the great Hercinian Forest then extended from the Black Forest across the whole of Germany, and the inhabitants, a mere hunter-race, only practiced the arts of husbandry when driven by extreme necessity. The forests were held sacred, and temples were erected on consecrated lakes, hidden in their secluded depths unprofaned by the hand of man. Similar sacred groves were found by Herodotus in the country of the Budini to the north of the Black Sea, and they were introduced by Hyperboreans into Greece; for instance, the sacred grove of Delphi, the famous Grecian oracle. In northern mythology, the ash tree (ygdrasill) is emblematical of the whole earth, and the first men, *esche*, ash, and *erle*, alder, also take their names from trees; hence particular trees were held sacred throughout Germany, nor has this ancient veneration yet entirely passed away.

The Romans regarded the forests of Germany with superstitious dread. There were said to be gigantic trees which, when hollowed into boats, held thirty men, and through the arches formed by their projecting roots a horseman could ride at full speed. The buffalo, the bison, and the elk, once numerous in these wilds, have now totally disappeared; and the bears, whose skins were the chief article of the dress of our forefathers, the wolves, boars, and innumerable other large game, daily become more scarce. The country possessed neither towns, roads, nor bridges, and it is easily conceivable that, dissatisfied with their meager forest fare, the people continually migrated to and took possession of the fruitful lands of neighboring nations. Solitude created a desire, or romantic longing, in the breast of the ancient inhabitant of these wilds, for what was distant and unknown, while the habits of the chase rendered him enterprising and hardy. The laws founded upon personal freedom, the virtuous manners and cheerful temperament of the ancient German, originated in those mighty wastes, where, forced to trust to his own resources, man necessarily became independent, and was secure from the corruption incidental to crowded communities. These wild forests also attached an idea of the marvelous, so novel to the Romans, to the character of the German, who, trained to war by the habits of the chase, associated piety with ferocity, and would still listen to the secret voice of Nature in the mysterious whisperings of the forest, now disposing him to deep musings, now creating strange forebodings, which were recognized as true prophetic inspiration in the women and maidens.

When Germany was first Christianized, the monks undertook to clear away the forests and to promote agriculture, and as the migrations had then ceased, those of the inhabitants who had remained in the country were gradually forced by necessity to exchange the life of the hunter for that of the peasant. Yet, notwithstanding this, and the great increase of population during succeeding centuries, a very considerable portion of these primitive forests still remains, and the stranger, who for the first time visits our country, still wonders at their extent; nor have the great union of states and the customs of city life been able to eradicate the ancient forest freedom, the love of nature, and the loyal character of our ancestors.

II. *Origin of the Germans*

WHO first trod the sacred forest? who for the first time rested beneath the shade of the German oak? The earliest account of the German people is very obscure. Civilized nations, distinguished by mighty deeds, had already long dwelt on the shores of the Mediterranean, while our northern land was still unknown. History, though still in its infancy, already recorded the vicissitudes of empires, while in our dark forests legendary lore still held its superstitious reign. Already had the sages of the East taught wisdom beneath the palm, the merchants of Phœnicia and Carthage weighed anchor and spread their purple sails on the distant ocean, the Greek beautified the earth with magic art, and the Roman founded his colossal and iron despotism, while the German, ignorant and naked, was still reigning undisturbed over the denizens of the wild. The first authentic account of the Germans dates scarcely a century before the birth of Christ, when the Romans first came in conflict with them. Before this period, their history is mere legendary fable, which, however, a peculiar character pervades. From this epoch the southern nations regarded them as a free and warlike nation. It has been attempted to unravel the genealogy of nations by referring them to the first book of Moses; and sometimes Gomer (Cimbri), with his sons, Ashkenaz (the Saxon Ascan), Riphath (the Frankish Ripuarii), and Togarmah (Germanii); sometimes Aram (Irmin, Hermiones), with his sons, Uz (the Asiatics), Hul or Chul (the Gauls), Gethen (Geten or Goths), and Masch (Massagetæ), have been supposed to be the ancestors of the German tribes; but these are mere nomenclatory hypotheses, by which we can arrive at no certainty. To this class also belongs the derivation of the Nibelungen from Niphilim.

There are clearer indications of an eastern origin, and traces of an affinity between our language and that of ancient India are still perceivable. Wodan, who was worshiped by the Germans as the father of the gods, is the Indian Buddha, the father of the twelve Diti, who, for a thousand years, fought against the Indian gods, and were driven into exile. Many are of opinion that Buddha was the most ancient and the only god of the Indians, until the religion of Brahma, together with the division into castes (hereditary privileges), was introduced, and the Brahmins, or caste of priests, usurped the whole authority. It is certain that, after this, the lower castes rebelled against the priests, and chose a new Buddha for their god, who is still worshiped in some parts of India. From the warlike castes, who thence migrated northward, may have sprung those brave and warlike nations met with, at a later period, in the north, as worshipers of Wodan, or Odin, from whom the German tribes trace their descent.[1]

In the oldest records of the German language, the Anten or Inten are often spoken of as an ancient nation, and particular buildings and weapons are mentioned as "works of the Anten." The word is also traceable in the names of places and people—Ant, Ango, Ent, Eng, Int, Intto, Indo—and India, in the German of the Middle Ages, is written Endia. See Mone's Derivations. The Grecian fable of Deucalion. Deucalion and his wife Pyrrha alone survived

---

[1] The Grecian fable of the Titans is somewhat similar. Chronos and the twelve Titans fought against Jupiter and the younger gods, and were destroyed by the thunderbolts of Jove. Chronos fled to Boreas in the Caucasus, whose highest mountain still bears the name of Elboreas. Prometheus, the eldest of the Titans, who stole the fire from heaven, was chained by offended Jupiter, for a thousand years, to the rocks of the Caucasus. The nations that, in the third century after Christ, under the name of Zenones, issued from the interior of Germany, and crossing the Danube overran Italy and Greece, were called by the Greeks, "The descendants of the Titans."

the flood. They threw stones behind them, whence sprang a new race of men, the Heraclidian wanderers, who peopled the country to the west of the Caucasus. To this many German legends bear resemblance. Tacitus heard, from the Germans on the Rhine, that the common ancestor of their people was called Thuisko or Thuisto, and sprang out of the earth. His son, Mammus, had three sons, from whom the principal tribes of Germany, the Ingavones, Hermiones, and Istavones, sprang. According to Pliny, the Cauci, Chaubi, or Chauci (from Caucasus), whom we meet with later as the Saxons, belong to the first. But the ancient Saxons had a legend that their nation, with their first king Ascan (perhaps Asian Khan, or Prince of Asia), originally sprang from the Harz Mountains. According to an old legend of the north, Buri, the father of the Asiatics, was licked out of a rock of salt by the sacred cow. With this agrees the northern legend, mentioned by Snorri, concerning the migration of the Asiatics, whose progenitor, Buri, dwelt at Asgard (Boreas in the Caucasus). His son, Bor, had three sons, Wile, We, and Odin (Wodan). The last, being driven by the gods out of the country, wandered through Gardaric (Russia) and Saxony to Sweden, where he founded Sigtuna (Upsala), as his new seat of government.

Other accounts of migrations seem to own a different origin. The chronicler, Hunibald, describes the Franks as fugitives, who wandered as far as the Rhine after the destruction of Troy, and who there founded Zante (so called from the Trojan river Zanthus). The old Saxon chroniclers ascribe the origin of the Saxons to deserters from the army of Alexander the Great, who fled to the country of Hadel. They have even discovered an affinity between the wanderings of Ulysses and of Æneas after the fall of Troy and the god Odin, and between his son, the first Saxon leader, Ascan, and Ascanius, the son of Æneas. The legends of Hercules, who is said to have visited Germany, and to have been honored there as a god, are even more obscure.

III. The Dark Ages

THOSE tribes which, at a later period, were classed under the general name of "Germans," were formerly known under separate names, and it is now impossible to distinguish them exactly from each other.—According to the earliest accounts of the Greeks, the Scythians, a simple-mannered and brave people, divided into several tribes, dwelt to the north of the Black Sea. It has been supposed that their name signifies "marksmen," and that they were, if not all, at least partly, Germans. Neither the Persian kings, nor Alexander the Great, were able to subdue them. The Greeks named the northern nations, on the other side of the great chain of mountains extending from Caucasus, by Hæmus, to the Alps, and dividing the south from the north of Europe, Hyperboreans, *i.e.*, people who dwelt beyond the abode of Boreas (the north wind). They also regarded them as "the most long-lived and the most just among mankind."

Somewhat later we hear of the Celts. They were supposed to dwell to the west of the Scythians, and the intermediate nation was named Celto Scythian. Their name has been sometimes supposed to signify "Heroes," and they are described as being extremely brave. The most remarkable of the Celtic tribes were the Cimmerii or Cimbri, who, migrating from the far west, from England and Denmark, where traces of them have been discovered, invaded Asia Minor and Italy. Their name was supposed to signify "Warrior."

I do not venture to quote the numerous legends of these northern tribes; in the first place, because they are merely a confused heap of religious notions and historical facts; in the second, because they have been only handed down to us by strangers, or by poets, those patrons of the marvelous; and thirdly, because it is impossible to distinguish how much is essentially German in the legends of the Scythians, the Hyperboreans, the Celts, and the Cimbri.

Under the name of Scythian are evidently comprehended not only the German, but also the Slavonian and Tartar races, now dwelling eastward of us.

To the Hyperboreans apparently belonged, not only the German, but also the Finnish races in Lapland, Finland, Courland, Esthonia, Livonia, and Lithuania, who were driven by the Germans to the icy northern cape, and to the rocky inlets of the Baltic.

Although there were many tribes that, notwithstanding their German origin, were generally comprised under the name of Celti, yet this name in reality belongs to another and a perfectly distinct nation, that migrated at an earlier period, and of whose peculiar language slight indications may still be traced in Scotland, Ireland, Wales, and Brittany. The Gauls, the Gælic and Welsh tribes, are the people whom we now commonly designate Welschen, Italians. Along the course of the Danube there are places that still retain their ancient Gallic names, none of which are to be met with further north. The Cimmerii who dwelt in England, the Ambrones on the Rhone, the Umbri in Italy, were all apparently of Gælic origin; and yet the Cimbri, conjointly with the Teutones, who dwelt at the mouths of the Elbe, and migrated into Italy, were apparently of pure German descent, and the Sicambri are well known to have been German Franks.

The Greeks never distinguished the German tribes from their neighbors by any particular name, and it was not until after the birth of Christ that they are mentioned under the new name of Germani by the Romans. The Latin word *Germanus* means brother, but the word may also be a German one, and signify a warrior, by which a number of secondary meanings are admissible, for instance, *guerre*, war; *ger*, a lance; *heer*, an army; *ehre*, honor; *gewehr*, security.

These Latin names were again lost amid the migrations of nations, when the Roman empire fell. Then innumerable new names appear, but no general designation, so that it is matter of doubt whether several tribes belonged to the German or Slavonian nations. After the great irruptions of the different tribes, many of the lesser ones disappeared, and were comprehended under the common designations of Goths, Franks, Bavarians, Germans, Thuringians, Burgundians, Longobardi, Angli, Saxons, Danes, Swedes, and Norwegians. It was not until the reign of Charlemagne that all these nations received the general denomination of Germans. The word *Thiot*, Diet, in the old German tongue, signifies the people. Before the time of Charlemagne, the Germans did not compose one nation, but were divided into distinct communities, allied by common descent, but politically independent of each other; so that they could not be classed under one name until they formed one nation.

IV. *The Division of the Germans into Separate Tribes*

THE bond by which the different nations of Germany were united, was formerly, as now, of very frail tenure, and even when drawn closer was ever liable to sever. The reason obviously lies in the national character, which, of too expansive a nature ever to be uniform, displays an infinite variety of striking peculiarities, differing according to the natural bias of the individual; hence, in ancient times, the unalterable love of freedom, and the wild chivalric spirit which animated our forefathers, who, equally independent and regardless of their native country, achieved single-handed the most daring exploits; hence, in our times, the extraordinary variety of talented individuals engaged in intellectual warfare as zealously as the German in times of yore in bodily combat. The consciousness of great physical strength produced a spirit of independence and a native indifference to danger which struck the Romans with astonishment, and which, by inducing a blind reliance on their own strength, caused the Teutons to weaken themselves by internal feuds, or with listless apathy to view each other's destruction. None pitied the vanquished. If nine fell, the tenth was confident of gaining success by the prowess of his single arm. The greater the slaughter of his brethren by the enemy, the fewer the competitors for glory, and so much the greater honor to the victor. Thus, instead of a neighbor being assisted as a friend, he was only regarded as a rival in heroic deeds; so that the action that would now be considered as the vilest perfidy was deemed by our forefathers the height of chivalric virtue; and it was not until the Romans had taken great advantage of this error that they discovered that their safety depended upon their acting in unison. But when danger no longer threatened, their ancient prejudices again produced disunion, and it was only when the evil was universally felt that they could be induced to enter into a bond of mutual protection. The forest life of the primitive Germans was one of the primary causes of this want of union; all intercourse in those immense and savage tracts being restricted to the nearest neighbors, as neither roads nor commerce existed as a means of communication between the more distant tribes.

In the first century after Christ, two Romans, Tacitus the historian, who makes honorable mention of our nation, and Pliny the great naturalist, wrote a genealogical account of the different tribes; which, according to Tacitus, descended from Thuisko, whose son Mammus was the common ancestor of the Ingavones, Hermiones, and Istavones; the first of whom are placed by Pliny on the North Sea; the second, in the interior of Germany; and the third, on the Rhine. He moreover mentions two great German nations, the Vendili on the Baltic, and the Peucini on the island of Peuce, at the mouth of the Danube in Hungary.

Thuisko is evidently an epithet derived from *Thuit*, *Thiot*, the people; like Mannisko, from *Mann*, a man; and nothing further is discoverable beyond the subdivision of these great nations into tribes. Whether Thuisko was also honored as a god, and was identical with Wodan, is not of much import with regard to the genealogy of these nations. He has been supposed to be the same as the Egyptian god

Thoth-Hermes, to whom Odin bears much resemblance in his works of invention, and the Romans in fact assimilate him with Mercury or Hermes, a name resembling that of the German deity Irmin, and that of the Hermiones.

About A.D. 1100, the monk Nestor, the earliest Russian chronicler, divided the Veragri or Scandinavians, who conquered Russia, into Suiones, Urmanni, Inglani, and Gothi. Could he have intended under these names to designate the Swedes, the Normans, the inhabitants of Ingermanland and Gothland, or did he refer to the yet earlier division of all the German tribes, as recorded by Tacitus and Pliny? An old manuscript in the Vatican library mentions Ermenius, Ingo, and Esco as the ancestors of the Germans, who in the sixth century are named by Nennius, the Englishman, Hisicio, Armeno, and Mugio.

These ancient names were soon lost amid the migrations of the tribes. In the north, the Ingavones gave place to the Saxons; in the west, the Istavones to the Franks; in the east and south, the Hermiones to the Goths, who, being the most considerable of the migratory tribes, gained the upper hand, and were consequently at enmity with each other. The hatred existing between the brother-nations is recorded in our old warlike legends, in which the Franks are called the Nibelungen; the Saxons, the Hegelingen; and the Goths, the Walfinger.

Gaupp has very ingeniously sought to refer all the German tribes to two original sources, the Suevi and the Non-Suevi, or High and Low Dutch. Under the denomination of Suevi he comprehends Suevi, Alemanni, Bavarians, Burgundians, Goths, Alani, Vandals, Gepidæ, originally wandering shepherd tribes attracted by the superiority of the country, and consisting of nobles, freemen and slaves, who, when converted to Christianity, embraced Arianism, which formed a still stronger bond between them, and more broadly distinguished them from the Non-Suevi, under which denomination he classes the Franks, Saxons, Lombards, Thuringians, and Frieslanders, who first practiced husbandry, had settled dwellings, and were divided into only one class of freemen, and two classes of bondsmen, Lazzi and Slavi or Servi, and who professing Catholicism were united, by a common faith, against the Arian Suevi. The whole of these divisions are apparently correct, nor are they contradictory. The Suevi collected into enormous masses, while the Non-Suevi separated, on account of their having fixed habitations, into numerous and much smaller tribes, of which the Romans have specified an enormous number, which, taken in the aggregate, may formerly have simply belonged to two great sources, the Istavones and Ingavones, who, at a later period, subdivided in a similar manner in Franconia and Saxony. Among the Hermiones, Tacitus first mentions the Suevi, to whom the Vendili or Peucini of Pliny doubtless belonged as Gothic tribes in the east. Thus the old account perfectly coincides with the modern mode of division. Many of the tribes were totally exterminated by intestine wars or during migration; many, on the contrary, raised themselves by their bravery from insignificance to considerable power; some incorporated themselves with nations to which they did not originally belong, as, for instance, the Lombards, who, severing themselves from the Suevi, united with the Saxons; finally, an intermixture of races took place, as in the case of the New Thuringians, who were some of Frankish, others of Suevian (Varini) origin.

The German tribes may with great justice be compared to a swarm of bees. The mere love of fighting occasioned continual wars between them, either on the pretext of defending their frontiers from the aggressions of their neighbors, or for the purpose of extending them; and they had the custom of sending the young men, whenever the population became too numerous for the soil, annually forth to seek an existence in foreign lands, so that the surplus of their warlike population was unceasingly pouring across the frontiers. The earliest and numerous migratory hordes, traveling from north to south, were apparently also German adventurers, such as the Cimmerii, Boii, and Senones; and in later times, the Cimbri and Teutones; the Suevi, under Ariovistus; the Marcomanni, Quadi, Getæ, and Bastarnæ. The opposition they met with from the Romans appears to have turned them eastward; a circumstance which perhaps reveals the origin of the immense empire founded by the Goth, Hermanarich, between the Baltic and the Black Sea. These fierce nations again poured with irresistible fury from the north to the south and west; opposition proved unavailing, and Goths, Alani, Vandals, Burgundians, Longobardi, Alemanni, Franks, Angli, and Saxons, spread like a torrent over the whole Roman empire. It was some time after this migration of these enormous multitudes before a large mass could again collect for a similar purpose in Germany, where they began to congregate into cities; when the surplus population again took possession of the Slavonian countries, which were conquered in the times of the crusades, and colonized the shores of the Baltic. Since that period the destructive religious wars prevented a too great increase of population, and filled Holland and the distant colonies with thousands, who fled thither from persecution at home; and within the last century several hundred thousands of German adventurers have gradually settled in America, on the Wolga, and in other parts of the world.

In their native country, the Ancient Germans were distinguished by the epithet of "Free," from the bondsmen, who apparently were not of German origin. These Sclavi (Slavi, Slavonians or Servi, Serbi or Servii) were doubtless prisoners taken from our Slavonian neighbors in the east. The other bondsmen, who rented their property from and were protected by a freeman, were called Lazzi, Lati, or Liti, in Germany, and Aldi, among the Longobardi in Italy. It is still uncertain whether, like the Sclavi or Servi, they were originally a conquered people, or whether the name is derived from the word *lassen*, to let (*freigelassenen*, those let free), or from *laz*, the last or lowest. The Longobardian *Aldi* evidently signifies the ancient (*alten*) and conquered inhabitants of the country.

V. *The Suevian Tribes*

SNORRI STURLESON, the earliest historian of the north, who wrote in the German (Icelandish) tongue, divides the ancient world into three parts, Asia, Suithiod, and Europe.[1] Tacitus also says that the Suevi possessed by far the greater part of Germany. Greek ships that visited the shores of the Baltic for the purpose of collecting amber, about three centuries B.C., brought back accounts of the Suiones in modern Sweden, of the mountain Sewo between Sweden and Norway, and of the Suevian Sea, the Baltic. The ancient name is still preserved in those of Swabia and Switzerland. The Hungarians call all Germans Swabians. It is impossible to discover whether the name was taken from *see*, the sea, or from *schweifen*, to roam about; on account of their nomad mode of existence, or from the long hanging *haar schweifen*, tails of hair, worn by them tied together behind the head, and which formed part of their national costume.

Fifty years B.C., when Julius Cæsar for the first time led his legions to the Rhine, he found the western Germans (Non-Suevi) under great apprehension on account of the numerical superiority of their eastern neighbors, the Suevi. From them he learned that they were divided into a hundred districts, each of which annually sent forth a thousand warriors, who migrated in one vast horde. A century later, Tacitus mentions these hundred districts, but says that the Semnones, the most ancient and the most considerable tribe of the Suevi, was the only one so divided, exclusively of the numerous other Suevian tribes.

The Semnones, and their allies the Boii, overran Greece and Italy at a much earlier period, settled in the north of Italy, and after a long and difficult struggle (the wars of the Samnites) were vanquished by the Romans. Their name resembles that of the royal race of Saming, the son of Odin,

---

.[1] Suithiod, the extensive country of the Suevi, lay between Asia and Europe.

the Samingri, in Norway. The same may be said of Samland. Perhaps the name may also be traced in that of the Cenni (Sens, Senn, shepherds in the Alps), who, Anno Domini 300, joined the Catti and Hermunduri and opposed the Romans.

A remarkable accordance exists between the names of the places and of the nations situated on the extreme verge of the north and the south of ancient Suithiod. In the north, the Suiones or Swedes, the Samingri and Samlanders, with the Guttones or Goths, Danes and Cimbri. In the south, the Swabians and the Swiss, the Semnones and Cenni, with the Getæ as far as the Danube; the Cimmerii, Umbri, etc. Besides these, there are the Gælic names which are evidently anterior to the German migrations. Snorri relates, that Odin found Norway already peopled, and that a nation called the Vani gave place to the German Vandali, who in their turn were replaced by the Slavonian Vendi. Again, we find in the south the names of Noricum (which may perhaps be also traced in those of Nördlingen and Nuremberg), and Vindelicia, in Augusta Vindelicorum, now Augsburg; also in Venice, the Vendian boundary. In the north, we find the worship of Thor, who was held in peculiar reverence by the Gælic and Finnish tribes, and who is anterior to Odin; and in the south, we meet with the Taurisci in the Alps, the Thurgau, etc. There also exists some similarity in name and language between the Lettish tribes in the north, and the Latins (whence the Latin or Roman tongue) in the south.

Tacitus mentions all the Suevian nations by the general name of Hermiones, a name that again appears in that of the Hermunduri, who dwelt in modern Thuringia, and in that of Ariminum (Rimini), a city founded by the Samnites in Italy. The German deity, Irmin, and the celebrated column of Irmen, a relic of paganism, destroyed by Charlemagne, show the same connection, and again call to mind the similarity between Hermes, Thoth, and Thuisko.

Besides the Hermunduri, other nations were said to belong to the Hermiones: the Cherusci in the Harz Mountains, the Catti in Hesse, the Longobardi on the Middle Elbe, the Marcomanni and Quadi on the Danube, besides several petty tribes in the direction of the Oder and the Baltic, who are buried in complete obscurity.

Pliny distinguished the numerous Gothic tribes by the generic names of Vendili on the Baltic, and Peucini on the Danube, from the more westerly Hermiones. The Peucini lay nearest to Asia, their native land, and took their name from an island supposed to have been held sacred, and which possibly may have had some connection with that of Samothrace, where the religions of the north and of Greece intermingled, or with the oracle of Delphi in Greece, which was founded by Hyperboreans in the earlier ages of antiquity. Zamolxis, the sage, who first taught the doctrine of the immortality of the soul, dwelt, at a very remote period, among the Getæ, the principal nation of the Peucini. These German tribes on the Danube were first subdued by Darius, the Persian king, and afterward by Alexander the Great. They consisted of Getæ, Daci, and Bastarnæ, and were in alliance with the Marcomanni in Bohemia, Böhmen, or Bojenheim, the ancient birthplace of the Boii.

The Quadi and Cenni defended the shores of the Danube against the Romans, who, at an earlier period, met with similar opposition from the Boii, and their constant allies, the Senones.

When the northern Vendili, consisting of Goths, Vandals, Burgundians, Alani, Gepidæ, Heruli, Rugii, etc., migrated to the south, overspread the ancient Roman empire, gave new inhabitants to Italy, France, Spain, and even to the north of Africa, the whole of ancient Suithiod, from the Elbe to the Vistula, was left bare, until repeopled by fresh Slavonian settlers.

The Suevi, who remained in Upper Germany, received the name of Alemanni, which is still preserved in that of the Swabian *Almanden*, public property, and evidently means all, or all sorts of men. The French call the Germans Allemands. The Bavarian Hessians, and a part of the Thuringians, were also originally Suevi, and Austria, when retaken by them from its Slavonian settlers, was again Germanized. Thus the whole of modern southern Germany is Suevian, and still makes use of the common High German or Dutch (oberdeutsch) tongue, though the long separation has rendered it very different to that spoken in the north of Sweden, with which it was once nearly allied.

VI. *The Tribes of Lower Germany*

THE Istavones were the Franks on the Rhine; the Ingavones, the Saxons on the North Sea; they always remained in their ancient dwelling-places, although they also sent forth immense hordes, which some centuries before Christ, under the name of Cimbri and Teutones, spread terror throughout Italy, and, at a later period, repeopled France and England. To the Istavones, who afterward appear as the Franks, belonged, most particularly, the Sicambri, Tencteri, Usipetes, Ubii, Marsi, Ampsibari, Angrivarii, Chamavi, Mattiaci, etc., on the Lower Rhine. The other small tribes on the Upper Rhine, the Nemetes, Vangiones, Triboci, Latobrigi, Rauraci; and on the Moselle and in the Netherlands, the Nervii, Treveri (Treves) and Belgæ (Netherlands), to which the Menapii, Marini, Gugerni, Eburones, Caninefates, and Batavians also belonged; all of which were certainly not of Suevian origin.

To the Ingavones belonged the Cimbri and Teutones, who migrated to the south; the Chauci, who afterward appear as the Saxons; the Frisii, Fasi, Dulgibines, Ambrones, Tubantes, etc.

Snorri says that Odin successively visited Saxony and Sweden. The most celebrated of his sons was Yngwi-Freyr, from whom the royal Swedish race, the Ynglinger, descended. According to this writer, Odin first founded in Sweden the sacred city of Sigtuna (Upsala), from Sigge, one of his own names, which leads us to the Sicambri, and to the legendary Frankish hero, Siegfried, who is also famous in the legends of the north, which in fact have generally originated from the Rhine. Odin is perhaps Ulysses, of whom Tacitus says that he founded Asciburgium (Odin's Asgard), on the Lower Rhine. Perhaps we must go back yet further. The Ambrones and Sequani dwelt on the Rhone and Saone, where, according to the Gælic legend, King Ambigat reigned, and sent the two sons of his sister forth at the head of immense armies; Bellovesus to Italy, where he founded Milan; and Sigovesus across the Rhine, where, together with the Tectosagæ (quod sagis tegerentur), he settled in the until then unpeopled Hercynian forest.

The Frankish-Saxon Odin-Sigge is probably Sarnote (Saxon Odin), who, in the form of abjuration anciently prescribed to the German pagans on their conversion to Christianity, is particularly mentioned after Wodan. In the temple at Upsala, the statue of the warlike Odin stood before a great golden sun, which was perhaps symbolical of the still more ancient Suevian-Gothic deity, Wodan (*Guodan*, God). The great annual festival in the north was called Sunarblot, Sonnen-blut (blood of the sun), Sonnen-opfer (sacrifice of the sun). Among the ancient Persians, *Thaout* meant sacred fire. Perhaps a more simple Suevian-Gothic adoration of the sun (of the ancient Wodan) preceded the more polished worship of Odin. Perhaps the Franks learned image worship in temples from the more civilized Gauls, or from the Grecian and Phœnician merchantmen, who visited those northern coasts. The twelve Drotlar, whom Odin appointed supreme judges over the Swedes, call to mind the Druids or Gallic priests.

VII. *The Germans*

THE character common to all the nomad tribes, or tribes of wandering hunters and shepherds, at the period of their settlement in Germany, soon obliterated all trace of difference in descent. There is an authentic account of the division of the land, by the Suevi, into Almenden (public property), belonging to whole tribes or communities, not to single families, which, in course of time, was exchanged for the Allodium, or private property, a mode of division which had been introduced at an earlier period among the lower Germans. This gradual transition, however, does not prove the existence of any essential difference between the German tribes, in which man, not property, was the chief consideration. All the Germans were warriors. Irman, in the Persian tongue, signifies a guest or companion in arms; Germanus, in Latin, a brother. They were all freemen and equal, united by a strong fraternal bond. The whole of the German tribes were early distinguished by their spirit of equalization from the other hordes to the north of the Caucasus, the Slavi and Tartars, as well as from those to the south, in Persia, Afghanistan, and Arabia, all of which, with the patriarchal reverence of children to their father, submitted to a single supremacy, and when, through increase of population or by conquest, they had attained considerable power, always erected magnificent palaces for their sovereigns, whose magic splendor was the astonishment of the world, and realized the fairy dreams of eastern imagination in the wonders of Babylon, Delhi, Bagdad, Ispahan and Stamboul. The Germans, on the contrary, regarded each other as brethren and equals, and even when they had become numerous and powerful, and were united under great leaders, always asserted their equality, and defended their free constitution. Every one enjoyed personal freedom, and had an exclusive right over his own property. In the popular assemblies of each district, the eldest man present presided, and the majority decided. It was only during war that they obeyed a leader, whom they selected by raising him on their shields. Even after the great migration, when the Germans, for nearly a thousand years, had, with various fortune, struggled against the Romans, and incessant warfare had consolidated the power of their leaders, we still find, wherever the German tongue was spoken, from Iceland and

Norway to the Gothic settlements in Italy and Spain, their ancient division into districts and their free constitution, which continued to exist long after the birth of Christ, and gave rise to the modern brotherhoods and societies of different orders of knighthood, and to the guilds and corporations of citizens. In England, Switzerland and Holland, ancient German freedom reigned almost uninterruptedly up to the present times, and in most of the other originally German or Germanized countries it has been revived under new constitutions.

The free intercourse between citizens, possessed of equal privileges and bound by the same duties, was the soul of the ancient German communities, and the foundation on which their whole history rests. Their liberty is of more ancient date than their servitude, for it owed its existence to the national character of the German, and though seemingly withered, still springs forth anew. "Liberty," said the Roman poet Lucanus, "is the German's birthright." "It is a privilege," wrote the Roman historian Florus, "which nature has granted to the Germans, and which the Greeks, with all their art, knew not how to obtain." Hume, the great English historian, says, "If our part of the world maintain sentiments of liberty, honor, equity and valor superior to the rest of mankind, it owes these advantages to the seeds implanted by those generous barbarians." "Liberty," observed Montesquieu, "that lovely thing, was discovered in the wild forests of Germany."

VIII. *Ancient German Heroism*

THE Germans were distinguished from all other nations by their blue eyes, light hair, and gigantic stature. They are said to have been generally seven feet in height, far overtopping the Gauls and Romans. Bones of an enormous size have been found in the ancient burial-places of the Huns, and people of extraordinary stature are even now to be met with on the coasts of the North Sea and the Baltic, and among the German Alps. The gigantic shepherd of Sens braving the Alpine regions of Berne and Unterwalden presents the truest image of our forefathers, whose strength was a national inheritance. Cæsar said that the Gauls fled at the sight of the Germans, and the emperor Titus, when commending them, said, "Their bodies are great, but their souls are still greater!"

In the remotest ages, it was customary among the Germans to destroy weakly, sickly, or deformed children, to drown in the morasses men whose bodies had been mutilated (*corpore infames*), and when become useless from old age, voluntarily to deprive themselves of life. An existence devoid of strength and beauty appeared to them to be worthless, and according to their religion, the joys of heaven were only granted to those who fell by the sword. Valerius Maximus relates that they sorrowed when dying on their beds, and rejoiced while expiring on the field of battle.

In the north, the sick were, at their own request, pierced with a lance, in order that a wound, and not disease, might be the cause of their death. In Norway there was a rock from which the old men threw themselves into the sea, after dividing their wealth among their children at a parting feast.

The bodily vigor with which the Germans were endowed was probably the result of the simplicity and purity of their manners, added to their continual exercise in the open air. War, the chase, and sometimes, though rarely, agriculture, were their only occupations. They despised, as effeminate, the refinements of civilized life; and as every wall appeared to them a prison, they built no cities, and destroyed those of the countries they invaded. To the south of the Danube, in Switzerland and in Gaul, the Romans had built splendid cities, communicating with each other by means of military roads, all of which were razed to the ground by the Franks and the Alemanni, and before long replaced by the low hut of the freeborn German, and the forest in which he loved to dwell. No towns, with the exception of a few sacred places, known by the name of Asenburgen, were to be found in Germany before the tenth century after Christ; the frontier towns of the Boii, in the Southern Tyrol, which are mentioned two centuries before Christ, having been merely built for defense during the wars, in imitation of those constructed by the Romans. With a mind free and bold, and a body inured to fatigue, the natural results of his wild forest life, the German was ever inspired with the almost hereditary ambition of distinguishing himself by heroic deeds: no danger could appall, no opposition deter him. A chivalric and unbending spirit pervaded the whole nation. "Who," asks Seneca, "is braver than the German?" And Sidonius says, "Death alone subdues them, not fear; they threaten even in death; their courage survives them!" They were, consequently, continually in arms. According to Libanius, they sat down to their meals in full armor, and slept helmeted. Weapons were the usual marriage gift between a bridal pair, for the women also learned to use them. They were even held so sacred that it was customary to swear by them. They are often mentioned in treaties of peace, and the old song of Wieland in the Northern Edda has the words, "Thou shalt swear to me by the deck of the ship, and by the rim of the shield, by the withers of the horse, and by the point of the sword." They were also considered as proofs of illustrious descent, and were handed down from one generation to another.

Over-population and famine, but still oftener their warlike propensities and thirst for adventure, seem to have been the causes that induced the Germans to abandon their forests; and if we compare the expedition of Brennus to Delphi, with the crusades; the irruption of Crocus, the destroyer of cities, with the venturous expeditions of the Normans to Winland (America) and Greenland, they will all be found to have been inspired by the same enthusiasm. In all, warlike customs preponderated over peaceful arts; the people were always armed, carried on private feuds, and preferred the trial by single combat to the decision of the law.

A malady, caused by superabundant health and strength,

and unknown among other nations, was common among the Germans, and in the north was called the Berserkerwuth. *Ber* or *bar* signifies without. *Serk*, like the Scotch *sark*, a gown or frock. In the mountainous Rhone country, a frock is still called *sarg*. This malady, or rather madness, seized them when at the height of their strength, more particularly when excited by anger, when they spared neither friend nor foe, and would even rave against themselves. Hence arose the legend of the were-wolf, or of men who at certain hours were changed into wolves.[1]

IX. *Ancient Fellowship in Arms*

THE civil institutions, the customs and superstitions of ancient Germany, arose from the peculiar and warlike form of government necessary for the guidance of a nation of free warriors, who owned no laws save those of chivalry and honor. This chivalric feeling is by no means sufficiently explained by ascribing it to the character common to all the wandering robber hordes, as it never rose in those of Asia to such a degree of sublimity. The cause must then be sought in the traits peculiarly characteristic of our race, which probably descended at a very remote period from some warrior caste of Northern India, from which they, in a degree, inherited a spirit of equality and fraternization which, strengthened by the lapse of centuries, became at length indelibly stamped on the national character.

The youthful warriors (Huns) generally took a mutual pledge as brethren in arms, and elected a leader from among their number by raising him on their shields, being guided in their choice by superior skill or courage, instead of high birth. It sometimes happened that a chief, already famous for mighty deeds, collected the young men into an army and placed himself at their head. The most implicit obedience was rendered to the chief, whom they were bound not

---

[1] This lupomania is still prevalent in the countries to the north and northeast of the Adriatic.—*Translator.*

to forsake even if he fell on the field, and if vanquished, to die with him. It was a common custom for the survivors to kill themselves, instead of seeking safety by flight, and it is authentically recorded that they even caused themselves to be buried alive in the tombs of their chieftains.

Many proofs of the severity of the laws by which these barbarians were governed were afforded during their wars with the Romans, and are still recorded by the traditionary chroniclers of the North. The same severity is also perceptible in the chivalric regulations of the knights of the Middle Ages, for the lists and in the field. The Cimbri, in their contempt for every stratagem of war, and for the Romans who defended themselves behind their intrenchments, always informed their opponents of the place and hour fixed for battle, exactly as was in later times the custom when a feudal combat took place, or as is now customary in dueling. The Germans rode without saddles and ridiculed the Romans for making use of them. By an ancient Danish law, whoever fled from fewer than four foes forfeited his honor, and the Norman laws were still more severe. The Jomsvikinger band was only allowed to make use of blunted swords an ell long, with which they were expected to overcome every foe. There was an association of pirates in the north, who were obliged by their laws to hoist their sails on the open sea during storms, in defiance of the elements, even when shipwreck was the sure result; and daring courage, allied with spotless honor and good faith, form the chief characteristics of all the heroes in the ancient legendary accounts; in the old song of the Nibelungen, for instance. Every one was declared infamous who made use of stratagem or took advantage of weakness; all dishonorable and cowardly artifices, such as falling on the enemy's rear, lying treacherously in ambuscade, making use of poisoned weapons, in short, whatever might render the contest unequal, was condemned as Nidingswerk, and forbidden under a heavy penalty.

Before iron and steel were used by the Germans for the manufacture of coats of mail, they covered themselves with the skins of wild animals, wearing on their heads those of the bear, the horned buffalo or the antlered stag, whence arose the custom of placing horns, wings, and other symbols on iron helmets and escutcheons. The shields, generally made long and narrow in order to guard the whole person, were either painted, ornamented with figures, inlaid with gold or silver, adorned with armorial bearings, or, when highly finished, with a representation of some battle or famous exploit. The colors of the dresses worn by the warriors varied according to those on their escutcheon. Iron rings placed round the body seem to have been the first approach to the use of armor, which is, however, of very ancient date, and was called Brinne, from *brehen*, to shine. The name of Brennus, so common among the Boii, apparently signifies "a man in armor." The Cimbri had numerous troops of mailed cavalry.

Warriors who fell on the field of battle were burned on funeral piles, together with their arms and the bodies of their enemies, and immense mounds, known as the tombs of the Huns, were raised over them. Naval chiefs were consumed with their ships either on shore or on the open sea. One of the heroes of the north, who had been brought on shore mortally wounded, ordered all the booty and the dead bodies of his enemies to be piled on the deck of his ship, placed himself on the summit as on a throne, and sailed into the midst of the ocean, where the whole was consumed.

Warlike deeds were celebrated in verse at every public festival; around every hearth resounded the praises of the fallen brave; and song alone preserved the memory of past deeds. The singers, who accompanied this legendary verse with the music of the harp, were in the south called bards, in the north scalds. Their songs were the forerunners of the more elaborate productions of the Nibelungen, the German legendary ballads, and the northern sagas.

In the popular religion war was regarded as a sacred and imperative duty; the gods were even supposed to ride daily on the plain of Ida, and to battle with each other, after which they held a joyous carousal in Walhalla, or "the hall of the dead," where the souls of warriors who had fallen honorably by the sword were received and permitted, under the name of Einheriar, to join in the battles and drinking feasts of the gods. Thus a warrior's death was the aspiration of every German, as that alone could unlock for him the gates of that blessed abode.

X. *Armed Communities*

IN the early German settlements, the customs of war were preserved even during peace time. The land was considered as lawful booty, and equally partitioned among the people, who nevertheless preferred the sports of the chase to agriculture. At stated times they assembled (in the open air and armed, as if encamped in a foreign land) in order to deliberate on their public affairs. The place of assembly was called Malstatt (from *mal*, time, and *zeichen*, a signal), or the Thing, or Dingstatt (from *dingen*, to counsel), and was generally distinguished by a great tree, either a sacred oak, ash, or lime, or by enormous stones, which were sometimes used as sacrificial altars, and sometimes as seats for the audience and rostra for the orators. According to the popular belief the gods held council (Thing), mounted on horseback, beneath the ash Ygdrasill. Even in the dark records of antiquity it is observable that the center of union in the great alliances between nations was not a king, but a popular assembly on some sacred spot. The different tribes appear to have been held together by a very frail federative system, and their chiefs seem to have merely represented our modern committee. As the authority was never vested in one individual, a plurality always existed, and the numbers three, four, and twelve, are generally found to predominate. In the north, Odin founded the government of the twelve Drottars; a number which may have arisen from the Asiatic idea of the twelve months or gods. It is certain that the people had, either at the same time the right of deliberating on the public affairs, or very soon gained it; for the same Ynglinga-saga which speaks of the twelve Drottars also records the meeting of the Swedish Bonden (free German peasantry) at Upsala, which decided all public questions, and was the exact counterpart of the meetings in the interior of Germany as described by Tacitus. The free Norwegians held similar assemblies at Throndheim. When the Galatæ, or Gallo-græci, who, 276 B.C., invaded Greece under Brennus, settled in Asia Minor, they chose a place of general assembly called Drynaimet, and divided their nation into twelve tetrarchies, over each of which was set a tetrarch who possessed either hierarchical or civil authority, a judge and a war chief, exactly as, in the interior of Germany, the civil and military authority was in later times divided between the landgrave and the duke. The Salic law was drawn up by four counselors chosen for that purpose out of a convocation of the whole Frankish nation, who even when ruled by kings and emperors retained the right of assembling in the Maifeld (Mayfield) in order to counsel the government. At the time of the Frankish conquest, the Saxons were divided into three tribes, in Westphalia, Enger, and Eastphalia; each tribe numbering twelve districts. They were also divided into three classes, the nobles, the freeborn, and the freedmen. Each class in each of these districts sent a representative, altogether six and thirty, to the general assembly held at Marklo, who, during peace, deliberated for the public weal. In time of war a duke was elected, who enjoyed unlimited power until peace was again concluded, when he resigned his authority. The Frisii were also divided into several districts, and held their annual popular assemblies at Upstalesbome (*Obergerichtsbaum*, tree of judgment), beneath a sacred tree. Until a very late period, the twelve freely elected representatives of the districts formed the deliberative assembly in Saterland. The number ten is elsewhere found predominant. The Suevi, or Semnones, had a hundred districts, each of which annually sent forth a thousand warriors; and sixty thousand freeborn Nervii annually elected a committee of six hundred, which managed all their affairs.

The number ten also predominated in the great English Anglo-Saxon Wittenagemot, or assembly of wise or aged men. These assemblies were common to all the German nations, the Suevi and Alemanni, the Danes, Burgundians, Boii, Vandals, the Ostro and Visi-Goths, and an additional proof of their primitive nature is furnished by their having continued to exist, long after the introduction of Christianity, under a monarchical and feudal form of government. During the great migrations, the name of the leader is often the only one mentioned, so that the relation in which he stood to the people has become a matter of uncertainty; but whenever his authority has been more fully spoken of, it is described as having been dependent on the will of the people: and even among those nations who wandered far and wide for many years, the power of whose chiefs became consequently more deeply rooted, as, for instance, among the Goths, the ancient division into districts and the free assembly of the people reappeared, as soon as they were permanently settled in any of the countries conquered by them. The only points of union in these federative states, in which each of the districts was independent, consisted in the meeting of the representatives in the general state assembly, and in the election of a common leader in time of war. It is not unusual to find many very small tribes completely independent; and even in the great states, the small district assemblies were co-existent with the diets.

XI. *Public Offices and Popular Assemblies*

THE present representative assemblies of Schwyz, Unterwalden, Uri, Glarus, and Appenzell, give the truest idea of the ancient German mode of government, the clerk and treasurer being the only modern additions. The Landamman, or magistrate, and the Landeshauptman, or captain-general of the country, correspond with the representatives of the primordial districts; and the accounts of Tacitus and Snorri prove that the power of the ancient rulers of the people did not surpass the limited authority of the modern Landamman and Landhauptman. Tacitus says, "Germanos non juberi, non regi, sed cuncta ex libidine agere"; and he makes Ambiorix, the leader of the Lower Germans, say, that among them the government was so arranged that he had no more power over the people than they had over him. Snorri relates that a Swedish king was forced, by the popular assembly, whose decisions he had opposed, to desist from an unjust war which he was carrying on against a neighboring nation; and that they threatened to throw him into a morass, where many of his predecessors had already been cast, on account of their opposition to the will of the people. Ulphilas, the Gothic bishop, who, in the fourth century, translated the Bible into German, says that these people were governed by a Reiks, or judge, during peace, and by a Thiudans, or leader, in time of war, the former being chosen on account of his high birth, the latter on account of his illustrious deeds; which agrees with the account given by Tacitus, "reges ex nobilitate, duces ex virtute sumunt; nec regibus infinita et libera potestas"; the people, however, always retaining the highest authority and the power of revoking their choice. The Reiks were always priests belonging to an ancient race held sacred on account of its supposed descent from the gods; as in the north, where many families derived their origin from Odin. The pre-eminence was always ceded to the hereditary high priest, whose duty it was to preside over the public sacrifices and ordeals, but whose authority merely rested on the superstition of the people, who, during war, always elected the bravest man as their chief, while every freeborn man stated his opinion unreservedly and without respect to rank in the public council. The Burgundians called their high priest, Sinist, or eldest, and their war-chiefs, Hendini. Other names have a similar origin. *Fürst*, prince, *princeps;* *Hersog*, from *heer*, an army, and *ziehen*, to lead; *dux*, a leader, duke. The word king is of later origin. The German *König* is derived from *Chun*, race, lineage, and was first used when families, distinguished from one generation to another by their illustrious deeds, united the double authority of judge and war-chief in themselves. The northern *Layman*, or lawyer; the English Alderman, *alter man*, or old man; the Swiss *Amman*, or magistrate; the Belgian *Ruwart*, from *ruhe*, peace, and *wahren*, to preserve, denote the officers of a peaceful civil government. There are probably also titles still extant that bear traces of the ancient form of government during war. The state assemblies were generally convoked on the great festivals, and were attended by all the members of the confederated provinces; besides this, on every fourteenth night, the customary unconvoked meeting was regularly held in each district, but when any urgent affair rendered a sudden convocation necessary, an arrow (the symbol of war) was sent from house to house, or one neighbor either shouted to the other or sounded the horn through the wide forests. This meeting extraordinary was called a bidden council (Ding), or a cried council (Schreygeding). These assemblies were held at night, the moon, or *Mana*, being the protecting divinity of the council (Things). From Mana is derived the word *man*, which originally signified not only the male sex, but also the privileges of an acting citizen. Hence also the word *mahnen*, to cite before the tribunal; Montag, Monday, or rather moon-night, followed by Dienstag, or day of council (Thing), Tuesday. The assemblies were held in the open air during the crescent moon, when the people, armed as if for battle, offered sacrifices of oxen, on which they also feasted, drank beer, mead, or wine, and gave their opinions with perfect freedom. But it was not until the morning that those who remained sober formed themselves into a circle, and deliberated over the councils of the night, "deliberant dum fingere nesciunt, constituunt dum errare non possunt." Every man had an equal right to speak, and the priest alone had the power of commanding silence, in the name of the gods, whenever the noise became overpowering; as at the present day in the Swiss assemblies, the *waibel*, or beadle, dressed in the colors of the country, calls out, "Peace by your oath!" Applause, rattling of arms, or groaning, accompanied the words of the speaker: the majority decided. The affairs of the state were here debated upon, war was declared, peace concluded, and judgment given. When no affairs of importance had to be transacted, the people only feasted and drank, while they sang the praises of fallen heroes.

XII. *Public Property, Meres and Guilds*

THE Germans only gradually exchanged their restless nomad existence (in the Slavonic tongue they are still called the Nemez, from *ne mesa*, without a boundary) for permanent habitations. The Suevi, with their division into a hundred Gauen or districts, were also comprehended in this change, and notwithstanding their subsequent migrations, this mode of division was retained; and even after their adoption of the Alemannic mode of subdividing the land into Allods (*allodium*), or private freehold estates, a considerable tract of common land (*almanden*) always remained for the benefit of the community. These tracts are at the present day frequent in Swabia, where they are in general used as sheep-runs. Meres were common to all the German tribes, and their origin is intimately connected with their free and military institutions. The largest tribes were divided into communities of a hundred men each, which were subdivided into tens. The whole of these communities were mutually bound by an offensive and defensive alliance, while the smaller divisions and the tens (Zehnmännerzahl, *tien manna tala*) were yet more closely united, by an obligation to assist each other in their private affairs as if they were their own. Owing also to these communities being obliged to become sureties for each other, they were called Freiburg-schaften, from *frei*, free, and *bürgen*, to bail; corporations or guilds for mutual security, the members of which were called Gildebrüder, Congildones, Eidhelfer, from *Eid*, an oath, and *helfen*, to help, conjuratores, who by law were accounted one and the same individual, whenever the actual criminal could not be discovered. The confederation of ten times ten, or of every hundred freeborn men, stood between the Friborg and the great community, and often held a particular assembly, as, for instance, the Hundredisthing in Norway. The chief man or president of a hundred was named by the Franks, Tunginus, by the Longobardi, Sculdais, and by the Anglo-Saxons, Hundredarius. In Swabia, the Hundreda appears at a later period under the name of Zent (*decania*). Even when the larger districts belonging to the Alemanni fell under the jurisdiction of the Frankish counts, many of the Zents in the mountainous country retained their freedom; among others, the peasantry of Leutkirch. As ten denoted a Mere, and Zent a canton, a thousand evidently stood for a district or Gau (*pagus*). The Suevi had a hundred Gauen, each containing a thousand men. The division into tens is most easily traced in the nation of the Visigoths, who named the president over tens, Taichunfath; over hundreds, Hundafath; and over thousands, Tiufath. The population of the Meres doubtless increased. The Allods, at first large, sufficed for the maintenance and settlement of the different families, which gradually became more and more numerous, and finally outgrew the land, especially in countries remarkable for fertility, or favorable for commerce. Each individual possessed a freehold within the limits of his Mere; but highway and byway, forest and fell, fish and fowl, wood and water, were the equal right of all. These common tracts, however, have no connection with those that surround our modern villages, which in general grew out of some enormous private estate. The ancient Germans, whose institutions were always founded on the principle of fraternization, possessed several other free guilds, besides the armed band of warriors already mentioned, who, like young swarms of bees, were driven forth from the parent hive, in search of a country wherein to settle; for instance, the Opfer guilds, consecrated to the service of some particular god (like the present Catholic brotherhoods, consisting of different gradations, from the superior to the servant, devoted to the service of some particular saint); the Singer guilds, scalds or bards; the soothsayers, Wahrsagergilden or Seidmänner, in the north. Probably also guilds of miners, armorers, and salt manufacturers (Halloren). The women also formed religious associations among themselves, connected with the worship of the gods, and with prophesying. They also held festivals, at which no man was allowed to be present, which gave rise to the legend of the assembly of witches on the Blocksberg on May-day eve (Walpurgisnacht). There were also bands of female warriors; and accounts of Amazons, or warrior-maids, called in the north Schildjungfrauen, or maidens bearing shields, are frequently met with in the ancient records of Germany.

XIII. *The Allod or Freehold Property*

IN whatever country the victorious Germans settled, the land was always equally divided among the freeborn warriors. The hereditary estates held by their descendants were termed Allods, from Od, an estate, and were so highly prized that, in later times, small freeholders have been known to refuse to part with their property in exchange for a large fief, which obliged them to render feudal service to the king. These hereditary estates were usually called Sonnenlehen, because they were said to have been originally granted to their possessors by the sun, whence the formula of later times, "This estate received from God and the glorious element of the suns."

As every freeborn man dwelt within the limits of his Allod, the habitations lay at scattered distances, and neither towns nor villages existed. The houses were built of wood, and usually consisted of one large apartment, called the hall or Saal, in the center of which stood the hearth, the housewife's seat of honor. In wealthy families, the women had a separate house, the Frauenhaus (Frauenzimmer, *Schrein*, a shrine; *Gadem*, a chamber); there were also a house for sacrifice, dwellings for attendants and slaves, cellars, barns, and stables. These houses were surrounded by gardens, cornfields, meadows, and forests. The boundaries of the Allods were carefully marked, and it was customary at the setting of a landmark, which was either a stone or a tree, to assemble all the children in the neighborhood on the spot, and to box their ears, in order to impress the circumstance and the locality more deeply on their minds.¹ An Allod could only be alienated with the consent of the family. Whatever the crimes of a freeborn man, the government could not deprive him of his estate, which was regarded as sacred, and as inseparable from the possessor, whose freedom, being derived from it, was alienable only with his property. It was illegal for any one to enter an Allod without the permission of the owner, who, if abused or maltreated by a stranger in his own house, or within his own limits, received double or treble indemnification. The state had no right to seize the person of any individual, or that of his guest, in his own house, a spot more sacred in the eyes of the ancient Germans than our churches are in ours. Even if the culprit had become the object of public vengeance by his crimes, and had been declared out of the pale of the law, no one ventured to cross his threshold, but the house was set fire to from without. England now alone preserves this ancient privilege, and realizes the saying, "Every man's house is his castle." The Allods were only hereditary in the male line, females being excluded from the succession on account of their being unable to exercise the privileges and duties of a freeholder, but every member of the family had a right to live in the house, and to be maintained on the produce of the Allod, nor could a father disinherit his children. When the eldest son took sole possession of the estate, he was obliged

---

¹ Until very lately, a somewhat similar custom, called "the bumping of the boundary," the spectators being bumped together on the occasion, was still kept up in some parts of England.—*Trans.*

to give to each of the other kinsfolk a portion of the personal property, and to apply part of his revenues to their maintenance. A family was called a Sippe, Sippschaft, or Magschaft, and was divided into Schwertmagen, kinsmen who carried swords, and Spillmagen, kinswomen who busied themselves in spinning. The father being the legal representative of the whole family, the slaves included, spoke for them before the tribunal, and was their guardian, *Mund*, mouth—*mundium*, to whom they owed implicit obedience, being under his jurisdiction, *bann—bannum;* the kinsmen remaining under his bann until they entered foreign service, or married, when they became selbstmundig, independent, and were freed from the bann; hence the word *freien*, to marry. The property received on these occasions was called Abban, appanage. Those who remained unmarried always continued under the bann of the paternal estate, the limits (Gehäge) of which they were not permitted to quit; hence the word *Hagestolzer*, old bachelor, from *hag*, hedge, and *stolz*, proud. The Spillmagen were always under tutelage; the bridegroom purchasing the right of guardianship from the parents of the bride, who henceforward submitted to his authority.

XIV. *The Division into Classes*

THE Suevian nations, when in their half nomad state, recognized but one description of slaves, viz., the prisoners taken in war, who were bound to serve them. But when the allodial system was introduced, many of the slaves were manumitted by the Frankish Saxon tribes, and furnished with houses and land, on condition of performing certain services, and of paying a certain tribute to their lord; it also sometimes happened that the inhabitants of a conquered country were permitted to retain a part of their landed property, for which they engaged to perform certain duties; thus a new class of bondsmen was created, distinct from the real slave, by their being merely dependent by their vassalage on the feudal lords. They were called by the Saxons, Lazzi; by the Franks, Liti; whence the German *Leute*, people; and their property, in contradistinction to the Allod (freehold), was called a Feod, or fief (*fe-od*, transferable property). The word *fe* comes from *Vieh*, cattle, as the Latin *pecunia*, from *pecus*, the only transferable property at first consisting of cattle; hence also the people were called Feodales, Vassi, Vasalli, and thus simply originated the feudal system, which spread so widely at a later period.

Tacitus speaks commendably of the treatment of the slaves in Germany. It is true that they were sometimes killed by their masters in moments of irritation, but it was illegal to strike or to ill-treat them. These slaves, at first few, gradually increased in such number as at length to necessitate the division of the large estates into numerous fiefs, and the feudal system became general. The freeborn man was named Germanus, Arimannus, Herimannus, Baro; and, among the Saxons, was distinguished by the designation of Friling from the Edeling or nobleman. It is not very clear in what nobility consisted in the pagan times; that there were two kinds is however certain, one derived from mythical descent, which naturally was restricted to a few families; the other, gained by conquest. When whole nations migrated, every man of whatever class received an Allod as his share of the newly conquered land; or when a horde overran a country, whose inhabitants they either could or would not completely reduce to submission, they tolerated them as subordinates, manumitted their former slaves, and promoting the freeborn to the rank of noble, created a purely political class of nobility far outnumbering that of the hereditary nobles. It is remarkable that the name Edeling, in the north, Oedling, is derived from Od, Allod, and therefore simply means the possessor of an estate. For the same reason, the Visigothic noble was entitled Garding, from the word *Gards*, which, according to Ulphilas, signifies an estate, as well as a garden. Perhaps the nobles were originally only the firstborn sons, or heirs to the estates, while the Frilinge denoted the portionless younger sons; but no sooner did the word Friling denote a separate class, than pride of birth asserted its claims, and even the poor younger sons of the nobility were called Edelinge. Yet it is nowhere to be found that the Frilinge were oppressed or domineered over by the Edelinge; among the Saxons, on the contrary, Edelinge, Frilinge, and even Lazzi, in equal numbers, and with equal right, conducted the public affairs; and when the Franks declared a war of extirpation against the Saxons, the Edelinge attempted, by betraying the Frilinge and Lazzi, to make friends of the Franks, and to get the whole of the formerly equally divided power into their own hands.

Among the Germans, who acknowledged no law as binding, in the framing of which they had not either assisted or to which they did not voluntarily and individually assent, there always existed men, who, naturally fierce and stubborn, resisted every law, and were unfettered by any moral obligation. These men were called Wildfange (wild animals), and were treated as wolves or outlaws. They were in the north Bärserkers, ravishers, or lawless Huns, whose wild daring caused them to be eagerly taken into foreign service. The owner of an Allod who, through caprice, remained at home and took no part in the state, was called Biesterfrei, Verbiesterte, bestialized (or Versessen, possessed by a demon), and was considered beyond the pale of the law, inasmuch as he recognized none; and if he committed a crime, he was delivered up to public vengeance; his well was choked up, his house destroyed by fire or unroofed, and then razed to the ground, but no one ventured to break open the door.

XV. *Single Combat and Fines* (*Wergeld*)

It is a remarkable fact that the ancient Germans had no public, but only a private law; all their oldest laws merely referring to the mutual rights of the freeborn, and to those of the freeborn over the unfree; the state assembly taking cognizance of and deciding all public and private affairs: beyond these decisions there was no law.

The laws chiefly aimed at providing security and indemnity. To every individual they secured his life, his liberty, his honor, and his property; or in case of injury and deprivation, an indemnity or commutation, of which there were only two kinds, single combat and fines. In the earliest times, every one avenged himself as he could, and it was the especial duty of a family, a member of which had been injured or murdered, to avenge him to the uttermost. Single combat, according to law (and the ancient laws were very strict in this particular), seems to have been intended as a check upon a custom conducing to so much disorder and bloodshed. According to the regulations, the advantages of ground, light, sun, and weapons, were to be equal on both sides; no Nidingswerk or underhand means were to be used, and no further vengeance was to be sought, however the combat, which was regarded as the judgment of God, might terminate. The Wergeld or fine seems to have been introduced at a later period, as, for instance, in cases where no single combat could take place, or for lesser injuries, when the injured person was compensated by the offender in cattle or weapons, according to the value of the injured object; for this purpose he could be deprived of all he possessed, except of his Allod, which, under all circumstances, was inalienable. There were even cases where the offender, unable to make full restitution, was obliged to serve the person he had injured for twenty years, and yet was never deprived of his Allod. In course of time, this system became more definite, and the value of the injured object was estimated in eight different degrees.

In the first place, according to the sex of the injured person. Injuries offered to women were not only estimated doubly or trebly higher than those offered to men, but the law in this respect also permitted private vengeance to be taken, and the offender to be deprived of his liberty or of his life.

Secondly, According to the rank of the injured person. The head-man of a district was estimated very highly, on account of the duties he had to perform. The noble was valued higher than the freeborn, the freeborn higher than the people, and they higher than the slaves.

Thirdly, According to the value of the injured object. Honor and liberty were valued higher than life, person, or property. Also all attacks on the property or person of an individual, which in any way entailed dishonor, received a much higher compensation. Rape, injuries to guests, embassadors, hostages, and especially to strangers, besides theft, robbing and insulting the dead, were doubly and trebly, nay, sometimes nine times more severely punished. In bodily injuries, every limb and every devisable sort of wound had its fixed value; toes and teeth were especially and individually prized; and injuries done to property were as definitely regulated; every article that could come under the head of goods and chattels having its comparative value.

Fourthly, According to the sex of the offender. A woman was punished more severely than a man, because she was considered less capable of the commission of a crime, and because, when injured, she received a higher indemnity.

Fifthly, According to the rank of the offender. When a Friling committed a crime, he paid more than a Laz, and a Laz more than a slave, according to the principle that he who enjoys higher privileges has higher duties to perform.

Sixthly, According to the intention of the offender. An unintentional injury was only lightly rated, and sometimes, according to the circumstances, completely passed over, on which account the mere intention of committing an injury was almost as severely punished as if the injury had in reality been committed.

Seventhly, According to the mode of injury. For instance, whoever killed another with an iron weapon was held less criminal than he who murdered another with a piece of wood or with his hands.

Eighthly, According to the place. Whoever injured another in his own house, had to pay doubly or trebly higher than if he had injured him elsewhere; and the offense was considered equally bad when committed on holy ground, in the assembly of the people, or on the highroad. During war time the Wergeld was trebled; discipline and good order being then of still higher importance.

However, notwithstanding the introduction of the Wergeld, single combat remained in full force in matters of honor and in doubtful cases; when, by ordinary means, the truth could not be discovered, the decision was left to God. Besides the ordeal by single combat, customary between freeborn men, there was also that by fire and water, to which women and slaves were subjected; the hand or the foot being held upon red-hot iron, or in boiling water.

The mundium or guardianship of the free owner of an Allod over his family, his people (the conditionally unfree) and his slaves (the personally unfree), whose reciprocal obligations have already been explained, was also regulated by the laws.

XVI. *Courts of Justice and Laws*

THE Germans had the axiom, "Where there is no accuser there is no judge." If the fine enforced by law were voluntarily paid, the case was not brought before the court. The master of a house, or a whole Sippschaft (kinsfolk), or two, in cases in which both were concerned, judged all family matters. The Friborg, Hundreda or Guild, took cognizance of all matters relating to Meres and Guilds, and all affairs of higher importance came before the great general assembly, and were decided by the freeborn members. It was not until a much later period, when the Christian monarchs increased in power, that the people were deprived of the right of holding open courts of justice, and the judges (*Schöppen*), who were bound by oath to administer justice, were restricted to a limited number.

In ancient times these courts were held in the open air, where all transactions were conducted by word of mouth, and they formed a principal part of the business of each community. The priestly judge of peace sat in a chair, staff in hand, with his legs crossed in sign of impartiality and tranquillity of mind, and his face turned toward the east during the new moon, in order to imply that the administration of justice was as sure as the increase of that orb. On the right hand stood the accuser, on the left the accused, encircled by the armed community, who pronounced the verdict; the kinsfolk and confederates of the Mere or Guild, to which the accused belonged, standing around him, as conjuratores; *i.e.*, they swore that they knew him to be an honorable man, and believed what he said. If the truth could not be discovered, the ordeal decided the point; but if it were proved by witnesses, the sentence was pronounced and executed. Corporeal punishment was unheard of among them, "neque vincire ne verberare quidem permissum," *Tac.* Adam Von Bremen says of the ancient Saxons, "decollari malunt, quam verberari." Prisons were equally unknown, all injuries being expiated by the Wergeld, except such as were considered irreparable, which were punished by death. The priest alone had the power of passing sentence on the criminal in the name of God. Capital punishment was awarded to all traitors, deserters, thieves, and adulterers; in a word, all crimes against man's honor or dignity and against female chastity. Beyond the sentence of being burned alive in his house or decapitated, passed upon men, and that of being hanged, drowned, or buried alive, passed upon women and cowards, there was no other mode of public punishment of death, and these were only awarded in extreme cases. The laws appear to have been, like other ancient customs, originally handed down by word of mouth; and in order the more easily to retain them in the memory, they were usually arranged in assonance and rhythm. Fragments of ancient versified laws are still extant, and a number of assonances are still made use of in our laws, such as

Bank und Bett, bed and board; *Bausch und Bogen*, in the lump; *braun und blau*, brown and blue; *Dach und Fach erhalten*, to keep in repair; *dick und dünn*, thick and thin; *Erb und Eigen*, heir and inheritance; *frank und frei*, frank and free; *gäng und gäbe*, current; *Gut und Blut*, property and person; *Haus und Hof*, house and land; *Haut und Haar*, hide and hair; *Herz und Hand*, heart and hand; *los und ledig*, free and single; *Hülle und Fülle*, plenty; *Kind und Kegel*, child and toy; *Land und Leute*, land and people; *Mann und Maus*, man and mouse; *Nacht und Nebel*, night and mist; *Rath und That*, word and deed; *Ruh und Rast*, rest and repose; *richten und schlichten*, to judge and adjust; *Schut und Schirm*, shelter and defense; *Stein und Bein*, stone and bone; *Stock und Block*, stock and block; *Weg und Steg*, highway and byway; *weit und breit*, far and wide; *Wind und Wetter*, wind and weather, etc. To these also belong the significant numbers, to summons three times, four roads, twelve confederates, fourteen nights, thirty days' respite; besides a number of signs, as, for instance, the right of fishing in a river extended as far as one could cast a hammer (the symbol of the god Thor) from the bank; another right extended as far as one could see a white horse, or hear the blast of the huntsman's horn. Indemnity for a wound was according to the distance the sound caused by the splintered bone taken from it, when thrown into a hollow shield, could be heard. The priestly judge held in his hand a staff (hence the scepter of a king), while adjudicating, which he broke asunder when passing sentence of death. Grass and earth were emblematical of submission. Whoever was charged with the debt of a deceased kinsman, which it was out of his power to pay, cleared himself by going to the four corners of his house and throwing dust behind him. A form of oath among men was by touching their beards; and among women, by touching their breast or plaited hair. A bargain was concluded by shaking hands, which was so commonly in use that "the German shake of the hand" has become the proverbial sign of loyal cordiality.

XVII. Hospitality

THIS virtue of ancient times was greatly esteemed by our forefathers, who regarded as a crime the dismissal of the peaceful wayfarer from their doors. A stranger no sooner appeared than he was invited to take shelter beneath their lowly roof, and offered food and a night's lodging; and it was considered disgraceful first to inquire of him who he was, whence he came, or whither he was going. As long as he remained in the house he was a guest, and any injury committed against him was severely punished by the law, even though he were a fugitive criminal; the master of the house was bound to defend him to the death, and as he was indemnified for every injury offered to his guest as if it were offered to himself, he was also liable to be punished in his stead if his guest committed a crime while dwelling beneath his roof; no one could dismiss a guest unless forced to do so by poverty, when it was incumbent on him to accompany him to the nearest dwelling, and there procure for him the comforts which it was not in his own power to bestow. The guest was presented on his departure with a parting gift, and if able gave something in return. In later times, hospitality and many other good customs fell into disuse, although attempted to be enforced by law, by which it was ordained that no one was obliged to harbor a guest longer than three days, whence arose the saying, "A three days' guest is everywhere cursed," for there is no doubt that, in later times, this good old custom was very much abused. The injurious treatment of a peaceful wayfarer on the public road was punished with double severity than when the offense was committed on a native. Every foreign wayfarer might pluck, as he went along, three fruits from a tree, or take three sheaves from a field, or three fish from a pond, if driven by necessity; whence came the saying, "Three are free." To deliver a man, who had fled for protection to a neighboring tribe, to his pursuers, was considered an indelible disgrace, and was unheard of among the Germans. The Gepidæ preferred total destruction to the commission of such an execrable crime as the violation of the rights of hospitality. A Norwegian queen once fled for safety to Sweden. The Norwegians demanded her surrender, and the Swedish king even sent his warriors to take her by force; but Hakon, one of his subjects, a wealthy peasant, with whom she had taken refuge, opposed them sword in hand, until she had reached a safer retreat.

The customs of hospitality greatly conduced to sociability, friendship, and marriage; and it was from the wayfarers, who carried intelligence of the occurrence of remarkable events from one district to another, that the people gained information of the changes that took place in distant countries.

XVIII. *Customs and Arts*

As a numerous offspring was considered honorable, celibacy was consequently a mark of disgrace. As soon as the children were born, they were plunged into cold water; their education was severe and hardy; they were taught swimming, wrestling, endurance of hunger, heat, and cold, the arts of the chase, and the use of weapons. It is recorded of a leader of the Teutones that he was able to leap, with the greatest ease, over six horses. A favorite amusement of the Germans was the sword dance, in which the young men danced naked, with the most expert and curious movements, between sharp swords and the points of lances, without receiving the slightest injury.[1] As soon as a young man attained sufficient strength, he was allowed to take part in military expeditions, and was solemnly declared capable of bearing arms. Among the Catti, every boy wore an iron ring on his arm, which he durst not take off until he had slain an enemy.

---

[1] The Scotch Highlanders and the natives of Hindostan still practice a sword dance bearing great similarity to that above described.—*Trans.*

Tillage was performed by the slaves, and the domestic concerns were managed by the women, while the freeborn men thought only of war and wild adventure, which, in time of peace, were, in some degree, replaced by the chase, of which they were passionately fond, and for which their enormous forests, well stocked with game, afforded free scope. They tried their strength in the rough encounter with the bear and the wild buffalo; and early introduced the more gentle art of falconry. The white falcon was held sacred, and was esteemed by its owner as his chiefest treasure. At home, the warrior slept on the bearskin; hence, whoever remained at home so long as to acquire a distaste for exertion was termed a Bärenhauter (*Haut*, a skin). Tacitus expressly mentions that they whiled away their leisure hours with gambling, which they carried to such a pitch that, in the delirium of excitement, they would stake their property and their persons on a throw of the dice. From the earliest down to the present times, the Germans have been reputed the greatest topers in the world. The present fashion of toasting arose from an ancient pagan custom. At every public banquet, the great Bragabecher was first drained, in honor of fallen heroes; then the Minnebecher, in honor of deceased kinsmen and ladye loves. Passing the cup round, drinking to a person or for a wager, trials of superiority in the power of drinking, etc., are ancient customs of guilds, that met for the purpose of carousing. Beer and mead were first made in Germany, where the use of wine was, nevertheless, early introduced. When Helico for the first time brought grapes across the Alps, the people rose en masse, and resolved to migrate to the land where grew this golden fruit, and many thousand Germans, on reaching Italy, fell victims to excess.

The mother of the family ruled the entire household, and was treated with the greatest deference by the women, slaves and children. She superintended the cleanliness of the house, the kitchens, the cellars, the table, and the beds; the making of the clothes, and the brewing of beer and mead; she was also acquainted with surgery, and busied herself with the preparation of balsams for the wounds of the men; and finally, she was the family prophetess, and on important occasions held communication with the gods, by means of mysterious signs, and the casting of lots. Whatever the Germans did, had merely reference to the present moment; even their arts aimed no further, and all their care was expended on their clothing and armor. Noble warriors fabricated costly weapons, and noble ladies spun and wove cloth for themselves and their households, an art brought by them to a high degree of perfection. In the earlier ages, the armor, weapons, shields, and war attire, drinking horns, and other articles, were skillfully and curiously ornamented with colors and various ingenious devices. In the north, the ships were built in the form of different animals, generally in that of dragons, and were adorned with golden images. Wealthy monarchs are said to have sometimes used purple sails. All these arts, however, merely conduced to temporary grandeur, and the Germans were totally unacquainted with works, such as public edifices, magnificent temples, and lordly palaces, calculated to immortalize their name.

XIX. *Honor of Women*

IN pagan times women were generally despised, and regarded as beings of an inferior order, but among the Germans, even in the earliest ages, they were considered as standing equal in point of honor to the men, and in many respects were even acknowledged to be superior (inesse quin etiam sanctum aliquid et providum putant, *Tac.*). The honor in which women were held exercised so great an influence over the customs and character of the Germans, and consequently over their arts and poetry, as to produce the romance by which their productions are mainly distinguished from those of the East, the Græco-Roman or antique.

The reverence in which women were held depended on the purity of their lives; hence by custom and by law they were judged not only by the outward honor they received, but also by their inward innocence. Tacitus, when extolling the unbending severity of German manners, and the sanctity attached to chastity, says, "that much as the German merits praise, his morality, as being the foundation of all his other virtues, deserves the highest commendation; nec ullam morum partem magis laudaveris."

Young maidens were brought up in the retirement of their homes, where they busied themselves in domestic employments, and only associated with the men whenever a guest arrived at the paternal abode. They did not marry so early, nor did their constitutions develop so rapidly, as those of the more luxurious inhabitants of southern climes; and it is still a fact, that the people of the north, especially those of the mountainous regions who have remained faithful to the hardy customs of their forefathers, do not arrive at puberty so soon as the inhabitants of cities. A German maiden seldom married before her twentieth year, or a man before his thirtieth, and it was to this custom that the Romans attributed the blooming health and robust strength of our hardy ancestors.

An insult offered to female modesty or honor was deemed an unpardonable crime, and punished with death. The virginal wreath, worn by the bride on her wedding-day, was apparently an ancient German custom; no maiden could wear it whose honor was not spotless. Slander, if proved, was punished with unusual severity; rape, under whatever circumstances, was punished by the most degrading death, and even late in the Middle Ages, we find decreed (in Schwabenspiegel's collection of laws), that in the house in which such a crime had been committed, all it contained, even down to the cattle, should be deprived of life, and the house itself razed to the ground. The untamable ferocity of the men often occasioned the commission of this crime, for that reason the more strictly guarded against by the laws; and the more ancient their date, the more certainly is the punishment of death decreed by them. But among the Frisii, the woman was placed between her parents and her ravisher; if she turned toward the latter, the crime was forgiven; but if she turned to the former, the criminal was condemned to death.

One of the best and wisest customs was that of daughters being portionless, so that a woman's attraction was her virtue and beauty, and not her wealth. Tacitus relates that the bride only brought some weapons, as a sign to the bridegroom that he must in future protect her; and that he, on his part, paid to her father, brother or guardian, a sum fixed by law, upon which the right of guardianship, or that empowering him to appear in her stead before the tribunal, was handed over to him. The affianced pair shook hands, and exchanged kisses and rings. In pagan times it was usual to place a drawn and sharp sword for three nights, between a newly married pair, from a religious superstition. The Hochzeit, or wedding (from *hohezeit*, high time), was regarded, as its name denoted, as the highest point in life, and was celebrated as publicly as possible, amid the shouts of the guests. The day after the wedding, the husband presented his wife with a gift, called the morning gift, of which she could not be deprived; and if any one disputed her right, she proved it by placing her hand on her breast, and swearing it was her morning gift. It was also customary after the wedding for the bride to exchange the virginal wreath for a cap.

Marriages between Frilings and Lazzi were illegal, and if they took place, the children lost caste, and were declared bondmen. A freeborn man could marry his slave after having given her her freedom; but a freeborn woman who united herself to a slave, being unable, on account of being herself always under guardianship, to give him his freedom, became a slave; and in order to render this dishonorable act impossible, it was punished with death.

Adultery was deemed another inexpiable crime. If the husband did not kill the guilty wife with his own hand, she was turned, naked and with shorn head, out of the house, and whipped by the women from village to village, until she sank from fatigue; a custom highly commended by Tacitus, and which, until a very late period, was in force among the Saxons (publicatæ enim pudicitiæ nulla venia. Nemo enim illic vitia ridet; nec corrumpere et corrumpi seculum vocatur, Tac.). The ancient Germans did not think the indulgence of these so-called weaknesses of the heart so urgent, as, for their sake, to relax public morals, and to cause the disorder of a whole nation. When better known to the Romans, and invariably told that their laws against adultery were much too severe, and a sign of barbarism, the Burgundian legislators took notice of this reproach, by adding to the decree in which this crime was then, as formerly, unsparingly denounced as worthy of capital punishment, these remarkable words, "rectius est enim, ut paucorum condemnatione multitudo corrigatur, quam sub specie incongruæ incivilitatis intromittatur occasio, quæ licentiam tribuat delinquendi"; and it was even said of the Goths and Vandals, that they not only retained their own purity, but also reformed the corrupt manners of the Romans.

The women were indeed held in such esteem that the fine or Wergeld for any injury committed against them was much higher than one committed against the men; among the Alemanni and Bavarians it was double the amount; among the Franks and Thuringians treble, and still higher if the injured woman were pregnant; among the Saxons, maidens and not married women were guarded against injury by a double fine. Every woman, possessed of sufficient strength, was free to carry arms. Women were also allowed to speak in council, and those noted for capacity and skill often headed great and important enterprises.

Fidelity unto death was vowed in marriage, and, according to Tacitus, a woman never took a second husband; "She can have but one husband, as she can have but one body and one life"; "sic unum accipiunt maritum quomodo unum corpus unamque vitam, ne ulla cogitatio ultra." Wela says of the Getæ, and Procopius of the Heruli, that the women killed themselves on their husbands' bodies; similar cases, but not as of common occurrence, are met with in the legends of the north, and it is a historical fact, that after bloody battles, the German women killed themselves in great numbers on the bodies of their slaughtered husbands.

XX. *Wolen and Walkyren*

THE immense strength and vigorous nature of the German people, which in the men produced an intense desire to distinguish themselves by bold and daring exploits, and, when stimulated to excess, engendered the Beserkerwuth, a species of wolf-like madness, aroused in the maidens and women that wonderful sort of inspiration, by which they became involuntarily intimate with the mysteries of nature. This inspiration, known in our times as animal magnetism, was, in all probability, of common occurrence in those ancient times, and evinced itself in a much higher degree. In the Middle Ages, this singular faculty was deemed witchcraft, and was condemned as a diabolical art, on account of the inability to explain it by natural means. There is now no doubt of its being caused by a peculiarly irritable condition of the nervous system, which sometimes appears in persons whose powers have been extremely reduced by sickness, sometimes in those possessed of a superabundance of health and strength. Clairvoyance, or the power possessed by a person in a mesmeric state of examining the whole of the internal organs of the body, and of involuntarily discovering the proper remedy, was, at that period, frequent among women, who were hence reputed to be possessed of the gift of healing. This faculty also extended to that of seeing what passed in remote places, and of foretelling approaching events, and altogether bore a close resemblance to modern mesmerism; hence the German women were believed to possess the gift of prophecy, and were regarded as sacred, from a belief of their being inspired by the gods.

The temple at Delphi, and, in fact, all the Grecian oracles, originated from these prophetesses, who, at a later period, were frequently met with by the Romans in the interior of Germany; the most celebrated among whom, Velleda, was worshiped as a divinity by the whole German nation, whom she unceasingly excited against the Romans.

These prophetesses were called Wolen, and when they foretold, or by their magic arts caused, evil, Hexen, in the north, Trollen, witches, who practiced sorcery by means of certain songs and drugs. These songs or incantations were in existence long after the introduction of Christianity, and were known by the name of Neitharte. It was believed that by means of them the witch had the power of raising storms, and of causing plagues. Caracalla, the Roman emperor, is said to have been deprived of his senses by these German incantations. These rhymes were so well known and so numerous, that in later times the repetition of them was strictly and repeatedly forbidden by the Church. Magic drugs or potions, especially love potions, were equally prohibited.

The Walkyren, or celestial women (from *Wal*, a dead man, and *küren*, to choose), were believed to be heavenly maidens, who hovered over every field of battle, and chose expiring heroes for their companions in the eternal joys of Walhalla; a belief which caused German warriors to look upon death as a nuptial festival in the skies. Earthly maidens were also regarded as Walkyren, when they girded on the sword and took part in the battle.

The poetical relation between the pagan warrior and his celestial bride changed, in course of time, to that between the Christian knight and his ladye-bright, who also was not always an earthly dame, but the Holy Virgin or some saint. Thus the romantic love, the enthusiastic service, vowed by knights in honor of a celestial being, or of an unknown, haughty, or eternally ungrateful dame, the Minnedienst and gallantry (in its noble sense) of the Middle Ages, all originated from the beautiful fable of the Walkyren.

XXI. Ancient German Poesy

IN writing, the Germans made use of singularly shaped letters, called Runic, that resembled little crossed bits of wood, or broken twigs thrown one upon the other; which, in fact, they were originally intended to represent. It was, at first, customary to augur from the position of such bits of wood, each of which bore a different meaning, which was retained by the Runic characters when used in writing, with which magic was always associated.

Paper being at that period unknown, the Runic characters were either engraved on stone or cut in wood. One of the Danish kings had a Runic writing, thirty ells in length, cut on a rock. Even in the present times, tombstones bearing Runic inscriptions are often met with. These characters were commonly cut in soft wood, particularly beech-wood (*Buche*, whence is derived the word *Buch*, a book, and *Buchstaben*—*stab*, a stick—letters), an art generally practiced by the women, on account of their superior dexterity. Many of these pieces of inscribed wood or Runic sticks have been preserved. The laws were also inscribed upon wood in these characters, and, on account of their lengthy contents, sometimes covered whole beams (*Balken*); and, at the present day, the books containing the laws are, in the north, called Balken.

Poetry was highly esteemed by the Germans, who, by reciting the noble deeds of their ancestors, kept up the national love of war and adventure. The bards, inspired by martial enthusiasm, transformed the fabled enterprises of the gods into legends recounting heroic exploits, in which the elements, the stars, and all the powers of nature bore a part. Descriptions of great battles, prophecies of pending destruction. the triumph of the victor, or the lament of the conquered, form the subject of almost all the songs that have descended to us from days of eld.

The harmony of two consonants, or alliteration; or of

two vowels, or assonance; or that of the last syllable in a verse, or rhythm; were peculiar to German poetry. All the ancient songs are also as remarkable for their proud and daring spirit as for their sublime and graphic brevity, which may be particularly observed throughout the northern Edda. Metaphor was so general, that a ship was commonly designated by a snake or a bird, a sword was termed fire, and *vice versa*. Diodorus mentions the bold figures and hyperboles in use among the northern Catti, as he designates the Scandinavians. Tacitus also speaks of the poetical genius of the Germans. The northern Saga describe the extraordinary influence exercised by song over the sympathies of the ancient warriors. The Danes formerly thought the composer of the best poem alone worthy of the throne, and the whole nation assembled, in order to judge of its merits. The Icelanders once composed a song in ridicule of the Danes, who felt the insult so deeply that a naval expedition was the result. Poetry was so all-powerful in exciting or in allaying the passions that a cruel Swedish king is said to have been suddenly transformed, by a single song, from a depraved and licentious despot into a just and valiant ruler. Love and hatred, grief and joy, were alternately swayed by the power of song. A celebrated Troll arriving at the court of a Swedish king sang before him and his assembled nobles. The first song excited such excessive delight that they danced and shouted for joy; when he sang the second they began to sorrow and weep; but scarcely had he sang the third than, frantic with rage, they drew their swords and slew one another.

Although the ancient melodies of Germany and Sweden were essentially of a martial character, they possessed great force and variety of sentiment, as may be seen in the Edda, in which violent anger, heartrending grief, and jocose delight, follow in rapid succession.

XXII. Public Worship

THE gods were generally worshiped in sacred groves and forests, or on heaths, whence, *zum Walde fahren*, to go to the wood, *wallfahren*, to go on a pilgrimage, and the name of "heathen," applied to unbelievers in Christianity. Tacitus relates that, at certain periods, all the tribes of the Semnones made a pilgrimage to a sacred grove, where human sacrifices were offered, and that whoever entered the groves wore chains in sign of submission to the deity.

Public worship was also solemnized beneath the shade of gigantic and solitary trees, on whose branches trophies and the heads of sacrificed horses were hung. The Upstalesboom, the point of reunion for the whole of Friesland; an aged nut tree at Benevento, held sacred by the Longobards; the great oak at Geismar, in Hesse, which Saint Bonifacio cut down; and the pear tree on the Malserheath; were once sacred to the gods. The names of Altaich (old oak), Eichstadt (oak city), Dreieich (three oaks), Sieben eichen (seven oaks), etc., have a similar origin; and, even at the present day, there is scarcely a village throughout Germany without its large tree, around which it was the custom, not long ago, for the young people to dance. The trees of liberty introduced during the French Revolution were merely fantastical repetitions of the long-forgotten customs of antiquity.

The gods were also worshiped on holy mountains, and, when Christianity was introduced, churches were generally built on heights. Even in our days, the mass is annually read, at the top of the Alps, to the assembled Senn shepherds. The procession of witches on the Blocksberg, the highest summit of the Harz Mountains, is probably a superstition derived from the ancient worship formerly offered on that spot to the god of spring. Not very long ago, the Johannisfeuer, or fires of St. John, were still commonly lighted on the tops of hills. Ancient altars have been found on the Odilienberg in Alsace. There are several Donnersberge, mountains so called from the god of thunder. One of the highest points of the Priesengebirge, famous in story, the Reifträger or Ringbearer, is quite bare, and surrounded with a regular circle of enormous stones. The Groteberg at Detmold is encircled with two great stone rings, and is the same as the ancient Teutoburg in the wood, the burial place of the legions of Varus.

Lakes, rivers, and springs were also held sacred. Tacitus mentions a grove with a sacred lake in an island to the north of Germany, apparently Zeeland. The image of the goddess Hertha, in a chariot drawn by cows, was brought in solemn procession to this lake, and there washed by slaves, who, immediately after the ceremony, were drowned. There were also places of sacrifice on the Bodensee, in the vicinity of the falls of the Rhine, and near to Bregenz. Petrarch, the celebrated Italian poet, relates, that so late as the fourteenth century, the female inhabitants of Cologne bathed in the Rhine on St. John's day, in order to wash away their sins; and that the superstitious custom of drawing water at midnight from holy wells was still practiced. The custom of the Swiss, at a yet later period, of dipping their colors before battle into running water, and of unfurling them before they were dry, was without doubt an ancient heathen ceremony.

The erection of temples is of later date; they were only known in the northern countries; as, for instance, the great temples at Upsala in Sweden, and at Lethra in Denmark. The worship of images also dates later, and was only partial, although it extended to Upper Germany, as has been already seen in respect to the Bodensee.

There were three high festivals in the year, which were held peculiarly sacred. On these occasions the whole nation assembled in order to offer sacrifice. They were all called Sunarblut, Sonnenopfer, sacrifice to the sun, or Suhnopfer, sacrifice of atonement, whence came the word Sinist, the title of the Burgundian high priest. But by far the holiest time was that answering to our Christmas, and the twelve darkest nights of the whole year, those during the winter solstice, after which the sun again approaches our hemisphere: during this period, the gods and spirits were supposed to descend upon the earth, while Wodan himself (Hermes, who, according to the Greeks, was the conductor of the souls of the dead), or in his place the chief goddess, Frau Hexe or Hölle, led the midnight procession of spirits hovering in the air. Hence originated the legend of the wild huntsman. The great festival, held at this time throughout the northern countries, was called the Yule feast, traces of which are still to be met with in Scotland. The second festival was celebrated in the spring; in the north, during Easter; in the south, at Whitsuntide or on St. John's day. The Franks held theirs at different times, having the great annual assembly, first in March, and at a later period in May. Great fires were lit (Easter fire in the north; St. John's fire in the south), through which the cattle were driven by way of purification, and in order to guard them against the powers of evil. A festival was instituted in honor of the first violet, around which they danced; there were also a feast of flowers, the president of which was, in Sweden, called the Flower-king; in Denmark, the May-king, etc. The image of Death or Winter was borne in solemn procession to the river. Many of these customs of olden times exist at the present day.

The third festival was held in the autumn, at the time of our *Kirchweih*, or church consecration, and appears to have been particularly dedicated to Thor, by whose horn it is designated on Runic stones. On this day wheaten cakes, in the shape of horns, were baked in honor of the god, which now, in some parts of northern Germany, are baked on the same day, in honor of St. Martin. St. Martin's goose also appertains to these ancient superstitions.

The Swedes every nine years celebrated a peculiarly solemn feast, which lasted nine days, during which 99 men, 99 dogs, 99 cocks, and 99 hawks were sacrificed. A similar sacrifice was customary in Denmark, which, A.D. 926, was abolished by the Emperor Henry the First.

That these festivals were bloody, is at once proved by the name Sonnenblut, and by the appellation of the priests, who throughout the north were called Blutmänner, men of blood. Warriors were held in high estimation who were also good Blutmänner, and could sacrifice beasts, a duty incumbent on every head of a family when no priest happened to be present. The Blutmänner, whose office it was to assist the king while offering sacrifices, were always twelve freeborn men, chosen from the people. They killed the beast, and sprinkled the sacred tree, the place of sacrifice, and all the bystanders with the blood; the flesh was then cooked and served at the banquet, the head of the animal being hung upon the tree. As they generally sacrificed and ate horses, the eating of horseflesh became a mark of distinction between the heathen and the Christian. A Christian king was forced by the pagan Swedes to eat horseflesh in sign of apostasy, and, at a later period, every one who ate horseflesh was regarded as a heathen, and was put to death.

It is equally certain that human sacrifices, though of rare occurrence, were nevertheless offered. The great Swedish and Danish sacrifices have already been mentioned. Tacitus also speaks of human sacrifices. The Cimbri sacrificed their Roman prisoners; and in times of dearth the Swedes sacrificed their king; but these were extraordinary cases.

Besides the great feasts and sacrifices, there were occasionally a number of other religious observances. During a storm the Swedes shot arrows into the air, in order to assist the god of thunder in his combats with the giants. During an eclipse of the sun the people crowded together and shouted, in order to scare the wolf attempting to eat the sun, which was supposed to be symbolical of the destruction of the world, when Odin would be devoured by the wolf Fenrir. In harvest time, a bunch of ears, tied up with ribbons, was left standing in the field for Odin's horse. On all important occasions divine counsel was sought by the examination of favorable or unfavorable omens. Jacob Grimm has, in his German Mythology, collected a number of these omens which were superstitiously observed long after the introduction of Christianity.

XXIII. *Pagan Superstitions*

THE learned Grimm has, with his usual laborious research, proved that the religion of southern Germany was, in the time of Tacitus, essentially the same as that of Scandinavia shortly before the time of Snorri, and that all the German nations, before their conversion to Christianity, called their superior gods by the same names, and had the same idea of nature, and consequently the same superstitions, fables, and legends.

The religion of the north, however, appears to have been, at a later period, of a higher and more polished order, and certain religious differences seem to have attached themselves to various localities and tribes. The German religion, like all those of ancient times, gradually fell from the simple adoration of one invisible Deity to the worship of the sun, moon, stars, elements, and other powers of nature, which, when the human race became more polished, were ingeniously and poetically humanized; a progression of the human imagination common to most nations, as may be proved by closely investigating the religions of Greece, Rome, and Asia.

The worship of the stars and of the elements was common to the Swabian nations, while that of the heroes, in which gods were represented under the form of men, was already practiced by the Frankish, Saxon, and particularly by the Scandinavian tribes. When Christianity, advancing step by step, uprooted pagan superstition, the worship of the heroes took refuge with the fugitive Norwegians in Iceland, where were preserved the sacred books of the Edda, in which the purer natural religion, and even the first doctrine of the existence of one invisible God, are again recognizable, among the ingenious fables of the heroes. According to these books, the most ancient god is Allfadur (*Allfater*, Father of all), the indivisible and eternal Creator and Preserver, the Father of the universe and of the inferior gods, whom he will survive, and who will one day destroy both them and the present world, and create a new one in its stead. The three Nornen, or goddesses of fate, the past, the present, and the future (beneath whose rule all temporal concerns stand fixed, and come but to pass away), are regarded as continually proceeding from him; while the whole of nature's creations, both gods and men, are regarded as merely temporary effluences from the one great and supreme being.

Allfater reigned alone over boundless void, which, by the power of his glance, split into two halves; one, Muspelheim, the world of light; the other, Nilfheim, or the abode of darkness. The spirit of Light was Surtur; the spirit of Night, Hela. Then Allfater commanded them to mingle, in order to produce a third and middle world, and a fiery shower of sparks fell from Muspelheim into the damp, cold Nilfheim, and fire and water battled together, fizzing and boiling, until from this fearful ferment two monsters sprang; first, from the dark and evil genius of Night came the giant Ymer, the symbol of brute force; then, from the light and good spirit of fire, the divine cow, Audhumla, the symbol of nourishing and preserving power. Ymer looked upon himself as the monarch of the world, and from his right and left foot issued a six-headed son, the father of the Hrymthursen, or wicked ice-giants, who inherited the cold nature of their progenitor, Night. The cow licked the good god, Buri, out of a rock of salt, from whose son, Bör, descended the three brothers, Odin, Wile, and We. These good gods slew the wicked Ymer, and, tearing his body into pieces, created the earth out of it. The giant's skull formed the vault of heaven; his brains, the clouds; his hair, the forests; his bones, the mountains; and his blood, the sea. But the gods made the first man and woman out of two trees, the oak and the alder. Henceforth men dwelt in the world, and good gods ruled over it; but the bad giants of the race of Ymer still existed, and the gods, foolishly intermingling with them, allowed Loki, one of the sons of the giants, to take his seat among them as the god of evil, who was one day destined to allure them to destruction. Thus the principle of evil was not entirely subdued by the death of Ymer, but still continued to struggle throughout all nature against the spirit of good.

XXIV. *The Ancient Idea of Nature*

ALTHOUGH the whole of nature was thus supposed to have been created out of the body of the giant Ymer, it was regarded as originally proceeding from the primary worlds of light and darkness, still existing beyond its limits. Muspelheim, the empire of Surtur, hung far above the heavens, and the sun, moon and stars were merely streams of light flowing downward from it. Far beneath the earth lay ancient Nilfheim, the kingdom of Hela, or hell, whose abode was Helheim; whose palace was Misery; whose table, Hunger; whose servant, Delay; whose threshold, Ruin; whose bed, Sorrow; and whose color was Decay. Nine long nights must the dead ride through dark valleys, when they reached Giöll, the river of hell, and rode over the bridge into Nilfheim, where all went who, instead of falling by the sword, died like cowards on their beds; all those also who had been thieves, or liars, or had acted dishonorably; but the deepest pit in Nilfheim was Huergelmir, completely built of snakes' heads, unceasingly spitting poison on the damned.

Between the middle world and Muspelheim lay another, inhabited by the good spirits of nature (Liosalfarheim, Lichtalfheim), born of the elves of light; the wise and tender genii of the elements, Fylgien, or guardian spirits; and the Walkyren, who were also the clouds, the messengers of Odin. Hence came the countless legends of elves and fairies, beneficent toward mankind, especially toward the poor, and children; hence also the stories of wood and water Nixen or nymphs; of the fantastical loves of sylphs and Undinen, and of river and tree elves.

The stars were sparks out of Muspelheim, directed by

Odin: thus the sun was called Odin's eye; the constellation of the Great Bear, Odin's chariot; and Jacob's Staff, the distaff of the goddess Freya. Odin also created day and night, and gave to the former, the horse Skinfari, the golden-maned; and to the latter, the horse Hrinfari, the mane of dew.

Between the middle world and Nilfheim lay also another world, Schwartalfaheim, belonging to the black elves, who dwelt in the interior of the earth, particularly in mountains. These are the Kobolds, who watch over subterranean treasures and metals, and generally attempt to hurt and to corrupt men. Tho numerous legends of the Venusberg, Kyffhäuserberg, Untersberg, Zobtenberg, Hörselberg, etc., prove that the mountains were supposed to be hollow, and to contain treasures or seductive spirits; and at a later period, to be haunted by the souls of the dead. The legend of the Tannhäuser, who entered the Venusberg, and there dwelt in joy and delight with the beauteous and mysterious mountain queen, is very old, and equally so are the stories of the mountain king, Rübezahl, who, under the form of a man, tempted maidens into the interior of the Priesengebirge. The water spirits were also supposed to be generally wicked, though sometimes only sportive. The word *necken*, to tease, came from Neck, Nickel, Nixe, the appellation of the water spirits; whence the River Neckar also derived its name.

Plants and animals were also connected in various degrees with the bright and black elves, by whom they were animated, and caused good or evil. The middle world, or earth, placed between these double worlds of light and darkness, was called Mannheim, the home of man, and was divided into an upper and a lower part; the former of which was Asgard, the heaven of the gods, with the beautiful Walhalla, whose windows overlooked the paradise destined for pious women and children; and the latter was the earth. The rainbow, the sign of union, was supposed to form a bridge called Bifrost, joining earth to heaven, by means of which the gods descended to the earth and the souls of men mounted to Walhalla. The earth was believed to be round, and to be surrounded by the ocean (Ymer's blood) or by the great Mitgard snake, Jormungardur; in the ocean dwelt the god Œgir and innumerable sea nymphs. As animals, plants, and metals were inhabited by elves and dwarfs, delicate and diminutive but powerful and cunning spirits, the mountains, seas, and ruder features of nature were naturally the abode of the giant race of Ymer. The extreme north was full of Hrymthursen or ice giants. Niord, the god of the cold air, is especially the god of the north; Uller, the god of winter; Kari, the god of the wind, and his sons, frost, ice, and snow. The manner in which the giants were identified with natural phenomena is visible in the following poetical Saga: When Gerdha, the daughter of the giants, closed her house door, heaven and earth were illumined by the reflection of her beautiful white arms; signifying the Northern Lights. As Hvenilda, the daughter of the giants, carrying earth in her apron, was wading through the ocean, the apron tore, and the earth, falling into the water, formed the island of Hven.

XXV. *The Gods*

THE polytheism of the Germans arose from the intermixture of this original idea of the cause of natural phenomena, with those borrowed from history and domestic life, or produced by their natural tendencies and lively imaginations. Allfater, primarily the one invisible God, afterward became the visible source of light, the sun, and finally, a demigod, Odin. Thus, in the golden temple at Upsala, the supreme deity of ancient Germany, who, from the Gulf of Bothnia to the Bodensee, was worshiped as the Father of all, the eternal God, in a word, as God, was first imaged as a beaming sun, and was afterward represented standing before this sun under the form of a human hero, Odin-Sigge. The wolf saga in the Edda is also twofold. A wolf swallows the sun, another swallows the hero, Odin, but both are one; hence the name of the year (as in the Greek, λυκάβας), Wolfgang, *i.e.*, the sun passing before the wolf. The Saga relates much of Odin that merely identifies him with man, and renders him ridiculous, so that the ancient pure belief in Wodan, Guodan, God, was almost forgotten, like the idea of the supreme divinity among the Romans, effaced by the image of the sensual and capricious Jupiter.

The idea of Allfater produced those of light and fire; of Surtur, the sun, the Persian Ormuzd, who was perhaps identical with Irmin; of Mannus, the father of all mankind; of Thaut, Thuisko, peculiarly the god of the Germans; and of Odin, the demigod, who, in the historical records, is spoken of as a man, the founder of kingly races, and from whom the Germans derived their customs, warlike habits, and arts; hence he was the god of victory (Sigge), and especially that of war and weapons; the god of wisdom; the inventor of letters, sciences, and arts. The invention of poetry is also ascribed to his having, in the form of an eagle, devoured the honey containing the poetical inspiration; but when flying back with it to Asgard, he was so closely pursued that he let a part of it drop from behind on the summit of the Asenberg, the tasting of which produced the bad poets, while the good ones were fed upon the honey that issued from his beak on the Himmelsberg. Drollery and sublimity thus go hand in hand throughout the Saga of Odin.

Odin's heavenly palace was the Walhalla, an enormous hall ornamented with golden escutcheons and lances, to which 540 doors led, each so wide that 800 heroes could march through them abreast. Here came all the souls of warriors, Einheriar (*einig, ein Heer bildende Waffenbrüder*, singly composing an army of companions in arms), who daily rode with the gods on the great plains of Ida, and battled with one another, in order to continue, after death, the heroic deeds they joyed in during life, and every evening returned to Walhalla, where, seated in a circle, they drank rich mead from golden goblets, presented to them by the beauteous

Walkyren, and fed upon the flesh of the boar, Sährimnir, which always remained whole, whatever number of steaks were cut from him, and upon the apples of Iduna, which preserved them in eternal youth, while the scalds sang in praise of the gods, of the charms of the Walkyren, and of past glory; Odin presiding over the feast, and rejoicing over his countless armies of heroes. The windows of Walhalla overlooked all the other heavens, which lay round about like beautiful castles, where the gods dwelt singly with their wives, and where the pious wives and children of mortals, who could not enter Walhalla, but might dwell in its vicinity, were transferred. Odin belonged to the world of light, his wife Frigga to that of darkness, but she was raised by her union with him to that of light. She was mother Earth, and stands in the same relation to the female black elves and Hela, as the goddesses of the earth, of Greece, Rome, and Egypt, did to the infernal powers; and, in the superstitions of Christian times, she was styled Frau Hölle (hell) or Frau Bertha, who, in her amiable character, was the prophetess of housewives and of households, and, in her fearful one, the leader of the night chase. In short, she personated the darkness of earth, and Odin the brightness of heaven; and as Odin was always imagined to be riding on the eight-legged horse, Sleipnir, Frigga is represented as seated in a chariot drawn by cows; horses being sacred to him, and cows to her. The image, washed in the lake, mentioned by Tacitus, was hers. She was also probably identical with Isis, of whom that writer says that she was carried about in a ship. In 1133 a ship was drawn overland, in solemn procession, with dancing and music, from Aix-la-Chapelle to Maestricht, evidently a pagan custom, in which the procession accompanying the chariot or ship was probably intended to represent the early migrations of the Germans.

Freyr and Freya were connected in the same manner as Odin and Frigga. Freyr was the son of Odin, in a stricter sense, the sun; and consequently the guardian of all the white elves. Freya was the daughter of Niord, and therefore belonged to the spirits of damp and darkness; she was the moon, and the goddess of love; and as Freyr, the sun, rode on a golden bear, she rode on a silver one, having in her train, Siofna, the first feelings of love, Lofna, happy love, Wara, true love, Snotra, shame, and Gefion, innocence; and, although in this manner belonging to light, she appears, from the above-mentioned Saga of the Venusberg concerning love charms and philters, to be in close connection with the black elves, over whom she probably reigned, as Freyr did over the white ones.

Thor or Dunar, the god of thunder, who was supposed to be drawn by black goats through the air, bearing in his hand Miölner, the hammer of destruction, and the great drinking horn with which he once nearly drained the ocean, thus causing the ebb and flow, bears much similarity to Odin, and is apparently a Gælic divinity of more ancient date, who continued to be worshiped by the Galli under the name of Taranes, and by the Finns and Lapps under that of Tiermes, the supreme god. Tyr, the god of war, is also identical with him, as well as Widar, the god of locomotion, who walked through and crushed everything with his iron shoes.

The rest of the Asen are bright gods of light; Wali, the spring; Balldr, beauty; Braga, the god of poetry; Saga, the goddess of history; Iduna, immortality; Heimdall, the god of the three classes, the nobles, the freeborn, and the slaves; and Forsete, the god of peace and justice. The twelve Asen, Thor, Balldr, Niord, Freyr, Tyr, Braga, Heimdall, Widar, Wali, Uller, Forsete, and Loki, were chosen from among all these various deities, and, assembled around Odin, assisted in governing the world; they also signify the twelve months of the year, and again appear in the seven days of the week: Wednesday, Odin's day; Thursday, Thor's day; Friday, Freya's day.

XXVI. *Historical Ideas*

As the outward frame of the earth was supposed to have been created out of the body of the giant Ymer, the ash tree, Ygdrasill, was supposed to represent its external growth and internal life. This tree reached from the bottom of Nilfheim far beyond all the heavens; it had three roots, by each of which there was a source; Urdarborn, the source of time; Mimer's well, the source of wisdom; and Huergelmir, the source of poison. Nidhöggur, the dragon, the father of all the snakes in Huergelmir, unceasingly gnawed the roots. The three Nornen or fates, the past, the present, and the future, sat around the source of time. Far above, at the top of the tree, perched an eagle, the symbol of perfection, perhaps as the fire eagle, the self-animating phœnix, while a squirrel ran busily up and down, making mischief between the dragon below and the eagle above. As soon as the dragon gnawed through the roots, the noble tree was to fall, and time and all earthly things were to cease. This beautiful world was not to endure forever; the gods, like men, mere creatures of Allfater, were subject to evil and destruction. All that was earthly would pass away, but Allfater would renovate earth and heaven. The ancient legends of the gods conclude with this doctrine, and this conclusion of the Edda is in extraordinary agreement with that of the old songs of the Nibelungen; in the former, the gods are destroyed; in the latter, men; and both, in the true old German heroic spirit, in expiation of a crime, but courageously despising death and fighting to the last. Thus the heroes and warriors imagined that all things would end in the manner in which they aspired to die, sword in hand on the battlefield. The ancient notions of the Germans, with regard to the intention of history and the moral to be deduced from it, are most clearly expressed by the symbol of the ash tree, the first Saga that speaks of the destruction of gods and men; nor can it be doubted that these ideas were continually present to the imagination of the Germans. The indifference with which they met death, nay, the eagerness with which they sought it, their high estimation of a virtuous and honorable life, and the unfaltering bravery with which they opposed irremediable destruction, are characteristics whose source is easily traced in the spirit of their religion, the fundamental principle of which was to die nobly. To die on the battlefield was sufficient atonement for any crime of which they had been guilty. They allowed their gods to sin, but made them die like heroes, which rendered them worthy of a future and glorious resurrection. But their gods were merely symbolical of themselves. Thus the oldest and first song of the Edda, the Voluspa, commences. A Wale advances into the circle of the gods, and in awful tones announces their fall and the destruction of the lordly Asgard, at the general conflagration of the world. This event will be caused by the gods, who will sin in common with the wicked of Ymer's ancient race, and will consequently be abandoned by the inward light which they derived from Muspelheim. However, the golden age is still of long duration; vengeance does not soon overtake their crime. Then the gods gamble in heaven, and, heated by play, do not perceive the approach of three daughters of the giants, who steal their golden Runic tables, upon which Allfater had himself inscribed the laws of the universe. Then the golden age is at an end. Care and anxiety take possession of the gods, who, forgetful of their given word, kill Angurbode, one of the three giantesses. Loki finds her out-torn heart, and falls in love with her; and as until now he was accounted one of the Asen, he goes over to the wicked giants in order to plot the destruction of his former companions. At the same time, a young wolf, Fenrir, which was brought up in Asgard, grows to such an enormous size that the Asen begin to feel uneasy. In vain they bind him; he breaks every chain. At length they try to bind him with a charm, but he does not allow the chain to be placed upon him until they swear that it is not a charm. They forswear themselves, and Tyr has the courage to lay his hand as security in the wolf's mouth, who instantly bites it off on discovering the deception. The gods are no longer worthy of life. Iduna, or immortality, is tempted from them by a giant; however, they still possess Balldr, or enchanting beauty; but the ugly quarrel with him, and his only brother, the blind Hödur, is unwittingly incited to kill him by Loki, and his wife, Nana, burns herself upon his funeral pile. Then the Asen take foul revenge on Loki, and, sinning against sacred nature, bind him with the bowels of his only son to three pointed rocks, and suspend over his head a snake distilling poison. His convulsions produce the earthquakes. The end of all things is now at hand. The rage of the gods and the wickedness of men increase. Enmity and hate have universal rule; then come fear and woe, the hatchet and sword age, the storm and wolf era. For three years there is unbroken icy winter, the frightful Fimbul weather, during which everything is buried in frozen sleep, before the awful end. The earth begins to shake; the dragon has gnawed through the roots; and the ash tree, Ygdrasill, will fall and crush the whole world. The wolf, Fenrir, madly struggles with his bonds, and bursts them. Loki also breaks away from the rocks. Across the sea come the giants, the Hrymthursen, in the ship Nagelfar, entirely built of the nails of dead men fastened together, a proof of the antiquity of the world. The Mitgard snake rises from the ocean like a gigantic ghost, and they all besiege Asgard from below. The Asen and all the Einheriar are armed and fight their last glorious battle, nor do they despair of success, until Muspelheim opens from above, and Surtur issues in flames at the head of his fiery squadrons, beneath whom the rainbow bridge, the symbol of union, breaks asunder, and everything is lost. Heimdall and Loki kill themselves; Thor slays the Mitgard snake, but dies of his poisoned wounds; Freyr is burned by Surtur; Odin is swallowed alive by the wolf Fenrir, whose open jaws reach from beneath the earth to heaven. Finally, the whole world is destroyed by the flames of Surtur, and becomes Ragnarok, or the incense of the gods. After this, Allfater will create a new world, devoid of evil.

PART II

THE WARS WITH THE ROMANS

XXVII. *The Romans*

IN the eighth century before Christ, Rome was peopled by fugitives from different parts of the country. The city was at first governed by kings, who might almost be termed robber kings, on account of the depredations they committed against neighboring nations. The Romans, however, strengthened by petty conquests, and rendered hardy and independent by continual warfare, soon drove out their kings, and founded a republic on the plan of the more ancient ones of Greece, whence they subsequently drew their refinement and arts, while from the brave Alpine nations, with whom they early came in collision, they acquired that heroic spirit which, at a later period, rendered them as formidable to the Greeks as their superior science and knowledge became to the Germans.

Rome was yet in her infancy when, four centuries B.C., two immense German hordes, the Senones and Boii, crossed the Alps, and settled in the fertile plains of Italy. Rome was taken and burned, but quickly recovered from this first attack, and the watchful cunning and steady courage of her inhabitants soon proved fatal to the warriors of the north, whose hardy habits had gradually degenerated in that luxurious climate. Their impolitic division into small and independent tribes was another cause of their ruin, and, after a long and bloody struggle, part of them were, one after the other, exterminated, and the rest incorporated with the now aggrandized republic, whose warriors had exercised their martial spirit, and improved their military tactics, during this long and difficult war. In the second century B.C., when Rome bore sway over the whole of Italy as far as the Alps, and had even subdued the southern provinces of Gaul on the Rhone, fresh hordes of barbarians, the Cimbri and Teutones, crossed the Alps, and again threatened the Roman power with destruction; but when, in their proud contempt of Rome, they again imprudently divided, they fell a prey to the sagacity and prodigious efforts of the Romans, who, compelled by necessity, reformed the ancient republic, and by conferring on the plebeians the privileges until now monopolized by the ancient and haughty patricians, gave an impulse to, and united the efforts of, every class; a measure by which the safety of the mass could alone be secured, and which added more citizens to Rome (for the inhabitants of neighboring states became ambitious to gain that honorable distinction) than she gained by the fame of her victories over the Cimbri.

Thus Rome a second time owed the increase of her power to German influence. Her insatiable ambition fed by conquest, she grasped at universal dominion, and after subduing all the countries in her immediate vicinity, boldly planned the reduction of the whole world. Greece, Asia Minor, the northern coasts of Africa, the whole of southern and western Europe, every Gallic and Celtic country, as far as Britain, submitted to the Roman eagle, which was alone defied by our elder brethren, the Persians, in the fastnesses of Asia, and by the Germans beyond the Danube and the Rhine. The fearful struggle between the Romans and the Germans, which lasted, almost unbroken, for nearly five centuries after the war with the Cimbri, extended along the shores of the Black Sea, and followed the course of the Danube, and of the Rhine as far as the Baltic. At one time, the Germans, quitting their wild forests, would lay waste the Roman frontier; or at another, the Romans would march their well-disciplined and ironclad legions to the Weser and the Elbe;

and in this manner the war was carried on, with various fortune, throughout whole centuries, until Rome, sated with the spoils of countless nations, sank into the lap of luxury, and her citizens, raised by unjust wars to unjust dominion, lost their ancient love of honor and liberty.

The legions, flushed with victory, ruled despotically over the helpless citizens, destroyed the ancient republic, and raised their generals to the throne, who, during successive centuries, turned the whole force of the mighty Roman empire against Germany. Millions of ironclad men, picked from every part of the world, well disciplined and practiced in every species of warfare, flexible and obedient to the will of their skillful leaders, thirsting for glory, or maddened by jealousy and revenge, besieged Germany on every side, and fell upon the poor half-naked native, whose only defense lay in the dark forest depths and the untaught strength of his arm. The event speaks for itself. These half-naked tribes, after the longest and most glorious struggle for liberty recorded in the annals of mankind, after crushing the masters of the world, and shattering their boundless empire, now form a great and powerful nation, while the very name of Roman is vanishing from the earth.

XXVIII. *The Senones and the Boii in Italy*

On the upper Danube, in modern Swabia, dwelt the Senones, and in modern Bavaria, their neighbors, the Boii. In the fourth century B.C., Helico, a carpenter, came to them, bringing with him the juicy grapes and golden fruit of Italy, which they beheld for the first time, and greedily desiring to possess a land that produced such luscious fruit, they migrated in immense hordes, under a leader named Brennus, and climbing the snow-topped Alps, descended into the smiling valleys of the Po, whence they gradually reached Rome, whose inhabitants, at that period, still weak, and depending more on their cunning than their strength, begged for peace, which was granted; but when, breaking their oath, they suddenly fell upon the unsuspecting strangers, Brennus, justly enraged, severely chastised their perfidy, and after totally defeating them, took the city [B.C. 389] and burned it to the ground. The aged senators, unwilling to survive the destruction of the city, had remained in the senate house, seated in state in their white and purple robes, with scepters in their hands; and when the Germans, armed with sword and brand, rushed tumultuously into the hall, they were seized with awe on beholding these venerable and motionless figures, which they imagined to be spirits or statues, until one of them, wishing to discover whether they were alive, took hold of the beard of one of the senators, who, resenting the insult, struck him to the ground with his scepter. The illusion was instantly dispelled, and the senators were murdered. The Capitol, which was commanded by Manlius, and still held out, narrowly escaped being surprised by the Germans, who, during the night, had scaled the rock on which it was built, when the sleeping garrison was aroused by the cackling of the geese, disturbed by their approach. One thousand pounds of gold purchased the departure of Brennus, who, with the insolence of a conqueror, threw his sword into the scales, and bade them add its weight to the ransom.

The Senones and Boii afterward settled in the north of Italy, but did not long remain at peace with the Romans, with whom they were so continually at war that every year produced a fresh list of battles, victories, and defeats. In these perpetual struggles with their belligerent neighbors, the Romans quickly acquired the military skill and discipline which in course of time rendered them so formidable, and so superior to their once-dreaded opponents, who, had they united in the pursuance of one settled plan of warfare, might have crushed the Roman empire in the bud.

XXIX. *The Senones and the Boii in Greece and Asia Minor*

IN the third century before Christ, the same nations, uniting with several others, migrated from the interior of Germany into Greece. They consisted of Senones, Boii, Cimbri, Teutobodiaci, etc., and had several leaders, among whom was another Brennus. Flushed with success, and greedy of plunder, they attempted to seize the treasures in the sacred temple at Delphi. Their impious daring was speedily chastised. A fearful whirlwind and storm suddenly arose; the earth quaked, the rocks fell, and, struck with horror and dismay, the barbarians fled. Vast numbers fell by the hands of the Greeks. Brennus was wounded, and the remainder of his army, being weakened by pestilence, and in danger of being captured, voluntarily burned themselves alive, to the number of 20,000 men, together with their booty, in their encampment. The soothsayers foretelling disaster to another horde when on the point of giving battle, they resolved to die like warriors, and after killing their wives and children, rushed into the midst of the enemy, and fell at the point of the sword. A third horde had, meanwhile, crossed to Asia Minor; the land pleased them, and settling there, they founded a nation, named, by the Greeks and Romans, Gallo-Græcians, or Galatians; the same to which St. Paul addressed one of his Epistles. They were distinguished by different names among themselves, and were divided into no less than 195 petty tribes, which were comprised under three heads within twelve districts, and had a general place of assembly, called Drynaimet. The twelve representatives of the districts, who formed the supreme council, were assisted by three hundred men; a hundred being chosen from each of the three heads or chief tribes; a form of government perfectly similar to those met with, at a later period, in Germany. In course of time, however, some men contrived to get themselves elected perpetual dukes of Galatia, and, at the time of the birth of Christ, this nation had shared the fate of its Asiatic neighbors, and had fallen under the Roman rule; but it always retained its original language, which, according to St. Hieronymus, was similar to the dialect spoken in the country round Treves. Fourteen hundred years after the settlement of these people in Asia, when the German crusaders passed through Galatia, they were astonished to find that the inhabitants spoke with the Bavarian accent. The greater part of the settlers were originally Boii.

XXX. *The Romans in the Alps*

ROME gradually increased in power, and ere long threatened destruction to the Senones and Boii in Upper Italy, who consequently besought the assistance of their brethren on the other side of the Alps. Accordingly, 200,000 German warriors, named Gæsatæ (guests, or *geeiseten*, ironclad), marched thence toward Rome; their leader, Britomar, a Boii, vowing not to loosen his girdle until he had taken the Capitol. The Romans twice suffered defeat, but the whole of Italy rising in the common cause, an army, consisting of 700,000 infantry and 70,000 cavalry, was raised, and, commanded by the brave Æmilius, made head against the invading host, which it succeeded in surrounding near the River Telamon, where, after a desperate conflict. victory sided with the Romans; 40,000 of the barbarians were slain, and their chief, Britomar, was taken prisoner [B.C. 225]. Another chief and all his followers killed themselves in despair; and a third, Ariovistus, took shelter in the mountains, where for two years he was supported by 20,000 Cenomanni and Heneti, but was finally overcome by the Romans [B.C. 223]. In the following year [B.C. 222], Wiridomar led 30,000 Germans from the Rhine, who were also defeated by the Romans. Wiridomar fell by the hand of the consul, Marcellus. Hannibal, the great Carthaginian general, who, with his gigantic elephants and dark Africans, traversed Spain, Gaul, and the Alps, with the design of crushing the ambition of Rome, already threatening to enslave the world, was received with open arms by the Alpine tribes. Some of the Senones and Boii fought under his command at Ticinum, where Cryxus, a descendant of Brennus, lost his life. Ducarius, the leader of the Boii, avenged the death of Wiridomar, by killing the consul Flaminius in single combat at the battle of Trasimene [B.C. 217], on which occasion the Boii buried 25,000 Romans in a wood, and used the skull of the consul Posthumus as a sacrificial cup. Hannibal was, however, no sooner called to Carthage, on account of the invasion of Africa by the Romans, than fortune again sided with the latter, and after several desperate and bloody battles, in one of which 35,000, and in another 40,000, of their number fell, the Germans were forced to retreat. The Boii long and obstinately defended the fortresses raised by them beyond the Lake of Como, but were finally obliged to cede them, together with their strongest fort, Felsina, to the Romans, and to take refuge in the mountains, whence they carried on a desultory and destructive warfare, until betrayed by their allies, the Cenomanni and Heneti, whose knowledge of the country and of mountain warfare proved of infinite service to the Romans; and at length, weakened by repeated losses, they were utterly annihilated in a battle, in which 32,000 of them were slain [B.C. 191]. This victory placed the whole of the southern side of the Alps in the hands of the Romans, who by skilfully exciting the mutual jealousies of the petty mountain tribes, some of which they took into their alliance and raised to the rank of Roman citizens, and by systematically exterminating others that offered resistance, quickly opened a route to the western side of the Alps, and, taking possession of Gaul, made the beautiful country on the Rhone into a Roman province, whence is derived its present name—*Provence.*

XXXI. *The Getæ and Bastarnæ*

It is uncertain whether the Budini, mentioned by Herodotus, inhabited the west or the north of Russia. Their name, blue eyes, light hair, and sacred forest lakes, indicate an affinity with the Goths of later times [B.C. 500]. The Getæ dwelt near the mouths of the Danube, behind them, further up the river, the Daci, and beyond them the Pannonians, at the time of the invasion of Darius, king of Persia, who, crossing the river, narrowly escaped total destruction on the steppes lying northward. His alliance was sought by the Pannonians, who sent to him a tall and beautiful girl, bearing on her head a vessel filled with water, and spinning while she led a horse by a bridle on her arm; on observing his surprise, they informed him that they were descended from the Teucri of Troy, and that all their women were as industrious and as useful as the maiden he beheld. On his penetrating deeper into the steppe, the Scythians (probably of Thracian or German, Tartarian or Slavonian origin) mockingly presented him with a bird, a mouse, a frog, and five arrows, signs that implied, "Unless you can hide yourself in the air like a bird, or under ground like a mouse, or in the water like a frog, our arrows will slay you before you reach our frontiers"; a threat they almost succeeded in executing, for, enticing the Persian army further up the country, it was surrounded, and only rescued from destruction by a successful stratagem. We learn from the Greeks that the wise Zamolxis taught the doctrine of the immortality of the soul to the Getæ, whose king, Diceneus, made him their legislator. Long after the disastrous expedition of Darius, toward the close of the fourth century before Christ, Alexander the Great, when attempting to extend his Grecian boundary as far as the Danube, overthrew the Getæ, and drove the Triballi, one of their tribes, from the island of Peuce, which was probably held sacred by them.

Pliny names all the German tribes of the Danube, Peucini, from this island.

The Romans had no sooner gained possession of the Alps, than they sought to extend their dominion further eastward, over Illyria, and to bring the German tribes of the Danube, as well as the Greeks, into submission. The Illyrian queen, the brave Teuta, whose ships spread terror and desolation along the coasts of Italy, cut off the heads of their embassadors and long bade them defiance, but being at length defeated, died of grief [B.C. 229]. Gentius, her third successor, struggled valiantly against them, and besought the assistance of Perseus, the Grecian king, who, influenced by avarice and indolence, left him to his fate, and he was forced to yield [B.C. 167]. The embassadors sent on this occasion to negotiate peace with the Romans were named Teuticus and Bellus. The wretched Perseus, when too late, sought to repair the consequences of his procrastination, and assembled the Getæ and their northern neighbors, the Bastarnæ, in order to make head against the Romans. One of their leaders was called Teutagonus. The avarice of the king, however, proved stronger than his apprehensions, and he refused the sum demanded by his allies; one of whom, Clondicus, king of the Bastarnæ, indignant at this baseness, devastated Thrace and returned to his own country, without offering any opposition to the Romans, who gradually subdued all the mountain tribes of Dalmatia and Croatia, one of which, the Stœni, rendered desperate by defeat, preferred death to slavery.

XXXII. *Irruption of the Cimbri and Teutones* [B.C. 113]

IN the beginning of the second century before Christ, a torrent of wandering hordes, the Cimbri and Teutones, descended from the Danube to the Styrian Alps, giving out that a flood had driven them from the North Sea, and that they were in search of a country wherein to settle. During their advance, they were joined by several of the southern

German tribes, among others, by the Boii, one of whose leaders was named Bojorix. Their progress was extremely slow, owing to their being accompanied by women and children, cattle, and an immense number of wagons laden with booty. The armed men alone mustered 300,000. The Cimbri had 15,000 horsemen, clad in polished steel armor, and armed with broad swords and long lances, their helmets ornamented with the horns of wild beasts, wings, and plumes of feathers. These people were of gigantic stature, and their long flowing golden hair, and fierce blue eyes, increased the majesty of their appearance. The Romans, panicstruck at their approach, dispatched an army to oppose the passage of the strangers through the Alps, and to secure the allegiance of their newly-acquired Alpine subjects. The wanderers received the Roman deputation peacefully, and said that they were only going into Gaul. But being treacherously misled by Carbo, the Roman general, who suddenly fell upon them during the night, while they were engaged in a narrow mountain pass, not far from the city of Noreja, a dreadful conflict took place, which terminated in the total discomfiture of the whole Roman army; the few who escaped with the general owing their safety to a storm, which suddenly arose and rendered pursuit impossible. After this event, the wanderers remained for several years in the Alps, slowly advancing toward Gaul; the sturdy mountaineers everywhere swelling their ranks. On reaching Helvetia they were joined by the inhabitants of two districts, the Tigurini (Zurichers) and the Toygeni (Toggenburgers), headed by the youthful Divico. The whole swarm now poured from the mountains into Gaul, and took possession of the country as far as the seacoast, the inhabitants flying for shelter within the walls of their fortified cities, which were fruitlessly besieged. Their attempts to subdue the German tribes, or Belgæ, inhabiting the Netherlands, proved equally futile. The Cimbri, either wearied by the protracted defense made by the cities, or perhaps merely incited by their roving and warlike habits, and attracted by the fertility of the southern countries, forgot their first intention, and, while the Teutones were busily engaged with the Belgæ, resolved to quit Gaul. On reaching the country near Marseilles, they fell in with a Roman army guarding the frontier, and commanded by Silanus, from whom they demanded permission to settle in Italy, which being refused, a battle took place, in which the Romans were worsted. Another frontier army, stationed near the Lake of Geneva, was attacked by Divico at the head of the Helvetians, and so completely defeated that all the Romans who escaped the slaughter were taken prisoners and forced to crawl ignominiously under a lance, placed horizontally on two low posts.

Another army, under Scaurus, sent to oppose them, was also defeated, and the general taken prisoner. He was afterward slain by Bojorix, the youthful German chief, in a fit of passion, excited by hearing the captive Roman proudly foretell that Italy would never become the prey of the German invader.

Shortly after these successes, they were rejoined by the Teutones, and the Romans were only able to dispatch against their now almost irresistible force a single and dispirited army, commanded by two generals, Manlius and Cæpio, who hated and finally abandoned each other. Cæpio, by plundering Gaul, imbittered the inhabitants against him, and venturing unaided an engagement with the Germans, was completely beaten [B.C. 105], and Manlius, who hastened to his succor when too late, shared the same fate. In this conflict, that took place on the banks of the Rhone, no quarter was given; every Roman was put to the sword, and the immense booty that fell into the hands of the victors was consecrated to the gods and cast into the river. The province now lay open and defenseless; victory had abandoned the Roman eagle, and Rome, amazed and helpless, saw herself doomed to certain destruction; one step more, and all Italy lay at the feet of the Germans, when, suddenly renouncing their project, they poured across the Pyrenees into Spain, then inhabited by the warlike Celtiberi, with whom they waged a futile war of three years' duration, while the Romans seized the unlooked-for opportunity to make fresh preparations for defense.

Marius, a renowned general, by birth a peasant, intrusted with the sole command, and armed with unlimited authority, raised, as if by magic, a fresh and immense army from the dregs of the populace, the slaves, and foreigners, which he daily exercised in military tactics, and accustomed to the endurance of the severest hardships, in which he set them an example. On the return of the Cimbri and Teutones from Spain [B.C. 102], he was strongly intrenched on the Rhone, and firmly resolved to dispute the passage into Italy, which three years before lay free and open before them. The two hordes now judged it politic to separate, and while the Teutones attacked Marius, the Cimbri entered the Tyrol, by which country they intended to enter Italy.

XXXIII. *The Destruction of the Teutones*

THE Teutones, presenting themselves before the camp of Marius, demanded land on which to settle in Italy, which was contemptuously refused; and, after vainly challenging him to battle on the open field, they made a furious but ineffectual attack upon the camp, whose strong walls and ditches withstood their irregular mode of assault, and the Romans soon became accustomed to the sight of their formidable opponents, who ere long, weary of the protracted siege, resolved to leave the camp in their rear, and to continue their route toward Italy. Their column was six days in defiling, nor did Marius obstruct their passage, although mockingly asked whether he had any message for Rome. As soon as their last ranks had disappeared, he broke up his camp, in the hope, by making forced marches along bypaths, of overtaking and surprising them in some favorable spot. The Teutones, meanwhile, followed the course of an Alpine torrent, and marched up the country to Aix, already celebrated for its medicinal waters, where they encamped in the valley, and were amusing themselves with bathing, feasting, drinking, and singing, when Marius suddenly appeared on the neighboring heights. His soldiers, although fatigued with a long march, were instantly ordered to erect a fortified camp. Evening had already fallen, and Marius, anxious to avoid a night attack, which might prove disastrous to himself, strictly prohibited any one to go down to the river to slake his thirst, lest, by that means, an engagement with the Teutones should be brought on; but some of the men, unable any longer to endure the thirst occasioned by a long day's march, disobeyed, and, descending to the river, were attacked by the Germans who were bathing. The alarm was instantly given, and Germans and Romans rushed eagerly to the spot. The Romans, dashing across the stream, attacked the wagoned encampment, which was bravely defended by the women, while the men rapidly assembled from the more distant parts of the camp, and almost succeeded in obstructing the retreat of Marius, who at length, though with great difficulty, regained the opposite bank. The Germans spent the night in drinking and gambling, and Marius, filled with horror as he listened to their wild shouts re-echoing along the mountains, vowed to sacrifice his daughter to the gods, if they granted him victory. The following day was passed on both sides in tranquillity, the Germans remaining peaceably in the valley, and Marius awaiting more favorable omens from the gods, which no sooner appeared than he prepared to attack the enemy on the following morning, and sent, under cover of night, a small chosen troop, commanded by his lieutenant, Marcellus, to take up a position to the rear of the barbarians. At sunrise Marius issued from the camp, and drew up his army in battle array, which was no sooner perceived by the enemy than, eager for the fight, they crossed the stream and stormed the hillside. The exertion of running so far, and their repeated slips on the steep, smooth surface of the hill, speedily rendered them weary and breathless, while the Romans, stationed in impenetrable masses on the edge of the cliff, easily repelled every attempt made to dislodge them. The immense numbers of the Germans now proved an additional source of disaster. Pressed upon from behind, unable to find a firm footing on the slippery ground, or to use their long lances and swords in the throng, their gigantic frames exposed to the short keen weapons of the Romans, who now pressed steadily down hill, while Marcellus fell upon their rear and fearfully redoubled the massacre, as many dying of suffocation as fell by the sword, they sought to extricate themselves from the fatal position into which their reckless daring and ignorance had hurried them, by flight.

The Teuton women defended the wagons to the last, when they offered to capitulate on condition of their honor being respected, which being refused, they murdered all their children, and then killed themselves. Marius preserved the most valuable of the spoils to grace his triumph, and collecting the remainder into an enormous pile, burned it in honor of the gods. The spot on which this battle took place, enriched by torrents of human blood and heaps of slain, in the following year produced wines, which afterward became celebrated, and the gigantic bones of the Teutones were long used for fencing in the vineyards. The greater part of the fugitives were taken by the Gauls and delivered to the Romans. Teutobach, the Teuton king, who was discovered and taken prisoner in a neighboring forest, was of such gigantic stature as to overtop all the other trophies in the triumphal procession. He was the same who is said to have leaped over six horses.

XXXIV. *The Destruction of the Cimbri*

THE Cimbri, meanwhile, traversed the narrow passes leading from the Tyrol into Italy, and viewed with delight the snow-capped mountains, which recalled to mind the winters of their northern home. Half naked and seated on their large shields, they slid down the glaciers, in those ancient times one of the favorite amusements of the Scandinavian mountaineers. The fertile vales of Italy, where they expected to meet their brethren, the Teutones, at length burst upon their view, and were greeted with shouts of joy. An army under Catulus, who had not ventured to oppose their passage through the Alps, fled, on their approach, as far as the river Adige, where, throwing up intrenchments on both banks of the stream, they awaited the enemy, who, encamping opposite the fortifications, tore up trees and built enormous rafts, which they loaded with pieces of rock, and floated down stream in such huge masses, and so quickly one after the other, as to cause the bridge connecting the two embankments to give way, and the river to overflow; whereupon they raised such a fearful war-cry that the Romans intrenched on the further bank of the river, deaf to the entreaties of their commander, fled panicstruck; while their countrymen on the opposite bank, imprisoned within their fortifications, defended themselves with such persevering bravery that the Cimbri, struck with admiration, gave them, unasked, peace and liberty. The wandering hordes, intoxicated with success, now spread themselves over the rich country around Verona, and madly reveling in the luxuries of the South, carelessly awaited the arrival of the Teutones, instead of whom Marius appeared at the head of his victorious army, strengthened by that of Catulus. The Cimbri, unsuspicious of the truth, sent a deputation to demand land for themselves and the Teutones, to whom Marius replied, "that their brethren had already land enough to rest upon," and, in explanation of his words, showed them the Teuton king in chains. In silent wrath, the Cimbrian embassadors returned to their encampment, and on the following day the youthful Bojorix, seated proudly on horseback, appeared as a herald before the camp of Marius, according to German custom, to challenge him to fix the time and place for battle. With a sneer at their frank and loyal chivalry, Marius named the third day, and the dusty plain of Vercelli.

The morning of the thirtieth of July, one hundred and one years before Christ, broke. A thick fog covered the whole country. The Cimbri were drawn up in a solid square, each side of which measured 7,500 paces. The foremost ranks were fastened together with chains, in order to render it more difficult for the enemy to break through them; and as each man bore a shield that covered his body, the whole mass resembled a wooden wall. Marius on his side provided the long spears of his soldiers with grappling hooks, with which to drag away the shields, the only defense of the Germans against the Roman short sword. The battle commenced, and the Roman cavalry, deceived by the feigned flight of the Cimbrian horse, and blinded by the fog, were drawn between them and the mass of infantry. In this moment of danger, Marius entreated the gods for assistance, and the sun suddenly beaming through the fog, which a high wind began to dissipate, the Romans discovered their perilous situation and retired, while Marius, joyfully exclaiming "The victory is ours!" made a vigorous charge upon the infantry, who, dazzled by the bright sunbeams which shone full in their faces, and suffocated by the clouds of dust, were speedily deprived of their shields, and a terrible carnage ensued. Unable to extricate themselves from the chain that bound them together, and fainting beneath the excessive heat and pressure, the living were dragged down by the dead. In this desperate situation, however, some contrived to stand their ground, and with impotent rage continued the struggle, until the shades of night veiled the scene of horror. Bojorix fell, sword in hand, with 90,000 of his followers; 60,000 were taken prisoners, and numbers killed themselves in despair. The women, dressed in black, with their golden locks in disarray, long defended the wagons, and slew every Teuton who fled from the enemy. When all was lost, they killed their children and then destroyed themselves. The Romans even then did not gain possession of the booty without a third battle with the dogs that guarded the baggage. The Helvetii, who had not quitted the narrow passes of the Alps, returned quietly to their own country on learning the disastrous fate of their allies.

The bravery evinced by the Germans so deeply impressed the Romans that the terror they had inspired became proverbial, and created a dim foreboding that their empire was destined to fall by the hands of the sons of the North. From this time, the Romans considered the Germans as, next to themselves, the bravest people in the world; a belief that was considerably strengthened during the subsequent wars, and rendered the Romans less confident in their own power. The wars with the Cimbri were also one of the primary causes of the gradual decay of the Roman empire, on account of the opportunity they afforded for the usurpation of the chief authority by plebeians, foreigners, and soldiers. The Cimbri and Teutones may thus be said to have conquered even in death, and although without the participation of the rest of the Germans, and on a foreign soil, not to have fallen in vain for their country.

XXXV. *Mithridates—The Insurrection of the Cimbrian Slaves—The Suevic Confederation*

THE Alps remained long undisturbed after the occurrence of these memorable events. Rome, meanwhile, became a prey to anarchy. Marius, supported by the soldiery, attempted to seize the government, but after a furious struggle was at length forced to yield to the young and haughty Sylla. When imprisoned in the city of Minturnæ, whither he had fled for safety, a Cimbrian slave, who was sent to cut off his head, was so struck by the countenance of the unarmed old man that the sword dropped from his hand, and the citizens, moved by the incident, restored the aged general to liberty. About the same period the Romans waged war with Mithridates, king of Pontus, who had boldly planned the deliverance of the nations subject to Rome. His youth had been spent among the Germans beyond the Danube, with whom he afterward connected himself by marrying his daughters to their chiefs, who assisted him in his enterprise against the Romans, and formed the chief strength of his army. But his brave and heroic spirit was destined to sink before the Roman eagle, and after losing three battles, being forced to seek safety by flight, a German, according to the custom of his nation, yielded to his desire, and deprived him of life [B.C. 63]. At the same time a war of a far more fearful character was occasioned in Italy by the insurrection of the slaves (who were prisoners, for the most part Germans taken in war), under their leader, Spartacus. Gannicus commanded the Cimbri. For three years they successfully repelled the veterans of Rome, filled Italy with terror, and even threatened the imperial city. But at length, rendered incautious by their rapacity and rashness, and becoming disobedient to their sagacious leader, they were all destroyed before they could succeed in crossing the Alps [B.C. 71].

The migration of the Cimbri and Teutones, which was doubtless caused by pressure from the North, had occasioned great disturbances throughout Germany, where a new power had probably either formed in their rear, or after their departure, as may be inferred from the fact that, shortly after the Cimbrian wars, the Suevic confederation, which devastated every country in its vicinity, and annually sent forth a thousand warlike adventurers from each of its hundred districts, is, for the first time, mentioned. While yet buried in the depths of their wild forests, their name spread terror through the Rhenish provinces and even reached the ears of the Romans. The Rhenish Germans also owned their inferiority to the Suevi, whom they considered superior to the rest of mankind, and only comparable to the immortal gods. Their separation from the western tribes, whom instead of succoring they attacked, and drove into the hands of the Romans, proved calamitous to Germany. Hemmed in on every side, they vainly sought to defend their liberty; and the tribes on the Upper Rhine that had united under Ariovistus, with those on the Lower Rhine under Ambiorix, were forced to yield to the victorious legions of the great Cæsar.

XXXVI. Ariovistus

Two Gallic nations, the Ædui and Sequani, dwelling on either side of the river Saone, quarreled for supremacy, instead of uniting against the Romans, who had already taken possession of Provence, and were only watching for an opportunity to seize the whole of Gaul. The Sequani, being worsted, called their neighbors from the Upper Rhine to their assistance, the Tribocci from Strasburgh, the Nemeti from Spires, the Vangiones from Worms, the Rauraci from Basil, the Tulingi from Tuttlingen, the Latobrigi from Breisgau, the Marcomanni from the Danube, the Sedusii, Harudi, and Narisci from between the Neckar and the Maine, in all 15,000 men, under the command of Ariovistus [B.C. 72], who, uniting with the Sequani, at the first onset completely defeated the Ædui, when, instead of returning whence they came, they resolved to settle in Gaul, and inviting multitudes of their countrymen over the Rhine, ordered the Sequani to cede to them the third part of their land. The Gauls, alarmed at this demand, sought assistance from the Romans. Julius Cæsar, the celebrated general, whose name descended to a long line of emperors, was at that period commanding in Provence, and delighted at the opportunity thus afforded for war and conquest, promised his aid and ordered Ariovistus instantly to quit Gaul; to which the German merely replied, "that the Romans were not concerned in his affairs." On marching up the country, Cæsar was informed by his spies that the German women having prognosticated evil to their nation on a certain day, the Germans would, on that day, either refuse to fight, or, if forced to do so, would be spiritless. Taking advantage of this circumstance, he attacked them on the day predicted, and they, imagining their gods to be against them, were easily put to the rout, and Ariovistus, whose two wives fell into the hands of the Romans, escaped across the Rhine [B.C. 58].

XXXVII. Cæsar on the Rhine

ARIOVISTUS was no sooner driven away than the Gauls discovered their error and found that they had only changed masters. Cæsar, after subduing the Helvetii, made the whole of Gaul, notwithstanding the rebellious spirit of the inhabitants, into a Roman province, and taking advantage of an interval of peace, attempted to extend the Roman dominion as far as the Rhine, the left bank of which had, for a considerable period, been peopled by a multitude of German tribes of greater or less importance. On the Moselle dwelt the Treveri at Treves; further down the Rhine the Eburoni and Tungri at Tungern; the Gugerni between the Maes and the Rhine; the Menapii to the south, and the Batavi to the north, of the mouth of the Rhine; the Caninefati on the islands. Joining these, to the west were the Toxandri and Marini on the coast of the North Sea at Dunkirk; to the south, the Atrebati, Atuatici (fugitive Cimbri); the Condrusi, Cœresii, Pœmones, the Nervii (a powerful people in Hainault), the Veromandui at Vermandois, the Ambiani at Amiens, the Bellovaci at Beauvais, the Suessiones at Soissons, the Velocassi, Caleti, etc. Although all these people were generally denominated Belgæ, each was distinct from and independent of the other, nor were they even in alliance. They did not all belong to the Frankish nation, several of them having migrated from different parts of Germany. Continually at feud with each other, they had only momentarily united in opposition to the Teutones. Fighting thus singly, their valor was powerless against so formidable an antagonist as Cæsar, who gradually subdued them, and easily suppressed their subsequent attempts to shake off the yoke [B.C. 57].

Shortly after this [B.C. 53] two nations, the Teucteri and Usipetes, who had been driven out of their country by the Suevi, crossed the Rhine, and demanded land from Cæsar, who, unwilling to tolerate so many warlike German tribes in Gaul, resolved to make a fearful example of them, in order to deter others from crossing the frontier, and treacherously seizing the German leader, who had come into his camp for the purpose of negotiating with him, suddenly attacked his unsuspecting followers, and drove them into the narrow tongue of land at the conflux of the Maes and the Rhine, where the greater part were either slaughtered, drowned, or taken prisoners. The remainder escaped to their native country. Throughout the Roman empire, there was but one man bold and honest enough to require that Cæsar should, for this scandalous breach of faith, be delivered up to the Germans. This man was Cato. Not long after this, Cæsar threw a bridge across the Rhine at Andernach, and marched into the country of the Sicambri, who had refused to deliver up the fugitive Teucteri and Usipetes. Unable to oppose him by force, the Sicambri laid their own country waste, and fled with their wives, children and property to the Wetterau, whence they watched the movements of the enemy. The great Suevian confederacy, meanwhile, flew to arms, and Cæsar, after an eighteen days' march through the silent forests, regained the Rhine without having seen a single enemy.

XXXVIII. Ambiorix

DURING the winter preceding the year B.C. 54, a dangerous conspiracy was set on foot by the conquered Belgæ, who hoped to regain their freedom by simultaneously murdering every Roman throughout the country. The plot was headed by an old man from Treves named Induziomar, and by the Eburoni, Ambiorix, and Cativolcus. The Romans had four well-fortified winter camps in the different districts, which it was resolved to attack on the self-same day. The stratagem, however, was only partially successful, but one of the camps falling into the hands of the insurgents, and the brave Induziomar was killed during the assault. The increased vigilance of the Romans rendered any other attempt abortive, and early in the spring [B.C. 54] Cæsar appeared, his ranks swelled by the Gallic tribes. The Ubii, a German tribe, dwelling among the hills on the right bank of the Rhine, being harassed by the Suevi, also joined him, and eventually proved themselves the firmest and trustiest allies of Rome, and the bitterest foes of their kindred tribes. It was a common event for the Germans to be at feud, but for a German tribe to shelter itself behind a more powerful ally was deemed so deep a disgrace that the name of Ubii became a term of reproach. Among the Treveri there were also several men belonging to wealthy families, who, in the hope of being able to usurp the supreme authority in their country by the aid of Cæsar, and of being created Roman governors or prefects, enrolled themselves beneath his standard, headed by the unworthy nephew of the patriotic Induziomar. The Belgæ no sooner came in sight of the immense army of the Romans, led by their victorious general, than many of the tribes, panicstruck, quitted the confederacy, and laid down their arms; but Cæsar, fearing lest the more powerful German tribes on the Upper Rhine might join the Belgæ, unexpectedly crossed the river, and made an inroad up the country, which was again unsuccessful, and after traversing uninhabited wilds, he hurried back to the forest of Ardennes, in order to destroy Ambiorix, who, unaware of his approach, was peacefully seated with his friends in front of his solitary dwelling, when they were suddenly attacked by the Romans. With desperate fury, he fought his way through the forest, and the Belgæ, believing him to be dead, and despairing of success, dispersed. His friend, Cativolcus, unable to survive his loss, killed himself. The whole country was laid waste by fire and sword. The Sicambri, allured by the prospect of booty, now took advantage of the general confusion and fell upon the Romans, whom they stripped of some of their ill-gotten wealth. Ambiorix also reappeared at the head of a small troop of patriots, which he had collected in the thickets of the Ardennes, and daily harassed and plundered the invaders. In the following year [B.C. 53] success at first attended the arms of the Belgian patriots, and the whole of Gaul rose against the Romans; but Cæsar was again victorious, Gaul was reduced into a Roman province, and the Belgæ were rendered tributary, and obliged to furnish a contingent to Rome.

XXXIX. *Boirebistas*

THE intestine feuds of the warlike tribes to the north of Mount Hæmus, the Getæ, Bastarnæ, and Daci, were of infinite service to the Romans while engaged in subduing the Alpine tribes, Illyria, and Greece. King Boirebistas, crossing the Hæmus at the head of the chief tribes of the Getæ, devastated Thrace, Macedonia, and Illyria; but, instead of turning his arms against the Romans, attacked the Boii, and Taurisci, remaining on the frontiers of Austria and Hungary, and, after a bloody battle, defeated their king Critasiros and laid the country waste. The mountain tribes of Illyria and Dalmatia, taking advantage of the quarrels that broke out between Cæsar and Pompey, Antony and Augustus, rose en masse, but, after a desperate struggle, were again reduced to submission. Teutimus, the Dalmatian chief, long defended the mountain fastnesses; and the Taurisci, taking possession of the narrow passes of the Tyrol, slew every Roman who attempted to pass into Switzerland, at that time a Roman province. At length, after a dreadful slaughter on both sides, the Romans advanced from the Lake of Constance into the mountains, and systematically exterminated the inhabitants. Every man fell sword in hand, and the women, maddened by despair, flung their children into the faces of the enemy. The Roman historian turns with horror from the monstrous crimes that blacken the page in which the destruction of the ancient inhabitants of the Tyrol by Tiberius, afterward emperor of Rome, is recorded.—About the period when Rome was erected into an empire under Augustus—at the time of the birth of Christ —all the countries to the south of the Danube, and westward of the Rhine, were incorporated with it. The petty German tribes of Frankish descent, on the Rhine, allured by the prospect of gaining wealth and distinction, enrolled themselves beneath the Roman standard. The Alpine tribes preferred death to bondage, while others awaited, in feigned subjection, an opportunity for revolt. As a means of preserving subordination, Cæsar loaded the Germans, who entered his army, with favors, and raised them to the highest honors. It was to the bravery of his German mercenaries that he owed his most brilliant victories over his rival Pompey. From this period, Germans were always employed in the Roman armies. The sons of the German nobility were also sent as hostages to Rome, where they were educated, and becoming enervated by luxury, caused these frontier tribes gradually to relax from the hardy manners of their forefathers. For still greater security, Roman colonies were planted along the frontier, who raised cities and fortresses, and introduced their religious rites, their markets, their laws, and their luxuries among the inhabitants; so that within a very short time all the countries, whose inhabitants were at first merely tributary to or in alliance with Rome, were completely transformed into Roman provinces, with a new language, new customs, and a new form of government.

XL. *Drusus*

AUGUSTUS, the first Roman emperor, dissatisfied with the limits of the Gallic frontier, and ambitious of extending his dominion beyond the wild forests on the right bank of the Rhine, which had offered an invincible obstacle to Sigovesus, the ancient Celtic king, and to the legions of Cæsar, sent Drusus, his valiant stepson, at the head of a powerful army, to conquer Germany. Between the Lower Rhine and the Maine dwelt several petty tribes. The Mattiaci, north of the Maine, on the Taunus Mountains; further north, down the right bank of the Rhine, the Teucteri, Usipetes, Cattuanes, and Chamavi; behind them, toward the interior of

Germany, the Catti (Hessians); the Sicambri, who traced their descent from the gods, in Sauerland, between the Lahn, the Lippe, the Weser, and the Rhine; the Bructeri, in Münsterland (not the Friesland Brockmen); the Marsi, in Osnabruck; the Fosi, on the Fuhse in Hildesheim; the Tulgibini, in the Duhlawald; the Ampsibari, on the Ems; the Angrivarii, in Enger; the Casuarii, in ancient Hasegau; the Tubantes, around Twenter, in ancient Twentegau; the Cherusci, in Harzgau, whose name belonged to a confederacy of several (*gauen*) districts, at the time of the Roman invasion, and who were bounded to the east by the Hermunduri, on the Saal; the Longobardi, on the Elbe; the Angli, Varini, etc., on the coasts of the Northern Ocean; beyond the Belgæ, the Frisii; in the country of the Dithmarsi, the Chauci; in Holstein, the Cimbri: all of which tribes were now attacked by Drusus, who, invading the country of the Frankish Usipetes, Teucteri, Mattiaci, and Sicambri [B.C. 12], laid them waste by fire and sword. The Catti, who, shortly anterior to these events, had separated from the Suevian confederacy, refused to assist their suffering brethren, who found equally powerful allies in the Saxon Bructeri and Chauci; and Drusus, alarmed at their immense numbers, prudently withdrawing from their neighborhood, took ship and sailed to the country of the Frisii, who entered into alliance with him, and agreed to attack their neighbors the Chauci, with whom they were at feud, and saved the Roman fleet, which had stranded on the low coast. The autumnal fogs and rains, however, caused the Romans to accelerate their return southward, and the only advantage gained by both these expeditions was the erection of a fort on the Taunus, and of another at the mouth of the Ems. In the following year [B.C. 11] the six allied tribes making an irruption into the country of the Catti, who had refused to assist them, Drusus seized the opportunity, and again devastated their now defenseless districts as far as the Weser, where, meeting with the Cherusci, the most warlike of the tribes of Lower Germany, whose impenetrable forests barred his further advance, he again retired, harassed by the tribes which had returned victorious from their expedition against the Catti. A great battle finally took place on the Lippe, in which the extraordinary discipline and courage of the Romans alone enabled them to keep the field. On the bank of this river, at the confluence of the Liese and the Gleene with the Lippe, Drusus erected the important fortress of Aliso (Liesborn), and extending thence a strong earthen wall across the morasses as far as the Rhine, secured a military road into the interior of Germany; after which he recrossed the Rhine, and built about fifty fortresses and towers along its banks.

The ensuing campaign was carried on in the country of the Catti [B.C. 10], where he succeeded in building some roads and bridges, which proved serviceable in his next expedition against this people, whose land he laid waste as far as the Suevian boundary; when, fearing to offend that powerful state, he turned northward, and pushed through the Cheruscian forests as far as the Elbe, on whose opposite bank he beheld a prophetess of gigantic stature, who, with a threatening gesture, exclaimed, "Ah! insatiable Drusus! to what do you aspire? Fate has forbidden your advance through our unknown regions! Fly hence!" Terror-struck at the omen, Drusus again retreated, but, before reaching Aliso, his horse fell, and he was killed on the spot. He was buried at Mayence, beneath the Eichelstein (from the Roman eagle, *aquila*). To the present day the peasants of Lower Germany curse in the name of Drus, whom they imagine to be something worse than the devil. After his death his brother, Tiberius [B.C. 8], invaded the country of the Usipetes and Teucteri, whom he subdued and threatened with extermination, unless they persuaded the Sicambri to yield. Upon this the chiefs of the Sicambri were sent to negotiate conditions, but were treacherously seized by Tiberius, who suddenly attacked and subdued the whole nation, whose imprisoned chiefs killed themselves, according to the custom of their country. After committing this **act of violence and** fraud, Tiberius sought to gain the hearts of the Germans by peaceable means, and by deceptive arts. For this purpose, he invited the most influential men from the neighboring districts, and giving them posts of honor in his army, loaded them with gifts, and incited them to usurp the chief authority in their several districts, and to rule despotically over their fellow citizens. Few, however, attached themselves to him. Domitius, another Roman general, who shortly afterward [B.C. 6] undertook an expedition to the Elbe, which he reached, rendered the Roman name feared by his boldness, and himself beloved by his gentleness and generosity. The Belgæ, on the coast, soon after revolted [A. D. 3], but were again subdued, and, in the following year, Tiberius sailed with a numerous fleet from the Northern Ocean up the Elbe, on whose banks a sharp conflict took place with the Longobardi, Senones, and Hermunduri [A.D. 4], in which he was victorious. On this occasion, an aged warrior of the Senones, approaching Tiberius, cordially offered him his hand, rejoicing that in his old age he had beheld such a warlike people as the Romans, a worthy opponent being the German's greatest glory. Sentius, who was afterward prefect of the Rhine, treated the people with such humanity that they voluntarily adopted the customs and acquired the useful arts of the Romans.

XLI. *Varus in Germany*

SENTIUS was succeeded by Varus, a confidential friend of the emperor Augustus; a man of high talent, and well acquainted with the systematic government of the subdued provinces. The remains of his magnificent villa, not far from those of his celebrated friends, Horace and Mæcænas, the favorites of the great Augustus, may still be seen in the beautiful vale of Tivoli. This able and learned man, blinded by his enthusiastic desire for the introduction of the customs of Rome among the barbarous Germans, imagined that civilization must be welcomed with joy and gratitude, and forgot that liberty is beyond price. As long as he remained peaceably in his headquarters, which extended from the left to the right bank of the Rhine, enriched the natives with gifts, made them acquainted with the costly and luxurious articles of the South, erected markets, and took their sons into the imperial army, they loved and treated him as a guest; but when, emboldened by success, he extended his forces across the Weser into the land of the Cherusci, and supported by Segestus, a treacherous chief of that nation, began to tyrannize over them, by rigorously enforcing the Roman laws, and chastising and executing the freeborn Germans, their goodwill changed into inveterate hatred, and they determined to rid themselves of the despotic stranger. Awed by the Roman army, which consisted of more than 30,000 picked men, encamped in impregnable intrenchments, they long brooded in silence over their wrongs; until a handsome athletic youth, named Armin, of the nation of the Cherusci, of noble descent and irreproachable life, skilled in the art of war, which he had learned from the Romans, in whose armies he had served with such distinction as to gain the honors of knighthood, gifted with eloquence and inspired by an enthusiastic love of liberty, appeared among his dispirited countrymen, whose courage he quickly roused, and a general conspiracy was set on foot in Lower Germany against the Romans, whose destruction was planned in midnight meetings in the silent depths of the forests, and Armin, whose brother and nearest relatives favored the Romans, became the leader and the soul of the confederacy. Notwithstanding the secrecy with which these meetings were held, they were discovered by Segestus, who, in the hope of increasing his power, and of avenging himself upon Armin, who had deprived him of his beautiful and patriotic daughter, Thusnelda, instantly betrayed the designs of his countrymen to Varus, who, confiding in his own power, and despising that of the Germans, treated the matter with contempt and incredulity.

XLII. The Battle in the Teutoburg Forest

AUTUMN had fallen [A.D. 9], bringing the long rainy season characteristic of the North, when Armin began to carry his long-cherished plan into execution. According to Dio Cassius, he first induced Varus to send a considerable number of troops into different parts of the country, in order to procure a winter supply of provisions, or to keep watch over the neighboring tribes, which had not submitted to the Romans, and then succeeded in drawing him with his whole force out of the fortifications, by secretly inciting a somewhat distant tribe, whose name is not mentioned, to revolt. Dio Cassius, whose account is by far the most precise, particularly mentions that Varus' road lay through the midst of apparently friendly tribes, who, by Armin's advice, joined him, in order to avert suspicion; and as there were no tribes lying toward the interior of Germany who had yet been subjected by the Romans, Varus could not therefore have marched in that direction, nor was it likely that he would undertake an expedition into those unknown regions at the commencement of the winter season; it is, consequently, far more probable that the revolt broke out in the opposite direction, and obliged him to advance toward the Rhine. It was also evidently the Catti who attacked him on his march thither, while Armin fell upon his rear; a supposition confirmed by the circumstance of his having quitted the camp at the head of the whole of his troops, accompanied by all the baggage, women, and children, which would not have been the case had he intended to maintain his headquarters on the Weser, while making an expedition against a distant tribe. According to Clostermeier and Ledebur, the summer quarters of the Romans lay below Minden in Prussia, in the vicinity of Reme, at the confluence of the Weser and the Werra, in the widest part of the valley of the Weser. While marching thence straight upon Aliso, Varus was accompanied some distance by Armin, who, under pretense of taking a shorter path, beguiled him into the narrow mountain passes between the Weser and the cities of Herford and Salzufeln, and, the instant the vanguard entered the forest, gave the signal for the general insurrection. The Roman soldiers, who had been distributed among the various districts, were simultaneously murdered. The ambushed Germans poured in thousands from the surrounding forests, breathing death and vengeance on their foes, against whom heaven itself seemed to conspire. A dreadful storm arose; the mountain torrents, swollen by the heavy rains, overflowed their banks; and while the Romans, encumbered with baggage, and wearied by the toilsome march, passed in long and irregular columns through the narrow valleys, the fearful war-cry of the Germans was suddenly heard above the roaring of the wind and waters. They halted, panicstruck, and were in a moment assailed with stones, arrows, and lances, while the Germans rushed like a torrent from the heights, spreading terror and destruction around. The well-disciplined Romans, quickly recovering from their surprise, formed into larger masses, and offered a determined resistance. The battle continued until nightfall, when they gained a more open spot, where they intrenched themselves; but surrounded by the enemy, and entirely without provisions, defense was useless, and their only safety lay in flight. Accordingly, at sunrise, after burning all their baggage, they commenced their retreat, and after passing through an open plain on the Werra in tolerable order, though not without considerable loss, re-entered the forest-clad mountains at Detmold, where, bewildered in an impassable valley, an immense slaughter took place; according to Tacitus, in the Teutoburg forest, "in saltu Teutoburgiensi," probably in the valley where the Berlebeche flows beneath the Groteberg or Teut, whose summit is surrounded with a double Hunnish ring of stones, and at whose feet lies the Teutehof, the owner of which is named the Teutemaier. The survivors again succeeded in reaching an open spot, where a small encampment was hastily thrown up for defense during the night. On the following morning, when not far from Aliso, fresh tribes, probably the Catti, stopped their further progress, and they were completely surrounded and annihilated between Osterholz, Schlangen, and Haustenbeck. Varus threw himself upon his sword. A few of the Romans escaped to Aliso, but afterward secretly abandoned that fort under the command of Lucius Cæditius, and fought their way to the Rhine.[1]

Armin now offered sacrifices to the gods, to whom he consecrated the booty, the slain, and the chief prisoners. He took bloody reprisals on the judges and lawyers, the chief objects of his hatred: "Viper, speak!" was said to one of them, as his tongue was being pierced. The rest of the prisoners were made slaves. The news of this defeat quickly spread, and the Romans, fearful lest the enemy, pursuing their victory, might cross the Rhine, hastily intrenched themselves, and sent to Rome for assistance. The terror formerly inspired by the German name, by the memory of the wars of the Cimbri and Teutones, and of the revolt of the slaves, awoke afresh. The imperial German bodyguard, and the Germans employed in the Roman service, were instantly sent into distant provinces, and recruits were raised in every part of the country for the formation of an immense army destined for the protection of Gaul; but so great was the universal terror that the Romans refused to serve, until forced under pain of death. These preparations proved, however, unnecessary; the Germans—satisfied with effacing every trace of the Romans, by the destruction of the forts and the military roads as far as the Rhine, which again became the boundary of the Roman empire—remaining peaceably within their frontiers.

XLIII. *Germanicus on the Rhine*

PEACE reigned a while. Tiberius was raised to the imperial throne [A.D. 14], and the son of Drusus, who after-

---

[1] Clostermeier's account—where Hermann overcame Varus. Lemgo, 1822, contains a full description of the locality of this celebrated defeat.

ward received the surname of Germanicus, was placed at the head of the forces on the Rhine, in the hope of revenging the discomfiture of the Roman arms, and of reconquering Germany. In the course of the year he suddenly fell upon the Marsi, while they were holding a sacred feast, and lying around the temple of Tanfana,[1] intoxicated and asleep. Immense numbers were slain, but the neighboring tribes coming to their assistance forced him to recross the Rhine.

The following year [A.D. 15], when he was setting out on a campaign against the Catti, Sigismund, the son of Segestus, came to implore his aid against Armin, who was closely besieging his father, into whose hands Thusnelda had fallen, and Germanicus, suddenly entering the country of the Cherusci, freed Segestus and took possession of his daughter. The youthful wife of Armin was far advanced in pregnancy when led in the triumphal procession, and bore her miserable fate without a tear;[2] her own father, whose treason had been rewarded, and whose avarice had been gratified by a gift of lands in Gaul, his life being no longer secure in his own country,[3] gazing unmoved on the wretchedness of his child. The news of this disaster soon reached Armin, who flew (*volitabat*) throughout Germany, rousing his countrymen to vengeance. Enraged at this insult to Thusnelda, the Germans rose to a man, and even Inguiomar, the ancient friend of the Romans, joined Armin, who soon again found himself at the head of a formidable army. Germanicus, meanwhile, had prepared for war, and sailed with a numerous fleet from the Northern Ocean to the Ems. while an army was dispatched to the coasts, and a third, commanded by Cæcinna, advanced through the country of the Marsi. Armin and his Germans now retreated with

---

[1] A name that has had many derivations, the most probable of which seems to be *Fahne*, or sacred standard, raised in *Tann*, or fir-wood.

[2] Mariti magis quam parentis animo, neque victa in lacrymas, neque voce supplex, compressis intra sinum manibus, gravidum uterum intuens.—*Tac. Ann.*

[3] The popular legends of Thusnelda are still extant, one of which relates how, when concealed in the old fort of Schellenpyrmont, a faithful bird warned her by his cries of the stealthy approach of the Romans.

their families and property, and the whole country was laid waste by the Romans, who advanced unopposed as far as the recent scene of slaughter, where, with lamentations and cries for vengeance, Germanicus caused the bones of the legions of Varus to be buried. Meanwhile, the Germans watched him from the mountains, intent upon destroying him in the same defiles in which Varus had fallen; and when he entered the narrow valleys, whose surrounding heights afforded ambush for the enemy, Armin at the head of a small troop retreated before him, until the whole army had entered the pass and was hemmed in on every side. The signal was given, and a dreadful slaughter ensued [A.D. 16], but the cautious Romans, though defeated, escaped annihilation by making an orderly retreat to the ships. A part of the army that had been dispatched to the coasts of Friesland was carried away by a flood on its march, and the whole narrowly escaped destruction. Cæcinna fared still worse, being overtaken by Armin while retreating through the country by the long bridges leading across the deep morasses of Munsterland, which were fast falling to decay; and yet, although surrounded by dangers and apparently insurmountable difficulties, shut up in a narrow dell[1] through which the Germans had turned the course of a mountain torrent, and defending their camp while the water rose to their knees and the tempest burst furiously over their heads, the valiant Romans succeeded in cutting their way through the enemy, and in escaping, though with considerable loss, to the Rhine. The winter months were employed by the Germans in besieging the fort of Aliso, but without success; and in the following year [A.D. 17] Germanicus sailed with a thousand ships up the Ems, and landing his army marched to the Weser, whose opposite banks were defended by the Germans. On reaching the river, Flavius, the brother of

---

[1] Probably in the forest-clad mountains of Caresfelt, where the ancient bridges of planks commenced, which in the fourteenth century still led across the morasses of Munsterland, in the country round Cologne, and were still called "the long bridges," as in the time of Tacitus. They have been now for the most part replaced by dams.

Armin, a Roman mercenary, stepping from the ranks, advanced to the riverside, and addressing his brother, described in glowing terms the advantage of being a Roman citizen, in the hope of inducing him to desert his people; but Armin, cursing him for a traitor, attempted to cross the stream with the intention of killing him, but was withheld by his followers. The Romans now prepared for battle, and Armin, again retreating, succeeded in surrounding and cutting to pieces the Batavian horsemen in the Roman service, who had ventured too far in pursuit. The next day the whole army advanced, but, on reaching the pass, Germanicus separated the troops and pressed forward at the head of one division, leaving the other at some distance to the rear, and the Germans, rushing from their ambuscade, were consequently surrounded, and, after a desperate conflict, entirely routed. This victory was recorded by Germanicus on a magnificent monument raised on the spot, although his loss was so considerable as to oblige him to fall back on the Ems. Roused to frenzy at the sight of this monument, and resolved to wipe off their shame, the Germans quickly rallied in pursuit, and another battle ensued, so obstinately contested that night alone separated the combatants, and the slaughter had been so terrible that when day broke neither army was able to renew the fight, and Germanicus, hastily retreating to his ships, set sail. Disaster still pursued this ill-fated expedition; a storm arose in which most of the vessels were wrecked, and when, shortly after this, Germanicus returned to Rome, the fort on the Taunus was the only one throughout Germany in the possession of the Romans.

XLIV. *Marbod*

WHILE these great events were taking place in the north of Germany, the south did not remain quiet. The tribes in the lower valleys of the Danube were continually at feud, thus rendering it easy for the Romans to subdue, one by one, those belonging to the Peucini, in the same manner that

Deldo, king of the Bastarnæ, was overcome by Crassus; and Boirebistas, the exterminator of the Boii, the powerful ruler of the Getæ and Daci, was defeated by Tiberius and Piso; on which account he was murdered by his subjects, the Getæ, by whom he had made himself hated; but who, after this event, quarreling among themselves, and being without a leader, fell an easy prey to the Romans. It was about this time, when Augustus was still emperor of Rome, that the Suevian confederacy, from which the Catti first separated themselves, was dissolved. Armin had, it is true, united the Frankish and Saxon tribes of Northern Germany in a temporary defensive alliance, and they carefully guarded the Rhine; but when the kingdom of the Getæ fell, as well as the Suevian confederacy, the Danube seemed no longer tenable. It naturally followed that the inhabitants of the exposed districts on the southern frontier voluntarily united under one leader, who was intrusted with great authority, in order to give unity and strength to their councils, the Romans having taught them of what importance it was to keep together in the fight, and to obey one commander. Marbod, who, like Armin, had passed his youth among the Romans, united the remaining Suevi of Upper Germany, the Boii, and all the petty southern frontier tribes, and led them far from the vicinity of the Romans into Bohemia, a beautiful, fertile country, surrounded by a natural rampart of mountains, where he was joined by the Getæ, who had fled from the East, and who aided him to subdue his Suevian neighbors on the Maine and the Saal, who had refused to league either with him or Armin. His people, collected from so many different Suevic and Gothic tribes, received the appellation of Marcomanni (mark or boundary), and he possessed the same power over them that was enjoyed by the Margraves of later times, that of commander-in-chief, with unlimited authority. He maintained a standing army of 70,000 foot and 4,000 horse, exclusive of the armed population. He had also a fortified castle in the interior of the country. The Romans beheld this newly-erected power with apprehension, and Tiberius marched against it at the head of a formidable army; but on his way, hearing of the revolt of the Pannonians, he hastily concluded peace with Marbod, who, more intent on his own aggrandizement than concerned for the liberties of the people, abandoned his neighbors. Commanded by Pinnes and Bato, they defended themselves, with the courage of despair, against 200,000 Roman troops, until Bato, seduced by Tiberius, betrayed Pinnes, but not long after again opposed the Romans, and a second time, yielding, the people shared the fate of the Taurisci, in the Tyrol. At Arduba, the women flung themselves and their children into the burning houses, and into the river, rather than fall into the hands of the enemy. These horrors, and the heroic struggles of Armin, were beheld unmoved by Marbod, who now openly manifested his intention of allying himself with the Romans, by whose assistance he hoped to usurp supreme authority in Germany. In order to remind him of his duty, Armin had presented him with the head of Varus, as a mark of honor, but Marbod sent it with a condoling message to the emperor Augustus. The Lower Germans were imbittered against him by his want of sympathy in the cause of liberty, while his very name was detested by the other tribes, over whom, not content with ruling despotically over the Marcomanni, he attempted to extend his dominion, and, consequently, he no sooner attacked the Senones and Longobardi, than the tribes of Lower Germany flew to their aid, and a powerful league, headed by Armin, was formed against him. Both sides assembled all their forces, and a great battle ensued, in which almost all the German tribes took part. Armin gained a complete victory, and Marbod, retreating to Bohemia, sent to Rome for assistance; but becoming intolerable to his own subjects, who elected the Goth, Catualda, for their king, he escaped across the Danube, and lived for eighteen years on the bounty of the Romans.

XLV. The Death of Armin

THUS Armin had saved his country from internal as well as external danger. For ten years he had been general-in-chief of the people, and his fame had spread throughout the whole of Germany; but as actions like his, before him unknown among the Germans, were the offspring of extraordinary circumstances, his fame naturally decreased in time of peace, and it became easy for those who envied his honors to instill the suspicion that he aimed at sovereignty into the minds of a people so jealous of its freedom, a suspicion strengthened by the example of Marbod, which served as a pretext to his enemies; and, at length, his own relations, who were most strongly influenced by envy, conspired against and murdered him, A.D. 21. From this moment the Germans no longer acted with unity, a circumstance of which the Romans, anxious to preserve peace on their northern frontier, did not take advantage. In the same year in which Armin was murdered, the Treveri, headed by Florus, revolted; but the attempt failed, owing to their want of unity. Some years later, A.D. 28, the Frisii shook off the Roman yoke. The friendly manner in which this simple-minded people had received the Romans had been ill-requited; they were treated as a conquered nation, and a tribute of ox-hides imposed upon them, which was endured until Olennius became prefect of the Rhine, and in the insolence of power demanded not only common hides, but also those of the buffalo, rare in Friesland, and moreover placed a strong garrison in the country, in order to enforce payment. The wretched people were consequently forced to sell all they possessed—houses, slaves, cattle, and even their children, in order to procure the hides in sufficient quantities from the neighboring nations. At length, rendered desperate by necessity and suffering, they suddenly rose en masse, and drove the Romans out of their country; an exploit which, for the first time, made their name famous in history. Their country retained its freedom, the Romans taking no revenge, probably because the conquest of these poor people would not have repaid the expense and danger of the war. Not long after this, the Caninefati revolted, but without success. The Cherusci were ruined by internal dissensions. The faithless relations of Armin attempted to introduce the Roman customs, and to usurp the whole authority, but were resisted by the people, A.D 47. The son of Flavius, surnamed Italicus, on account of his having been born and bred in Italy, was chosen king, but made himself so disliked by his Roman manners that he was deposed; but, aided by the Longobardi, he regained his throne, and the people gradually lost their ancient power and love of honor. The Catti made continual excursions across the Rhine, A.D. 50, until, rendered careless by success, they were attacked and cut to pieces by the Romans, when in a state of intoxication. In the same year, Agrippina, the daughter of Germanicus, led a great Roman colony to the Rhine, and erected an important fortress on the frontier, called, after her, Colonia Agrippina—now Cologne.

On the right bank of the Rhine, between the Roman and German frontier, was a narrow tract of country, which had long remained uninhabited, partly on account of the migrations, and partly on account of the wars. The Friedlanders, whose population, as has ever been the case in Germany, was too redundant for the land, coveted the possession of this empty tract, and, in order to negotiate the matter, sent Veritus and Malorix, two of their chief men, to Rome, where they were well received. The magnificence of the capital of the world did not tame the free and haughty spirit inspired by their forest homes. When, in the theater, the seat of honor was not assigned to them, they took possession of it, saying, "The German nation is the bravest in the world, and therefore the highest honors are its due." Their request was refused.

The petty tribe of the Ampsibari, driven out by the Catti (who gradually sought to extend their limits), wandered along the Rhine, and begged land of the Romans. Their request met with a haughty refusal; and when rich possessions were offered to Boiocal, their chief, who had served in the imperial army, he nobly refused them, and, swearing to remain true to his people, exclaimed, "We may want land on which to live, but it is never wanting for those who die." He returned with his tribe to Germany, where, being everywhere rejected, part of it dispersed among different nations, and the rest fell victims to hunger and misery. Soon after this, a great war broke out between the Catti and the Hermunduri, who disputed the possession of the salt-springs of the Saal, even at that period held in great estimation. The Hermunduri were victorious in a pitched battle, and sacrificed all their prisoners to the gods. During this year, A.D. 58, a great subterranean fire broke out on the banks of the Rhine, with which the layers of peat found there may perhaps have some connection. After the death of Nero, the Roman tyrant, who paid very little attention to Germany, several Roman generals strove for empire. Vitellius, who commanded in Cologne, was the first who made use of the Germans when attempting to seize the imperial crown. He favored them so much as to allow them, when enrolled beneath his standard, to wear the costume of their country. After causing himself to be proclaimed emperor in Cologne, he marched to Rome, where the appearance of his warriors created great astonishment. He always carried about with him a German prophetess, whose predictions were to warn him of future events. An unsuccessful speculation, as he was murdered. Vespasian became emperor. His son, Titus, when subduing Judea, had also Germans in his army, whom he praised highly, saying "that their souls were even greater than their bodies." But there still were noble hearts that throbbed with indignation at the baseness of their free born countrymen, in thus selling themselves to the destroyers of their fatherland.

XLVI. *Civilis and Velleda*

THERE lived a young man among the Batavians who was called by the Romans Civilis, or the friend of the people, and who had lost an eye in their service. Becoming suspected on account of his love of freedom, he was thrown into prison, together with his brothers, who were shortly afterward beheaded. On his restoration to liberty, he swore eternal enmity against his oppressors, and vowed, according to the custom of his country, not to trim his beard or head until he had taken ample vengeance on them. Finding that his fellow countrymen groaned secretly beneath the Roman yoke, which unity and energy on their part might easily cast off, he appeared among them during a sacred feast at midnight in a forest, and with enthusiastic eloquence excited them to open revolt. The standard of rebellion was raised, and the Romans were simultaneously murdered throughout the country; an example that was quickly followed by the Caninefati and Frisii. Victory followed victory, and one by one every Belgian tribe, even the Treviri, encouraged by the success of their neighbors, joined in driving out the common enemy, or in besieging him in his strongholds. The Germans also in the imperial service deserted in troops to the friends of liberty. The country of the Ubii was completely laid waste, and the most fearful vengeance was wreaked upon all who had been faithless to their fatherland; the city of Cologne, which submitted to the conquerors, being alone spared, A.D. 69.

At this period, Vitellius and Vespasian were battling for empire, and consequently the whole strength of the Romans could not be poured upon Belgium, where the cause of freedom speedily progressed; and although the fortress of Vetera (Zante) was unsuccessfully besieged during the whole of the winter, the affairs of the allies prospered,[1] and several other

---

[1] The exact site is uncertain, but with great probability is placed, by Ledebur, on the Velsberg (Wellsaup) near Flaersheim.

German tribes evinced a disposition to make common cause with Civilis, while Velleda, a maiden prophetess who dwelt in a lonely tower in the Bructerian forest, and was regarded with veneration throughout Germany, announced victory to her people and destruction to the Romans. The most valuable part of the booty was always sent to her in sign of honor, and she became as it were the inspiring genius of the Germans in their struggle for freedom. The Gauls also seized this opportunity to cast off the chain, and united their forces with those of the Belgæ, who, unluckily for their cause, were persuaded by their new confederates to found a great Gallic empire, which excited the jealousy of the Germans on the other side of the Rhine, and cooled their zeal, while the steady alliance of the Gauls could not be counted upon, although for the present everything prospered, and the flag of liberty ere long floated on the Alps, and the Roman arms again suffered defeat in Helvetia.

The following year, A.D. 70, affairs took a different turn, Vespasian overcame Vitellius, and civil dissension ceased. Cerealis, a veteran general, whose name struck the Germans with terror, was dispatched into Gaul at the head of a powerful army, and, on reaching Treves, easily subdued the Gauls, who abandoned Civilis; while the people of Cologne murdered all the Germans who were in their city, and delivered up to him the wife and child of Civilis, who had been intrusted to their care. Notwithstanding these disasters, the Belgæ were not yet disheartened, and in the first battle drove the enemy from the field. Another followed, in which so many of the Germans went over to the Romans that Civilis was forced to retreat, and throwing himself into the Batavian islands, opened the canals, and caused a great inundation, by means of which he long bade defiance to the enemy; but finding opposition unavailing, and honorable conditions being offered, he at length concluded peace. His name was honored by both friends and enemies. According to a short account by Statius, Velleda was taken prisoner by the Romans.

XLVII. Internal Dissensions Among the Germans

THESE disturbances were followed by a long peace on the frontier. In the interior of Germany feuds broke out between the brother tribes, which afforded a delectable spectacle to the Romans. The Catti fell upon the Cherusci, and drove king Chariomer from the throne. There were also disturbances among the Suevi, and Masyus, a king of the Semnones, and the prophetess Ganna, who was almost as famous as Velleda, fled to Rome, where they were honorably received. Tacitus mentions the extermination of 60,000 Bructeri by their neighbors the Chamavri and the Angrivarii, while the rest of the Germans looked on with indifference, as a late and very remarkable event, and concludes his account with this exclamation, "May dissension ever reign among the Germans, and thus prevent the danger with which they threaten Rome!" Similar disturbances, occasioned by military despotism and the discordant Gothic and Suevic tribes who composed the nation, prevailed in the kingdom of the Marcomanni. The Goths, under Catualda, the successor of Marbod, oppressed the Suevi, who, rebelling, drove them out and elected Vibilius, one of the Hermunduri, for their king. Catualda went over to the Romans, and assembled a great number of his adherents, to whom the Quadi, dwelling in Moravia behind the Daci, associated themselves, who were allowed to settle in Pannonia, which lay waste and uninhabited, on condition of aiding the Romans against their countrymen. Thus the new kingdom of the Quadi, on the right bank of the Danube, served as a guard against that of the Marcomanni, on the opposite bank. Catualda was succeeded by Vannius, who, evincing an inclination to make terms with the Marcomanni, was, at the instigation of the Romans, seized by his own nephews, Sido and Wangio, who were assisted by the Jazyges, the first Slavonian tribe that crossed the Danube. Roman policy triumphed. The united

Marcomanni and Quadi were beaten, Sido was rewarded with the throne of Vibilius, and Wangio with that of Vannius, for their devotion to the interests of Rome. But the hatred of the Roman rule was deeply rooted among the Germans, and their friendship was more apparent than permanent. No sooner was one nation subdued, or gained over by the enemy, than another instantly rose to renew the struggle for the glory and liberty of their fatherland.

XLVIII. *Dezebal*

THE ancient Dacian-Getic kingdom, which had been dissolved after the murder of Boirebistas, again rose. The king, Durias, voluntarily abdicated in favor of Dezebal, a brave and intelligent man, his superior in the art of government, who speedily united all the tribes, known earlier under the general name of the Peucini, beneath his command. Apprehensive of the event, the emperor Domitian sent Sabinus with a numerous army across the Danube, which was annihilated by Dezebal, and the emperor, marching against him in person, was also beaten, A.D. 89. The Marcomanni and Quadi, ashamed of assisting the Romans against their brethren, had, meanwhile, preserved a strict neutrality, and Domitian, imagining that he could subdue them more easily than the Daci, put their embassadors to death, and invaded their country; but, emboldened by the example of Dezebal, they offered him battle. A complete victory was gained, which at once put an end to their base alliance with the Romans, and, uniting their forces to those of the Daci, they became so formidable that Domitian sued for peace, and agreed to pay Dezebal a heavy annual tribute, A.D. 90. The weak Nerva succeeded Domitian, and Dezebal remained in undisturbed tranquillity until the accession of the warlike Trajan, when war once more broke out. Trajan, judging it to be as dishonorable to allow the discomfiture of the Roman arms in Dacia to remain unrevenged as it was impolitic to tolerate so enterprising a neighbor, refused to pay the tribute, A.D. 100, and marching at the head of a strong army against the Dacians, conducted the war with such skill and energy that Dezebal was finally overcome and forced to conclude a shameful peace, A.D. 103. Filled with mortification at his defeat, and with fears for his country, he once more attempted to arm the neighboring tribes against Rome, setting before them the danger to which they were exposed, unless they united against their common enemy. His entreaties were vain, and he was forced to stem the torrent unassisted and alone, A.D. 106. A long and obstinate struggle ensued, and at length, completely defeated and driven to desperation, he killed himself, after making a vain attempt to poison the emperor. His treasures, which had been secretly buried in the bed of the river Sargetia, were betrayed to Trajan, who took possession of them, and Dacia became a Roman province. A stone bridge, the wonder of the times, was thrown across the Danube, in this part of immense width, and records, together with the bas-reliefs of the beautiful column still preserved at Rome, the name and warlike deeds of Trajan.

XLIX. *Roman Provinces on the Rhine and Danube*

HADRIAN, the prudent and pacific successor of the warlike Trajan, followed the plan commenced by Cæsar, and continued to Romanize the provinces lying on the frontiers of Germany, besides completing their defense, by erecting fortifications along the left bank of the Rhine, and the right bank of the Danube, virtually surrounding that frontier of the empire with a chain of castles. At the most important points, strongly fortified encampments, garrisoned by Roman legions, connected by straight, high, damlike roads, and provided with watch-towers overlooking the distant country, were constructed. The Rhine and the Danube generally marked the boundary. Their banks were thickly studded with castles and fortified towns, and their streams were traversed by bridges, the remains of which may still be seen at

Cologne and Mayence, besides the ruins of the one already mentioned, built by Trajan over the Danube.

The Romans had thus already crossed both rivers, and had built two gigantic têtes-de-pont to bar the further progress of the Germans. After the expulsion of the Dacians, Trajan and Hadrian led powerful colonies into Mæsia (modern Moldavia and Wallachia), in order to repeople that country with Romans, and to prevent the Germans from crossing at the point where the Danube falls into the Black Sea. The corner where the Black Forest penetrates into Basil was a still more important position, on account of the obstinacy with which the Germans defended the mountains between the Danube and the Rhine, which at once hindered the junction of the Romans, and rendered them liable to surprise on either side. Neither labor nor expense were therefore spared in erecting the fortifications of the Black Forest, which were completed by Hadrian, who built a great wall that extended from Pfarring on the Danube to Mittenberg on the Maine, and is now known as the Teufelsmauer, the Heidenmauer, or the Pfahlgraben. It appears to have been completely fortified, and to have defended the whole of the country lying to its rear. The roads of communication between the forts were carried along the edge of the mountains, instead of running through the valleys, in order to secure the garrisons against ambush or sudden attacks in their route through the forests. Modern tacticians have been struck by the astonishing science displayed by the Romans in their choice of positions for encampments, and lines for mountain military roads, etc. German liberty could not possibly exist within reach of these fortresses, and the whole frontier lay waste and desolate, until by slow degrees repeopled and cultivated by Roman colonists, or by poor German fugitives and deserters. These lands were called *agri decumates;* it is uncertain whether on account of a tenth paid by the cultivator, or from a Roman measure for marking out the fields, or from the usual plan of recruiting among the peasantry. When the emperor Henry the First raised the first fortresses in Germany, one out of every ten peasants was chosen to form the garrison of the fort, whom the rest were obliged to maintain by their labor; and it seems probable that these *agri* were, in like manner, intended for the maintenance of the Roman garrisons.

As countless legions were continually quartered on the frontiers, the conquered tribes soon adopted the language, customs, and luxurious manners of their masters, and a number of Roman towns were either built behind the forts, or the latter gradually swelled into cities. All the large cities on both sides of the Rhine and the Danube were originally Roman; the most considerable of which was Treves, the capital of the whole of the northern province, celebrated for its magnificent temples, palaces, amphitheaters, etc., the ruins of which still exist. The remains of an immense aqueduct are still to be seen at Mayence. Besides these, but few traces of the ancient splendor of the Roman cities are now visible above ground, but enormous foundations of walls, mosaics, single statues, and quantities of coins have been discovered beneath its surface. Numbers of old Roman towers, easily distinguishable by their stones, which exactly measure a Roman foot, still remain, and possibly owe their preservation to their inutility. They were formerly single watch towers, around which, in later times, towns and cities sprang up.

The whole of the conquered country was placed under the Roman form of government. The proconsul had unlimited power and authority in the province, and was ordinarily a general, on account of the continual war with the Germans. The government was, consequently, completely military, and as the regulations merely referred to the maintenance and recruiting of the legions, the civilization introduced by the Romans simply extended to the economy of the barracks and markets. During peace, the levying continued; the feuds between the German tribes, idleness, and curiosity, always sending a crowd of fugitives or adventurers to the frontiers, who entered into the Roman service and formed its bravest legions. Many of these deserters were attracted by the vanity of affecting Roman customs, which led them to despise their native simplicity; others, by the hope of revenging themselves on their former foes in Germany; but by far the greater number were instigated by mere love of fighting, while all seemed alike unaware of the guilt they incurred by aiding the stranger to lay their country desolate. The division of the Roman frontier provinces was as follows:

The right bank of the Danube was divided into four provinces: First, Rhætia, which extended from the sources of the Rhine and the Danube to Salzburg and Ratisbon. The capital of this great province, which was connected with Italy by the Alpine passes, and with Helvetia and Gaul by military roads, was Augusta Vindelicorum, now Augsburg. The other considerable towns were, Brigantium, now Bregenz, on the Bodenese; Campodunum, now Kempten; Regina Castra, now Ratisbon, etc. At a later period, this province was divided into Upper Rhætia, the Alps, and Vindelicia, the country of the Lower Danube. Second, Noricum, to the east of Rhætia, with the cities Juvavia, Salzburg; Lintia, Linz; Celeja, Cilly, etc. Third, Pannonia, which extended from the Ems in the direction of Hungary, where lay Vindobona or Juliobona, Vienna. Fourth, Mæsia, which stretched as far as the mouths of the Danube, and formed throughout its whole extent the line of boundary between the Roman empire and Germany.

The left bank of the Rhine was also divided into four provinces: First, Helvetia, now Switzerland. Here were built two magnificent cities, Vindonissa (the bridge on the Aar) and Aventicum, Wiflisburg, or Avenche; Augusta Rauracorum, Basil. Second, Germania Prima, on the Upper Rhine, with its capital Moguntia, Mayence; Argentoratum, Strasburg; Tabernæ, Rheinzabern; Nojomagus, Spires; Borbetomagus, Worms, etc. Third, Germania Secunda, on the Lower Rhine, with its capital, Colonia Agrippinæ, Cologne; and Confluentia, Coblentz; Bonna, Bonn; Juliacum, Juliers; Aquæ, Aix-la-Chapelle, etc.; Bacharach has been derived from *Bacchi ara*, a stone used as an altar to the Rhenish Bacchus. Fourth, Belgica, with its capital, Augusta Trevirorum, Treves; and many cities whose French names still betray their Latin origin, viz.. Soissons, Augusta Suessionum; Vermandois, Augusta Verumanduorum; Cambray, Cameracum, etc. A catalogue of the roads raised by the Romans in Germany during the earlier part of the third century, now known as the Peutinger Table, has been discovered.

PART III

THE MIGRATIONS

L. *Revolt of the whole German Nation against Rome*

THE conquest of Dacia turned the scale in the great struggle between the two nations, and victory quitted the standards of Rome for those of Germany. A whole century had passed since the destruction of Velleda, marked, on the western frontier, by no occurrences of more importance than a few inconsiderable incursions. The Dacian war had scarcely affected the southern frontier. In the far interior of Germany no Roman army had again penetrated, and the Germans, rapidly increasing in number, quickly regained their diminished strength. Rome, meanwhile, was fast falling to decay. The mighty empire tottered beneath its own weight. The union of the numerous and various countries and nations of which it was composed could only be effected by the despotic extirpation of their national characteristics, their courage and their worth. Enslaved by luxury, and demoralized by a despotism based on the degradation of the people, these degenerate nations henceforward supplied weak and worthless troops, who, although superior in numbers and discipline, vainly sought to cope with the personal strength of their intrepid opponents, or to protect the sinking empire.

To the increasing population of Germany, and the growing corruption of Rome, may be ascribed the great events which took place during the second century after Christ, when a sudden and terrific irruption burst like a torrent from the interior of Germany, drawing after it fresh and countless hordes, before whose irresistible might Rome was at length forced to yield. This sudden irruption of the German nations was undoubtedly, like that of the Cimbri and Teutones, caused by movements in the north. The first impulse was apparently given by the Goths on the Baltic, whose descendants, at a later period, boasted of having gone, under the command of Berig, from the island of Skanzia (Schonen, the southern promontory of Sweden) to the south. But these northern Goths could not have been very numerous, and the enormous masses that poured in every direction across the Danube and the Rhine into the Roman provinces must have issued from the whole breadth and width of Germany, while a very small portion could have come from the north.

It is a circumstance of much greater importance, that from this period the countless minor tribes disappear, and are replaced by the great German nations, the Franks, Alemanni, Saxons, and Goths, which could as easily have sprung from the air, as from the cold and impoverished north, and are the identical nations which, a century earlier, inhabited the countries already mentioned. During the long peace, they had increased in numbers, and had become more civilized in their form of government, their laws, and their religion; and, after a long silence, are again mentioned in history as the same, but a more polished, people. All the tribes of the Lower Rhine were gradually known only as the Catti and the Sicambri; all those on the Northern Ocean, as the Frisii, Chauci, and Angli; all those of Southern Germany, as the Alemanni and Bojoarii; all those of Central Germany, as the Hermunduri, Longobardi, and Burgundians; all those of Eastern Germany, as the Goths, Gepidæ, and Vandali. The Franks and Saxons soon afterward appear in the place of the Sicambri and Chauci; and all these changes prove, that the small districts, formerly separate from and independent of each other, had everywhere united, and had formed into large communities. For instance, it would not have been possible for the great nation of the Franks to have sprung from the Sicambri alone. A union of all the numerous minor tribes in the neighborhood, mentioned at an earlier period, but whose names have since disappeared, must first have taken place. The cause of this alliance is extremely obscure, but may have been induced by several circumstances, such as common origin, the superiority of a powerful tribe over its weaker neighbors, and finally, the necessity of leaguing together on account of the renewal of the war with Rome.

LI. *The War of the Marcomanni*

It is a remarkable fact that the Roman empire was simultaneously attacked, on the Rhine and Danube by the Germans, and in Asia by the Parthi or Persians, A.D. 162. The Rhenish tribes first rose. The Catti, formerly so inconsiderable, suddenly invaded Rhætia in immense numbers, and advanced as far as the Alps, where they were opposed, and, after an obstinate battle (several women being found among the slain), defeated by Pertinax. About this time, the Chauci appeared on the Northern Ocean, and, landing from their pirate vessels, devastated the coasts of Gaul and Britain. Shortly after these events, the Germans rushed in enormous masses across the Danube, headed by the Marcomanni, whose name was given to the war, accompanied or followed by the Quadi, Bastarnæ, and Hermunduri; the Vandali and Goths, with numerous minor tribes, the Astingi, Narisci, Burii, etc.; and probably also the Slavonian Jazyges, and Roxolani. These countless hordes first besieged Aquileia, A.D. 166, a large fortified town on the Adriatic.

The brave defense of this place, and the sudden appearance of Marcus Aurelius, the wise and spirited emperor of Rome, returning at the head of his victorious legions from the Parthian war, induced the Germans to retire across the Danube, whence they soon returned, and again laid waste the Roman provinces. A dreadful plague at the same time ravaged the interior of the empire.

The emperor, undismayed by these calamities, collected indiscriminately all who were capable of bearing arms, even slaves and thieves, and marched to the Danube. It had been foretold to him, that if he caused two lions to swim across that river the enemy would flee; and he accordingly did so, when the Germans, mistaking them for a couple of dogs, killed them with their clubs. Two migrating Vandal tribes were afterward persuaded by the emperor to assist him against the other Germans, and after a desperate contest he was victorious over the Marcomanni and Jazyges. The battle with the latter took place in the middle of the frozen Danube. They were completely routed, and from this single nation were regained no less than 100,000 Roman prisoners; a circumstance calculated to give an idea of the magnitude of the war. The emperor followed up his victory by an attack upon the Quadi, who, retreating far into the interior, drew him gradually further into the vast wilderness, where his army was threatened with starvation from thirst, the long heats having dried up all the springs, and their fate seemed inevitable, when their fainting strength was revived by a sudden storm. A Christian legion, said to have worked this miracle by their prayers, hence received the name of the fiery legion. The Quadi were afterward forced to make peace, A.D. 174, and the emperor, taking advantage of the momentary tranquillity, restored the ruined fortresses on the banks of the Danube, built several others, and garrisoned them with 200,000 men. The Romans, presuming on their strength, now neglected to fulfill all the conditions of the peace, and began to annoy the Germans, who again revolted, and a battle was fought, which lasted an entire day. Before the war was concluded Marcus Aurelius died, and was succeeded by his son, Commodus, A.D. 180, a licentious youth, who, anxious only to continue his debaucheries at Rome, instantly concluded a shameful peace with the Germans.

LII. *The Alemanni*

THIS nation belonged to the ancient Suevi, and were the ancestors of the Swabians. The petty tribes dwelling to the south of the Catti and Hermunduri appear to have confederated with them, and early in the third century to have formed a mighty nation, which passed the Heidenmauer, destroyed the Roman cities and colonies, and made their name feared throughout the whole of the Black Forest as far as the Rhine. Although appearing under the name of the Alemanni as one distinct and individual nation, they were held by no firm political bond, and, as in earlier times, were divided into several districts, each completely independent of the other, and governed by its own council, laws, judge, or duke. Even in war time they oftener fought singly than in unison, and only on particular occasions elected a temporary war-chief. They were bounded on the north by the Catti and Hermunduri; on the east by the Cenni (the ancient Senones, who had mingled with the Alemanni when pursued by the Burgundians, who, issuing from Silesia, gradually advanced toward the west) and the Boii—Marcomanni (from whom descended the Bojoarii or Bavarians). In front of them, behind the Rhine, lay Germania Prima, Helvetia, and Rhætia, against which they always, and with increasing boldness, directed their attacks.

They first appeared in modern Swabia after the great war of the Marcomanni, when peace reigned on the frontiers. Caracalla, the Roman emperor, took them into high favor, wore their dress and a light-colored wig in order to resemble them the more closely, and is said to have been deprived of his senses by the magical songs of the Alemannic women; often telling the Germans that they ought to come over and destroy the Roman empire, and then putting the interpreters to death, lest the Romans should discover what he had said. This mad emperor, nevertheless, often ill-treated his German friends. On one occasion he sent for a number of the young Alemanni, under pretense of enrolling them in his army, and then, with a scornful laugh, ordered them to be put to death. A general insurrection, in which the Catti joined, was the immediate result. The emperor was victorious, and, after the battle, asking the captured women, "which they preferred, death or slavery?" was answered by their murdering their children and then destroying themselves. A.D. 213.

During the campaign of his successor, Alexander Severus, in Parthia, the Germans again crossed the Rhine, and occasioned such universal terror that the emperor was obliged to hasten his return to Italy, where he was greeted with delight, but expired before the opening of the campaign, A.D. 234.

The name of the next emperor is traced in German history in characters of blood. Public spirit no longer existed in any part of the empire. The soldiers, numbers of whom were Germans, usurped the chief authority and raised Maximin, a Goth, a man of extraordinary bodily strength, and accounted the bravest in the army, to the imperial throne. In order to prove to his subjects that he had renounced his former kindred, and was a thorough Roman, he instantly continued the Rhenish campaign with unusual vigor, and carried war and desolation into the very heart of his native country. At the head of an innumerable army, which he had himself conducted from the sands of Africa and the steppes of Parthia, he marched triumphantly about four hundred miles in different directions through Germany, burning and destroying all before him. A great battle took place in a now unknown morass or lake, in which the emperor narrowly escaped with his life. He is a proof of the truth of the axiom, "that the renegade is ever his country's bitterest foe." The ingratitude of the Romans fearfully avenged his crimes, and he[1] and his son, who is said to have been the handsomest youth of his time, and who was on the eve of wedding the noblest and most beautiful of the Roman maidens, fell by their hands, A.D. 235.

LIII. *Alemannic Warriors*

THE Alemanni invaded Gaul A.D. 253. A young warrior inquiring of his mother how glory was to be gained, "There are only two ways," she replied, "one by creating grandeur, the other by destroying it." The latter possessed the higher attraction, and leading a large army across the Rhine, A.D. 259, he utterly destroyed more than sixty Gallic cities, of which not one stone was left upon the other. He subsequently fell into the hands of the Romans at Arles, and, imprisoned in an iron cage, was carried about the country, a fit object of contumely and scorn. Gallienus, who was then emperor, married Pipara, the beautiful daughter of a king of the Marcomanni. Roman history, the only one that touches upon these events, is neither graphic nor precise in respect to them, and merely speaks of a battle, near the Lake of Garda, where 300,000 of the Alpine Alemanni were defeated by 12,000 Romans; and records that not many years after the same nation again swarmed from the Rhine and the Alps, until checked by the bravery and skill of Probus, the warlike Roman emperor, who even, for a short time, restored the Heidenmauer, and the fortresses of Hadrian, A.D. 277.

Christianity, meanwhile, progressed. Crocus is said to have found some Christian clergy in Gaul, whom he obliged to sacrifice to the gods. According to the legend, the emperor, Maximian, caused a whole legion, named the Theban, with their leader, Mauritius, to be cut to pieces, A.D. 287, on account of their profession of the Christian faith, with which

---

[1] To this emperor is ascribed the transplantation of 11,000 British maidens into Gaul, who, on their way, were killed by the arrows of the wild Saxons near Cologne, on the Rhine.—*Legends of St. Ursula.*

he feared they might infect the rest of the troops. This event took place at Sitten, or Sion, in Valais, on the spot where the large monastery of St. Moritz now stands. About the same period, at Augsburg, then a Roman city, St. Afra, a dissolute female, who had been suddenly converted to Christianity, which she zealously preached, suffered the death of a martyr, and was afterward canonized. Maximian, unable to stem the torrent that threatened to overwhelm Italy, now shared the imperial throne with Diocletian, who invaded Swabia, while he opposed the Franks and Saxons on the Lower Rhine; but so little was effected that the civil feuds among the Germans alone protected the Romans from destruction, A.D. 288. The Goths and Vandals pressed forcibly onward, opposed by the Thuringi, Burgundians, and Alemanni. "Holy Jupiter!" exclaimed the Roman, Mamertius, "at length they bathe in their own blood!" But the exultation of the Romans was only momentary; Helvetia was before long again invaded by the Alemanni, who, during this irruption, destroyed all the works of the Romans, particularly the magnificent cities of Vindonissa and Aventicum, A.D. 303, which were so completely razed to the ground that, fifty years later, a forest, known as the Helvetian Wilderness, covered their sites. The Alemanni were in such force on the Upper Rhine that Constantine the Great, the first emperor who professed Christianity, which he established throughout the empire, owed his elevation to the throne to their friendship, and particularly to that of their leader, Crocus. Proclaimed emperor by the troops on the Rhine, A.D. 306, he defeated his rival by the assistance of the Germans, whose services were afterward requited with ingratitude, as will hereafter be related. After waging a cruel war against the Franks, he erected a fortress, named after him, Constance, on the Bodensee, with such a hostile intention against the Alemanni that they finally joined the Franks, but were defeated, and for some time after remained in tranquillity.

Constantius, the son and successor of Constantine, being

furiously attacked by his father's bitter enemies, the Franks, anxiously sought the alliance of the Alemanni, whose chief, Chnodomar, a gigantic warrior, aided him in subduing them and their leader, Magnentius; but scarcely were they vanquished than the faithless emperor, uniting with a part of them, attacked his allies, A.D. 353, who revenged his treachery by devastating the Roman frontier. They were victorious on the Alps, but were afterward defeated near the Bodensee by Arbetius, the Roman general, A.D. 355. Shortly after this, the emperor Julian the Apostate, who commanded on the Rhine, and his lieutenant, Barbatius, simultaneously invaded Swabia, from opposite quarters; upon which the Alemanni marched boldly between the invading armies as far as Lyons, destroyed several cities on their route, and then, returning to the Rhine, suddenly attacked Barbatius, over whom they gained a complete victory, and retreated to their own country laden with spoil. Julian raised the fortress of Tres Tabernæ, Zabern, as a rendezvous for the troops, and collected a numerous army, which induced the whole nation of the Alemanni to join the standard of Chnodomar, who, mounted on a fiery horse, his helmet adorned with red plumes, and an enormous lance in his right hand, crossed the Alps at their head, and solemnly demanded the cession of Alsace from the emperor, who dismissed his embassadors, and gave him battle near Strasburg. An immense slaughter ensued. As soon as victory began to side with the Romans, the infantry of the Alemanni obliged their princes and nobles to dismount and to fight on foot, so that none could save themselves by flight. Chnodomar, becoming entangled in a morass, was taken prisoner, and two hundred of his companions in arms, who formed his bodyguard, voluntarily yielded to the conqueror, in order to share his fate. He was carried to Rome, where he died of nostalgia. Julian then sailed up the Maine, wasting the country of the Alemanni on the right bank as far as Spessart, where the natives made a valiant defense behind an impenetrable abatis. The greater part of the nation was, however, forced to submit, and to deliver up 20,000 Roman prisoners, besides furnishing wood from their forests for the reconstruction of the cities they had destroyed on the Rhine, A.D. 357. The Alemanni were now hard pushed by Julian, who, following up his victory, and contriving to render their leaders suspected, and to set them at variance, took some by stratagem, and made the rest submit by force. On their again meeting, as was their custom, for the purpose of planning a conspiracy, during one of their midnight festivals, he attacked them so suddenly that they escaped with great difficulty by flight, A.D. 359. Vadomar, whom he invited to a banquet and treacherously seized, afterward served in Asia, and distinguished himself as a Roman general in the Parthian war. After the departure of Julian, the Alemanni regained courage, crossed the Rhine on the ice, and devastated Gaul, but were surprised near Chalons, while bathing in the Marne, by Jovinus, who put them to the rout, and hanged their leader, A.D. 360. The following year they made another incursion under Rhando, and attacked the city of Mayence; upon which the emperor Valentinian, assisted by Jovinus, invaded the Black Forest, A.D. 361, where he was skillfully opposed by Viticabius, the sickly but energetic son of Vadomar, and by Macrian, the equally sickly, but intelligent leader of the Catti; the former of whom he caused to be murdered. The latter defied his attempts. The Alemanni and Catti made a desperate defense on a high mountain near Sulz, A.D. 368. The emperor, unable to reduce them to submission, now incited the Burgundians against them, and a quarrel, similar to that between the Catti and Hermunduri, arose between them, on account of the salt-works on their frontiers, and the Burgundians marched against them to the number of 80,000 men. Upon this, Macrian prudently made terms with them, and avoided a battle; and the Romans, afraid of their new guests, breaking the treaty, the Burgundians murdered the Roman delegates, A.D. 370, and returned to their own country. The indefatigable emperor then incited the Franks against the

Alemanni, while Macrian, with equal perseverance, sought to confederate the whole of the northern Germans against him. The emperor, discovering some of his letters to Hortar, a conquered Alemannic prince, tortured him to death, and nearly succeeded in capturing Macrian (*in aquis Mattiacis*) at Wiesbaden, where he was lying sick, A.D. 371. The repeated and bloody defeats suffered by the Romans on the Danube, in their war with the Goths, now forced them to withdraw from the Rhine, where the faithless Mellobaudes, who favored the Romans, laid wait for Macrian and murdered him. Two years after, A.D. 375, the Alemanni, under Priarius, invaded Alsace, but were defeated and cut to pieces at Colmar by Mellobaudes. Although the power of Rome was forever annihilated, the Alemanni were forced to quit Gaul, and, wandering southward, peopled the Alps, where their descendants, the Swiss, still dwell. In the fourth century, Ausonius, the Roman poet, whose works are still extant, immortalized the charms of Bissula, an Alemannic maid.

LIV. *The Franks*

AMONG the Low German tribes, who fought under Armin, appear the Catti and the Chauci, who, in the third century, although the names of the individual tribes were not yet entirely lost, were gradually included under the general denomination of Franks and Saxons. *Frank* signifies free, and the tribes that confederated for the preservation of their freedom were distinguished by this name. The experience gained in the Roman war taught them the value of union, and their ancient book of laws boasts in its preface that the confederated Franks were powerful enough completely to cast off the galling Roman yoke (gens Francorum, firma pacis fœdere, quæ Romanorum jugum durissimum de suis cervicibus excussit pugnando). Their name, although not mentioned by the Roman historians until the third century after Christ, may, with great probability, be ascribed to the time of Civilis, who roused all the Lower Germans in the name of Freedom, and, according to Tacitus, said expressly to the people of Cologne, "You will be free (*frank*) among the free" (*franken*); liberi inter liberos eritis. Nazarius, the panegyrist of Constantine, says that all the Lower German tribes had formed a strong league (conspiratione fœderatæ societatis exarserunt). The Franks, like the Alemanni, were for a long period a simple federation of independent tribes, composed of the Sicambri, Chamavri, Bructeri, Catti, Cherusci, etc., and all the other petty Low German tribes, which, with the exception of a few that united with the Saxons, were, at a later period, included under two heads, as Salic and Ripuarian Franks. They had also among them many petty leaders or dukes, who were even oftener at feud with one another than those of the Alemanni. They are first mentioned as fighting against the emperor Gallienus, by whom they were defeated, A.D. 256. They subsequently made a great irruption into Gaul, A.D. 260, and thence penetrating into Spain (according to Aurelius Victor, who merely mentions the fact), destroyed the great city of Tarragona, and for twelve years maintained their position on the other side of the Pyrenees, whence they were driven by Posthumus. Their ships are said, even at that early period, to have visited Africa. Aurelian repelled a fresh irruption of the Franks into Gaul, A.D. 265. After his death, A.D. 273, they again invaded that country, and found a powerful opponent in his successor, Probus, who defeated both them and the Alemanni, A.D. 277, repaired the old Roman fortresses, walls, and roads, and subdued the Gothic Lygii and Arii, whose prince, Semnus, fell into his hands. He also reduced the Burgundians and Vandals, in the interior of Germany, to submission, took Igillus, the Vandal prince, prisoner, and settled the vanquished tribe in the country of Vandelsburg, in Britain; his policy being to remove the Germans to distant countries, when he engaged them in the Roman service. He valued the Germans at a gold piece a head, and carried on a regular plan of kidnapping. He caused several thousand Frankish men and youths to be transported to Asia, where he settled them on the borders of the Black Sea. He remained for some time on the Rhine, fortifying the banks and adorning them with vineyards. The fortifications were afterward destroyed by the Franks and Alemanni, who carefully preserved the vineyards from injury, and cultivated them with the greatest assiduity. These improvements were fatal to the emperor Probus, who was murdered by his own soldiers, impatient of the hard labor imposed upon them in the cultivation of these vineyards. At the same time, the Franks, who had been transported to Asia, being pressed beyond endurance, suddenly rose, and after murdering all the Romans in their vicinity, seized a considerable fleet, which lay at anchor in the Black Sea, sailed to the Archipelago, plundered the wealthy maritime cities and landed in Sicily, where they took the great city of Syracuse, and returned to their ships laden with booty. Landing in Africa, they battled with the Romans beneath the walls of Carthage, and being worsted, retreated to their ships, sailed unopposed through the Mediterranean, and coasting Spain and Gaul, as far as the Northern Ocean, returned laden with wealth to their native country.

LV. *Frankish Upstarts and Traitors*

AFTER the death of Probus, the Franks again crossed the frontier, and attacked the emperor Maximian at Treves, where he held his court, but were repulsed, and compelled to replace their prince, Genobaudes, whom they had driven away, on his throne. In the hope of winning them over, the emperor ceded the waste country lying on the frontiers, and entered into an alliance with them. This narrow-sighted policy produced most important results. The Franks, taking advantage of their central position, aided the Romans against the other Germans, or *vice versâ*, as better suited their own projects of aggrandizement, while they imperceptibly increased in power and in political weight.

Constantine the Great, although a Christian, was cruel,

false, and treacherous, and the instigator of treason in others. When celebrating his victory over the Franks at Treves, he caused a number of the prisoners, among others two Frankish princes, Ascar and Ragais, to be thrown to the wild beasts in the amphitheater, where, smiling in scorn, they met their doom with the utmost intrepidity. The whole of the Germans, Franks, and Alemanni, enraged at this act of cruelty and thirsting for revenge, united against the emperor, who, entering their camp in disguise, gave them false information of his departure, and of the place and time when he would be most open to attack. The stratagem succeeded, and the allied Germans were completely beaten, A.D. 310. He now plotted their entire reduction, and pretending to be on the point of undertaking an expedition against the Alemanni, suddenly changed his course, and marching down the Rhine unexpectedly attacked the Franks, A.D. 318. The erection of a great bridge near Cologne afforded him for the future free ingress into their country. (This bridge was standing until 955, when it was broken up by order of Archbishop Bruno, and the stones were used in building the monastery of St. Pantaleone.) Notwithstanding this ill treatment, the Franks again befriended the emperor, and flocking beneath his standard, aided in vanquishing Licinius, the competitor for the imperial throne. It was on this occasion that he invoked the God of the Christians to grant him the victory, and in consequence of his success embraced their religion. The importance to which the Frankish nation had already risen is clearly demonstrated by the circumstance of a soldier named Magnentius having set himself up as a candidate for the imperial throne, in opposition to Constantius, the successor of Constantine. He was betrayed by Silvanus, one of his countrymen, who deserted to the emperor with part of his followers at the decisive moment. On the eve of the great battle of Mursa on the Drave, Magnentius entreated the gods for victory, and after sacrificing a maiden on the altar, mixed her blood with wine, which he distributed to the whole army. His defeat was decisive, and he killed himself. His brother,

Deventius, who had remained in Gaul, defended himself for some time, but, finding opposition useless, also deprived himself of life, A.D. 353. Silvanus, after assisting in driving his fellow countrymen back to the frontier, incurred the suspicion of having connived at a fresh and unexpected irruption on their part, in which they destroyed forty cities, and Constantius lending an ear to the insinuations of his secret enemies, he was compelled to seek safety by flight, and rejoined his countrymen, who received him with delight, and solemnly proclaimed him emperor at Cologne. He was murdered by a certain Nosicius, A.D. 356, a pretended deserter, employed for that purpose by Constantius. The emperor Julian also combated the Franks, who, for thirty days, fruitlessly besieged him in Sens, when dissension again broke out among them. The ancient Sicambri, who dwelt close to the Roman frontier, were pressed upon by their neighbors the Chamavri. Charietto, the leader of the Sicambri, aided by Julian, defeated the Chamavri, and took their chief, Neliogast, prisoner, A.D. 360. The whole frontier of the Netherlands was afterward held by the Sicambri as a Roman fief, and they are henceforward known as the Salic Franks. Charietto became their first prefect, and afforded great assistance to the emperor against the Alemanni. He was succeeded by Mellobaudes, who was also in alliance with Rome.

Somewhat later, the Franks were governed by three princes, Marcomir, Genobald, and Sunno; and it appears that at that period a reaction took place in the feelings of the people, who once more began to feel ashamed of the treasonable part they enacted by thus affording assistance to the enemies of their country. Their countryman, Arbogastes, the zealous ally of Rome, was their most violent opponent during their heroic struggle for freedom.

The emperor Maximus sent Quintinus at the head of a powerful force into their country, where they lay in wait for him in the forests, as is expressly related, armed with poisoned arrows, and he suffered a discomfiture as complete as that of Varus, but few of the soldiers escaping to bear news of the disaster. The conquerors followed up their victory by the invasion of Gaul, A.D. 388, when they were at first opposed by Arbogastes, who soon after, changing his plans, arbitrarily set up a new emperor, by name Eugenius, a rhetorician, and negotiated for peace and alliance with the invaders, whom he finally persuaded to lend their aid to Eugenius, upon which a destructive war broke out between them and the rival emperor, Theodosius, who was supported by the Goths. A great battle took place between the two nations at Aquileia, in which the Goths were victorious. Eugenius was executed, and Arbogastes fled to the Alps, where he put an end to his life, A.D. 394.

The difference between the national character of the Franks and that of the Alemanni is visible even at this early period; and to the close alliance that so long subsisted between the Franks and the Romans may be justly ascribed the traits which, at a later period, distinguished the former, whose upstart warriors have ever been noted for treachery, ambition, and love of luxury. "Choose the Frank for a friend, but not for a neighbor," was even then a proverb. Salvianus says, "The Franks, instead of deeming perjury criminal, call it a mere *façon de parler*." "They laugh, and break their word," observes Vopiscus. A practice they had probably acquired among other Roman customs, and which was unknown to the other nations of Germany, who, uncontaminated by an alliance with the enemies of their country, ever retained their love of simplicity and truth.

LVI. *The Saxons*

THE Saxons dwelt beyond the Franks, and consisted of the Chauci, Frisii, and the remnants of the tribes collected on the coasts of the Northern Ocean and the Baltic. Their name has been variously derived from the ancient Sacæ [1] on

---

[1] Probably the Siks.—*Trans.*

the Indus, from *Sachs*, race, or from *Sassen*, freeholders. According to tradition, they came by sea (from the army of Alexander the Great) to Hadel, where they landed, and buying from the Thuringi, who at that period stretched far down toward the Northern Ocean, a gownful of earth, spread it over a large territory, to which they laid claim, and then inviting the Thuringian chiefs to meet them unarmed for the purpose of negotiating the affair, murdered them during the banquet with knives worn for that purpose, concealed beneath their dresses. According to a legend somewhat similar to that of the Edda, the Saxons and their first king Ascan sprang from the rocks of the Harz Mountains; and the proverb, "There are Saxons wherever pretty girls grow out of the trees," is still in use. The ancient account of this people is very obscure. Odin went from Saxony to Scandinavia, and his descendants at a later period from that country to England. In the beginning of the third century, the Chauci were powerful by sea, and plundered the Roman coasts; and somewhat later, the Saxons were continually at war with the Normans in Denmark and Norway. When the Roman empire was under the joint rule of Diocletian and Maximian, the former of whom defended the Danube, the latter the Rhine, the subjection of the Saxon pirates, who had long and unopposed infested the northern seas, was planned, and toward the close of the third century, Carausius, an experienced sea captain, attacked and overcame them. He subsequently entered into a strict alliance with them, and set himself up as emperor, a title which he, for some time, maintained by their assistance.

The connection between the Saxons and the Vindili, or the Gothic tribes on the Baltic, is also buried in obscurity. When the latter, migrating in a body to the south, left their ancient place of abode completely unoccupied, they were succeeded by the Slavian tribes, who, settling there, became the eastern neighbors of the Saxons. It is only known for certain, that a part of the Saxons accompanied the Longobardi to Italy, but by far the greater number migrated to England. It was customary for the old men to remain at home, while the surplus population, consisting of young and hardy warriors, was annually sent forth to seek a settlement elsewhere, and to win a new country by their swords. Godfrey of Monmouth, the English chronicler, relates that the first Saxons who visited England alleged this custom as the reason of their migration. An annual meeting of all the chiefs of the people was held at Marklo in Saxony, and the young men, chosen by lot, were, according to law, obliged to bid an eternal farewell to their native country.

LVII. *The Goths*

TOWARD the close of the second century, the great nation of the Goths, accompanied by countless other northern tribes, descended from the north to the coasts of the Black Sea. Tradition records that the ancestors of the Goths sailed in three ships, commanded by King Berig, from their ancient home, Gothland in Sweden, to the German side of the Baltic, and landed at Gothiscantzia (Dantzig). One of their ships arriving later than the rest, the men on board of it received the name of Gepidæ, from the word *gapan*, to stare idly, to delay, to gape. Gradually spreading along the coast, they conquered the Ulmerugi and Vandali, but meeting with opposition from the Saxons in their advance toward the west, they turned southward, conquering the tribes or forcing them along with them on their route, and at length reached the Black Sea. Many of the Goths were, however, left in the north, in the part of Sweden that still bears the name of Gothland. The preponderance of the Gothic name over those of the other eastern German tribes perhaps arose from an ancient religious superstition, as well as from their intellectual superiority. The civilized manners of the Greeks and Romans, and, in later times, Christianity, rapidly spread among them, and the regulations they introduced, during the peace consequent on the cessation of migration, were followed by all the other German tribes, and laid the foundation of a new era. In other respects, the Goths had the same form of government with the other Germans. Each tribe was sometimes headed by an independent chief, who was either a judge, a duke, or a king; sometimes several of these tribes obeyed a common head, or it happened that a king, who had gained the upper hand, reigned over several minor and tributary chiefs; but this sort of authority was never of long continuance, and the tribes became once more independent. At length, the chiefs of the most considerable tribes succeeded in retaining during peace the authority intrusted to them during war, and rendered their dignity not only perpetual, but also added to it a power which soon threatened the ancient liberties of the people; the natural result of protracted warfare and of encroaching military rule. In the great Gothic migrations, the Goths seem to have been the most considerable nation, and appear after the Marcomanni, Quadi, Getæ, Peucini, and Bastarnæ, who must have been gradually incorporated with them, as they also were generally denominated Goths, and were divided into Ostrogoths, of which the Gruthungri formed the most considerable tribe, and Visigoths, the chief tribes of which were the Therwingri and Taiphali. Connected with the Goths were the Gepidæ, who are said to have accompanied them; the Longobardi, from Denmark; the Heruli, also from the Scandinavian north; the Vandali, from the Baltic; the Rugii, from the island of Rügen; the Burgundians, from the Oder. The Alani, Hirri, and Scirri, are of dubious origin; and the Jazyges and Roxolani, who joined the Goths in their march, were without doubt Sclavonians.

LVIII. *Great Irruption against Rome*

THE Goths were already known at the time of the war with the Marcomanni, to whose rear they had been long settled before they made a direct attack upon the Roman empire. During the discussion of this project in the popular assembly, three of their chiefs were struck by lightning, and the unlucky omen caused its renunciation, A.D. 192. In the commencement of the third century, they had become extremely powerful, and compelled the emperor Caracalla to pay them an annual tribute; and shortly after, Maximin, a Goth by birth, was raised to the imperial throne, who, however, was so devoid of patriotism, as to include his fellow countrymen in the fierce and cruel war carried on by him against the western Germans. After his death, the tribute was again exacted from the Romans, and the Goths invaded Greece under Ostrogotha, Argaith, and Guntherich, A.D. 245. Ostrogotha subsequently became a powerful monarch. Fastida, the great Vandal king, rendered insolent by his victories over the Burgundians, insisted upon the partition of the kingdom of Ostrogotha, who vainly represented the folly of the demand, and advised him to beware of attacking his brethren, but Fastida, deaf to reason, persisted in his ambitious schemes, and was overthrown.

A formidable Gothic army under Cniva now invaded Mæsia, A.D. 250, defeated the Romans in a great battle at Beræa, and took possession of Philippopolis, where 100,000 men were put to the sword. During their march toward Greece, the emperor Decius fell upon their rear and attempted to cut them off; a fierce struggle ensued, in which Cniva proved victorious. The emperor and his son were drowned in a lake, and Gallus, his successor, bribing him to make peace by the payment of a large sum of money, the Gothic chief departed, laden with booty. In 258, several hordes, under different chiefs, crossed the Black Sea, and after plundering and destroying the cities of Asia Minor, returned to their country; and, reappearing the following year, A.D. 259, stormed and sacked the city of Trapezus by night. The cities of Nicæa and Nicomedia were burned to the ground during a subsequent incursion, A.D. 260. In 266 they again crossed the Black Sea, under Respa, Veduco, Thuro, and Bato, and overran the whole of Asia Minor, plundering and devastating that rich and fertile country. On their return home, laden with booty, they were attacked in the Euxine and defeated by a Roman fleet. In the following year, 267, a numerous horde, under King Naulobates, undertook a similar expedition, plundered the Asiatic coasts, and afterward landed in Greece, where they destroyed a number of magnificent cities. Athens, the seat of ancient learning, was taken, and the stupendous collection of Greek books contained in that city was on the point of being burned, when an old man, rising up, advised them to leave the Greeks all their books, "for," said he, "so long as they use their pens with so much diligence, they will never understand the use of their swords." The emperor Gallienus, after attacking and defeating them on their return home overland, entered into alliance with them, and since that period the Heruli were almost constantly engaged in the imperial service. Two years later, A.D. 269, two fresh expeditions were undertaken by the Goths. An enormous horde crossed the Black Sea with 6,000 ships, and landed on the banks of the Danube, whence, being forced to retreat by the Romans, they sailed into the Archipelago, and laid waste the whole of Greece; but, when attempting to return overland to the Danube, they encountered the emperor Claudius, and being defeated at Naissus, took refuge on Mount Hœmus, where, hemmed in on every side, they fell victims to hunger and pestilence. Another horde, after coasting along Asia Minor, landed in Cyprus, spreading desolation wherever they appeared, and destroying all the cities. It was by them that the celebrated ancient temple of Diana at Ephesus, reckoned one of the seven wonders of the world, was burned. On their return home through Greece they were also cut to pieces. These considerable losses for some time checked the inroads of the Goths, and several warlike emperors successively mounting the throne, who personally conducted the war on the Danube, they were compelled to remain within their own limits. Aurelian, whose wars, although probably some of the most remarkable that took place, are only lightly mentioned in history, gained several signal victories over them. While the Goths, as usual, made an incursion into

Greece, the Marcomanni and Vandali invaded Italy; the former were defeated with immense slaughter by Aurelian in Hungary; the latter, meanwhile, advanced as far as Milan, and caused such terror in Rome that extraordinary human sacrifices were offered, in order to appease the anger of the gods. Aurelian overtook the enemy at Placentia, where he suffered a defeat; but the Romans, whose courage rose with the danger, fought on subsequent occasions with such intrepidity, that after winning the battles of Fano and Pavia they forced the Marcomanni to retreat. Aurelian's triumph was graced with singular trophies; besides the car of a Gothic king, drawn by six stags, there were several Amazons, who had been captured sword in hand, among whom the youthful Hunilda, celebrated among the Romans for her wit, was particularly distinguished. She afterward became the wife of a man of rank named Bonosus, who, aided by the Goths, aspired to the imperial throne, and, on discovering the inutility of his attempt, deprived himself of life. Aurelian owed his victories over the Goths to his German mercenaries, chiefly Franks, some of whose generals are mentioned by name, Hartmund, Haldegast, Hildomann, Cariovist. The emperor Probus watched the Danube as carefully as the Rhine, refortified the banks of both rivers, and introduced the vine into Hungary. The emperor Galerius valiantly opposed the Goths, and Constantine the Great did not belie the cunning he had practiced on the Rhine, by his conduct toward them. When defeated and forced to seek safety by flight by their king Ararich, he incited the Slavonian Sarmatians against them, A.D. 331; but his project being foiled by the sudden revolt of the Slavi against their own nobles, whom they had no sooner driven out of the country than they concluded peace with the Germans, he induced the Vandals to attack the Goths, and upon the defeat of their king Vidumar by Geberich, the successor of Ararich, he took them under his protection and employed them in his service. At Constantinople, the new capital of the eastern empire, there were no less than 40,000 Varingians, or mercenaries, in his pay. Among the countless Roman prisoners carried by the Goths into the interior of their country, were several Christians, who succeeded in converting a great part of the people to Christianity. The Goths in the imperial service were also, for the most part, Christians; and when, on the conversion of Constantine, that religion was established throughout the empire, a grand convocation of the whole of the Christian clergy was held at Nice, in which the Catholic Church was recognized as the only true one, A.D. 325.

Several Gothic bishops, present at this assembly, opposed this decision, from a conviction of the incompatibility of Catholicism with the pure doctrine of the Saviour.

LIX. *The Great Empire of Hermanarich—Origin of the Huns*

PEACE was no sooner established with Rome than internal feuds broke out among the Germans. The Ostrogoths under Ararich and Geberich had already subjugated the Burgundians, Alani, Vandals, and Gepidæ. Geberich's successor, Hermanarich (the royal family of the Ostrogoths was called the Amali—the immaculate?), also subdued the Heruli and several Slavonian tribes, besides including the Visigoths beneath his rule, although Athanarich, their prince or judge, was permitted to retain something of his independence, and was a viceroy rather than a subject. The empire of Hermanarich spread from the Baltic to the Black Sea, and this great king, of whom there unfortunately exists but a very meager account, entered into an alliance with Rome, and carried his victorious arms far to the northeast; the treaty being alone infringed by Athanarich, who waged a three years' war against the emperor Valens, whose rival, Procopius, was supported by the Visigoths. When Hermanarich was very old, his empire was threatened by the Huns, an immense swarm of misshapen barbarians, who gradually advanced from the depths of Asia toward Europe. The

Slavonian tribes took advantage of the opportunity thus afforded to free themselves from the Gothic yoke. The prince of the Roxolani went over to the Huns, and his wife Sanieth, being, by Hermanarich's command, torn to pieces by horses, her brothers attempted to revenge her death on the aged king, whom they grievously wounded, but did not succeed in depriving of life, and who, when he beheld his kingdom a prey to discord within, and threatened by the Huns from without, when, helpless from his wounds and the infirmities of old age, he was no longer able to ward off defeat, voluntarily put an end to his existence in his one hundred and tenth year.

The Huns (Monguls, Calmucks, wandering shepherd tribes) were natives of the north of Asia, and inhabited the immense steppes lying between Russia and China. Divided into tribes and families, and unpossessed of either cities or houses, they wandered from place to place, seeking pasturage for their cattle, and dwelt in tents, in which they also stabled their horses. From being constantly on horseback, their legs were weak and crooked. They were short of stature, extremely broad-shouldered, with strong muscular arms; had coarse protruding lips, small flat noses, yellow complexions, and thick short necks; in a word, they were quite as hideous as the Calmucks of the present day. Their horrid ugliness, immense numbers, activity on horseback, and skill in archery, struck terror even into the hearts of the brave Goths, who deemed them the descendants of wicked demons; a superstition that greatly conduced to their success. Hermanarich had no sooner taken his seat among his ancestors in Walhalla than his great empire was dissolved. Part of the Ostrogoths remained faithful to his son Hunimund, while the rest raised Winithar to the throne. The pagan Visigoths attached themselves to Athanarich, who belonged to the ancient race of the Balti, but those who had embraced Christianity were ruled by their dukes Fridigern and Alavius (Olaf). Dissension, meanwhile, prevailed. Athanarich, accusing the Christian Goths of having abandoned the ancient manners and customs of Germany for those of Rome, fanatically persecuted them, and, on one occasion, had an idol carried in procession before their houses, and put all those to death who refused to fall down and worship it.

Balamir, the great prince of the Huns, overcame Hunimund and marched against Winithar, who, after twice defeating him, fell in a third engagement, and the Ostrogoths were constrained to fly. Part of them subsequently submitted to the Hun, who had married the beautiful Waldamara, the widow of Winithar, whose son Widerich, together with Alatheus and Saphrax, two Ostrogothic chiefs, assembled the remnant of the people and fled. The Visigoths, who had beheld the defeat of their brethren unmoved, perceived, when too late, the danger to which their supineness exposed them, but boldly and resolutely taking the field, marched in a body to oppose the passage of the Huns across the Dniester; the enemy, however, crossing the river at another point, surrounded and defeated them, and they were driven behind the Pruth, where, for some time, they valiantly defended themselves behind a long wall which they had hastily thrown up; but, at length, finding opposition futile, they severally dispersed; Fridigern and Alavius seeking refuge within the Roman frontier, while Athanarich, who viewed the Romans as the hereditary foes of his country and despised them on account of their being Christians, and who, moreover, had taken a solemn oath to his father never to set his foot on Roman ground, took shelter in the valleys of Transylvania.

LX. *Migration of the Goths into the Roman Empire*

ON reaching the Danube, Fridigern and Alavius sent Ulphilas (Wolflein, little wolf), the pious and learned Gothic bishop, to entreat the emperor Valens for land on the Roman side of the Danube, as an asylum from the Huns. This bishop was the first translator of the Bible into German. Part of this translation is still extant, and forms a curious record of the ancient Gothic language and state of civilization.[1] He persuaded the emperor to allow the Goths to pass the frontier, on the ground of its being far more dangerous to repel them by force; and his consent was at length gained, on condition of their delivering up their arms, and regularly paying for their provisions. The superintendent, sent for this purpose to the Danube, took advantage of their blind confidence in his honesty to cheat them in every way, and, when their money was spent, deprived them of their beautiful women and children; in his rapacity overlooking the fact that a great number of the Goths had, in their impatience, crossed the river without yielding up their arms. Deceit, ill-treatment, and the scanty allowance of food, ere long forced them, although the greater number were unarmed, to assume a threatening posture, which caused the Romans to concentrate all the forces quartered on the Danube on one point. While the banks were in this defenseless state, the Ostrogoths under Alatheus and Saphrax arrived, and crossed the river unquestioned and unopposed. The Visigoths meanwhile advanced as far as the great city of Marcianople, where the governor, Lupicinus, invited the chiefs to a banquet. Their prolonged absence from the camp caused the people to suspect foul play, and they began to storm the closed gates of the city, upon which the treacherous Roman instantly ordered his guests to be put to death. In this strait, Fridigern, with great boldness and presence of mind, calmly represented to him that, if he and his companions were murdered, the city would in-

---

[1] The so-called Codex Argenteus, an old Gothic translation of the Gospels, written in silver characters on a purple ground, now preserved at Upsala in Sweden, where it was brought in 1648 by General Konigsmark, who had stolen it from Prague. It came originally from the monastery of Worden, to which it had probably been presented by some munificent Frankish chief, and doubtless fell into the hands of the Franks when they seized the empire of the Visigoths. The only question is, whether it is the genuine translation of Ulphilas. That he translated the Bible is most certain. Still, may not the silver characters be the invention of some other translator, and date about two centuries later? It is possible; but the fame of Ulphilas warrants its being at least a strict imitation of the original work.

evitably be destroyed by their avenging countrymen, but that, if they were set at liberty, they would quickly be appeased. These reasons induced Lupicinus to allow them to quit the city, and Fridigern, true to his word, caused the Goths to retire. But suspicion and enmity had now replaced their former confidence, and they found themselves abandoned to misery and want. The Romans repented of having permitted the entrance of such a numerous horde into their territory. Lupicinus at length resolved to have recourse to arms, and marching with his whole force against them, suffered a complete defeat. This victory placed the country at the mercy of the Goths, who seized the weapons and the produce of the land. The Ostro and Visi-Goths united in one body, and were joined by the Varingi, or Gothic mercenaries, who had been in the Roman service since the time of Constantine, and were commanded by Sueridus and Colias. They had been quartered at Adrianople, and the Romans, apprehending their desertion, intended to have sent them to Asia Minor, but impolitically refusing the payment of their arrears, they quitted the imperial service and went over to their countrymen. The inhabitants of Mount Hœmus, and the rest of the population who groaned beneath the heavy Roman yoke, hailed the Goths as their deliverers, joyfully guided them through the country, and delivered up to them the concealed treasure and provisions. Their further advance was impeded by the city of Adrianople, which long withstood the attack of assailants ignorant of the mode of besieging fortified places. While they were thus engaged, the emperor Valens returned from the Persian war, at the head of a great army, strengthened by innumerable Frankish auxiliaries under Richomer, Mellobaudes, and Frigeridus. Even at that early period a hatred existed between the Franks and the Saxons, which until very lately remained unabated. Valens and the Franks were at first victorious, but when the defeated Goths entered into an alliance with the Alani and the Huns, who, at that juncture, poured across the Danube, an engagement such as

Europe had never before witnessed, in which a million of men strove, took place on the plains of Adrianople. The Roman army was completely annihilated, and Valens, who had been carried wounded into a hut, was there burned to death, 9th August, 378. The Romans, burning to revenge their defeat, now collected their whole force, and simultaneously murdered all the Goths that remained in Asia Minor, whether Varingians or private individuals. Theodosius the Great, the newly-elected emperor, a mighty warrior at the head of a numerous and exasperated army, aided by the Franks under Bauto and Arbogastes, wiped off the disgrace that had befallen the Roman arms in the plains of Adrianople by several brilliant victories, and chased the invading hordes across the Danube, where they fell into the hands of the merciless Huns. In the confusion of the time, the brave Fridigern, who, until then, had kept the Goths united, is lost sight of; and the aged Athanarich was induced to quit his forest abode in order to form a rallying point for his dispersing countrymen. The Huns, whom a part of the Ostrogoths had already joined, appeared to him more dangerous than the Romans, and, forgetful of his oath, he sought an alliance with the latter, and strove to assemble all the Visigoths within their territory; a proposal gladly assented to, as, by this means, the Visigoths became a bulwark against the Huns. Theodosius treated Athanarich with great honor, gave him a magnificent palace at Constantinople, and, at his death, which took place soon after these events, followed the aged warrior to his grave. The greater part of the Visigoths remained in Greece in close alliance with the Romans, and were again formed into a corps of mercenaries or Varingians, commanded by their own chiefs, and governed by their own laws. Capable of a higher degree of cultivation than the other German tribes, they ere long acquired all that was elevated and refined in the Roman manners, without becoming enervated by luxury or losing their natural nobility of character, and were consequently so highly esteemed by the Romans as to be preferred, on account of

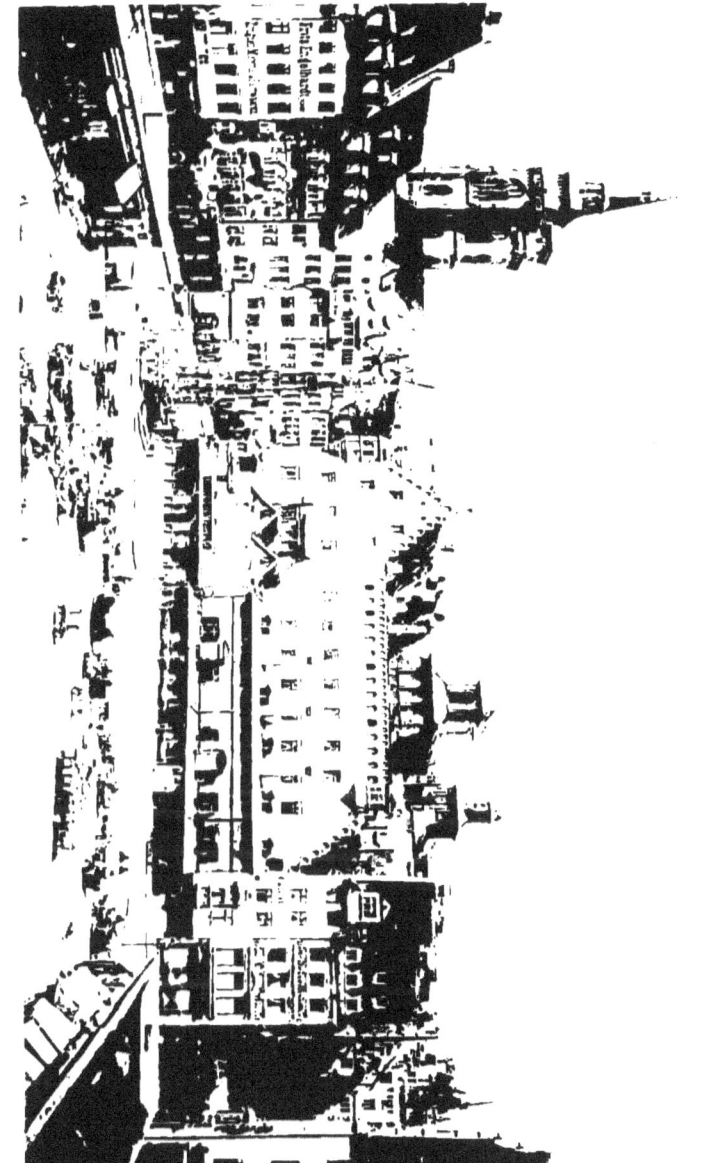

NUREMBERG

their capacity, to the highest offices of state. The Roman historians of that time even acknowledge that the Germans were deemed men, and the Romans women. Their influence even extended to dress. The fops of that period wore a light-colored wig, and the Roman senators did not disdain to adopt the Gothic furs in the place of the ancient toga. Saul, Gainas and Alaric are mentioned as warriors serving in the imperial army, whose prowess gained the important victory over Eugenius, the rival emperor, the traitor Arbogastes, and the Franks. Christianity received a fresh impulse through the alliance of the Goths with Rome. Fritigil, a prince of the Marcomanni, visited Milan, during the reign of Theodosius, in order to see St. Ambrose, the archbishop. The Ostro-Gothic Gruthungri, who had retreated across the Danube under Alatheus and Saphrax, alone refused to come to terms, and again making an incursion for the purpose of plunder, were defeated and driven back by Theodosius. Alatheus fell on the field of battle.

The position of the empire, and the double danger to which it was exposed from the Danube and the Rhine, convinced Theodosius the Great of the expediency of dividing the government, and he accordingly willed that the empire should be divided after his death, which happened in 395, between his sons, Honorius and Arcadius, the former of whom reigned at Rome as Emperor of the West, and the latter at Constantinople as Emperor of the East.

LXI. *Alaric*

MANY of the Gothic chiefs in the Roman empire raised themselves to high distinction, more particularly Alaric, a descendant of the Balti, who, on being elected king by the majority of the Visigoths, instantly planned the most daring enterprises, and, suddenly invading Greece, plundered and destroyed the most considerable cities, A.D. 396, sparing Athens alone, owing to a superstitious notion that he beheld Pallas, the patroness of the city, standing before the gates.

Arcadius being unable to oppose him, Honorius sent Stilico, a Vandal (who had been raised by Theodosius to the highest dignities of state), to his assistance, who succeeded in inclosing Alaric within the mountains of the Peloponnesus, but afterward allowed him to retreat from a desire of injuring Arcadius. A bitter jealousy had arisen between the eastern and western empires, of which Alaric skillfully took advantage, and fixed himself in Illyria, where, placed between Rome and Constantinople, he lost no opportunity of promoting his own interest in both quarters. At this time another Goth, named Gainas, who had gained considerable power in Constantinople, and was plotting the seizure of the imperial crown, happening to absent himself on a recruiting expedition, the Romans suddenly attacked and murdered all the Goths in the city, and Gainas being discomfited by another Gothic army under Frajuta, that remained faithful to the imperial standard, fled across the Danube, and fell into the hands of Uldes, prince of the Huns, who put him to death. Shortly after this event, Alaric undertook a great invasion of Italy, and at the head of numerous German tribes and of his allies, the Alemanni, fell upon Aquileia, A.D. 400, while Stilico was engaged in withdrawing all the troops from Gaul in order to oppose him; but, notwithstanding his exertions, Alaric, who continually received encouragement from Constantinople, pressed gradually onward. During the solemnization of Easter festival at Pollentia, the Goths were suddenly attacked by Stilico, and a battle ensued, in which Goth opposed Goth, A.D. 403, and Saul lost his life fighting on the Roman side at the head of his mercenaries A second and not less bloody engagement took place at Verona, when Alaric, being forced to retreat, was again shut up in the mountains by Stilico, who once more allowed him to make terms.

Radagais, at the head of an enormous horde of pagan Alemanni and other German tribes, now rushed from the Upper Danube over the Alps, A.D. 405, swearing to offer all the blood of the Romans in one great libation to his gods, and advanced as far as the Apennines, where, hemmed in by the whole army of Stilico (who, by skillful treaties and promises, had succeeded in combining beneath his standard the Huns under Uldes, and a Gothic force under Sarus), he and his followers were destroyed by famine, pestilence, and the sword, near Fiesole in Tuscany. Alaric did not long remain quiet. Stilico, his brave opponent, accused by Honorius of carrying on a secret understanding with him, and even of grasping at the purple, was put to death, together with the wives and children of 30,000 Germans in his service. The payment of the tribute, which had been agreed to at the treaty of peace, was also refused, and Alaric, burning for revenge, quickly seized the favorable moment afforded for the long-planned conquest of Italy, by the destruction of Rome's best general; and being joined by the 30,000 widowers, marched straight upon the imperial city, whose possession he deemed would secure to him that of the whole of Italy, leaving Honorius, to his rear, shut up in Ravenna. Terror-struck and helpless, the Romans entreated for peace, which was granted by the invader on the payment of 5,000 pounds' weight of gold, 30,000 pounds' weight of silver, and a proportionate quantity of the costly articles of commerce which, at that period, flowed into Rome from every quarter of the known world. Entreaties were unavailing. "What will be left us?" asked they. "Life," was the stern reply. "We are still numerous," they threatened. "Then come out," rejoined the Goth. "the thicker the hay the easier it is to mow!" The terms were enforced; the golden statue of Victory was melted to meet the demand, and the Romans, who still retained their heathen superstitions, foresaw in its destruction the impending ruin of their city. Satisfied with the booty thus gained, Alaric now left Rome in order to attack Ravenna, and conferred the imperial dignity on one Attalus, whom he sent to Africa to prepare for his arrival in that country, and whom he afterward deposed for having, aided by the Romans by whom he was accompanied, attempted to assert his own independence. Honorius was aided in the defense of Ravenna, which was well fortified, by a part of the Goths under Sarus, the hereditary enemy of the Balti; Alaric, meanwhile, ruled unopposed in the open country, and after annihilating the last Roman army, united his forces with those of Ataulph, his son-in-law, who had brought fresh tribes from Germany; but failing in his attempts against Ravenna, he resolved to wreak full vengeance upon Rome. He is said to have presented three hundred youths to the wealthiest Romans for slaves, who secretly opened the city gates to him; but, however that may be, it is certain that he took Rome by storm during the night of the 24th of August, 409. For the first time since the invasion of Brennus, the capital of the ancient world beheld the enemy, who had so often been led in triumph through her walls, enchained, thrown to the wild beasts in her amphitheater, or doomed to cruel slavery, now appear as a bloody and inflexible conqueror, armed with the sword of vengeance, repaying all the crimes committed by her against the liberties of nations, which, unatoned by her first punishment, were afterward bitterly visited upon her. Yet, although murder and pillage filled the city, Rome was not destroyed, and the defenseless ones were spared. A Goth, who discovered some valuable golden vessels in the house of a pious maiden, when told that they had been left with her for safety and belonged to the church of St. Peter, left them untouched, and gave information of the discovery to the other Goths, who came in multitudes to the spot, and bore the golden ornaments in a solemn procession, in which the people joined, to St. Peter's: the war-cry ceased; the voices of the conquerors and conquered rose in unison, and the pillage terminated in hymns of devotion.[1] Leaving Rome, Alaric marched into Lower Italy with the intention of visiting Africa, but his fleet was wrecked off Messina,

---

[1] When Honorius was told at Ravenna that Roma was lost, he gave signs of the deepest despair, believing that a pet bird of his called Roma was alluded to, and was instantly consoled on discovering that it was merely the capital of the world.

and he died suddenly, in his fifty-fourth year. The river Busentom (Baseno) was diverted from its course by prisoners, and the Gothic monarch was buried with an immense treasure in its bed; after which, the stream was restored to its natural course, and the secret of his burial-place, which remained as unknown as the projects that died with him, was sealed by the murder of the laborers.

LXII. *The Vandals, Alani, Suevi, and Visigoths in Spain*

AFTER the destruction of Radagais, the tribes from which his army had been raised, instead of invading Italy, moved toward Gaul, whence the troops had been withdrawn. The Vandals under Godegisel, the Alani under Respendial, and a horde of Suevi under Hermanarich, crossed the Rhine during the last days of the year 407, never to return, and, after plundering Gaul for some time and unsuccessfully combating the Franks, suddenly traversed the Pyrenees and entered Spain, where they were well received. The Basci, a remnant of the ancient Celts, and the Iberi in the mountains, offered no opposition, preferring poverty and freedom beneath the German rule to the splendid tyranny of Rome. The Vandals under Gunderich, the successor of Godegisel, ruled at Hispalis (Seville), and gave name to the province of Andalusia. The Suevi inhabited Castile and Gallicia, and the Alani settled on the Ebro. The departure of these wild tribes from Gaul did not, however, relieve that province from the horrors of war; a new emperor, Constantine, who had set himself up in Britain, crossed the Channel and was supported by the Franks under Edobic, in opposition to Sarus, who, aided by the Alemanni under Goar, and by the Burgundians under Gunthachar, proclaimed Jovinus emperor, A.D. 412. The dispute was settled by Constantine being deprived of his throne and his life.

Honorius, desirous of freeing Italy from the Visigoths, dexterously seized upon these events as a pretext, and solicited the aid of Ataulph, the successor of Alaric, against Jovinus, flattering him with the possession of Gaul and Spain if he would quit Italy; but the strongest motive for conciliation between the Goth and the emperor was the passion cherished by Ataulph for Placidia, Honorius's beautiful and talented sister, who had been taken prisoner at Rome by Alaric; he accordingly acceded to the emperor's proposal, and abandoning Italy at the head of his whole nation. marched against Jovinus and Sarus, whom he defeated; and, after taking possession of the south of Gaul and of the north of Spain, celebrated his nuptials with Placidia at Narbonne, A.D. 414; the ceremony being performed by Sisegar, the Gothic bishop, whom the king also appointed preceptor to his children; a proof of the civilization to which the Goths had already attained. A high bed was constructed, around which all the booty gained by Ataulph and his late father-in-law, Alaric, was heaped. Attalus, the deposed emperor, who was in his suite, composed songs for the occasion, in which he pointed out to him the events that might possibly result from the union of the mightiest of the German princes with the sister of the Cæsars, and the foundation of a new Gothic-Roman empire on the ruins of the ancient one was consequently projected. But the time had not yet arrived, and it happened as was prophesied by Daniel: "In the end of years they shall join themselves together; for the king's daughter of the south shall come to the king of the north to make an agreement; but she shall not retain the power of her arm, neither shall he stand, nor his arm: but she shall be given up, and they that brought her, and he that begat her, and he that strengthened her in these times,'' chap. xi. 6.[1] A forest known as la selva Gothesca now covers the site of the ancient city of Heraclea, in the south of France, where Ataulph and Placidia held their splendid court. The Goth, Sarus, having been cruelly put to death

---

[1] According to Bishop Newton, this prophecy relates to the marriage of Berenice, the daughter of Ptolemy Philadelphus, the second king of Egypt, with Antiochus Theus, the third king of Syria.—*Trans.*

by Ataulph, Dubios, a servant of the former, probably incited by Sigerich, the brother of Sarus, murdered him at Barcelona, A.D. 415. Sigerich usurped the Gothic throne, and exterminated the whole race of the Balti. In pursuance of a policy completely contrary to that of his predecessor, he broke with Rome, perhaps with the intention of flattering the national pride of the Goths. The beautiful Placidia was sentenced to run on foot for twelve miles before the car of the usurper, who a few days after fell by the hand of Wallia, whom the Goths had raised to the throne, and who, renewing the alliance with Rome, sent Placidia back to her native country, with 800,000 measures of wheat. He carried on a successful war in Spain, and subdued the Alani, whom he incorporated with the Goths, which gave rise to the Gothic-Alani nation, and to the name of the province of Catalonia. Toulouse became the capital of the Visigothic empire under Wallia, who left an only daughter, the mother of the celebrated Ricimer, who was closely connected with the family of the Cæsars (continued by Placidia, who married Constantius, and gave birth to the emperor Valentinian the Third, and to the infamous Honoria). The brave Theodorich, who succeeded Wallia as king of the Goths, greatly extended his dominions, and defeated Rechiar, the king of the Spanish Suevi, but met with a powerful opponent in Ætius the Roman general, who attempted to reconquer Gaul. Arles and Narbonne were vainly besieged by Theodorich, who, after a long war, was finally obliged to league with Rechiar against their common and far more formidable enemy, the Hun.

In the south of Spain, the Vandals bade defiance to the attacks of both Goths and Romans, and rose to considerable importance under Geiserich, the brother of Gunderich. Geiserich had married his son Hunerich to a daughter of Theodorich, whom, on mere suspicion, he deprived of her nose and ears, and, fearing the vengeance of the Visigoths for this act of barbarity, invited the Huns, who were already on their way thither, into Spain.

LXIII. The Alemanni in Switzerland—The Burgundians in Alsace

TRANQUILLITY had for a short period once more visited the Alps, and ruins, scattered along the path of the devastating hordes, alone remained to tell the tale of bygone splendor. Helvetia no longer existed; the green forest waved over heaps that were once cities, while the Alemanni, proud of their freedom, fed their flocks, and built their scattered cottages, in the sheltered valleys. Civilization and oppression had disappeared with the Romans, and Christianity was unknown to the savage Swabains, who remained faithful to their ancient religion and customs in the new settlement. The lake into which the Rhine flows from the Alps was probably again called by its ancient name, the Boden-see, from Odin (Wodan, Buddha), to whom a place of worship was erected on the shore. The Thurgau and Frickthal, from their deities Thor and Frigga, lay in its vicinity. The name of the Odenwald, between the Maine and the Neckar, has a similar origin, and the freedom so long preserved in Switzerland is a proof that ancient German liberty co-existed with paganism. Independent war-chiefs or dukes also appear amid the obscurity of those times. The Alpine countries finally received the name of Schweiz (Switzerland), identical with that of Suevi or Swabia, whose inhabitants owned the same origin. The people of Schweiz, Uri, Unterwalden, and Hasli, have a tradition of their having been driven by famine out of Sweden, which agrees with that of the Longobardi, and the migration of the Goths; and it is possible that, at the period of the commingling of different tribes, a Gothic or Longobardic horde, straying among these mountains, mixed with the Alemanni; or perhaps the legend has been clothed in a new form, and originally referred to the earliest immigrations of the Suevi.

The Burgundians (tribe of Bur?) originally dwelt on the Riesengebirge, which was perhaps also an Asenburg, and connected the Caucasus with the north. Forced along by the advancing Goths, the Burgundians turned toward the west, and appeared to the rear of the Alemanni. At a later period they joined the Vandali (originally Vindili), and invaded Gaul, as has been already related, when Honorius, for the sake of peace, finally bestowed upon them Alsace, as a fief of the empire. Immense sacrificial altars, the remains of which are still to be seen, were erected by them on the Odilienberg, which was doubtless sacred to Odin, whose name was subsequently changed to the Christian one of Ottilia. The name of Worms, which the Burgundians, on reaching the southern Alps, renewed in that of the city of Bormio, has also reference to the ancient deity, Bör. This comparatively small tribe bore a high traditionary fame among the Germans, and holds a prominent place in the songs of the Nibelungen, which is probably owing less to its later history than to the religious veneration with which it was anciently regarded.

LXIV. *The Salic Law*

IN the beginning of the fifth century, the history of the Franks took a new and important turn; the Roman armies were completely driven out of Gaul by Stilico, and the country fell a prey to the Vandals, Burgundians, Alani, and Suevi. The Franks, in order not to remain behindhand, took possession of the neighboring lands as far as the Moselle, and divided themselves into the Salii on the Moselle and the Meuse, and the Ripuarii on the Lower Rhine. All the ancient and various names of the tribes disappear in these two, which are evidently derived from the Latin. *Salii*, leapers, from *salire*, had long been the appellation of the Frankish mercenaries in the imperial service; a name not at all in unison with the ancient titles and nicknames of the Roman legions and mercenary troops. The Salii were the Franks who dwelt nearest to the Romans, whom they for a long period served, and who, very probably, made use of this name for the sake of a quibble, which may first of all have been derived from the Saal (Yssel), and the Saal-land (Ober-Yssel) in the Netherlands, where the Franks, tributary to the Romans, formerly dwelt. It has also been deduced from the Wurzburgian Saalgau (the subsequent Ostro-Franci), and even from the Thuringian Saal (on account of the ancient connection between the Thuringians and the Franks), or from the word *Saal*, a hall (Allod). The name of the Ripuarii is clearly Latin, from *ripa*, a bank, and was the general appellation of the Franks who dwelt on the banks of the Rhine. The Salii, who affected the Roman party, were long at feud with the Ripuarii, who were more German in their customs, and it is probable that at that period the Bructeri, Cherusci, etc., tribes that dwelt further eastward toward the Weser, and that were formerly accounted Franks, formed a closer connection with the Saxons (with whom they subsequently intermingled), when forced to defend their ancient liberty and religion against the despotism and zealous Christian proselytism of the Franks. The abandonment of Gaul by the Romans necessarily occasioned a great change in the affairs of that country; the Salii, no longer supported by Rome, became independent, and their newly-acquired possessions, which extended as far as the Moselle, afforded them an opportunity for remodeling their government. Long accustomed to the rule of a war-chief, and well acquainted with the advantages of union, as well as jealous of the splendor and fame of the great king of the Goths,[1] they elected a monarch after the demise of Genobald, Sunno, and Marcomir, instead of continuing to be governed by various petty and independent princes, and raised Faramund, the son of Marcomir, to the throne, A.D. 420. . Before submitting to the authority of the new monarch, they solemnly guaranteed their ancient privileges, by the prescription of certain conditions, whence originated the Salic law,

---

[1] Sigebert of Gemblours says plainly that they wished to follow the example of other nations: "Franci in communi deliberant, ut et ipsi sicut aliae gentes regnum habeant."

which was drawn up in writing. Up to this period, the laws had been merely traditionary, but when the new settlements within the Roman territory caused a wider extension of the people, ancient customs were endangered by new, their privileges seemed likely to be encroached upon by the monarch, and a written code became necessary. Four elders, chosen by the people, were intrusted with the completion of this important work, as was afterward set forth in the preface of Chlodwig, appended to this celebrated code. "The renowned nation of the Franks, the chosen of God, strong in battle, wise in council, mighty by their union, noble and virtuous, of surpassing stature, bold, vigorous, and firm, caused the Salic law to be drawn up, while they were yet pagans, by the chiefs by whom they were at that period governed. Four men were chosen from among the elders, named Wysogast, Bodogast, Salogast, and Windogast, who came from the countries then called Salagheven, Bodogheven, and Windogheven. These four men met three times in the Malberg, weighed the origin and peculiarities of all the laws, and then laid them down in writing. But when the long-haired, beautiful Chlodwig, the first of the Frankish monarchs who received Catholic baptism, lived, whatever seemed unfitting in this code was expunged. Vivat Christus, who chose the Franks unto himself, for this is the people that, by its bravery and power, cast off the oppressive yoke of Rome." Faramund was succeeded by Chlodis (Louis), whose successor, Merowig, was, according to the legendary account, suckled by a sea-monster, which attacked his mother on the shore. Chlodis introduced the custom of wearing long hair, which afterward became a sign of royalty, and was adopted by his successors, hence named the long-haired kings. The descendants of Merowig were the Merovingians.

LXV. *Etzel*

ABOUT this period a powerful leader arose among the Huns, who was named by the Romans Attila, by the Germans, Etzel; the center of whose kingdom was in Hungary, where his throne stood in an enormous wooden palace. He united beneath his rule not only all the Huns, but also all the Ostro-Germanic tribes. The Ostrogoths, whose history is very obscure at this period, were forced to follow their example. They were governed by several leaders, and were continually at war with the Sarmatians (Slavi). Fidicola, one of their princes, had been defeated by the Sarmatians shortly before the appearance of Etzel, in whose train were Theodomir, the father of the celebrated Diettrich of Bern, Widimir and Walamir, at the head of the Ostrogoths, and Ardarich, king of the Gepidæ. Etzel was one of those mighty spirits, who, like Cæsar and Napoleon, were born to captivate every heart, to rule millions with a glance, and to use their giant strength in crushing a world. Adored by his followers, whom he led to victory, and a chieftain eagerly hailed by the warlike nations, which, habituated to battle and long estranged from their homes, were inimical to peace, he was the cruel despoiler of all who opposed his despotic rule.

Rome trembled at the approach of the destroyer, rightly termed "The scourge of God," who seemed destined to mete out the reward of the crimes accumulated during the thousand years' reign of the ancient mistress of the world. The Eastern empire first suffered. The whole of Greece was laid waste, and Constantinople was alone delivered from destruction by the policy of Pulcheria, the mother of the helpless emperor, Theodosius, who bribed the Huns, by the payment of an immense ransom, to spare the capital, and to turn their course westward, A.D. 451. The storm now burst upon Germany. Desolation, rapine, and slaughter marked its advance toward Gaul. Obscure legendary accounts of the horrors of that period are still extant. All the relics and jewels belonging to the Church, still in its infancy, were saved at Andecks, on the mountain, from the rapacity of the invaders. Wimpfen owes its name to Wibpin (*Weiberpein,* women's pain), all the women of this place having been cruelly murdered by Attila's command, and several Hunnenberge, Hunnengräben (fortifications against the Huns), are still to be met with in Germany, although it is uncertain whether they ought not to be ascribed to the Hungarians of later date, who were also called Huns. History records but one attempt made to oppose the progress of Attila on the right bank of the Rhine, the heroic opposition of 10,000 Burgundians under Gunthachar, who fought and fell like a second Leonidas.[1] The Franks under Merowig, and the Alani under Sangipfan, vainly strove to stem the torrent, and all the nations of the West, Germans and Romans, became at length aware that a great general confederacy could alone preserve them from destruction. Placidia, the experienced and strong-minded mother of the weak emperor, Valentinian, governed Rome, and Ætius, the famous warrior, then commander-in-chief of the Roman forces, collected the remaining strength of the empire and entered Gaul, where he was joined by the Visigoths under Theodorich, the Franks under Merowig, and the remnant of the Alani. Claudebald, the brother of Merowig, went over to Etzel with a part of the Franks. The protracted siege of

---

[1] The circumstances attending this brilliant action are unknown, but evidently form the groundwork of one of the songs of the Nibelungen, in which they have received the following poetical embellishment. "Once upon a time there lived a handsome Frankish warrior named Siegfried, or the Horned Knight, on account of his whole body, with the exception of a small spot on his back, being as hard as horn and perfectly invulnerable. This knight came to Worms, and wooed and won the beautiful Chriemhilda, the sister of Gunthachar. His wonderful strength and dauntless courage soon raised the jealousy of all the Burgundian knights, and one of them, Hagen the Grim, secretly encouraged by the king, murdered him (one day when weary with following the chase, as he stooped to quench his thirst at a brook) by running his sword through his back. Chriemhilda, inconsolable for his loss, became hateful to the Burgundians, who refused to restore to her the great treasure won by Siegfried in the Netherlands, and which Hagen sunk in the Rhine, where it still lies. Soon after this, Etzel, king of the Huns, attracted by the fame of her great beauty, dispatched embassadors to Worms to ask her in marriage, with whom she returned into Hungary, and was made queen. But her heart remained constant to the memory of Siegfried, and demanded vengeance. Gunthachar, his brothers, Hagen the Grim, and a crowd of Burgundian nobles, were invited to the court of Etzel, where, at the instigation of the queen, they were put to the sword by the Huns and their German allies, headed by the youthful and valiant Dieterich, the Ostrogoth, who afterward filled Europe with his fame.

Orleans, which was desperately defended by the Romans, long retarded the advance of the invader. At length, pressed by famine, the garrison resolved to capitulate, if their prayers for succor were unheard; but before the prayer was ended, clouds of dust appeared on the horizon annunciatory of the approach of their allies, the Visigoths, and Etzel was compelled to retreat, in order to draw up his innumerable horse near Chalons, on the broad plains of the Marne, where the nations of the East and West arrayed their forces, and stood in momentary expectation of an action decisive of the fate of Europe. Etzel was superior in the numbers, military skill, and confidence of his troops, while those of his opponents were inspired by the memory of their ancient fame, by zeal for the cause of Christianity, and by the danger which threatened their freedom and their homes. In this contest, German opposed German, with the deadliest hate; consequently whichever side might prove victorious, the German was sure to suffer. The battle at length commenced on both sides, with equal animosity. The death of the brave Theodorich was bloodily avenged by his son, Thorismund, and the Visigoths gained a decisive victory. After losing 200,000 men, Etzel retreated and the Western empire was saved. An enormous funeral pile, composed of horses' saddles, had been erected, on which Etzel had intended to burn himself alive, if unable to escape. Thorismund, raised on his reeking shield, was proclaimed king of the Visigoths amid the shouts of the victors. But prosperity speedily severed those whom adversity had united. Ætius, jealous of the glory and power of Thorismund, drew off his troops, and persuaded him to return to his country, giving him, as indemnity for the anticipated booty, a golden charger, weighing five hundredweight, set with precious jewels, supposed to have been the tablet of Solomon's table, taken by the Romans from the celebrated temple at Jerusalem.

Etzel, invited by Honoria, the sister of Valentinian, who, for having offered to marry him, was imprisoned at Rome, crossed the Alps into Italy, A.D. 452. For three months,

Aquileia, ever the stumbling-block of the invader, detained him, but was finally taken and destroyed. Many of the Romans fled for refuge to the little marshy islands of the Adriatic, on which they founded the city of Venice. Etzel came in sight of Rome, whose destruction appeared inevitable, when an unlooked-for incident averted her fate. Leo, the bishop of Rome, an aged and dignified man, set forth to meet the savage and rapacious Huns, at the head of the Roman clergy, arrayed in priestly attire and chanting devotional hymns. None ventured to oppose the pious priests, and they presented themselves before the king, who, influenced by Leo's aspect and words, promised to spare the city and instantly to retire. According to the legend, the appearance of this saintly man so powerfully affected the mind of the Hun that, in imagination, he beheld an enormous giant tower above the head of the bishop, and, with a threatening gesture, motion to him to retire. Etzel died on his way out of Italy, according to some accounts, by the bursting of a blood-vessel, according to others, by the hand of a maiden named Ildegunda, who may have been confounded with Chriemhilda; but the whole occurrence is involved in obscurity. He was buried with great pomp; the whole army on horseback encircling his body, which was placed in a golden coffin within a silver one, and the whole inclosed in one of lead. Those who prepared his grave were put to death, in order to render impossible the discovery of the locality. The sons of Etzel did not inherit the genius of their father; bitter feuds, in which the Huns joined, arose between them, and the Germans speedily found means to throw off their yoke. Ardarich, king of the Gepidæ, was the first who raised the standard of rebellion. He was followed by the Ostrogoths under the Amali, Walamir, Theodomir, and Widomir. A victory was won on the river Netad in Hungary; and another was gained by Walamir at the mouths of the Danube, when the Huns were forced to retreat beyond the Black Sea. The Goths again threatened the Eastern empire. Theodomir, bribed by the emperor, sent his son, Theodorich, who was born on the day of the last victory won by Walamir, as a hostage to Constantinople, but still maintained his position on the Danube. Widomir was also persuaded, by means of a large bribe, to turn his course to the west, where his people intermingled with the Visigoths.

LXVI. *Geiserich*

GEISERICH, or Genserich, had placed himself on the Vandal throne by the murder of his brother Gunderich. Although lame from a fall from horseback, he was noted as being the most active of all the German leaders. Being driven from the Pyrenees by the Visigoths, and invited into Africa by Bonifacius, the faithless Roman governor, he resolved to quit the theater of war in Europe, and to erect a new and splendid kingdom in the luxurious South. The whole of his subjects, together with some of the Alani and Goths, in all 80,000 men, had already assembled on the shore for the purpose of embarkation, when he was informed that Heringar, the king of the Suevi, was attacking him in the rear, and, instantly returning, drove the enemy into a river, in which the king was drowned. In May, A.D. 429, Geiserich sailed to Africa, where he conquered the whole of the northern coast, and drove out the Romans who had invited him thither. The large and well-fortified city of Carthage became his capital, and all the other fortresses were demolished, lest they might serve as strongholds for the Romans. The natives were well treated, and public immorality was checked; prostitutes being compelled to marry, and adultery punished by death; morality was, in fact, so strongly enforced by Geiserich that it was commonly said, "The Romans are licentious when compared with the Goths, but they are worse when compared with the Vandals." Landed estates in the vicinity of the capital were bestowed upon the Vandals, with the view of hindering their dispersion during peace, and of facilitating their assembling in case of danger. With political foresight, Geiserich, whose favorite title was that of Sea-king, sought to sway the Mediterranean, named by his subjects the Vendilsee. The plans formed by Alaric, whose early death prevented their completion, were now carried into execution by the Vandal monarch, who, as if by enchantment, created a powerful fleet, and, in 439, besieged Palermo with the intention of conquering Sicily, his vessels at the same time sweeping the Atlantic and plundering the coasts of Spain. Rome, at that period threatened by the Huns, offered little or no opposition to his schemes. The death of the gallant Ætius, her brave defender, who fell a victim to court cabals, hastened her ruin. Valentinian was murdered by Maximus, who forced the widowed Eudoxia to become his wife, and seated himself on the imperial throne. Eudoxia, animated by revenge, secretly invited Geiserich to destroy Rome and to carry her away, and, in 455, he sailed for that purpose with an enormous fleet to Italy, where he landed and took Rome by storm, but spared both the city and the inhabitants, and contented himself with a systematic pillage, which lasted fourteen days. The treasure was appropriated to the maintenance and increase of his fleet; and the splendors of Rome were transported to Africa to adorn her ancient rival, Carthage. The ships were laden with gold and jewels; even the golden roofs were carried away. That the Vandals were not insensible to beauty and art, and that the term of Vandalism has been wrongly used in order to indicate coarse barbarity, the enemy of refinement, science, and civilization, are clearly proved on reference to history, which records their having deprived Rome of her finest marbles, and that a ship laden with them was wrecked; had they not appreciated the value of these statues, as miracles of art, they would either have been wantonly destroyed or passed by unheeded. Geiserich, preferring his African kingdom to the possession of Italy, returned to Carthage, accompanied by the empress Eudoxia, whom he regarded as part of the booty. Her daughter, who was also named Eudoxia, was given in marriage to his son, Hunerich. The Vandals now ruled the seas, and annually devastated the coasts of Spain, Italy, and Greece. The Romans and Goths in Spain armed a great fleet against them, which Geiserich attacked when lying in the harbors, and carried away from the roads. Leo, emperor of the East, A.D. 460, manned a formidable fleet at Constantinople, and sent it, under the command of Basiliscus, against Carthage. Geiserich, instead of opposing it on the open sea, prudently retreated into the harbor, and as soon as the Greeks had drawn up their ships in a close circle round the entrance, suddenly sent fire ships among them, which destroyed the greater part, and put the rest to flight, A.D. 468. Geiserich died, ten years after this event, in extreme old age, A.D. 478. After the migration of the Vandals to Africa, the Roman peasants, headed by Merobaudes, the Roman poet, in whose honor columns were raised, revolted against the Suevi, who, numerically weak, and shaken by disaster, gradually sank, while the dominion of the Visigoths increased, and finally spread over the whole of Spain.

LXVII. *Odoachar*

AFTER Geiserichs' departure from Rome, Ricimer, the Sueve, grandson to Wallia, king of the Visigoths, and the hereditary enemy of the Vandals, held undisputed sway in Italy, and conducted all the measures taken against Geiserich by both the Western and Eastern empires. His authority, however, was not displeasing to the weak emperors of Constantinople, with whom he entered into alliance, because, satisfied with possessing the power without the title of emperor, he bestowed it upon men whom he one after the other deposed, as soon as they disobeyed his injunctions. Majorian, Severus, Arthemius, whose daughter he married, but whom he soon after disagreed with, and finally, Olybrius, were successively proclaimed emperor, and kept in awe by his German troops, chiefly composed of Heruli and Rugii, who had settled in the Alps to the northwest of Italy, A.D. 472. His death left the throne defenseless.

Odoachar, one of the Heruli (of whom when yet a youth it had been foretold by St. Severinus that he would exchange his rough furs for the imperial purple), was distinguished for his boldness and valor, and soon caused himself to be elected prince of his nation, and leader of the Roman mercenaries. He first united with Childerich, the Frank, against the Alemanni, whose prince, Gibuld, he overthrew, A.D. 466. He then planned the conquest of Rome, and easily succeeded in dethroning Romulus Augustulus, an amiable but weak youth, the last of the Roman emperors, when he caused himself to be proclaimed king of Italy, probably as much from a superstitious dread of the fatal destiny which seemed attached to those who bore the imperial title as from a desire of flattering his countrymen. A.D. 476.—A.U.C. 1229. Order was quickly established throughout the kingdom. The Germans received a third of the landed property, and were distributed among the Romans, who were allowed to retain their customs and laws. Ravenna, which became the capital, kept the Tyrolean Rugii and Heruli in check. Thus was the fall of the Roman empire accomplished, after a struggle of eight centuries against the Germans, from the time of the first Brennus to that of Odoachar, by whom their colossal power was finally crushed. Order was restored; but it was long before the ferment entirely ceased. After the fall of Rome, the Latin tongue and the refinements of the South greatly influenced its conquerors, and drew a broader line of distinction between them and their brethren who still inhabited the wild and trackless forests; Christianity also caused a still wider separation between the converted and the pagan nations. These circumstances, combined with the hereditary feuds and the restless, war-loving character of the Germans, were turned to advantage by their kings, who, influenced either by zeal for religion or by ambitious motives, carried on the struggle, now terminated with Rome, among themselves.

PART IV

THE TRANSITION FROM PAGANISM TO CHRISTIANITY

LXVIII. *The Propagation of the Gospel*

IN THE midst of the tumult of nations, rushing onward in their migrations as madly as the raging waters of the lordly Rhine beneath its black and aged cliffs, Christianity, the spirit of eternal peace, appeared, like the celestial bow hanging unmoved and calm, softly radiating through its misty veil, over the dark and foaming abyss. While the Roman empire, in the decline of age, shaken to its very foundations by savage and invading hordes, was slowly sinking to decay, while those mighty hordes, solely intent on pillage, filled the world with horror and despair, a mild and gentle spirit of love and peace sought refuge in the hearts of a few, as in a sanctuary, uninfluenced by earthly power, gradually gained a mastery over the passions of mankind, and, by its invisible but benign influence, spread peace around. The gospel was preached and proclaimed in the East and West by the apostles and followers of the Saviour, who sealed their profession with a martyr's death.

Small Christian communities disseminated themselves to the utmost verge of the empire, and although cruelly persecuted by the Roman emperors, Christianity rose again with renovated strength, like the phœnix from the pyre. Before its doctrines, replete with eternal truth, the dark fables of paganism fell; while the firmness shown by its adherents in preferring a lingering death, torture, and the stake to a renunciation of their faith impressed even their persecutors with a conviction of the truth of the religion they professed, and aided its diffusion. In the commencement of the fourth century, the new religion had taken such deep root in the empire that the emperor Constantine deemed it politic to adopt it, and, by so doing, rendered it the religion of the state. Under the first Christian emperors, the German countries lying within their jurisdiction were entirely Christianized, and the heathen temples were either converted into churches or new places of worship were erected.

Before the conversion of Constantine, while war was raging on the Danube, a great number of the Goths were converted by their Roman prisoners, and Christianity spread so rapidly among them that Gothic bishops were present at the great council of Nice, convoked by that emperor, and several distinguished theologians shone among the earliest Gothic bishops, one of whom, Ulphilas, as has already been mentioned, produced a Gothic translation of the Bible. In the progress of the migrations, all the Gothic tribes, after their settlement in the Roman territory, embraced Christianity; an example shortly afterward followed by the Franks, who imparted its doctrines to the other nations of Germany.

LXIX. *The Spirit of Christianity*

THE fundamental doctrine of the Christian religion, "Love thy neighbor as thyself," was a command of love by which it was at once distinguished from the different religions, founded upon egotism, practiced by the heathens. The Jews, Greeks, and Romans, like the ancient priest-castes of the East, that kept themselves apart from the rest of the people, regarded themselves as chosen nations, all others as barbarians, strangers, and enemies, whom they were not only permitted but commanded to treat with cruelty or to exterminate. Hence slavery was universally practiced. The ancient Germans, who only respected the rights of those with whom they were in immediate alliance, and the laws of hospitality, were not free from a similar charge, and habitually treated every stranger, nay, even their own countrymen and nearest neighbors, as enemies, and made it their chief occupation to attack and oppress each other. Christianity first taught equality and fraternal love. The spirituality of its doctrines was also directly opposed to those inculcated by paganism, which, referring merely to the external world, degraded men's minds by sensuality and superstition. To many of the nations of antiquity, the doctrine of the immortality of the soul was utterly unknown, while others formed their notions of a future state on the same principle as the Germans, who imagined their heavenly Walhalla to be merely a more joyous continuation of their earthly existence. Christianity first taught the doctrines of the Divine origin, and of the eternal duration of the soul. Deeply impressed with the truth of these two great doctrines, whole nations renounced their ancient superstitions and customs, and egotism, so deeply rooted in the nature of man, alone opposed the fulfillment of the great injunction of universal love that has ever been so universally disobeyed. Nations continued to butcher each other, nay, they even carried on the butchery in the name of the very Saviour who enjoined peace and love; while slavery not only continued, but even gained ground among the Germans, who framed their excuse on the humility inculcated by the gospel. But the good seed had been sown, and gradually produced better fruit. Centuries passed away; and, as the doctrine of mercy, the knowledge of the common rights of man, of the value of civilization and of peace, imperceptibly gained ground, ancient barbarism disappeared. Although the precept of universal philanthropy taught by Christ found a slow and difficult reception among the conquerors of the earth, the second aim of Christianity, inward contemplation, met with universal encouragement; souls oppressed by crime or misfortune sought peace in the bosom of the church, or the egotism and pride of man led to a haughty contempt of the world, and immoderate mortification of the body. The Roman, whose sense of guilt was sharpened by the ever-recurring recollection of his ancient empire, now trampled beneath the foot of the savage invader, sought to expiate the past and to forget the present in the contemplation of eternity; while to the German, hurried away by his fervid imagination and enthusiastic zeal, Christianity presented a bright and joyous view, and he regarded himself as a soldier of Christ, whose glory he must seek to promote on earth by fighting and conquering in his cause. An inspiring and encouraging faith also pervaded the doctrines of the first German theologians, recluses, and ecclesiastical orders, whose renunciation of the world, and disdain of its allurements, far from being the result of sorrow or remorse, originated in religious enthusiasm, and an ecstatic contemplation of future and eternal joy.

LXX. *The Catholic Doctrine*

THE false interpretation of the figurative expressions with which the Bible abounds has ever been owing to ignorance or to willful perversion. In the earlier times of Christianity, the new doctrine was tainted with paganism and the ancient philosophy of Greece; the former, in direct contradiction to the words of the Saviour, requiring many outward forms, while the philosophers sought to build some theory of their own imagining on some fancied interpretation of the gospel. Two of the religious sects, to which these various interpretations gave rise, whose animosity greatly influenced the history of the world, and whose dispute was settled by the great council of Nice, convoked by the emperor Constantine, A.D. 325, may be more particularly remarked. The sect of the Arians, so named after their founder, Arius, maintained that God only consisted of one person, and that Christ was not God himself; while the opposite party professed that Christ, the Son of God, was also God the Father, only appearing as a second person under his earthly form, but united to the Godhead by the eternal Spirit. They also divided the Godhead into three persons, God the Father, God the Son, and God the Holy Ghost, and named them the Holy Trinity. The latter sect triumphed, and took the appellation of Catholic or universal.

The German bishops could not yet compete in learning with the countless clergy of Greece and Rome. One of them, named Theophilus, a Goth, distinguished himself at Nice in defense of Arianism; two others, Sunnia and Fretela, asked the advice of St. Hieronymus on the subject. Unila, Nicetas, and Theotimus are also mentioned as celebrated Gothic bishops, but the only Gothic book extant is the Bible translation of Ulphilas. It is merely known that all the Goths regarded Arianism as the simpler and better doctrine, and that their zealous profession of it gave rise to a Catholic alliance between the Greeks and Romans (which the Franks, who, although Catholics, at first inclined to the simpler doctrine, and objected to the worship of images, soon afterward joined), which ultimately proved too powerful for them, and greatly contributed to their calamities. An extraordinary multiplicity of doctrines and ceremonies was gradually introduced into the Catholic church. At first, tradition had greater influence than dogma, or rather, examples were cited without the precepts they inculcated being much commented upon. Piety was demonstrated by actions of self-denial, of bold heroism, of fidelity unto death, etc., which were transcribed and held up for imitation, and with a little poetical embellishment were converted into legends, which, in the first centuries after Christ, had already become very numerous, and formed the chief literature of the times. The naivete and profound thought that distinguish the legends of Germany prove that Christianity was originally in that country entirely practical, and free from subtle speculations. Their moral is ever noble and elevated, and they inculcate every Christian virtue through the medium of interesting and attractive tales, generally founded upon fact. At a later period, the legends became less natural, and the moral they inculcated more ecclesiastical. Simple practical Christianity was lost amid the artificial and complicated ceremonies of the church, which were chiefly introduced by the exaggerated and perverted practice of worshiping the saints, and men, instead of being roused by the example of the martyrs to emulate their piety and virtue, instead of seeking to live and to act in the same spirit by which they were animated, actually began to worship their dead bodies, their ashes, and their relics, to raise chapels and churches in their honor, and to invoke them, as the heathens formerly did their household deities, as the patrons and guardians of their country, their nation, their houses, and their families. Still, notwithstanding these heathenish practices of the church and the subtlety of theologians, the living spirit of Christianity was not entirely lost, and long breathed in the simple and unadulterated forms of the church in Germany. A spirit of austerity and of reverential awe, modified by a faith of almost child-like simplicity, may be traced throughout our earliest legends. The strict morality practiced by the German while yet a heathen was now ratified by the commands of the gospel, and more strictly enforced by religious zeal. The legends of this period chiefly record the pious fidelity of men, and the holy chastity of women, and clothe ancient German virtue, as in the beautiful legend of Genoveva, in a more religious garb. Christianity, while still in its infancy, presented a bright contrast with the dark religions of antiquity, and inspired every mind with confidence. A light had burst upon mankind; the dark clouds veiling futurity had passed away, and the brightness of heaven was disclosed to view. The combats of the gods and their carousals in Walhalla were exchanged for the promises of Christian bliss, of spiritual glorification. The ferocity of the warrior was tamed; for a while the clash of the weapon and the din of war ceased, while the iron-bound knee bent at the sound of the vesper bell. Rapine and bloodshed had devastated Europe for centuries, and the most sudden vicissitudes of fortune had become common during the great migrations; to-day a slave, to-morrow an emperor; now the ruler of the North, now dragged in chains to the far South, the land of the dark

African; and so general had been the suffering that the first dream of the convert, the first hope of the Christian, was that once again he might behold those from whom he had been so cruelly torn; a hope that forms the groundwork of the interesting legend of St. Faustinianus, so deeply characteristic of the age, and of all the legends of those times, now so lightly esteemed, although valuable as historical documents, and replete with beauty.

LXXI. *Commencement of the Hierarchy*

THE only Christian communities were scattered and oppressed; and even when the whole Roman empire embraced Christianity, no spiritual superior was allowed by the emperor. Each community had its priest, a certain number of whom were controlled by a bishop. The bishops were all of equal rank, and formed a council (*concilium*), which was presided over by the emperor, and which deliberated upon and fixed the doctrines of faith, the forms of worship, and the ordinances of the church.

The necessity of unity in the church, the division and gradual decay of the imperial power, afforded an opportunity for ambitious churchmen to increase their authority, and the bishops were ere long controlled by the patriarchs, or heads of the church, four of whom were created; viz., the patriarch for Western Europe, who resided at Rome; for Eastern Europe, at Constantinople; for Asia, at Antioch; for Africa, at Alexandria. The highest authority was, however, in reality still exercised by the councils. In the seventh century, the patriarchates of Antioch and Alexandria were destroyed by the Turks, by whom Mohammedanism, which speedily supplanted Christianity in Asia and Africa, was introduced.

The long and violent contest carried on between the patriarch of Constantinople, whose power sank with that of the Eastern empire, and his Roman rival, naturally roused the sympathy and passions of the different nations that owned their supremacy, and while Rome was supported by Germany, the Eastern Romans, Greeks, Asiatics, and Slavi sided with Constantinople. A difference, at first hardly perceptible, in the dogma and form of the Greek church, gradually produced a schism, which at length caused its complete separation from that of Rome, whose patriarch usurped the unlimited control of the church, and gave it a monarchical form. The entire West, including the whole of Germany and the northern countries, embraced the tenets of the Roman church, whose authority mainly rested on the interpretation of a certain verse in the New Testament, which it was alleged proved the intention of the Saviour to found the new church upon St. Peter, as upon a rock; as a logical sequel to this doctrine, this foundation stone was the martyrdom of St. Peter at Rome, where he preached the gospel. The chair of the Roman patriarch was consequently called that of St. Peter, whom he was supposed to succeed, and, like whom, he was also supposed to hold the keys of heaven. The pontiff, or pope (*papa*, father), was at first subordinate to and protected by the temporal monarchs, and it was some time before he usurped any temporal power, or ventured to interfere in any great degree with the internal regulations of the German church, whose bishops, although subject to the decisions of the general council, held independent convocations in their own country, and, having the first voice in the national assembly, were united in one common national interest, and had not yet become blindly submissive to Rome. The archbishops (among whom those of Mayence and Rheims were the first who extended their authority) had each several bishops under their control. The common clergy were always chosen by the people, and slaves were not allowed to enter into holy orders. In default of schools, the monasteries and the service under priests afforded the only means of spiritual tuition. The priests were obliged to be confirmed in their offices and to be ordained by the bishops, who, although chosen by the priests, were confirmed in their dignity by the people, the king, and the pope. In the same manner that the vote of the monarch became more influential, as democratic power gradually decayed, monarchical power at a later period yielded (in its turn) before the despotic vote of the pope, who was at first very irregularly chosen, his election being greatly influenced by the people of Rome, until its final regulation in the eleventh century. The pope was surrounded by a chosen number of dignitaries of the church, who, according to statute, consisted of archbishops and bishops, and who acted as counselors, officers, and legates, and, under the title of Cardinals, elected his successor. As early as the eighth century, a similar regulation existed in some of the bishoprics, the bishops being elected by a number of canons (*canonici: Domherrn*, from *Dom*, church). The popes, during their assumption of power, added their decretals to the laws or canons of the church, compiled by the council, and sanctioned by the monarch, which, gradually creeping into the civil law, influenced both public and private life. All pagan customs, with the exception of those incorporated into the Roman ceremonies and belief, were interdicted by the church, not by the state, under penalty of public penance. Domestic life in Germany was also greatly affected by the laws laid down by the church concerning marriage between relatives, which was merely allowed to be contracted by persons five or six degrees removed from each other, and which was denounced as incest when contracted by persons more nearly allied by blood; thus, many things which, until then, had been considered lawful, were now punished as criminal. By these means, the church acquired a fearful degree of influence, yet further increased by the sale of indulgences, or the remission of sin on payment of a certain sum of money. An additional hold was gained upon the people by means of the judiciary power exercised by the monastic orders, and by the higher church dignitaries over their dependents and slaves.

The clergy were generally maintained by tithes. Every landowner, in obedience to the old Jewish law, gave a tenth of his produce to the church, which was also enriched by gifts to the saints, or by pious offerings, either voluntary, or imposed by law. The churches and monasteries necessarily required land for their support, and as extensive and uncultivated tracts were, at that time, everywhere to be met with, the clergy were at first remunerated with grants by the monarch or the people, and speedily vied with the laity in influence and magnificence. The superior knowledge of the Roman priesthood, and more especially their improvements in agriculture, early disposed the governments of Germany in their favor, and it was to the priests and monks, who introduced the use of the plow while they taught the gospel, that our rude forefathers owed the peaceful arts of tillage and the knowledge of a Saviour. It was no unusual occurrence for pious or guilty men of rank to bestow their Allods or freeholds upon the church, whose dependents and slaves, secure from the ravages of war, were ever blessed with peace, which, added to the consideration in which the clergy were held on account of their knowledge of agriculture, and to their being everywhere in possession of the most productive soil, rendered it an enviable distinction to dwell beneath the shade of the crosier.

LXXII. *The Monasteries*

THE first hermits, or recluses (men who, shunning society, and despising worldly pleasures and grandeur, dwelt in dark caves, fed upon roots, and passed their lives in prayer and meditation), are met with in the vast deserts of Egypt, whither they had either fled for safety during the bloody persecutions of the Christians, or had resorted for devotional purposes. St. Antony was the first hermit. Soon after him, St. Pachomius founded the first community of recluses, A.D. 305, who bound themselves to the observance of the severest rules. Women also formed similar communities; and monasteries and nunneries soon became numerous. About the fifth century, Benedict of Nursia founded a new and powerful monkish order in Italy, distinguished as the Benedictins, or

Western monks, from the earlier Basilians (who took their name from St. Basilius), or Greek monks. Although the trinal vow, of obedience, poverty, and chastity, was common to all monkish orders, they were reasonable enough to perceive the impossibility of enforcing it, and it is expressly stated in the rules of the Benedictins, an order including all the monks and nuns of the West, that those who found the vow too severe might quit the cloister and return to the world: "Si non potes servare, liber discede." Benedict also ordained that the monks, instead of being idle, should *work*, cultivate the land, write useful books, etc.; a law which proved extremely beneficial, and greatly tended to spread the knowledge of agriculture, which received many useful improvements from the monks, and of the cultivation of useful plants, facilitated by the mutual intercourse between adjacent monasteries; and it must be confessed that whatever has been handed down to us of the science and literature of Greece and Rome, of the history of the world and of that of Christianity, is owing to the labors of the pious and learned monks of those times, who preserved and copied the manuscripts that escaped the destruction caused by the migrations, and who penned the histories of their monasteries, or recorded the political events of their times.

Rome was, at that period, the center of the learned world, and the Latin tongue was, consequently, in general use in the monasteries. An attempt made, in later times, to replace it by the language of the country, failed, owing to the influence of the pope, whose power had already reached a dangerous height, and by whom the use of the Latin tongue was prescribed in all ecclesiastical matters as a means of increasing the dependence of the laity upon the priesthood, and of curbing the independent spirit of the Germans. The monasteries and convents, governed by abbots and abbesses, originally under the control of the bishops, were no sooner enriched by endowments of money or land, and rendered powerful by the number of their dependents, than they asserted their independence, in which they were upheld by the popes, who made use of these co-operative societies, whose influence extended throughout Christendom, as a check upon the ambition of the bishops.

LXXIII. *The Catholic Form of Worship*

GOD, no longer adored on the mountain or in the forest, was now worshiped in temples consecrated to his service. The Christian or Byzantine style of architecture, so called from having been first introduced at Byzantium (Constantinople), was general throughout Germany until the Middle Ages, when it attained a higher degree of perfection, and was called the German or Gothic style. The introduction of pictures and images into churches early became a source of contention, and was as strongly censured by one party, who feared lest the veneration in which they were held might endanger the spiritual purity of the Christian faith, and degenerate into idolatry, as it was strongly upheld by another, who argued that they were merely venerated as visible representations of the objects of their mental adoration, the Saviour, the holy family, the martyrs, and their sufferings, etc., and that the effect produced by an elevated style of architecture, by sculpture, paintings, music, illuminations, processions, and ceremonies, upon the senses, was highly conducive to devotion. The latter opinion prevailed, and the churches were gorgeously decorated. Vaulted roofs and lofty towers lent an air of imposing grandeur to the edifice, adorned within with columns, statues, and pictures. In simple but deeply stirring hymns, the priests chanted in the Latin tongue the praise of the Most High; lamps and waxen tapers burned day and night before the sacred pictures and images; while holy water and incense, genuflections, folding of the hands, the sign of the cross, the measured and solemn movements of the richly attired priests before the splendid altar, placed to the east, where shone the natal star of Jesus, the harmony of the choristers, etc., added solemnity to the scene. In the ceremonies and in the dress of the priests much was borrowed from the pagan worship of ancient Rome, and from the Jewish ceremonial. All important affairs, for instance, those transacted in the national assembly, opened with prayer.[1] The elected monarch was solemnly anointed and crowned; the ordeal was still retained in the laws; in every important private affair counsel was sought of God or of a saint by prayer, and by the casting of lots; much of the pagan belief in natural powers, omens, etc., was also retained by the Christians in their various superstitions, such as belief in magic, witchcraft, etc. The ancient feasts of the heathens were now replaced by, or rather changed into, Christian festivals, the chief of which, Passion Week and Easter, in memory of the sufferings and resurrection of the Saviour, were partly borrowed from the ancient Passover of the Jews, and partly from the spring festival of the ancient Germans. Whitsuntide, like Easter, was a movable feast; Easter always falling on the first Sunday after the first full moon during the equinox, sometimes earlier, sometimes later; Whitsuntide always falling forty-nine days after Easter. The church-ale (*Kirmess*, consecration of the church), corresponding with the autumnal festival of the ancient Germans, was of equal importance; and lastly, Christmas, or the birth of Christ, fell in the middle of winter, and was a repetition of the great Yule feast. Many of the numerous other festivals, in honor of the Saviour, of the holy Virgin, and of the saints, corresponded with those of pagan times, to which several of the customs practiced at those periods bear great resemblance; for instance, the practice of carrying palm branches and green boughs; St. John's fire; St. Martin's goose; horns, etc. Sunday was a regular festival, on which, as on all others, peace, joy, and rest were enjoined. Fasts, or the prohibition of meat, although taken from a Jewish custom, accorded with the Christian spirit of self-denial, and fell on several feast days, on every Friday, and lasted several weeks before Passion Week.

---

[1] As in the English houses of parliament at the present day.—*Trans.*

The institution of certain sacraments, or holy acts, such as baptism, the confirmation or consecration of adults, the marriage benediction, the last unction, and confession, which, under pain of eternal condemnation and excommunication, ordained that all crimes should be confessed to the priest, who, bound to secrecy, awarded penance or gave absolution, greatly influenced domestic life. The clergy, as they increased in importance, arrogated to themselves the right of excluding rebellious members from the church, the most severe of all ecclesiastical punishments, which, formerly, consisted merely of penance within or without the church, corporeal chastisement, offerings, and fines. The supposed sanctity of certain localities to which pilgrimages were made (*Wallfahrten*, a name derived from the pagan custom of visiting distant sacred forests), gave rise to another peculiar mode of worship. The saints, supposed to preside over these localities, were either invoked by people when in danger, who, on such occasions, vowed to make a pilgrimage to their sanctuaries, or they were visited by others in the hope of a miracle being performed in their behalf, in order to free them from mental or bodily ailments. Some of the saints were held in such high estimation that their admirers deemed it incumbent upon them to make a pilgrimage to their graves at least once during their lives, and sometimes imposed severe penance upon themselves, by going barefoot, or crawling the whole way on their knees.

LXXIV. *The Christian Kings*

THE struggle between the migratory nations and those among whom they attempted to settle, had, by necessitating implicit obedience to the dukes or chiefs, greatly increased their authority and gradually consolidated their power. The servility of the Italians, accustomed to the despotic rule of Rome, ere long inspired the German chieftains with a wish to tame the independent spirit of their followers. The example of a Jewish king, recorded in the Scriptures, at that period diligently studied, greatly tended to strengthen this wish, and while fierce and warlike kings coveted the purple of the Roman tyrant, gentle-minded and pious ones deemed themselves, like David, the anointed of the Lord, and the vicegerents of God upon earth. The ancient Jewish ceremony of anointing with oil was countenanced by the priesthood, on account of the opportunity it afforded of flattering royalty, and of increasing their own power, they alone having the right to perform this sacred function. These ideas, however, were not prejudicial to the ancient privileges of the people, the kings being still dependent upon them for their election, and presiding, not ruling, over the general assembly. When the throne became hereditary it was made so with the consent of the people, and was by no means granted from an inclination on their part to increase the royal prerogative, but with an intention of diminishing it, by imposing fresh conditions on each successor to the crown. Nor was the person of the king considered inviolable; the crime of murdering him being, in the Anglo-Saxon and Bavarian laws, merely punishable by a fine of considerable amount. The royal allotment of the conquered land was larger than that of any of the freeborn warriors, and consisted of a large Allod (freehold) or domain, where the king had his palace (Hofburg) and held his court. He also possessed other Allods, of smaller extent, in different parts of the country, on which he had little Pfalzen (palaces) or country houses (villas), which served as resting places for him and his household on his journeyings; and on these occasions, in order to render the charge of his maintenance less burdensome to the people, the king and his court were supported by the revenues of these lands, to which royal dues, such as tolls, mines, fines, etc., were gradually added. Taxes and duties upon freeholds, private property, person, or commerce, were utterly unknown, the loyal nation presenting gifts of honor to their monarch on occasions of national festivity or of royal weddings, when a considerable tribute was often imposed upon the conquered nations. The kings, chiefly enriched by the pillage of the wealthy Roman provinces, expended great part of their wealth upon their numerous followers, the splendor of whose appearance contributed to their pomp and magnificence, besides insuring respect for their authority when presiding over the general assembly, and also served as a means of alluring the youthful warriors into their service, to which, dazzled by courtly splendor, and lured by ambition (the nobles and leaders of the army being chosen by the monarch from their number), they willingly attached themselves.

LXXV. *State Assemblies, Dukes and Counts*

THE new kingdoms retained much of the ancient Germanic constitution; for instance, the division of freeborn men into tens and hundreds. The tens (*decania*) disappeared in course of time, and the hundreds (*centena*) became cantons, several of which formed a Gau or province. The popular assembly was, as in former times, held every fourteen days, but, instead of the president being a judge elected by the free voices of the people, he was a Graf or count (*comes*), who was nominated by the king, and headed the contingent furnished by the Gau in time of war. Every post of honor, not only in the army and in the provinces, but also in the court and around the royal person, being filled by the Grafs, gave rise to different titles, such as, Pfalzgraf, Waldgraf, Landgraf, Markgraf, etc. The word *Graf (gravio)* has been falsely derived from *grau* (gray, old). Grimm has rightly deduced it from *Ravo* (*tectum*), and makes it synonymous with *Geselle*, a companion (from *Saal*, a hall), which also signified a companion in the house and in the field; hence a Graf in Latin was always called *Comes*, and had sometimes a proxy called *Vicecomes ;* whence are derived the modern French and English titles of comte, vicomte, count, viscount. The army consisted of the whole nation, headed by its Centners and Grafs. The great extent of the territory gained by conquerors, like Etzel, etc., who, in order to facilitate the government of their enormous kingdoms, allowed the subdued nations to retain their former rulers, on condition of their furnishing a contingent in the field, gave rise to the ducal dignity. The Frankish monarchs pursued a similar policy toward the subjugated Germanic tribes, either allowing them to be governed by their own princes, or setting dukes over them; but in either case allowing them to retain their native laws, whether Alemannic, Bavarian, Saxon, or Thuringian. All the Dukes, Grafs, Centners, and the higher dignitaries of the church, were bound to call the freemen of the state to a general assembly, presided over by the monarch, once a year, and in extraordinary cases, more frequently. These assemblies took cognizance of the judiciary proceedings in which an appeal had been made to their tribunal from the lower courts; framed and improved the laws; elected and deposed the king, who was responsible to them for his actions; declared war, and concluded peace, unless civil war happened to be raging. Each man's vote bore equal weight with that of the king; each individual also possessed an equal right to state his opinion, and to lay petitions before the court, beyond which there was no appeal. The chief alterations in the laws related to the confirmation of the royal, ducal, and ecclesiastical power, which affected the whole state, and was consequently decided by the assembly, which also regulated the particular laws relating to dukedoms and provinces. These state assemblies were, under different names, common to all the Germanic kingdoms. The Anglo-Saxons named theirs the Witenagemots (council of wise men, elders, or gray heads), aged, wise or distinguished men being next in rank to the dignitaries of the church and state. The Franks, whose assemblies were held in the open air during the month of March, styled them the fields of March.

The conduct of the war, as soon as declared, was intrusted to the king, who, on that occasion, received, as was the case with the ancient German leaders, a great accession of authority, and the strictest obedience was enforced to his bann or right of compulsion. The Arimannia, from *mannire*, to cite, were the armed community convoked to the national assembly during peace, which, in time of war, formed a Landwehr (militia), called the *arrier-ban* (Heerbann, from *Heer*, an army, and *bannire*, to summon). The monarch summoned the dukes; they, the counts; who, in their turn, summoned the centners; and so on throughout the several degrees. Each man served the same chief in the field by whom he was governed in time of peace. Every canton, county and dukedom furnished its contingent, which was distinguished by a particular banner (*Panner, Panier*, a standard, whence comes the Banner-herr or banneret). Every man provided himself with arms and provisions until the conclusion of the campaign, which was settled beforehand. Non-appearance in the field, and the still graver crime of *Heeresliz*, or desertion on the field of battle, were severely punished. Obedience was strictly enforced by the king and the subordinate leaders, who had the right of inflicting instant and summary punishment on the person of the criminal, a right they durst not exercise in time of peace. The civil laws were also thrice as severe during war time.

LXXVI. *The Laws*

THE example of the Romans, the increased extent of the states, and the novelty of many of the new laws imposed upon the people, gradually produced the necessity of possessing written codes, which were to a certain degree disadvantageous to the people, who were rendered unfamiliar with their contents as soon as the necessity of committing them to memory ceased, while the facility with which the number and intricacy of the laws could be increased soon required them to be interpreted by lawyers or expositors of the law, whose power depended on their knowledge and capacity. The people were, consequently, on account of their ignorance, deprived of the right of judging in legal matters, upon which, in ancient times, every freeman had a right freely to state his opinion and to vote, but which were now decided by a select committee of the Rachimburgen, who, in difficult cases, referred to the opinion of a learned professor or Sagibaro, who had no casting vote. The Rachimburgen were members chosen from the national assembly. They were continually changed, until the reign of Charlemagne, by whom their office was rendered permanent, and they were entitled Schöffen, whose nomination rested with the Grafs. The system of Wergeld, or fining, was retained in the new constitution, which was constructed upon the ancient one, and which, owing to the constant insertion of new and often contradictory laws, became at length extremely intricate and confused. Many of the Roman civil laws were either entirely or partially adopted into the civil code, and the Mosaic ecclesiastical laws were mixed up with the ordinances of the church, until, at length, the erection of states into hereditary kingdoms, and the universal adoption of the feudal system, rendered a new constitution and new laws necessary. The most important alteration was the partial suppression of the ancient perfect and pure Wergeld system, which was replaced by the Roman laws regarding imprisonment, corporeal and capital punishment, the latter of which was supposed to be upheld by the scriptural maxim of "An eye for an eye, and a tooth for a tooth." Actions injurious to ducal, royal, or ecclesiastical dignity were especially punished by corporeal chastisement and death: new crimes punished by new laws. The old Wergeld system was still retained by the people, with this single alteration, that the Wergeld was now always paid in money. The highest coin current at that period was the shilling (*solidus*). The trial by single combat also still continued to be legal, and the other ordeals were merely altered to suit them to the more enlightened ideas of the age.

As everything modern originated from the South, and everything ancient from the North, the codes of the southern nations, the Ostro and Visi-Goths, for the most part contain Roman laws imbued with the principles of Roman and biblical legislature, which exercised power over the life, person, freedom, honor, and freehold property (Allod) of the criminal, while the codes of the northern nations, particularly those of the Anglo-Saxons, still retain traces of their genuine German origin. The Salic is the oldest written law, and was first adapted to the new system by Chlodwig, almost all of whose successors either added to or modified it. The original manuscript was in German, but the only complete copy now extant is in Latin, and besides containing the oldest preface, records many of the barbarous customs of ancient Germany, which, at that period, were still practiced. The antiquity of the Thuringian code is proved by its barbarity; it is still perfectly heathenish, and chiefly treats of revenge for bloodshed, and of trials by single combat. The contrast between the nations of Lower and Upper Germany, or the Frankish Saxons and Goths, is perceptible throughout the laws which have descended to our times; those of the Franks, Thuringians, and Longobardi, and those of the Saxons, Anglo-Saxons, and Frisii, forming two connected codes, widely differing from those of the Ostrogoths, Visigoths, and Burgundians, and those of the Alemanni and Bavarians. All the German nations anciently acted upon the principle of judging every man by the laws of his native country, for which reason the Franks allowed the different tribes subdued by them, and incorporated into their kingdom, to retain their national laws, merely introducing others referring to the church and state, and to the new situation of affairs in general. The Longobardi alone deviated from this principle. Under the Merovingian dynasty, the several codes of the Ripuarii, Alemanni, Thuringians, and Bavarians were transcribed. In the fifth century, Dietrich von Bern gave a code of laws to the Ostrogoths, and King Eurich one to the Visigoths, in both of which much was borrowed from the Roman law. The Burgundian code was drawn out during the reign of Gundebald, and when the Franks took possession of Burgundy merely received some slight alterations. The first code of the Longobardi was drawn up in the seventh century, during the reign of King Rotharis, whose successors, and at a later period the Franks, added to it many new and Roman laws. Originally the laws of the Longobardi were essentially German, nor were any others at first tolerated in their country.

The Saxons and Frisii were, at the end of this period, compelled by the Franks to commit their laws to writing with the addition of the new Frankish ordinances. In England, the Anglo-Saxon law, in which the spirit of the genuine old Germanic code has been faithfully preserved, was gradually introduced by the kings. Latin transcripts of all the codes of ancient Germany are still extant.

LXXVII. *The Feudal System*

FEUDAL tenure (or the manner in which slaves, emancipated slaves or freed-men, and poor freemen, held part of an Allod, for the use of which they rendered certain duties to the owner, who, if the feoffee failed in fulfilling his engagements, had the power of depriving him of the use of the property, which was only lent upon certain conditions, and not given away) was general among the Germans in pagan times. Tacitus mentions that the German slaves who cultivated a small parcel of land formed a class distinct from the household slaves. The wars, at a later period, introduced another description of feudal tenure among the subdued nations, who were constrained to pay tribute and to swear allegiance to their conquerors, whenever the latter did not take immediate possession of the lands; or, sometimes, a whole nation held its lands in fief from another on a system similar to that which bound the slave to the freeman. When the migrations had ceased, the feudal system was perfected by the Frankish monarchs, who divided the extensive lands they had gained in Gaul, as fiefs, among their armed followers or dependents, who, by their services, had become their Angetranten (confidants, *Antrustiones*) or Getreuen (*fideles*), who, either on account of the royal fiefs being as large, and often larger, than the Allods of the freemen, or on account of their holding offices as Grafs, were not only admitted into the state assembly on an equality with the freemen, but were also estimated higher in Wergeld. By their success in war they gradually increased in wealth and influence, and were at length formed into a class of nobles, who bore precedence, as royal feudatories, over the ancient nobility merely composed of freemen, the majority of whom, either influenced by the ambition of shining at court, or anxious to escape from poverty and debt, made a voluntary cession of their Allods to the monarch, to whom they swore allegiance as their liege lord, from whom they held their lands in fee (*feudum oblatum*), and were thus received into the class of nobles or vassals of the crown. In this manner the feudal system gradually gained ground, and the freemen, now the minority in point of numbers, bearing little weight in the state assembly, oppressed by the arrier-ban, which continually summoned them to the field, the whole of their little property either swallowed up by the necessary expenses, or ruined by neglect, compelled to endure contempt, tyranny, and poverty, and often deprived of their estates by cabals, became completely subservient to the vassals, whom increasing wealth and power had rendered proud and insolent. Besides the crown vassals, there were also the church feudatories, who held their land on similar conditions, and the underfeudatories to the vassals, mesne-lords or valvasors. All the crown vassals were originally Comites, companions in arms; but the other Comites, or Grafen, before long merely signified those who were distinguished by the offices they held from the crowd of dependents, while the immediate personal servants, or ministeriales, were distinguished from the indirect servants by their feudal tenure, which imposed certain duties upon them as vassals of the crown. The ministeriales originally consisted of the Mareschalk, or groom; the Truchsess, he who set the Truke or dish upon the table; the Mundschenk, or cup-bearer; the Kammerer, or chamberlains; the Küchenmeister, or master of the kitchen;

the Kellermeister, or superintendent of the cellar; and the Hausmaier, or major domus, who, on account of the ministeriales being composed of the chief vassals and of the heads of the nobility, was naturally considered as the highest dignitary of the state, and, being himself a noble, was the representative of his class on all state occasions. At first, all these ministeriales were merely common servants, and long after the introduction of Christianity these offices were performed by slaves; as the royal prerogative increased, these offices gradually became of higher importance, and their titles being eagerly sought by men of distinction, became attached to the highest offices of state, to the ducal dignity, and to the great fiefs.

The service rendered by the vassal was the only bond between him and his lord. The fiefs, at first held only for a certain time, were afterward held for life, and returned to the mesne-lord upon the death of the feoffee, a grievance that was speedily removed by the vassals, as soon as they became powerful enough to compel the monarch to make the fiefs hereditary.

LXXVIII. *Migrations and New Languages*

THE whole of eastern Germany, as far as the Elbe and Saal, had been depopulated by the migrations of the Germans, who were replaced by the Slavian nations, the Wendi, Sorbi and Bohemians, while the great hordes of the ancient Ostro-Germanic or Gothic nations spread over the south and west as far as Africa. The Saxons, Thuringians, and the Bavarians, whose name now suddenly starts from its long oblivion, the Alemanni in Swabia, Alsace, and Switzerland, and the Franks on the Rhine, retained their ancient positions in Germany until the migration of the Saxons to England; of the Franks, to northern and central Gaul; of the Burgundians, to the Rhone and the Alps; of the Ostrogoths and Longobardi, to Italy; of the Visigoths, to the Pyrenees and Spain; and of the Vandals, to Africa.

All the tribes that settled within the limits of the Roman empire at first formed a separate and warlike class of nobles, who governed the inhabitants in the despotic manner in which the Turks governed the Greeks, but ere long mixed with the Romans, and more or less adopted their language. This change was more rapidly effected in Italy, where Roman influence was most powerful, on account of the memory of past grandeur and the policy of the popes, who sought to render the Latin tongue universal, in order to facilitate the subjection of the barbarians of the North to the crosier; and, in fact, the Italian language retains more of the ancient Latin tongue, and has been less adulterated with German, than any other of Western Europe.

In Spain, where the Germans formed the minority of the population, the Latin tongue, which had been orientalized by the Moors, who crossed over from Africa, was the common language of the country. In Gaul, the Franks retained the pure German tongue until the time of Charlemagne; but, at a later period, when a separation took place between the Roman West Franks and the Ostro-Franks of pure Germanic descent, the Latin tongue was, through the influence of the Roman clergy, generally adopted by the former. Various dialects of the new French tongue sprang up in Burgundy, in the Visigothic South, in central Gaul, and in the North, where the population was partly composed of Britons, who had fled thither from the Saxon in England, and partly of Normans from Scandinavia (Brittany and Normandy). In England, which had never been entirely subdued by the Romans, the Latin tongue had not taken deep root, and was quickly supplanted by that of the Angli and Saxons, who migrated to that country, which at once accounts for the great similarity that exists between English and German.

I shall merely trace the steps of the migrating Germanic tribes until they mingle with the inhabitants of the country in which they settled, and touch upon the affairs of England and of the Scandinavian North in so far as they are illustrative of those of Germany (whose influence has ever spread far beyond her natural limits, and after affecting the histories of Italy, Spain, and France, after stamping an indelible character on the Middle Ages, has traveled with the Spaniard and the Englishman to the far West, and spread along the shores of the Mississippi, the La Plata, and the Ganges, and over the boundless plains of New Holland), lest in following the winding of the stream we may stray too far from the source. Our mother country, invigorated instead of weakened by the migrations, those great drains of her strength, has imparted a noble heritage of moral and physical power (which in former times proved invincible to the assaults of Roman corruption) to the remotest branches of the great nations she still fosters in her bosom.

PART V

THE CONTESTS BETWEEN THE GOTHS AND FRANKS

LXXIX. *Theodorich the Great*

DIETRICH VON BERN (Verona), named by the Romans Theodorich the Great, was sent by his father, Theodomir, as a hostage to Constantinople, where, notwithstanding his Roman education, he retained the customs of his country, and, after his father's death, succeeded to the Gothic throne. On the fall of the Western empire, Zeno, emperor of Constantinople, set up a claim to the possession of Italy, but being too weak to reconquer that country, and being, at the same time, anxious to free himself from the Goths, proposed to Theodorich to make himself master of it in his name, to which the cunning Goth, who secretly intended to gain the prize for himself, easily acquiesced. On his line of march lay three nations: a Slavonian race, under King Babai, then devastating Greece, whom he subdued; the Gepidæ, under King Gundarich, whom he defeated on the right bank of the Danube; and the Rugii, in the mountains leading to Italy. Their king, Fava, had just been overthrown by Odoachar, and his son, Frederich, sought refuge and protection in the camp of Theodorich, A.D. 487. The Ostrogothic army, encumbered with women and children, and swelled by numbers of the Rugii and other Germans, slowly wound its way through the mountain passes, unopposed by Odoachar, who awaited its approach on the Isonzo, not far from Aquileia on the Adriatic, where a bloody engagement took place, which was followed by another near Verona, A.D. 489, in both of which Theodorich was victorious. Tufa, the commander of Odoachar's troops, deserted his master, but both he and Frederich appear to have been disappointed in their expectations of reward, as before long they again suddenly changed sides, and Tufa betrayed a number of Gothic nobles into the power of Odoachar, who had taken shelter behind the fortifications of Ravenna, and who, a third time venturing a battle on the open field near the Adda, was once more compelled to retreat to the city, which, after enduring a three years' siege, was at length forced by famine to capitulate. Odoachar and his followers were murdered at a banquet by order of Theodorich, who suspected them of treason, A.D. 493. During this contest, the Burgundians, under Gundebald, crossed the Alps and plundered the country to the rear of the Goths. Several thousand Romans, who had fallen into their hands, were restored to liberty at the entreaty of St. Epiphanius, who begged for mercy for them in the name of Christ. The Burgundians were afterward held in check by Theodorich, who fortified the Alpine passes, humbled the Gepidæ, the Heruli, and the Rugii, protected the Alemanni in the mountains opposite Graubündten, whither they had fled from the Franks, and sent his general, Pitzia, to the assistance of Mundo, who had formed a small robber state, composed of people of every nation, and who was at feud with the Bulgarians, a powerful Slavonian tribe menacing Greece and Italy. The frontiers of his new kingdom thus rendered secure from attack, Theodorich now turned his thoughts to peace, and to the internal regulation of the state, and astonished the world, so long habituated to scenes of bloodshed and treason, with the unusual spectacle of a rude warrior transformed into the wise legislator of a new and flourishing empire. The population had been almost entirely swept away by the devastating wars, and the third part of the lands, which had already been seized by Odoachar for his followers, sufficed for the settlement of the Goths. The ancient laws and warlike constitution of Germany were retained. The army was composed solely of the Gothic population (the rest being prohibited to carry arms), commanded by the Grafs. The Goths, being Arians, had their separate church. They were recommended, by Theodorich, to imitate the polished manners of the Romans, who retained two-thirds of the lands, and generally the cities. The prohibition to bear arms was the only change in their ancient privileges. The Catholic religion was protected. All theological disputes were put an end to by the practice of universal toleration; and, on one occasion, when a Catholic, with the intention of flattering the king, professed Arianism, Theodorich condemned him to death, "for," said he, "he who can betray his God will betray his king." The morality practiced by the Goths was, on the other hand, recommended to the corrupt Romans. Protected by a thirty years' peace, agriculture, manufactures, and commerce flourished; the devastated provinces regained their former prosperity; and the great work of draining the Pontine Marshes was commenced, and personally overlooked by Theodorich from his fortress, part of which is still standing on the high rock of Terracina.

In the year 500, during his visit to Rome (where he did not fix his residence, probably owing to his desire to be within reach of the northern frontier), he held public games, in imitation of the ancients, and adorned the city with public buildings. His council was composed of the most learned men, among whom Cassiodorus, his historian and first minister, and the philosopher Boetius, are pre-eminently distinguished. The latter, however, with his father-in-law, the bishop Symmachus, and the pope Johannes, happening to incur a strong suspicion of having abused the confidence of the king, by plotting with Justinus the Greek emperor against the Goths, the two former were executed, and the pope was thrown into prison, where he died. Dietrich, although a great war-chief and ruler like his predecessors, is manifestly the first German monarch who sought to unite these apparently dissimilar qualities with the attributes of a scriptural king, of a shepherd chosen by God to lead his people. Many of his letters, and the records of the judgments pronounced by him, are still extant, and might serve as models for any sovereign. They also prove the zeal with which he strove to promulgate his conception of the duties of a monarch, among other royal families, and among other nations than his own; and although the German monarchs continued to be elected by the people, and to be dependent on the state assembly, yet the belief of the divine majesty of kings, and of their being the representatives of God upon earth, may be traced to this period. Dietrich, in his abhorrence of the cold, stern despotism of imperial Rome, had conceived a far more elevated project, which he deemed the noblest aim of every true-born German; viz., the union of the states of Germany. In pursuance of this scheme, he sought, by promoting intermarriages between the different royal families of Germany, to unite them in one common interest, and by this means to render peace general. For this purpose, he married his daughters, Theodicusa and Ostrogotha, to Alaric, king of the Visigoths, and to Sigismund, son of Gundebald, king of Burgundy; his sister, Amalfreda, to Thrasimund, king of the Vandals; and Amalberga, her daughter by a former husband, to Hermanfried, king of Thuringia; all of whom he sought, by his letters, to incline to his project. The reverence he universally inspired, as the father of kings, was so great that his fame spread even to the distant nation of the Aesthri on the Baltic, who sent him gifts. The union and pacification of the royal houses of Germany was prevented, and his great plan destroyed, by the jealousy of the Franks, who, although allied with him by his marriage with Audifleda, the sister of Chlodwig, the great Frankish monarch, continued to cherish their ancient enmity against the Goths. The kingdom of the Visigoths was invaded by Chlodwig. The brave Thorismund, the conqueror of Attila, fell by the hand of his brother Theodorich, who, in his turn, was murdered by the third brother, Eurich, a prince famed for his valor and code of laws. Alaric, his son and successor, being defeated and killed by the Franks at the battle of Vougle, A.D. 507. Theodorich sent an Ostrogothic army, under the command of Ibbas, to the assistance of his daughter, the widow of Alaric, and of her young son, Amalarich. Ibbas defeated the Franks on the Rhone, and compelled them to subscribe to a treaty of peace, by which Gascony and Guyenne were ceded to them, and Languedoc was left in the possession of the Visigoths. Gasalrich, Alaric's natural son, who had caused himself to be proclaimed king of Barcelona, and had usurped the throne of Amalarich, was also defeated by Ibbas.

Theodorich the Great is said to have died of fright, A.D. 526, at sight of a fish's head placed before him at table, which bore an imaginary resemblance to the countenance of the innocent bishop Symmachus, whom he had murdered. According to the popular tradition of Italy, the soul of this great king was doomed to suffer eternal torment amid the flames of Ætna.

LXXX. *Chlodwig*

REMARKABLE events were, meanwhile, passing among the Franks, who still remained divided, Childerich, the son of Merowig, reigning over the Salii, and Sigismir, the son of Claudebald, over the Ripuarii, at Cologne. The Franks, outraged in their domestic honor by the voluptuous and licentious Childerich, drove him from the kingdom and bestowed the crown upon Ægidius, the last Roman governor of Gaul; a choice only possible among the Salii, who had long been accustomed to serve under Roman generals. The deposed monarch fled to his relative, Bisinus, king of Thuringia. The Thuringians appear to have been originally connected with the Franks, and at some later period to have mixed with the Saxons and their Gothic neighbors, the Varini and Angli. A faithful servant of the exiled king, named Wiomad, undertook to restore his master to the throne, and breaking a gold piece with him, half of which he was to send in token of the time having arrived for his return to his native country, insidiously attached himself to Ægidius, whom he persuaded to tax the Franks according to the Roman custom; an innovation which he rightly judged would cause his expulsion. Childerich, meanwhile, repaid the hospitality of Bisinus by debauching his wife, Basina, with whom he carried on a clandestine intercourse. The broken bit of gold was at length delivered to him by a trusty Frank, and he secretly returned to his country, where he was gladly received and replaced on the throne by the discontented Salii. Basina, enslaved by passion, soon after escaped from Thuringia to the court of her lover, who made her his wife, and she became the mother of Chlodwig the Great. The Thuringians, enraged at this breach of hospitality, invaded and laid waste the country of the Salii, fearfully revenging on the subjects who tolerated such disgraceful conduct in their ruler the injury offered to their king. Two hundred Frankish maidens were crushed beneath their chariot-wheels, as an expiatory sacrifice to violated chastity. Childerich, aided by Odoachar, subdued the Alemanni. His tomb, which was discovered at Tournay in 1653, contained a golden bull's head and several golden bees, evidently heathen symbols.

Chlodwig, brave, energetic, and warlike, turned his thoughts to more ambitious projects than his father, and, taking advantage of the distressed state of the Ripuarii, at that time oppressed by the Alemanni, imposed an oath of fealty on their king, Sigebert, the son of Sigismir, and reunited the whole Frankish nation. He then attacked Siagrius, the son of Ægidius, who still maintained an independent Roman government in central Gaul, and, after gaining a decisive victory at Soissons, took possession of the whole of Gaul as far as the Visigothic frontier. This success attracted the attention of his German neighbors, the Burgundians, Alemanni, and Visigoths, all of whom he attempted to circumvent. Chlotilda, the daughter of Hilperich, king of Burgundy, who had been murdered by his brother Gundebald, was at that time living in retirement in a nunnery at Geneva. The fame of her beauty reached the ears of Chlodwig, who resolved to get her into his possession, and to set up a claim to the throne of Burgundy. He accordingly dispatched the trusty Aurelian to Geneva, where, disguised as a beggar, his feet were washed by the royal nun. Dropping the monarch's ring into the water, he discovered himself to her, and she joyfully consented to wed the brave Chlodwig, upon which the beggar disappeared, and in due time a splendid embassy arrived at the Burgundian court to demand the bride. Chlotilda produced the token, and Gundebald, fearing the consequence of a refusal, gave his consent. She set out for the frontier in a chariot drawn by oxen, burning and destroying the dwellings of the Burgundians as she advanced, in revenge for the murder of her father, and being closely pursued by Gundebald, fled on a swift horse to the palace of Chlodwig. Her firstborn son died in his infancy. On the birth of the second, she entreated her husband to allow him to be baptized in the Christian faith, to which she belonged. He consented, and the life of the child was spared.

The execution of Chlodwig's plans against Burgundy was delayed by the revolt of the Alemanni, who viewed the introduction of the feudal system into the provinces, and his armed followers, with suspicion and dislike, as indicative of a design upon their national liberty and independence. United under several leaders, they attacked the Franks, who had also united beneath the standard of Chlodwig, at whose side fought Sigebert of Cologne. The battle of Zulpich decided the contest, A.D. 496. At one moment the enthusiastic spirit of the Alemanni threatened to overpower the superior discipline of the Franks, and Chlodwig, excited by the peril, invoked the God of his wife, and vowed to forsake the religion of his fathers if he proved more powerful than Odin, the war-god of the Alemanni. He was victorious, and the majority of his subjects, converted by the supposed miracle in their favor, were solemnly baptized with the king. The ceremony took place at Rheims. The legend relates that the vial of oil with which St. Remigius anointed the monarch's head was brought for that purpose by an angel from heaven, and that the saint exclaimed, while pouring the contents on the head of the king as he knelt before him, "Bow down thine head, O Sicamber, and adore what hitherto thou hast destroyed; destroy what hitherto thou hast adored!" The whole transaction was probably a wily invention on the part of Chlodwig, who, hoping, by the assistance of the priests, to bring his wild Franks into subjection, seized this opportunity to convert them without endangering himself. From this period, the Roman bishops, or popes, and the Frankish monarchs mutually supported each other, either against the Arian Goths, the Greeks, or the German pagans. Ere long, the whole of the Frankish nation embraced Christianity, and the Alemanni gradually became converts to the God of victory.

Chlodwig, urged by the revengeful spirit of his queen, and, moreover, anxious to secure the Alpine passes in Upper Burgundy, at length declared war with that country, but finding that Gundebald was too strongly posted for him to hope for success, contented himself with receiving his oath of allegiance, and incited by the Catholic bishops, who impatiently desired the extirpation of Arianism in Gaul, turned his arms against the Visigoths, whom he expected to overcome with greater facility. Alaric, the unworthy son of the brave Eurich, fell in the battle of Poictiers by the hand of the victorious king of the Franks, A.D. 507, by whom he was justly held in contempt for the cowardice with which he had delivered up to them his guest, Siagrius, who had fled to him for safety. Theodorich the Great, king of the Ostrogoths, now took up arms in defense of the youthful son of Alaric, and a second engagement took place near Arles, which proved disastrous to Chlodwig, who was forced to retreat, after leaving 30,000 of his men on the field of battle. Finding himself compelled to leave the Visigoths in peace, he fell upon Brittany, A.D. 509, and constrained the Britons, its new inhabitants, who had been driven from England by the Saxons, to do him homage. It was a fortunate circumstance for Chlodwig that his neighbors, instead of uniting, fought singly, in self-defense. Had they confederated against the Franks, the rising power of that nation must have been completely checked. The ancient name of Gaul was changed by this monarch to that of France.

Chlodwig, whose conquests and largesses had given him unlimited control over his troops, and had consolidated his power, now turned his attention to the internal regulation of his kingdom, and sought, by the removal of the subordinate kings, and by the more general adoption of the feudal system, to keep the nation united beneath his jurisdiction in time of peace as well as war. His treatment of his Merovingian relatives, the subordinate kings, was one tissue of treachery and cruelty. His ancient ally, Sigebert of Cologne, who was disabled by a wound received at the battle of Zülpich, was, at his instigation, murdered by his own son, Chloderich, whom he deluded by promises, and also caused to be put to death. He was stabbed in the back by an assassin, when in the act of bending down to look into a chest that contained his father's treasures, which he deluged with his blood. Ragnachar of Cambray, and his brother, two of the Merovingians, fell by Chlodwig's hand. Chararic of Flanders and his son, a little child, were condemned to the cloister. While being deprived of their long hair, the symbol of royalty, the boy remarked, "Our hair will soon grow long again!" upon which Chlodwig, provident of the future, caused them both to be murdered.

By means of the imposition of feudal service, the discipline habitual in war time was continued during peace, and shackled the freedom of the people. At the commencement of this reign, the Franks were extremely republican in their manners. It is related, that after the battle of Soissons the booty had been equally divided among the troops. One of the men, a common Frank, had received for his portion a sacred jar, which he obstinately refused to restore when entreated to do so by one of the bishops, and upon its restitution being requested by Chlodwig, insolently replied, "that he was only bound to obey him during battle, and not afterward," and broke the jar into pieces. Some time after this occurrence, the king, who had not forgotten conduct which he was legally unable to punish, took advantage of the army being drawn up in battle array to ride up to the insolent soldier and to cut him down under pretext of misbehavior.

The feudal system was universally adopted throughout France before the conclusion of this reign. During peace, Chlodwig was surrounded by his Antrustiones, or trusty followers, whom he rewarded with rich lands in the conquered provinces, and who formed a new order of nobles, from whom he selected the Grafs. This class of nobility ere long possessed all the honor, all the influence, and, by means of the feudal system, all the wealth of the country, and leaguing with the priests, at length succeeded in crushing popular freedom. Thus Chlodwig, who died in 511, laid the groundwork for a complete revolution in the internal policy of Germany.

LXXXI. *Gundebald*

WHILE the Burgundians, weakened by the destruction of Gunthachar, and pressed by the Huns, were driven to the banks of the Rhone, Alsace, with their capital, Worms, fell into the hands of the Alemanni. In their new kingdom, which, traversed by the Rhone, extended beyond Lyons, they founded the city of Bormio (named after their ancient capital, Worms), on the other side of the Alps, where they bend toward Italy. The history of this new settlement is somewhat obscure. The Burgundians are said to have been converted to Christianity by a bishop who preached to them for seven successive days. They were, at one time, in alliance with Ætius, who granted the highlands to them. After the fall of the Western empire, they treated with Constantinople. In their new kingdom, two-thirds of the land was allotted to them, the remaining third to the Romans, and each nation was governed by its own laws. The land was divided into Gauen, or districts, under the jurisdiction of Grafs, whose authority was unlimited, while that of the king or chief did not exceed that of a duke. The first king of Upper Burgundy who succeeded Gunthachar was Gundioch, a descendant of the Visigothic Balti. At his death, the kingdom was divided between his four sons; Hilperich, who reigned at Geneva, Godegisel, at Besancon, Gundebald, at Lyons, and Godemar, at Vienne. Harmony was not of long duration. Gundebald, a man of higher talent and enterprise than his brethren, grasped at sole dominion (his daring invasion of Italy, while Theodorich the Great was engaged with Odoachar, has been already mentioned), and quarreling with Hilperich, defeated and cruelly murdered him, together with his family, with the exception of Chlotilda, one of his daughters, who subsequently married Chlodwig, A.D. 499. After a short contest, he swore allegiance to the Frankish monarch, but, emboldened by the lenity with which he was treated, and trusting in the strength of his mountain fastnesses, he again attacked his brothers, and, after destroying the kingdom of Godegisel, once more retreated to his mountains on the approach of the Franks and the Ostrogoths from opposite quarters, who finally concluded peace with him, and Dietrich gave his daughter Ostrogotha in marriage to Sigismund, the son of the usurper. Gundebald was the reformer of his country. Gifted with more than ordinary talent, and with a mind highly cultivated for the age in which he lived, he saw the advantage, and incessantly aimed at the realization, of union in the state and the increase of the royal prerogative, but, incautiously venturing too far, he was vehemently opposed in his projects by the Grafs of the districts, A.D. 502, who, on one occasion, at Geneva, forced him to withdraw his code of laws, which they replaced by another, entitled the Lex Gundebada, which is still in existence, signed by thirty-six Grafs. Gundebald died in 516.

LXXXII. *The Extension of France Under the Sons of Chlodwig*

THE superiority of the Franks over the other nations of Germany was owing to both their natural and acquired advantages. Ingenious, brave, and enterprising, trained to war, accustomed to victory, fired by ambition, and favored by their position in the center of the German states, they easily acquired and maintained a power with which, taken singly, none of the other states was able to compete, and which their religious zeal rendered peculiarly formidable to the Saxons, while their central position, between the Ostrogoths in Italy and the Visigoths in the Pyrenees, offered every facility for taking advantage of the want of unity between the two nations. Nor were these circumstances overlooked by the bishop of Rome, whose influence over the other bishops of the West, and the Catholic populations of Italy, Gaul, and Spain, was gradually increasing, and who accelerated the downfall of the Arian Goths by exciting the fanatical spirit of the Franks and their allies against them.

Chlodwig divided France into four kingdoms, the largest and most important of which, the Rhine country, Austria or Austrasia, with its capital, Metz, was bestowed upon Theodorich, his eldest son; and Neustria, with its capital, Orleans, on Chlodomir; while Childebert reigned at Paris, and Chlotar at Soissons. The separation of Austria from Neustria was subsequently widened by the different manners of the two nations, the former remaining faithful to the ancient customs of Germany, while the latter adopted those of Rome. Each of the sons of Chlodwig bore the title and exercised the authority of king, although they were in a manner dependent upon each other, and were bound together by the union of the Frankish nation, the general state assembly, the laws, and their own interest. This strange and dangerous division of the kingdom of Chlodwig, destructive to the power and unity of the state, arose from the political inexperience of the Franks, whose kings were of very recent date, and who had made no provision (beyond that of the law common among the Salii, by which the inheritance was equally divided between the sons) for the succession to the throne. This law was also in practice among the Thuringians and the Burgundians, and had, at a very remote period, been common to all the Scandinavian nations. It was retained by the Franks for more than three centuries after the death of Chlodwig.

The kings of Neustria and Austria extended their possessions by the sword. Chlodomir subdued the Burgundians, and strengthened his dominion in the West, while Theodorich and his son, Theobert, conquered Thuringia, drove the Ostrogoths from the Alps, and compelled the dukes of the Bojoarii to take the oath of allegiance.

Saxony, still as formidable as in ancient times, was the only German state left undisturbed by the Franks, notwithstanding the vicinity of their frontiers, which at some points ran parallel; a circumstance highly obnoxious to France, which, before long, strove to crush the neighboring state with an unremitting animosity equaling that displayed by Rome in her attacks upon the free nations of Germany.

LXXXIII. *Fall of the Kingdoms of Thuringia and Burgundy*

THE origin of the Thuringii has been derived from the Hermunduri or from the Therwingi. The name bears a resemblance to that of the god Thor. The derivation from the name given to the Cherusci, who, according to Tacitus, were called Thoren, fools (*stulti*), on account of the depravity of their manners, is a mere play upon sounds. They seem, at a later period, to have been connected with the Suevian Angli and Varini (on the Werra), the latter of whom maintained an independent monarchy until 595.

Bisinus, to whom Childerich had fled for safety, was related to the Merovingians, and this part of the Thuringian nation appears to have been originally connected with the Franks. The kingdom of Bisinus was divided between his sons, Hermanfried, Berthar, and Baldrich; the first of whom married Amalberga, the daughter of Dietrich the Ostrogoth. This wily princess contrived, by half covering his table, in sign of his only possessing half a kingdom, to rouse the ambition of her husband, who surprised and killed Berthar, and in order to strengthen himself against Baldrich, who was more on his guard, entered into an alliance with Theodorich, king of Austrasia, by whom Baldrich was subsequently defeated and slain. Hermanfried afterward refusing to divide his ill-won kingdom with the Franks, they united with the Saxons and defeated him in a pitched battle near Scheidingen, A.D. 529. A plot, laid by Iring, a cunning Thuringian, who attempted to sow discord between the allies by persuading the Franks to make peace with his nation and to deprive the Saxons of their share of the booty, was discovered by Hadegast, the old Saxon duke, who instantly attacked and completely subdued the whole of Thuringia. Theodorich, under pretense of an amicable settlement of affairs, invited Hermanfried to Zülpich, where, while engaged in conversation with him on the castle wall, on which they were walking, he had him suddenly pushed, as if accidentally, down the precipice. Thus ended the unfortunate dynasty of the kings of Thuringia, A.D. 530.

The northern part of the country fell a prey to the Saxons, and the Franks seized that to the south of the Unstrutt, but during the subsequent disturbances in France, Thuringia regained much of her former independence, and was again governed by heathen dukes, who paid an annual tribute of five hundred pigs to the Austrasian monarch.

One noble and interesting character presents a bright contrast with the coarse brutality that distinguished these royal dynasties, that of Radegunda, the daughter of Berthar, the only descendant of the royal house of Thuringia, who was celebrated for her extraordinary beauty, and whose possession was disputed by Theodorich of Metz and Chlotar of Orleans, the latter of whom gained the prize. Regardless of worldly splendor, Radegunda sought only to indulge in seclusion her grief for her murdered family, and to spend her days in prayer and in acts of beneficence. Chlotar, at length weary of her piety, repudiated and imprisoned her in a convent, where she was honored as a saint. Venantius Fortunatus, the Latin poet, sang her praise in glowing verse. Nicetius, bishop of Treves, and Sidonius, bishop of Mayence, vainly emulated the attempts of this unfortunate princess to moderate the savage passions of the brother kings. Theodorich murdered Siwald, a descendant of a side-branch of the Merovingian race, but spared his son, Garibald, then a young child, and sent him to be educated at Rome. He afterward made him duke of Bavaria. Garibald was the father of the celebrated Theodolinda, and the founder of the Agilofingian dynasty. The Bavarians (*Bajuvarii*) evidently derive their name from the ancient country of the Boii, and date from the Gothic migration. They are first met with in history as seeking protection from the Franks and Alemanni against the Avari, who then devastated the country in their advance westward, and from whom they were no sooner delivered than they became insolent and rebellious. The elevation of Garibald to the ducal dignity was probably occasioned by a fresh invasion of Bavaria by the Avari. Siegmund succeeded his father, Gundebald, on the throne of Burgundy, and, on the death of his Ostrogothic queen, married her waiting-woman, who, being mocked, on account of the awkwardness with which she moved in her royal robes, by her little stepson, Siegerich, revenged herself by persuading his father to murder him in his sleep. The Burgundians, horror-struck at the deed, rebelled; the Franks, headed by Chlodomir of Orleans, invaded the country, and Siegmund, universally deserted by his subjects, fled to the monastery of St. Maurice in Valais. His retreat was discovered, and he was carried to Orleans, where he was murdered, and his wife and child were drowned in a well, A.D. 524. His uncle Godemar, meanwhile, headed the Burgundians against the Franks, and Chlodomir was defeated and killed. Chlotilda, undeterred by the fate of her son, continued to incite his brothers against Burgundy. The brave Godemar at length disappeared, after a last and desperate battle, and the country, which however still continued to be governed by its national laws, was annexed, by Childebert and Chlotar, to France.

LXXXIV. *Fall of the Kingdom of the Vandals*

AFTER the death of Geiserich, Hunerich, his son, mounted the throne, and instead of carrying into execution the ambitious projects of his father, instantly concluded peace with Rome. Conscious of the disgust with which he had inspired his subjects by his vicious propensities, and suspecting that they intended to depose him in favor of his brother, Theodorich, he caused him to be murdered, together with his wife and children. His father, although an Arian, had treated the Catholics with the greatest lenity, in the hope of winning them over. They were now cruelly persecuted by Hunerich, who condemned Iodocus, the patriarch of Carthage, to be burned alive in the market-place, closed all the monasteries and Catholic churches, and sentenced the priests, monks, and nuns to be broken on the wheel or driven naked out of the country. His wife, the pious Eudoxia, the Roman captive, fled for protection from his tyranny to the sepulcher at Jerusalem. At length, the warlike Moors of Mount Atlas, taking advantage of his unpopularity, poured in thousands from their valleys, and carried on a war of extermination against the strangers of the North, A.D. 486. Hunerich was succeeded by his nephews, Gundamund and Trasamund. Amalfrida, the sister of Theodorich the Great, became the wife of Trasamund, and brought over 5,000 Gothic nobles to assist her husband against the victorious Moors. Trasamund was succeeded by Hilderich, the son of Hunerich, who imprisoned Amalfrida, put her Gothic followers to death, and entered into an alliance with the emperor Justinian, his hereditary foe. The Vandals before long discovered their folly, and, deposing Hilderich, raised Gelimer, a distant branch of the royal family, to the throne. But treason was already at work. Godas the Goth, who had been intrusted by Gelimer with the government of Sardinia, went over to Justinian, who dispatched Belisarius, his celebrated general, at the head of an army more than 100,000 strong, including numbers of Huns and Heruli, to Africa, A.D. 533. Ammatas, Gelimer's brother, fell a victim to his own impetuosity in the first battle, and the king, after bravely defending his brother's body to the last, was finally compelled to retreat to the mountains, instead of throwing himself into Carthage, which yielded at discretion. Too weak singly to face the enemy, Gelimer anxiously awaited the return of his friend, Tzazon, whom he had sent, at the head of a Vandal force, to Sardinia, where he was victorious over Godas. On his return, Gelimer once more took the field, and another battle was fought, in which Tzazon was killed, and the royal treasure fell into the hands of the conqueror. Accompanied by a few faithful adherents, Gelimer again fled to his mountain stronghold. Pharos, a Herule in the imperial service, who was sent to persuade him to yield and to enlist beneath the imperial standard, vainly sought by bribe and flattery to bring him to submission. The Vandal king replied that he only wished for three things, a loaf, as it was long since he had tasted bread, a sponge, with which to bathe his eyes, scorched by the glare of the noontide sun on the bare rocks, and a lute, to soothe his sorrows, all which Pharos brought to him. At length his position became intolerable, and one day seeing one of his nephews fighting, as if for life, with another boy, for a small piece of dough, their last remnant of food, he was completely discouraged, and surrendered to Belisarius, who treated him with great respect, but made him grace his triumphal entry into Constantinople, bound with silver chains. The Vandal prisoners entered into the imperial service, and were employed against the Persians. Some thousands of their countrymen, who had scattered themselves among the mountains, reassembled under Stotzas, and made common cause with the Moors against the Romans. A long and harassing war ensued, during which Stotzas was killed. He was succeeded in his command by Gontharis, who retook Carthage, where he maintained himself for some time. The Romans, at length, succeeded in putting him and the rest of the Vandals to the sword at a great banquet, when they were helpless from intoxication.

LXXXV. *The Ostrogothic War—Vitigis*

THE downfall of the kingdom of the Ostrogoths in Italy was partly occasioned by similar causes. The death of Theodorich the Great, the signal for disunion between the Goths and Romans, was quickly turned to advantage by Justinian on one side, and by the Franks on the other. Amalaswintha, the learned daughter of Theodorich, and the widow of Eutharis the Goth, took possession of the kingdom in the name of her youthful son, Athalarich. Amalaswintha had been educated at Rome, and was consequently anxious to place her son beneath similar tutelage. A violent opposition was raised to her schemes by a party in the kingdom, which, under pretext of rescuing the young prince from the degrading effects of Roman effeminacy, encouraged him in the grossest vice, and the queen, finding her life no longer secure, had already entreated the emperor Justinian for a place of refuge, when her son fell a victim to excess, and her opponents raised Theodatus, the son of Amalfrida, to the throne, who caused her to be suffocated in a bath. The Romans, oppressed by the tyranny of the barbarous Gothic party, now recalled with regret the comparatively mild government of Theodorich, once deemed by them so intolerable, and anxiously sought assistance from the Greek emperor, who, elated by his recent victory over the Vandals, acceded to their petition, and, under pretext of avenging the murder of Amalaswintha, turned his arms against the Goths, who were doubly obnoxious, on account of their profession of Arianism, to the Catholic Romans, by whom he was zealously aided, while the Franks, from political motives, offered no opposition to his project. Theodatus, panic-struck at the arrival of Belisarius in southern Italy, offered to exchange his crown for a pension from the emperor; a proposal rendered null by his subjects, who, despising him for his cowardice, convoked a general state assembly at Regeta, near Rome, which deposed him and placed Vitigis on the throne, by whose orders he was put to death. Vitigis, in the hope of securing himself on the throne by an alliance with the last of the Amali, A.D. 536, forced Malasuntha, the daughter of Amalaswintha, to become his wife, and sent embassadors into Asia with the intention of persuading the Persians to attack the eastern frontier of Greece. He also entered into alliance with the Alpine Alemanni and Burgundians, who to the number of 150,000, almost all mailed cavalry, advanced into northern Italy, where, instead of aiding him, they plundered and laid waste the country. Belisarius, meanwhile, approached, the Romans swelling his ranks as he advanced upon Rome, whose gates were flung open by the inhabitants to welcome his arrival, and to receive a Roman garrison. Vitigis instantly besieged the faithless city, at the head of the whole of his army. Wooden scaling towers, drawn by oxen, were placed close to the walls, which the Goths furiously attacked, but were repulsed with great loss by Belisarius, who, when all the common stones were exhausted, flung several thousands of the marble statues, which at that time adorned the city, upon the heads of the besiegers, who fought with such extraordinary fury that 30,000 of them are said, on one occasion, to have fallen in a skirmish that took place beneath the walls.

Johannes, Belisarius' lieutenant, meanwhile, carried on the war to the rear of the Goths, and being invited by the injured Malasuntha to Ravenna, the Gothic capital, took Ariminum, and garrisoned Milan, whose gates opened to receive him on his passage to that city. News of these disasters quickly reached the Gothic king, who, setting fire to his camp, raised the siege of Rome, and marched in pursuit of Johannes; but, being unable to draw him out of the fortified walls of Ariminum, he suddenly attacked Milan, with the intention of revenging himself upon the inhabitants, and of attracting the procrastinating Burgundians and Alemanni beneath his standard, by the hope of plunder. The city was soon taken by stratagem; and Vitigis, allowing the garrison to march out unharmed, put 300,000 of the inhabitants to the sword, and yielded the city a prey to his Burgundian auxiliaries, who slew indiscriminately both Goths and Romans. Their king, Theodobert of Austrasia, who had been simultaneously applied to for assistance by the Greeks and the Goths, now invaded Italy with the intention of taking possession of it for himself. Although for some time professing Christianity, he afforded another striking proof of the ferocity of the times, by offering, according to pagan custom, a sacrifice of young children (those of the Goths) to the river-god, and casting their bodies into the Po. The Franks, armed with battle-axes, fell indifferently upon the Romans and the Goths, both of whom had implored their protection. Johannes was defeated, but a pestilence, breaking out among them, so greatly reduced their number, that a retreat became inevitable, and they quitted Italy at a moment when Vitigis was closely besieged by Belisarius in Ravenna, where he bravely defended himself, until at length, worn out by the perseverance of the enemy and hopeless of success, the Goths voluntarily offered to place the Greek general on the throne of Italy. The offer was accepted, and Vitigis was betrayed into the hands of Belisarius, who entered Ravenna, but, true to his allegiance, refused to be proclaimed king. The Gothic women, indignant at the treachery and folly of the men, contemptuously spat in their faces. Vitigis and several other prisoners of distinction were taken to Constantinople, where the emperor, struck with admiration by their bravery, treated them with great honor. The extreme beauty of the Gothic women is highly extolled by a Greek writer of that age, A.D. 539.

LXXXVI. *Totilas—Tejas—Fall of the Kingdom of the Ostrogoths*

BELISARIUS was, at this conjuncture, recalled from Italy, fortunately for the rest of the Goths, who, placing Ildebald on the throne, took the field against the Heruli and Rugii, their hereditary foes, immense robber hordes of whom had joined the Romans. Ildebald defeated their two chiefs, Vitalus the Roman, and Wisand the Herule, but was shortly afterward killed, at a banquet, by a Goth, whose jealousy he had excited. His head was cut off at one stroke and rolled upon the table. Eurarich, one of the Rugii, succeeded him on the Gothic throne and was also murdered. The Goths then elected Totilas, A.D. 541, Ildebald's cousin, who again attempted to drive the Greeks out of Italy. On his march southward he is said to have encountered St. Benedict on the Casino Mountains, who foretold to him the approaching downfall of his kingdom. Undeterred by this prophecy, he attacked and took Naples, and captured the great Grecian fleet which had been sent to the assistance of the city, and which lay at anchor in the bay. His treatment of the famished Neapolitans was remarkable for a humanity rare at that period, and he superintended in person the distribution of small quantities of food to each person, in order to guard against the fatal consequences of eating too freely when in a state of starvation. A Goth who had abused a Roman maiden was, by his orders, put to death, and he strove, by the practice of strict justice and of humanity, to conciliate the people. But this wise policy was adopted when too late for success. Belisarius again arrived from Greece at the head of a powerful army; and Totilas, who, meanwhile, had taken Rome by surprise, retreated northward, after demolishing the walls, which were rebuilt by Belisarius, who placed the city in so complete a state of defense as to enable it to withstand a three days' storming by the Goths, who, in the course of the protracted siege, attacked and defeated the army of Johannes and murdered all the inhabitants of Tiber (Tivoli), in the vicinity of Rome, in revenge for their having supplied Belisarius with information of their movements.

Belisarius, again recalled by the emperor, quitted Italy for the last time, and Totilas once more took possession of Rome. After defeating the allied army of the Greeks and Romans under Verus, not far from Ravenna, he returned southward, made himself master of the whole country, built a fleet, conquered Sardinia and Corsica, and plundered the Grecian coasts. Ancona alone remained in the hands of the Greeks. Emboldened by success, he demanded the daughter of Theodobert in marriage, but met with a refusal, and the Franks again attempted to gain possession of Upper Italy. At the same time, the eunuch Narses, who had succeeded Belisarius in the command of the imperial troops, of which he had been deprived by the cabals of the jealous courtiers, entered Italy from the north, and, re-enforcing his army with the Heruli and Gepidæ under Philemuth, and with 6,000 of the Longobardi, who for the first time entered Italy, attacked the diminished forces of the Goths at Taginas, near Ariminum. The battle raged for two days, when Totilas, mortally wounded by the arrow of a Gepidæ, fled from the field, followed by the remnant of his army, and, after riding 84 stadia, fell dead from his horse, A.D. 552. His blood-stained robe was presented, as a trophy, to Justinian. The Goths now chose Tejas for their leader, who, resolving not to fall unavenged, marched, sword in hand, through Italy, murdering every Roman that crossed his path; Narses, meanwhile, pursuing a similar plan toward the Goths, whom he hoped to exterminate. The Goths, in revenge for the surrender of Rome to the Greeks, murdered 500 children belonging to the first Roman families, whom they had taken as hostages. At length, closely pursued by Narses, Tejas fled for safety to the beautiful valley that extends from Salerno to the sea, where, strongly posted on the Monte di Latte, he for some time kept the enemy at bay. Barricading the entrance to the intrenchments with his body, the brave Goth defended himself with one hand while guarding himself with a long shield with the other, and, after a valiant defense, was killed when in the act of changing his shield, bristled with arrows and lances, for the third time. The Romans, struck with the bravery of their foe, granted free egress to the thousand Goths that alone survived the fight. The death of Theodobert took place about this period, and his son, Theodobald, remaining inactive, the Alemanni, who dwelt in the mountains, deemed the occasion favorable, on the dispersion of the Goths, for an invasion of Italy, and attempted to carry into execution the project that was shortly afterward undertaken with such signal success by the Longobardi under more experienced leaders. They divided into two enormous hordes, commanded by Leutharis and Butilinus, the former of which coasted the Mediterranean, the latter the Adriatic. These hordes were composed of foot-soldiers, armed with shields and swords, and merely clothed with long trousers, the upper part of the body being naked, from an idea that by that means they should suffer less from the heat of the climate. The army under Leutharis was destroyed by pestilence, and that under Butilinus was surrounded and cut to pieces by Narses, five men alone escaping the fate of their comrades, A.D. 554. In the following year, Ragnaris, a Hun, headed 7,000 Goths against Narses, whom he treacherously killed during a conference, a fate which not long afterward awaited him at Conza. The tyrannical conduct of the Romans toward their former masters, the German land-owners, now scattered throughout the country, and the insolence of the German mercenaries, sufficiently account for the futile revolts of the Goths under Widinus and Amingus in Verona, A.D. 563, and of the Heruli under Sinduval, a man whose bravery had chiefly contributed to the victories gained by Narses, under whom he had served, and who ended his life on the gallows, A.D. 566. According to the chronicle of Franke, some of the fugitive Goths crossed Mount St. Gothard, and settled in a wilderness on the spot where Uri now stands.

LXXXVII. *Origin of the Longobardi—Fate of the Heruli and Gepidæ*

THE legendary account of the Longobardi or Langobardi is as follows:—A famine having been caused in Denmark by a great flood, the people assembled in order to deliberate on the best means of alleviating the general distress, and had already come to the resolution of putting all the old men and women to death for the sake of sparing the food for the young and able, when a wise woman, named Gambara, proposed that lots should be cast for the migration of a third of the population. Her advice was followed, and the chosen number of Danes, then known as Vinili, afterward as Longobardi, on account of the prodigious length of their beards, departed, under the command of Gambara's two sons, Ibor and Ajo. Upon the Vandals refusing them permission to settle in their neighborhood, war was declared. On the eve of battle, Gambara besought the aid of Freya, while the Vandals invoked Wodan, who promised to grant the victory to whomever he first beheld at sunrise. At the appointed hour, the Danish women, with their long hair hanging over their faces, stationed themselves along the front of the army, drawn up in battle array. The sun rose, and Wodan asked, "Who are these with long beards?" Thus Wodan gave them a new name, as well as victory. Their name has also been derived from the word *Hellebard*, a halbert. They are supposed to have formerly settled on the extensive corn-lands now surrounding Magdeburg. Although conscious of their common origin, they kept apart from the Suevian confederacy, and notwithstanding their numerical inferiority, maintained their independence among the Saxons (some of whom migrated with them to Italy) by means of their extraordinary bravery, which is justly praised by Tacitus. Their other legends are totally devoid of interest. Agelmund, one of their kings, chanced to be riding along the banks of a stream, into which seven boys, born at one birth, had been cast. He stopped, and plunging his lance into the water, drew out one who had grasped it. This boy became his successor, and founded a royal dynasty. The family of the Welfs claims a similar origin. After the cessation of the migrations, the Longobardi are first mentioned as a powerful nation in the neighborhood of the Rugii, Scirri, and Gepidæ, and of the Slavian Bulgarians and Avari, in the mountains of Austria. The Rugii and Scirri, after their subjection by the Ostrogoths, are no longer met with in history, although there is great probability that the Bavarians descended from both these nations, and that the word *Scirri* may be traced in the name of Scheyer. Jornandes, the Gothic historian, mentions Edico and Wulfo, as princes of the Scirri during the fifth century, and the same names, Ethico and Welf, recur, at a later period, in the celebrated family of the Welfs. The Heruli were remarkable for their obstinate adherence to paganism, and for their extreme ferocity. As late as the commencement of the sixth century, they put all their old men to death, and the widows voluntarily burned themselves alive. Rumentruda, the daughter of Tato, king of the Longobardi, fearing the revenge of the crippled brother of Rudolf, king of the Heruli, whom she had mocked, caused him to be murdered. Rudolf, burning for vengeance, attacked the Longobardi, at the head of the Heruli, who, like genuine Berserkers, fought perfectly naked, and on being defeated were seized with such madness, that, coming in their flight to a field of flax in full bloom, they imagined it to be a lake and attempted to swim through. They afterward entered into alliance with Constantinople, A.D. 500, where their king, Graitis, received baptism, and was consequently murdered on his return by his pagan subjects, who, in order to strengthen their party, sent to Thule, Scandinavia, their ancient birthplace, A.D. 528 (which, according to an obscure tradition, was at that period inhabited by pirates, also Heruli, who devastated the coasts of France and Spain), for a king of the ancient mythical race, whose arrival being delayed, the Christian party, aided by the emperor Justinian, gained the upper hand and raised Swarta to the throne. At length Todat arrived from Thule at the head of 500 young men, and Swarta was deposed; but the pagan part of the nation were unable to maintain their independence unassisted and alone, and finally. became incorporated with their allies the Gepidæ. The Christian Heruli long served with distinction under the Greek emperors, as mercenaries against the Persians, Vandals, and Goths.

The Gepidæ boast of having been the first nation (under Ardarich, whose gold coins are mentioned in the Burgundian code) that threw off the yoke of the Hun, and what little has been recorded concerning them in history speaks greatly to their praise. Although continually at feud with the Ostrogoths, they maintained their independence; and when Ildechis, the son of Tatus, king of the Longobardi—who had been murdered by his nephew, Wacho—fled for protection to their king Turisend, who put it to the vote in the national assembly whether they ought not to avoid a contest with their powerful opponent and comply with his demand for the delivery of their guest, the people unanimously replied, "that annihilation was preferable to the violation of the laws of hospitality." This magnanimous resolution was, notwithstanding, powerless to save the life of the unfortunate Ildechis, who was murdered by his enemies. Wacho was succeeded by Audoin, whose son, Alboin, killed Thurismund, the son of Turisend, in battle, but, forgetting to carry away his arms and returning home without a trophy, was deprived of his seat, as one unworthy of the honor, at his father's table. In order to repair his negligence, he went openly to Turisend and demanded the arms of his son. The aged king entertained him with the greatest hospitality, and even protected him from the anger of his subjects, whom he had treated with the utmost insolence. Turisend died, and was succeeded by his son, Kunimund, who was killed in battle by Alboin (against whom he was seeking to revenge the seduction of his daughter, Rosamunda), and the whole nation of the Gepidæ was incorporated with that of the Longobardi, A.D. 566.

LXXXVIII. *Alboin in Italy*

IN 552, a number of the Longobardi accompanied Narses into Italy during his expedition against the Ostrogoths. Some time after this, the services of Narses, like those of the unfortunate Belisarius (who is said to have wandered over the scenes of his former exploits, blind and starving), were rewarded with ingratitude. Being tauntingly advised by the Greek empress to carry a spindle instead of a sword, he replied "that he would shortly spin her a thread, the end of which she would not easily find," and invited the Longobardi into Italy, that land ever coveted by the German, which was probably doubly attractive to Alboin, owing to the security afforded by the Alps against the increasing and encroaching Slavonian hordes. Their ranks swelled by 20,000 of their ancient allies, the Saxons, the Longobardi descended the lofty Alps, A.D. 568, and for the first time beheld the immense plain, to which they were destined to give the name of Lombardy, or the land of the Longobardi. Four years were spent in warfare with the Romans, who defended themselves within their fortified towns, which, at first, offered an insurmountable difficulty to these wild warriors, unacquainted with the mode of conducting a siege; while the Burgundians and their duke Mummulus, who beheld with apprehension the arrival of a numerous and warlike nation in the vicinity of the western Alps, continually harassed, and probably might eventually have succeeded in subduing them, had they been assisted by the Franks, who, fortunately for the Longobardi, were at that time too busily engaged in civil broils to be able to turn their attention to the affairs of their neighbors. The whole country of the Po and the fortified city of Pavia at length fell into the hands of Alboin, A.D. 572, who, warned by the fate of the Ostrogoths, occasioned by the dispersion of their forces in central and southern Italy, took up a strong position on the Po, and made Pavia his capital, whence he could watch the movements of the Burgundians, the Alemanni, and the Franks, while he kept the Bulgarians and the Avari in check by the erection of strong fortifications in the Frioul. Instead of treating the conquered Romans with the generosity they had met with at the hands of the Ostrogoths, he deprived them of the whole of the land, and reduced them to a state of servitude, to which they submitted without a struggle, although they had formerly disdained the equality offered them by their Gothic conquerors.

Shortly after these events Alboin fell a victim to his own brutality. During a festival held at Pavia, when flushed with success and wine, he forced Rosamunda, the daughter of Kunimund, to drink from a cup formed from the scull of her father. In order to revenge this insult and to gratify her hatred against her father's murderer, Rosamunda, without hesitation, sacrificed her honor for the attainment of her purpose. One of her attendants had a lover, named Peredeo, a strong and active man, whom she unwittingly ensnared, and then threatened to denounce to the king, unless he consented to deprive him of life. Peredeo, worked upon by the wily queen, was conducted by her into the royal chamber, where Alboin, unable to snatch his sword from the wall, to which it had been artfully fastened by the queen, defended himself for some time with a footstool against the attack of his murderer. He was no sooner dead, than Helmichis, Rosamunda's confidant, married her, in the hope of gaining the crown; but the Longobardi, enraged at the murder of their king, attempting to seize their persons, they fled for safety to Longinus, the Greek governor of Ravenna, who, struck by the great beauty of the queen, offered her his hand. Rosamunda, habituated to crime and detesting the tool of her revenge equally with its object, now administered poison to Helmichis, who no sooner tasted the cup, than, discovering her treachery, he forced her to drain it to the dregs, and to share his fate, A.D. 573.

The Saxons, dissatisfied with the treatment they received from the Longobardi, quitted Italy, and being defeated during their passage across the Alps by the Burgundians under Mummulus, were constrained to purchase freedom with the sacrifice of their whole booty. A worse fate awaited them on their arrival in their native country on the Bode (now Swabia), which they found occupied by the Alemanni, who had been invited thither by the Franks, and whose peaceful offers being scornfully rejected, a war ensued, in which the Saxons were completely worsted, and 30,000 of them slain.

LXXXIX. *Theodolinda*

AFTER the death of Alboin, the Longobardi raised Kleph to the throne, who fell, in 575, by the hand of one of his subjects, and an interregnum of ten years ensued, during which the thirty-six Gauen were governed by an equal number of independent dukes, who invaded France, in 576, and were defeated in the mountains by Mummulus. In the ensuing year, three of these dukes, Amon, Zadan, and Rodan, again invaded that country, but were defeated and obliged to abandon their baggage on the Alps. They afterward gained a victory over a Roman army under Baduarius, A.D. 577. The dukes, apprehending a double invasion on the part of France and Greece, A.D. 584, now elected another king, Autharis, the son of Kleph, who restored peace to the kingdom and made a treaty with Smaragdus, the exarch of Ravenna. In order to strengthen himself against France by an alliance with Bavaria he demanded Theodolinda, the beautiful and pious daughter of Garibald, in marriage, and accompanying the embassy in disguise, succeeded in gaining her affections. On quitting her father's court, he discovered his rank to her, by saying, as he struck his battle-ax into a tree, "Thus strikes the king of the Longobardi!" Garibald, secretly influenced by the Franks, withdrew his consent to the marriage, upon which Theodolinda fled across the Alps to her royal lover, and the wedding was celebrated at Verona. The Franks, enraged at the failure of their scheme, accused Garibald of having connived at the flight of his daughter, and a war ensued, in which Autharis, protected by his fortresses, was victorious. The Franks, harassed by internal dissensions, deferred their revenge, and Autharis, turning his arms against the Romans, overran Italy and raised a monument at Reggio. He died early, A.D. 591, and the Longobardi, wrought upon by the beauty and address of Theodolinda, intrusted her with the choice of a successor to her bed and to the throne. A handsome Thuringian named Agilulf, whose political principles coincided with her own, became the object of her choice, and on his bending to kiss her hand one day as she sat at table, she said with a blush, "You have a right to kiss my cheek, for you are my king!" The influence obtained by this queen over the minds of the people was so unlimited that the same nation which, in 579, had murdered four hundred Romans for refusing to sacrifice to their gods, embraced Christianity at her request. She was on friendly terms with the pope, Gregory the Great, and not only concluded peace with the Franks, but strengthened the alliance by promoting marriages between the two nations. Under her peaceful reign, the constitution of Lombardy was finally arranged. The warlike form of government, consisting of dukes and their subordinate chiefs or *decani*, who exercised the judiciary power in time of peace, was at first retained. The Romans, deprived of their freedom, managed the estates of their lords, and held a particular office as Gastalden (*Gast*, guest; *ald*, *alt*, old '), dependent, like that of the *decani*, on the dukes.

---

¹ See Chapter IV. The word *Aldi*.

The new kingdom extended from Savoy to the Frioul, and from the Southern Tyrol to Benevento. A part of Upper Italy, the cities of Ravenna, Rome, and Naples, with Calabria and Sicily, alone remained in the hands of the Greeks, and formed an exarchate, of which Ravenna was the capital. The church, meanwhile, supported by Theodolinda, increased in power, the pope exercising almost uncontrolled authority at Rome. Frioul and Benevento, on the eastern and southern frontiers, were governed by powerful and almost independent dukes. The republic of Venice, then in its infancy, already emulated Greece in the knowledge and practice of navigation, a science unknown to the Longobardi, whose invasion of the country had driven fresh fugitives to the little islands in the Lagune, first peopled by refugees in the time of Attila.

Agilulf died, and Adelwald, his youthful son and successor, rendering himself obnoxious, was murdered by his subjects, A.D. 615, who, in gratitude for the benefits conferred on them by Theodolinda, elected Ariowald, the husband of her daughter, Gerberga, as her successor on the throne, A.D. 625.

XC. *The Crimes of the Merovingians*

THE success of the Frankish kings of the race of Merowig, who by violence and fraud had risen from obscurity, and had become the most powerful monarchs in Europe, led to the indulgence of the deepest moral depravity. Their policy, widely differing from that of the enlightened and generous-minded Dietrich of Bern, was solely based on oppression and murder, and the bloody feuds between the numerous descendants of Chlodwig, each of whom, dissatisfied with his portion, grasped at the whole of the immense inheritance, equaled in treachery and cold-blooded cruelty the horrors they had already enacted in their wars with neighboring nations. Some of these feuds may have arisen from an idea of the political unity of the nation being necessary for its protection against foreign aggression, while others may have been caused by a desire of gaining sole possession of the enormous treasure, composed of the booty taken from many nations, preserved at Paris, which is beautifully and truly designated in the Nibelungenlied as the source of all their corruption. On recurring to those olden times, when the Frank, poor, ignorant, and barbarous, suddenly came into possession of enormous wealth and power, the scenes of horror that ensued, one brother turning his hand against another, lest he should first fall a victim to treachery, may almost be anticipated. The tragedy was commenced after the deaths of Theodorich and Chlodomir, two of the four sons of Chlodwig, by their brethren, Childebert and Chlotar, who seized the inheritance of the sons of Chlodomir, whose mother, Chrodogilda, being offered the alternative of their death or of their seclusion, with shorn heads, in a monastery, proudly replied, "Rather let them die than be deprived of their royal right!" upon which they were instantly stabbed by Chlotar; Childebert, moved to pity, when too late, vainly attempting to rescue them from his murderous grasp. On the death of Childebert, the whole authority was vested in Chlotar, the close of whose reign is marked by an incident which proves that a nation cannot be rendered entirely and blindly subservient to the ambition of its rulers. During the invasion of Saxony, the Franks suddenly protested against the injustice of the war, and threatened to put their king to death unless he desisted from it; but it was not until his tent had been destroyed by the enraged multitude that Chlotar yielded and terminated the campaign.

Chlotar was succeeded by his four sons, A.D. 561, who divided the kingdom; Charibert reigning at Paris, Guntram at Orleans, Sigebert at Metz, and Chilperich at Soissons. The horrors committed by these four brethren cast the depravity of the four sons of Chlodwig into the shade. Never has one family amassed such a heritage of crime! The nation, influenced by the changes consequent on the introduction of the feudal system, either beheld with indifference or favored the dissensions between their rulers, of which they took advantage in order to obtain concessions and additional privileges in return for their assistance (the majority of the people having been deprived of their Allods, and the tenure of the fiefs depending on the will of the sovereign, and being alienable on the demise of the feoffee), although in general they required no stronger incentive than the hope of booty; while the clergy, ever on the watch for an opportunity of increasing the power of the church at the expense of that of the temporal sovereigns, participated in the guilt of this royal house by promoting disunion between its various branches.

XCI. *Fredegunda*

THE disorders in the family of Chlotar were commenced by Charibert, king of Paris, who, in defiance of the interdict pronounced against him by Bishop Germanus, took unto himself four wives, a crime to which, in the superstition of the times, his early death was attributed. Guntram, king of Orleans, followed his example and took three wives. This base polygamy was turned to advantage by Sigebert, king of Metz, who, after gaining a victory over the Avari in the east, raised himself above his brothers by an alliance with the princess Brunehilda, the daughter of Athanagild, king of the Visigoths, whose youthful charms and immense dowry filled all France with her fame, and the heart of Chilperich, king of Soissons, with envy. This wretch had already sacrificed his wife Audodeva and her two children to his mistress, Fredegunda, a woman celebrated for her beauty and ferocity. Solely influenced by jealousy and avarice, he now demanded the hand of Galaswintha, Brunehilda's sister, whom, at the instigation of Fredegunda, he caused to be murdered in her bed, soon after her arrival in Soissons and the reception of her rich dower, and a few days after the commission of this crime proclaimed his artful mistress queen. He then suddenly entered the territory of Sigebert, in the hope of gaining possession of it by surprise, but met with a sturdy opposition from the Austrasians, Sigebert's true-born German subjects. During this contest, letters were addressed by St. Radegunda from her convent to both the brothers, adjuring them to peace, and reminding them of the evils that had befallen her family, the bitter consequences of disunion; but her voice was unheard. The war proved disastrous to Chilperich, whose son, Theodebert, was killed in battle, and Sigebert had scarcely been seated by the Neustrians on the throne of Paris than he was slain by assassins in the pay of his treacherous brother, A.D. 576, who, taking advantage of the consternation caused by this event, re-entered the city, placed himself at the head of the Neustrians, drove out the now chiefless Austrasians, took the unfortunate Brunehilda prisoner, and almost succeeded in gaining possession of her son, Childebert, a child of three years of age, whose life was saved by a trusty servant, named Gundobald, who frustrated the search of the murderers by secreting him in a game-bag, by which means he contrived to escape with him to Austrasia, where he was proclaimed king. Brunehilda, now a prisoner and in the power of Fredegunda, the murderess of her sister and husband, had already prepared for death, when a deliverer appeared in the person of Merowich, the son of Chilperich, who, happening to see the beautiful prisoner at Rouen, became deeply enamored of her and drew her from her prison. Influenced by gratitude for this proof of devotion, the queen bestowed her hand upon him, and, aided by the faithful bishop of Prætextatus, who pronounced the nuptial benediction, the lovers escaped to Austrasia, where the great vassals of the crown, unwilling to place their youthful sovereign under the guardianship of a step-father, and unmoved by the tears and entreaties of Brunehilda, refused to receive her husband, who was, consequently, compelled to return to Neustria, where, fearing his father's vengeance, he raised an army, and being defeated by a ruse de guerre, preferred receiving death from his companions in arms to the fate that awaited him, as a prisoner, at the hands of the hateful Fredegunda.

This queen, whose propensities were as licentious as they were bloody, had, in the meantime, carried on a criminal intercourse with Landerich, her husband's major-domus, which was by chance discovered by Chilperich, who, one day entering her room softly when she was dressing, heard her utter the name of Landerich, for whom she had mistaken him, but not daring to put her to death, was himself shortly afterward deprived of life by her adherents, when following the chase, A.D. 584. Chlotar the Second, the only son of Fredegunda, who governed in his name, succeeded to the throne. The peace-loving Guntram of Orleans, struck with horror at the bloody deeds of this Megæra, sent embassadors to Childebert of Austrasia, and an interview took place between them on a bridge, when the childless old man, tenderly embracing his nephew, declared him his heir, hoping, by this means, to save his kingdom from the bloody grasp of Fredegunda. The dotage of the aged king was, meanwhile, turned to advantage by the great vassals and the bishops of Neustria and Austrasia, who, during the minority of Childebert, frequently made the old man the umpire of their feuds, and found means to gain many great privileges. The brave Mummulus, the most powerful of the Burgundian chiefs, was, by the intrigues of his enemies, sentenced to death by his ungrateful master, and the whole nation became gradually infected with the egotism and cruelty characteristic of the race of Merowig.

The increasing power of the great vassals for some time kept the authority of Fredegunda and of Brunehilda in check, but the latter at length succeeded in forming a party in Austrasia, by which she was placed at the head of affairs. The success attending her first enterprise, undertaken against the Longobardi, at once gained the confidence of her warlike subjects and confirmed her newly acquired power. With a heart hardened by former adversity, she bloodily revenged herself upon the nobles, the authors of her cruel fate, who, after depriving her of her husband, Merowich, had compelled her to part with Lupus, her only faithful adherent. These occurrences are mentioned in the song of the Nibelungen as the revenge of Chriemhilda. Fredegunda, enraged at her success, attempted to assassinate her, but was frustrated in her scheme, and her emissaries were put to death. She then, in the hope of gaining the chief power in Neustria, secretly caused the nobles to be murdered one by one, but, nevertheless, only reached her aim on the death of Guntram, A.D. 595, when she and her paramour, Landerich, set up a claim to the throne of Burgundy, in opposition to that of Brunehilda and her son, Childebert, who, after his first campaign against the Longobardi, had subdued the petty nation of the Varini and incorporated it with that of Thuringia.[1] This youthful monarch, basely deserted by the Burgundian nobles, whom Landerich had bribed by lavishing upon them the accumulated treasure of the Merovingian kings, died shortly after his defeat at Soissons, not without suspicion of having been poisoned by Brunehilda, who coveted the possession of the sole authority, in order to reign undisturbed with her paramours. Childebert left two sons, Theudebert, who inherited Austrasia, and its capital, Metz; and Theuderich, who claimed Burgundy, and its capital, Orleans; the possession of which was again disputed by Fredegunda. A second battle took place on the Seine, in which Brunehilda was victorious, whereupon Fredegunda, stimulated by revenge, stirred up the Avari and the Saxons, who invaded Thuringia, A.D. 596, but, before the contest was decided, her criminal existence reached its close.

---

[1] Radigis, king of the Varini, had deserted his Anglo-Saxon bride for a Frankish princess. The Anglo-Saxon, in revenge for this insult, landed on the coast of Germany, and, after a long search, succeeded in taking her faithless bridegroom prisoner in a wood, when she compelled him to repudiate the Frank and to marry her. This little incident was the cause of the ruin of the whole nation, which was subdued by the avenging Franks.

XCII. Brunehilda

THEUDEBERT, after repulsing the Avari and the Saxons, turned his arms against Chlotar, whom he defeated, after a desperate engagement, in which 30,000 Franks fell. Brunehilda, deprived of one object of her hatred by the death of her old enemy, Fredegunda, now sought to revenge herself upon the Austrasian nobles by whom her influence had formerly been impaired, and after causing Ægila, the majordomus, to be murdered, bestowed that office upon Protadius, the paramour of her old age, whom she raised to the highest dignities of state. Enraged at the disapprobation of her tyrannical and licentious inclinations manifested by her grandson Theudebert, she remorselessly flung the brand of discord into her own family, by persuading Theuderich that his brother, instead of being the son of Chlotar, owed his existence to a miller, and a quarrel had already broken out between them, when Uncelin, duke of Alemannia, raising a sedition among the Germans, slew the Roman Protadius in his camp, and brought about a reconciliation. Brunehilda, furious at the restraint imposed upon her by Theuderich, caused the bishop Desiderius, who had ventured to preach repentance to her, to be stoned to death, and revenged the reprobation with which the Irish saint, Columban, had denounced her crimes, by driving him out of the country. This artful wretch at length succeeded in setting her grandsons completely at variance, by persuading the credulous Theuderich to deprive his brother, on the plea of his illegitimacy, of the beautiful province of Alsace. Two dreadful conflicts took place at Toul and Zülpich, the latter of which proved fatal to Theudebert, who fell into the hands of his unnatural grandmother and was confined in a monastery, where he was shortly afterward murdered by her order, and the brains of his little son, Merowich, were dashed out against a rock, A.D. 612. Theuderich, inspirited by this success, now invaded Neustria, and Brunehilda was gloating on the prospect of speedily sating her revenge on Chlotar the Second, whose mother death had placed beyond her reach, when the retribution so long delayed at length burst upon her head. Theuderich, struck by the beauty of Theutelana, the daughter of Theudebert, was on the eve of marrying her, when his grandmother, who dreaded the consequences of this alliance, contradicted her former assertion of Theudebert's illegitimacy, in order to prove that the marriage was forbidden by the church. The fratricide, filled with remorse at this avowal, drew his sword and threatened the life of his hateful grandmother, who soon after revenged herself by administering poison to him.

Theuderich left four sons, still in their infancy. Sigebert, the eldest, was placed by Brunehilda, who intended to govern in his name, on the throne of Austrasia, but her expectations were frustrated by Pipin von Landen, who, at the head of a numerous party of discontented nobles, went over to Chlotar the Second, who prudently convoked a general assembly of the Frankish nobility, to which he submitted his cause, and the means of putting an end to the feuds which for so long a period had desolated his family. Brunehilda, meanwhile, alarmed by this general desertion, fled from Metz into the interior of Germany, whence she attempted to rouse the jealousy of the Austrasians against the Neustrians. The fidelity of Warnachar, her major-domus, appearing to waver, she conspired against his life, but discovering her intention he counterplotted with Chlotar, and when she recrossed the Rhine at the head of a numerous army, and entered the broad champaign around Chalons on the Marne (famous for the meeting of conflicting nations in the time of Attila), where she encountered Chlotar, her followers deserted her to a man, and she was delivered up to her adversary, who, after causing her to undergo the most excruciating torture for three days, had her placed on a camel's back and paraded through the camp; the punishment being terminated by her being tied by the hair of her head, by one arm and one foot, to the tail of a wild horse. Thus miserably ended the life of the Visigothic princess, A.D. 613, whose arrival in France was attended with such splendor, and hailed with such universal delight. Her crimes were visited upon her descendants. Sigebert and his second brother, Corvus, were murdered by order of Chlotar; Merowich, the third, being his godson, was spared; and the fourth, Childebert, fled the country and was never heard of more. Frideburga, a noble maiden, daughter of Gunzo, duke of Alemannia, lost her senses on hearing of the death of Sigebert, to whom she was betrothed, and being restored to reason by St. Galus, the disciple of St. Columban, he was, in reward, permitted to found the monastery of St. Gall in the country of the pagan Alemanni, by whom St. Columban had a short time previously been driven away for having ventured to throw three of their deities (probably Wodan, Thor, and Frigga, who gave name to the Bodensee, the Thurgau, and the Frickthal), whose images stood on the banks of the Bodensee, into the lake.

The use of carriages was introduced into France by Brunehilda, during whose reign the roads were made, long known as the chaussées[1] de Brunehault, the only benefit she ever conferred on her subjects. With her the legitimate line of the Merovingians ceased, and the bastard brood of Fredegunda, Merovingians only in name, mounted the throne in the person of Chlotar the Second, whose slothful effeminacy, bigotry, and sensuality, were unredeemed by the energy which so eminently characterized the lineal descendants of Merowig. The great vassals of the crown and the bishops, anxious to obtain a confirmation of the privileges they had gained during these disturbances, now sought to establish peace throughout the kingdom, reunited beneath the scepter of Chlotar the Second, and convoking a general state assembly at Paris, A.D. 625, compelled him to render the feofs hereditary and to grant fresh privileges to the clergy, who

---

[1] On the Feldberg, the highest summit of the Taunus, a large mass of stones, called Brunehilda's bed, is still to be seen, whence this queen is said to have often gazed on the delicious prospect.

henceforward shared with the people the right of electing the bishops, whose office was merely confirmed by the king.

The power of the Hausmaier, or mayor of the palace, a post of great importance whenever the scepter was in the hands of women and children, had also risen during these long disturbances, and had become, as will hereafter be seen, the object to which the nobility most ambitiously aspired.

XCIII. *Grimoald*

THE Avari, a wild and savage race that had settled in Hungary, advanced under the command of their prince, Cacan, through the mountains of Illyria and Lombardy, A.D. 611, and after slaying Gisulph, the grandduke, and all his adherents in battle, laid siege to the city of Frioul, where Romilda, the widow of Gisulph, had taken refuge. One day when gazing from the battlements, the duchess beheld the young khan, and becoming enamored of his beauty, offered, regardless alike of honor and duty, to betray the city into his hands on condition of being made his wife. The compact was made and fulfilled. The city was delivered up, and Cacan took Romilda with her four sons and four daughters into Hungary, where the marriage was celebrated; but on the following morning, with a perfidy worthy of the husband of such a woman, he caused her to be impaled alive. Her daughters, Appa, who subsequently married a duke of Alemannia, and Gaila, who wedded a duke of Bavaria, preserved their honor by the singular precaution of polluting their persons with the putrid flesh of a fowl. The four sons found means to escape. Grimoald, the youngest, who was mounted behind his eldest brother Tafo, was thrown to the ground during the flight, and Tafo, fearing lest he might be taken alive by their pursuers, was in the act of transfixing him with his lance, when, moved by the entreaties of the boy, he changed his resolution, and replacing him on his horse, continued his flight. Grimoald again fell and was seized by an Avar, who mounted him on his horse with the intention of carrying him off, when the brave child, drawing a dagger from the man's belt, suddenly stabbed him to the heart, tossed him from the saddle, and galloped after his brethren, whom he speedily rejoined. Tafo was hospitably received by Ariowald, king of Lombardy, and succeeded his father in the dukedom of Frioul. A certain Adalulf, whose criminal advances had been scornfully rejected by Queen Gundeberga, revenged himself by rousing the suspicion of the king against Tafo, whom he falsely accused of carrying on an illicit intercourse with the queen. Tafo was put to death. The innocence of the queen was afterward fully proved, and, on the death of Ariowald, she was treated by the Lombards with the same respect that had formerly been shown to her mother, Theodolinda, her second husband being left to her choice, which fell upon Rotharis, a man distinguished for prudence. He bestowed an admirable code of laws upon Lombardy. On his death, A.D. 643, the Lombards, wishful to show their devotion to the memory of their beloved queen, Theodolinda, and of her virtuous race, raised her brother, the Bavarian Aribert, to the throne, A.D. 654. His sons, Bertarit and Godebert, disputed the succession, 661, and a struggle ensued between the rival parties, which terminated at Benevento in favor of the Lombards.

The brave little Grimoald was adopted by Duke Arigil of Benevento, and became a famous warrior. He greatly distinguished himself, under the command of his patron, against the Greeks in Lower Italy, and, on succeeding to the throne of Benevento, declared in favor of King Godebert. A man who was secretly in the pay of King Bertarit succeeded, however, in persuading the two friends that each was plotting the other's destruction, alleging, in support of his assertion, that each wore armor beneath his dress, through fear of the other. The fear of assassination now induced them in reality to take this precaution, which Grimoald no sooner perceived than, confirmed in his suspicions, he slew his supposed enemy, thinking to save his own life. Bertarit still maintained his right, but the Lombards, persuaded of Grimoald's innocence, placed him on the throne. Constans, the Greek emperor, taking advantage of the discord that prevailed in Lombardy, marched thither in person from Naples and laid siege to Benevento, which was, at that time, defended by Romuald, whose father, Grimoald, was engaged in the north, but who dispatched Sesuald, his trusty adherent, at the head of some troops, to his assistance. Sesuald fell into the hands of the emperor, who promised to load him with honor and wealth, on condition of his giving Romuald a false account of the death of Grimoald, and of persuading him to capitulate; but the faithful man, when led to the walls for that purpose, cried out, "Be firm! Grimoald approaches!" His head was instantly severed from his body and cast into the city. It fell at the feet of Romuald, who pressed it to his lips and deeply deplored his death. Instead of awaiting the arrival of Grimoald, the emperor retreated upon Naples. He was pursued, and a battle was on the point of commencing, when Amalong, a gigantic Lombard, lifting a Greek from his saddle with his lance, held him poised in the air, and the rest of his countrymen, terror-stricken at sight of this feat, fled to Sicily. Bertarit at length, finding resistance futile, submitted to Grimoald, who, either mistrusting him or being again misled, laid a plan for murdering him in his bed, which was discovered by one of Bertarit's servants, who aided his master to escape and placed himself in his bed. Grimoald, struck by this proof of fidelity, attempted to attach him to his own person, but, finding his endeavors unsuccessful, yielded to his entreaties, and restored him to his master, who had taken refuge in France. His cause was embraced by Chlotar the Second, who took up arms against the Lombards, and was defeated at Asti by Grimoald, who, feigning to desert his camp, which he left well stored with provisions, suddenly returned and put his feasting opponents to the sword, A.D. 665. In the following year, he defeated the Avari, who also invaded Lombardy, by marching and countermarching his little army, each time dressed in different colors, within sight of the enemy, so as to give them a false impression of his numbers. Grimoald gave many new laws to his country. In his old age he was remarkable for his bald head and long white beard.

After his death, A.D. 671, the Lombards recalled the exiled Bertarit, and Romuald contented himself with the possession of Benevento. Cunibert, the son of Bertarit, was greatly disquieted by the rebellious dukes, and his son, Liutprand, was set aside by Reginhart, a descendant of Godebert. Aribert the Second, his son and successor, in order to revenge himself upon Ansbrand, the guardian of Liutprand, who had taken refuge in Bavaria, deprived his son of his eyesight, and mutilated his mother and daughter. Ansbrand being assisted by the Bavarians and joined by the Lombards, by whom Aribert was universally detested, in the first encounter the latter fled from his camp, but, unwilling to part from his treasures, loaded himself so heavily with gold that, when crossing the river Adige on horseback, he sank beneath the weight and was drowned, A.D. 711. Ansbrand mounted the throne, and was succeeded by his son Liutprand, who gave laws to the Lombards favoring the emancipation of the slaves, in order better to dispose the ancient Roman inhabitants toward the Lombard rule. He also projected the conquest of the whole of Italy, where the Romans were attempting to make their exarchate independent of the Greek emperor; but an insurmountable obstacle presented itself at Rome, where the pope, Gregory the Second, who disdained to submit to a king of Lombardy, and was moreover desirous of dividing Italy into petty sovereignties, in order to increase his own independence, was powerfully supported by the Franks, who, forgetful of the generosity of Liutprand in assisting them against the Moors, compelled him to restore Ravenna to the pope. Liutprand died in 744, and was succeeded by Rachis, whose brother, Aistulf, on coming to the throne, attempted to carry out the plans of Liutprand, and pressing hard upon Rome, was attacked and defeated by the Franks.

XCIV. Fall of the Suevian and Visigothic Kingdom in Spain

AFTER the death of Theodorich the Great, the protector of the Visigoths, Amalarich, their king, attempted to cement the friendship of the Franks by an alliance with Chlotilda, the daughter of Chlodwig, but the ancient hatred existing between the two nations was too deeply rooted, and the haughty princess, ill-treated by her husband, sent a cloth stained with her blood as a token to her brothers, and Childebert, hastening to avenge her wrongs, slew Amalarich near Narbonne, A.D. 531. The Goths elected Theudis, and the Franks were waylaid on their return to France, and defeated by Theodisel, his general, who succeeded him on the throne, and was assassinated in consequence of his licentious habits. He was succeeded by Ægila, who was deposed by Athanagild, the father of the celebrated Brunehilda, whose successors were Liuba and Löwigild, a furious tyrant, against whom the Basques, in the Pyrenees, rebelled. His son, Hermenegild, married Ingundis, the daughter of Brunehilda, a pious, gentle princess, and zealous Catholic. Her husband had been reared in the same faith by his mother, Theodosia, who was a Greek Catholic. Goiswinda, his step-mother, an equally zealous Arian, enraged at the obstinacy with which her daughter-in-law adhered to her religious tenets, caused her to be thrown into a tun full of water, in order to baptize her according to the form of her church. Hermenegild, revolted by this treatment of his young wife, refused to embrace Arianism, and rebelling against his father, joined the ancient Roman Catholic inhabitants of Spain, the Suevi and the Basques. The rebels were defeated; Andeca, king of the Suevi, was confined in a monastery, and the whole nation reduced to submission. Hermenegild surrendered himself to his father, who condemned and put him to death. The Catholics worshiped him as a saint. Ingundis, while attempting to escape by sea into France, fell into the hands of the Greeks, and died in Africa, A.D. 585.

Fredegunda, delighted at this catastrophe, and hoping to gain the Visigoths over to her party in opposition to that of her arch-enemy, Brunehilda, offered her daughter, Rigundis, in marriage to Reccared, Hermenegild's brother, and the richly-dowered bride, sadly foreboding that the evil fate of Ingundis might prove her own, set out for Spain, but before she reached the Pyrenees, was despoiled and sent back by Guntram's vassals; an insult which was afterward bloodily revenged by Löwigild. Reccared, who succeeded his father, favored the Catholics, and foreseeing that the Arian Visigoths must finally yield to their antagonists and share the miserable fate of the Ostrogoths, made a public confession of the Catholic faith. He afterward defeated a conspiracy formed against him by the Arians, A.D. 590, headed by Goiswinda and her ally, Guntram, who had sent a Frankish army under Desiderius, duke of Toulouse, into Spain, and Goiswinda killed herself in despair. Reccared introduced several new regulations into the government, which, by lowering the pride of the Gothic nobility, and by conferring great privileges upon the Romans, essentially contributed to the gradual extinction of the German language and free constitution, and to the promotion of Italian ascendency, which was materially assisted by the efforts of the Catholic clergy, whose influence had greatly increased during the long interregnum that occurred after the death of Alaric. The subsequent rapid change of sovereigns on the throne, and the schism in the church, had also added to the importance and pretensions of the bishops, who now held a casting vote in the diet or council, which promulgated both civil and ecclesiastical law, and formed among the Visigoths one and the same assembly. Reccared died in 601. His son, Liuba, was dethroned by Witherich, who, rendering himself obnoxious by his tyranny, was assassinated at a banquet. In this manner sovereigns rapidly succeeded each other, all of whom were unable to transmit the throne to their descendants without a violent struggle, were murdered by their rebellious subjects, or dethroned by a successful rival; the ecclesiastical and temporal lords, meanwhile, taking advantage of the confusion that prevailed to gain a firm footing in the state. The Basques were in almost continual revolt, and the country lay open to the Franks, who, fortunately for their neighbors, were at that period busily engaged in their own civil dissensions. The most distinguished among the Gothic princes of that time were—Sigebert, who drove the Greeks from their last strongholds in some of the maritime towns, and who died in 620; Chindasuinth, who, by putting 500 nobles to death, annihilated the power of the ancient aristocracy, A.D. 652; and Reccesuinth, who chastised the Basques, and restrained the hierarchical power by reinstating that of the dukes, A.D. 672. After him, Wamba the Wise was unanimously chosen king. During his reign, the Moors, whom he successfully repulsed, first landed in Spain. He was projecting the imposition of further restrictions on the power of the bishops, when he fell a victim to their treachery. A great rebellion of the Romans, under Paulus the Greek, which may be regarded as a Roman reaction against the declining Gothic empire, had been happily quelled, when Erwig, a young man whom he had loaded with benefits, administered a sleeping draught to him, and the priests, during his stupor, deprived him of his long hair (a loss which, according to the Gothic custom, rendered him incapable of reigning), and consigned him to the cloister. On regaining his senses, fearing lest the prosecution of his claim might occasion a civil war, he had the rare self-denial calmly to take the vow which separated him from the world. Erwig, struck with remorse, followed his example. He was succeeded by Egiza, A.D. 687, during whose reign the Moors again invaded the coasts, but were repulsed by the brave duke, Theodorich. Witiza, the son of Egiza, succeeded his father, and imposed fresh restrictions upon the clergy, A.D. 698. His unbridled licentiousness rendering him obnoxious to the people, an insurrection broke out, and Roderick was elected in his stead, against whom the son of Witiza and Count Julianus conspired.[1] Roderick is said to have dishonored the daughter of Julianus, who, in revenge, invited the Moors over from Africa. The whole of the north of that country was, at that period, in the hands of those zealous propagators of the religion of Mahomet, who had put an end to the Greek dominion, which had been re-established there by Belisarius. Taric, the Moorish chief, landed with a great army on the celebrated rock which forms the most southern point of Europe, and is named after him Gebel-al-Taric, Gibraltar. Roderick marched against him, and although in the commencement of the battle his army was weakened by the desertion of Count Julian, who went over to Taric, the engagement lasted eight days, from the 19th to the 26th of July, A.D. 711. It took place near Zeres de la Frontera. The victory was at length decided on the eighth day in favor of the Moors, by the sudden disappearance of Roderick, whose horse and crown were found on the bank of a river. The flower of the Gothic nation strewed the field of battle. The bodies of the nobles were distinguished by the golden rings they bore, while those of the freemen bore silver ones, and those of the bondmen copper ones. At Sidonia, a brave defense was made by Egiza; and, in Cordova, four hundred Goths sustained a siege of three months in a church with unexampled bravery. At length Toledo, the capital, fell into the hands of the invaders, who soon became masters of the whole country. The numerous Jewish population, formerly cruelly oppressed by the Christians, now revenged their sufferings by acting as spies and auxiliaries to the enemy. The Goths, persuaded that the Moors, solely intent on plunder, would shortly evacuate the country they de-

---

[1] One day as King Roderick was beholding the sports of the maids of honor from a balcony of his palace, Cava, the daughter of Count Julian, accidentally lost her footing and fell. The king, struck with her remarkable beauty, became passionately enamored of her, and, being unsuccessful in his suit, offered her violence. According to another legend, an ancient chest, which contained the destruction of Spain, was opened with bold curiosity by Roderick, and the instant that the lid flew up, the enemy entered and laid the country waste.

spoiled, did not exert their utmost energy in order to drive them out, and were only convinced of their fatal error when the enemy had settled in the land and opposition was unavailing. Fresh armies continually crossed the Strait, repeopled the desolated provinces, built new cities, and plunged the majority of the inhabitants into slavery. Among others, thirty thousand Gothic maidens were carried away from Spain, as a present to the caliph. A number of Gothic warriors took refuge in the mountains of Asturia and Gallicia, and at a later period again emerged from their rocky fastnesses.

XCV. *Mahomet and the Arabians*

THE Arabians, a people distinguished from the other Asiatic nations by superior elevation of character and fervor of imagination, were destined to play a part in Asia and Africa, after the fall of the Roman empire, similar to that enacted by the Germans in Europe. Christianity, although spread at an early period over Asia Minor and Arabia, became gradually less adapted in its doctrines and form of worship. to the peculiar temperament of the Eastern nations. The various characters impressed upon the Western and Eastern churches by the deeply-searching intellect of the meditative German, and by the subtle sophistry of the Greek philosopher, were lost amid the burning wastes of Asia. The Asiatic, unacquainted with the higher intellectual necessities of the European, with physical powers more rapidly and fully developed than his moral faculties, with an imagination warmer than the feelings of his heart, ignorant of liberty, whether in polity, religion, or science, accustomed to cringe beneath the despot's power, shackled in his religious creed by severe laws, which governed not only the actions but the thoughts of his every-day life, beheld Christianity in a very different light to the European. Deprived of vitality, its further development checked, to him it appeared a mere dead letter, a stern and inflexible law. The religion of love and liberty no sooner became one of passive obedience and hard necessity than it lost its dominion over the minds of the people, and its influence on government, society, manners, and daily life.

Christianity was first imbued with an Asiatic character by the Arabians, the most imaginative of the Eastern nations. Mahomet, a man of energetic and creative intellect, who represented himself as the messenger and prophet of God, founded upon it a new doctrine, Islamism, or Mohammedanism, adapted to the temperament of his countrymen, and replaced the Bible by the Koran, which commands belief in one God, recognizes Moses, Christ, and Mahomet, as his prophets, announces the first duty of the true believer to be the promulgation of this doctrine by fire and sword over the whole world, and promises voluptuous joys in heaven to those who fall in battle against unbelievers; an idea probably drawn from the Walhalla of the North, as it is possible that the mythology of the Goths and Vandals may not have been entirely unknown in Arabia. After death, the Mahometan heroes, attended by houris (exactly similar to the Walkyren), caroused in eternal delight; the only difference between the Arabian paradise and that of the North being the absence of warlike sports, the heroes being merely rewarded with sensual pleasures. In 622 the Mahometan war of proselytism commenced. The accordance of Islamism with the Asiatic character, the heroic deeds of Mahomet, the valor and enthusiasm of his followers, and the promises of celestial bliss, all conduced to the rapid propagation of the new religion, and involuntarily biased the minds of their opponents in its favor, even while still opposing them sword in hand. Islamism, consequently, speedily predominated throughout Asia, but was met by another spirit more powerful than its own in Europe, against which it vainly battled. Mahomet subdued the whole of Arabia, and became the caliph of the faithful. His successors followed in his steps, and after conquering Persia, Syria, Palestine, Egypt, and the whole northern coast of Africa, shook Constantinople, Sicily, and Spain, everywhere compelling the conquered nations to embrace Islamism. During the reign of the great caliph, Walid, Spain was conquered by Taric.

The foundation of a new and gigantic empire, animated by a spirit hitherto unknown, unlimited in its aspirations, and forcibly attempting to domineer the world, was not without its influence on Germanized and Christianized Europe. The appearance of the Moors and their new religion interrupted the civil contests of the Germans, and forced them to turn their attention and their arms to the South, in order to defend France and all Christendom from the destruction which threatened them from Spain. The long contests that ensued steeled the heroism of the Germans, elevated their minds, contracted by the petty feuds between kings and vassals, and fired them with religious enthusiasm; nor did the benefit cease with the danger; the sciences introduced by the Moors, more especially their natural philosophy, mathematics, and mechanics, their knowledge and active pursuit of commerce, their wealth, refined sense of the enjoyments of life, and their fertile and vivid imagination, exercised a powerful influence over the arts and social existence of the Germans during several succeeding centuries. Their kings imitated in their courts the pomp and splendor of the caliphate, and the customs of chivalry attained to a high degree of refinement, more particularly in Spain, where every action was inspired and sanctified by religious enthusiasm, and where the Moors emulated the Germans in the practice of every knightly virtue.

XCVI. *The Anglo-Saxons*

ABOUT the period of the migration of the Suevi and the Visigoths to Spain, of the Franks and the Burgundians to Gaul, of the Ostrogoths, the Heruli, and, later, of the Longobardi, to Italy, Britain was also newly peopled by Germans. The Romans had been obliged to quit this island, never entirely subdued by them, in order to defend their empire from the irruptions of the barbarians, and the ancient inhabitants, the Britons in the south and the Scots in the north, were disputing its possession, when Hengist and Horsa, two Saxon leaders, landed with a considerable force on the coast, A.D. 450, in search of a settlement, for which purpose they had quitted their country, under oath never to return, as was customary in Germany, whenever the population became too numerous for the land. Being well received by Vortigern, the British king, they entered into an alliance with him against his enemies, the Scots, whom they speedily compelled to retreat to their mountains. They settled in the country, and Vortigern contracted a marriage with Rowena, the beautiful daughter of Hengist. Their friendship, however, was not of long duration. The Saxons, coveting sole possession of the land, treacherously murdered the Britons during a conference, with knives concealed for that purpose beneath their dresses. Fresh hordes continually arrived from Saxony, and Hengist became king of Kent, A.D. 455, the first Saxon kingdom founded in Britain, where, notwithstanding the obstinate opposition of the Britons and Scots, seven kingdoms were gradually founded. The Saxons, who were accompanied in their migrations by numbers of the Angli, received the general appellation of Anglo-Saxons, and the name of Britain was changed to that of Angelland or England. Some of the Britons took shelter in the mountains of Wales, and others, escaping to the coast of France, gave name to Brittany. The Britons, ennobled by misfortune, gathered strength in their fall, and the legends and poetry of that period celebrate their heroic deeds and wild chivalry, more particularly those of King Arthur and his knights. An incident, unimportant in itself, occasioned the introduction of Christianity into England. Two young Angli prisoners, who had been carried to Rome, were standing for sale in the market-place, and the Romans, attracted by their singular beauty, had collected around them, when Gregory the Great, then in a private station, chancing to pass, also stopped, and asked to what nation they belonged, and on being told that they were Angli, said, "They are not Angli, but Angeli, and we must endeavor that the praises of God be sung in their country."[1] Shortly after this incident, he was raised to the papal chair, and sent a number of missionaries to England, where the gospel was willingly received; and, as conviction, untainted by intrigue or violence, had alone induced conversion, the Anglo-Saxons became in consequence distinguished by their zeal and enthusiasm in the cause of religion, above any of the other German nations, and the most celebrated preachers of the gospel went from England to Scandinavia, Germany, and France. The seven kingdoms retained the division into (*Gauen*) districts, the only change in the constitution being the greater power assigned to the king and his adherents. In 825, Egbert, king of Kent, united these seven states into one kingdom, that of England, notwithstanding which, the people still retained their ancient liberties, the inviolability of their homes, the right of electing the aldermen (*Alter mann*, old man), their public administration of justice, and their Witenagemot, or popular assembly, presided over by the king, the origin of parliament; principles which have been to the present day preserved in the British constitution, the rock on which the strength and glory of England rest, while the internal and external decay of the power of Germany during past centuries may be justly attributed to the gradual extinction of her freedom.

Although recognizing a brother nation in that of Britain, we must, in pursuance of our plan, here take our leave of that great people, and confine ourselves solely to the history of Germany. Still it ought never to be forgotten, whenever the power and glory of England form the theme, that these proud islanders own a common origin with ourselves, and that the civil government of which they so justly boast sprang from the ancient free constitution of our fatherland.

---

[1] Hume.

PART VI

CHARLEMAGNE

XCVII. The Austrasian Mayors of the Palace

THE degenerate Merovingians, alike unworthy and incapable of ruling, weakened by family dissensions, by their effeminacy, and by the system of monkish education, gradually sank beneath the sway of the mayors of the palace, who, as the hereditary representatives of the vassals of the crown, from whose number they had originally been chosen, and whose interests they consequently forwarded, found means to usurp the control of the state in time of peace as well as of war, and, by craftily surrounding the kings with the pomp and external show of the power they wielded in their stead, by freeing them from the burden of government, and by favoring their love of idleness and pleasure, rendered themselves ever necessary to and generally beloved by their nominal sovereigns. Forbearing to place the crown on their own heads, from a fear of becoming obnoxious to the majority of the people, and of the security of their position being endangered by the vassals, their jealous adherents, whom such a step would inevitably change into ambitious rivals, it was not until the mayoralty had been gradually and firmly established, by dint of good fortune and of great talent, as a hereditary dignity, that they ventured by slow and sure means to prepare for its seizure. By countenancing the disputes for the succession to the throne, and the murderous and treacherous propensities of the Merovingians, whom they corrupted and weakened from their early childhood, both mentally and physically, by indulgence and religious superstitions, they

COLOGNE

succeeded in rendering them contemptible to their subjects, while they removed every suspicion of the existence of their ambitious projects by their apparent submission to their puppet sovereigns, and gained the hearts of the nation by flattering the vassals, by their impartial administration of justice, by their warlike deeds, the glory of which redounded to the honor of France, by their extension of the limits of the state, and by their promotion of the public weal.

The supremacy of the Austrasians was closely bound up with that of the mayors; both rising at the same time, and mutually assisting each other. The true-born German Rhenish Franks, Thuringians, Alemanni, and Bavarians, with whom the Burgundians at first coalesced, presented a vivid contrast, under the general denomination of Austrasians, to the more Romanized Neustrians, who consisted of the West Franks, Romans, Goths, Basques, and Bretons. The Austrasians, gifted with all the energy of the genuine German character, and endowed with the valor and strength of their ancestors, whose customs and language they faithfully retained, despised and gradually became estranged from the Neustrians on account of their weakness, licentiousness, and treachery, and as the difference between their character and language became more marked, a reciprocal and bitter hatred arose between them. The Austrasians, happily governed by able monarchs, covered themselves with glory and increased their skill in warfare in their contests with the other nations of Germany. It was also their mayors of the palace who seized the supreme authority, which they alone held through the favor of their countrymen.

XCVIII. *Pipin von Landen*

In 622, Chlotar the Second made his son, Dagobert, king of Austrasia, and the brave Pipin von Landen, the first of the vassals who had rebelled against Queen Brunehilda, became his mayor of the palace. Pipin, whose family came from the Netherlands, was the founder of the powerful race of subsequent mayors, which two centuries later mounted the imperial throne of Germany, and assumed the name of Carlovingian, from Charlemagne, his most illustrious descendant. Chlotar was still alive when a war broke out between Dagobert and the Saxons, whose duke, Bertoald, is said to have wounded him in battle in the head, upon which he sent one of his blood-stained locks to his father, who instantly marched into Saxony and took a most fearful vengeance. Duke Bertoald fell in battle, and every prisoner who was taller than the length of Chlotar's sword was put to death. Peace was at length concluded on condition of their paying a tribute of five hundred stallions. The Saxons were also much disturbed by the Normans. Sifrit, the Saxon duke, while solemnizing his marriage with Giritta, a beautiful Dane, was suddenly attacked and slain, and the bride carried off by the pirate Haldan, a Swedish sea-king.

On the death of Chlotar, Dagobert became king of the whole of France, A.D. 628. The wound he had received in the Saxon war had disgusted him with warfare, and he lived in voluptuous and splendid indolence at Paris, surrounded by his three queens and numerous concubines; a mode of life he attempted to palliate by alleging the example of King Solomon, and by lavishing wealth and favors on the clergy. Among the numerous churches built by this king, that of St. Denis, whom he elected as the patron saint of his kingdom, is most remarkable. The incessant pilgrimages to the shrine of St. Denis soon attracted commerce, and a large market, the chief emporium of Europe, was erected in its vicinity. About this time, Samo, a Frankish merchant, who had gained great popularity among the Slavian Wendi, was elected their king, and succeeding in uniting them beneath his rule, repulsed the Avari. Some Frankish merchants happening to be killed while passing through his territory, Dagobert seized that occurrence as a pretext for attacking the new Slavian kingdom, and declared war against him; but Samo offering a brave and determined resistance, and defeating the Franks in a great battle, near

Wodgatisburg, which lasted three days, gained so much renown that the Slavian Sorbi and their king, Dorwan, voluntarily submitted to him, A.D. 630. Pipin, who, until now, had not taken part in the contest, proffered his services in this moment of necessity, and wisely releasing the Saxons from their tribute, besides yielding to the request of the Thuringians, to place Radulf, their fellow countryman and a pagan, at their head, united the heathen and Christian Germans in a national war against the Slavi, in which he was victorious. Samo's kingdom fell as rapidly as it had been raised, and the Slavi were henceforward necessitated to seek assistance from the Germans against the Avari.

Dagobert died, A.D. 638, and the kingdom was again divided among his sons; Sigebert the Third reigning over Austrasia, and Chlodwig the Second over Neustria. On the death of Pipin, A.D. 639, who during these changes had retained his mayoralty in Austrasia, his son, Grimoald, was removed from his office (the influence possessed by his family having already alarmed the jealousy of the king), and Otto was created mayor in his stead; upon this, the old party of Pipin, and the dukes, Radulf of Thuringia and Fara of Bavaria, asserted their independence, and Otto, marching against them with Sigebert, slew Fara, but, being compelled by Radulf to retreat, lost his ascendency over the vassals, and Grimoald was recalled. No sooner was Sigebert dead than Grimoald, regardless of the warnings of an aged monk, ventured to place his son Childebert on the throne; but it was still too early; the mutual jealousies of the Merovingians and Carlovingians still presented too many advantages to the clergy and the vassals, and Grimoald fell, with his unfortunate son, beneath the poniards of the rivals his ambition had evoked.

XCIX. *Pipin von Heristal*

DAGOBERT the Second, the son of Sigebert, had been confined by Grimoald in an Irish monastery, where he was allowed to remain; the clergy and the vassals agreeing to reunite the whole of France under Chlodwig the Second, who had been driven out of his senses by remorse for having broken off the arm of St. Dionysius, in order to carry it about with him as a relic; an action he was afterward induced to regard as a deadly sin. Nanthilda, his mother, who governed in his name under the direction of Floachat, the mayor of the palace, swore to maintain all the clergy and the vassals (who were already powerful enough to carry on their machinations openly and in defiance of the people) in their dignities and lands during her lifetime. The death of Chlodwig, A.D. 656, occasioned fresh disturbances, the kingdom being again divided among his sons. Chlotar the Second was placed on the throne of Neustria, where Ebroin, the mayor of the place, afterward raised himself to great power. Chlotar died early. Childerich, who became king of Austrasia, infringed the liberties of the people by causing a freeman, of the name of Badillo, to be whipped, and was murdered by his exasperated subjects, A.D. 673. Theodorich the Third, who had been destined for the cloister, inherited his brothers' kingdoms, over which Ebroin ruled in his name. The Austrasians rebelled against him, and drawing Dagobert the Second from his seclusion, attempted to place him on the throne, to which two Merovingians, both of whom were monks, disputed the succession. Ebroin was at first unsuccessful, but escaping from a monastery in which he had been imprisoned, was again victorious, and caused Dagobert to be put to death. Pipin von Heristal, the grandson of one of the daughters of Pipin von Landen, now placed himself at the head of the Austrasians, and Ebroin was defeated and killed. He was succeeded in the mayoralty by the brave Berchar, who had in his camp Theodorich, the legitimate sovereign, and the only remaining descendant of the house of Merowig, against whom Pipin and the Austrasians were arrayed in open rebellion, in which they were countenanced by the people, who, weary of intestine feuds, and indifferent to legitimacy, were inclined to side with the party that gave proof of greater bravery and capacity, which explains the remarkable battle of Testri, in which victory sided with the Carlovingians, A.D. 687. Pipin won this battle by stratagem. Setting fire to his own camp, he suddenly fell upon the Neustrians, who had hastened to pillage it under the impression of his having retired, and put them so completely to rout that no further opposition was raised. Although universally recognized as the only man capable of reforming the state, he merely compelled Theodorich to acknowledge him as mayor of the whole of France, and, warned by the fate of Grimoald and Ebroin, permitted him to retain the shadow of royalty while he held the substance. Dating from this period, the Merovingians no longer intermeddled with the government. The monarch, a mere cipher, shut up in his palace, contented himself with frivolous amusements, and showed himself occasionally to the people on the Marzfeld, where, sumptuously attired and wearing his long golden hair, he graciously received the gifts of his subjects, or nodded approbation to the transactions conducted by the mayor of the palace. Pipin survived two Merovingian kings, the successors of Theodorich, whose death did not lessen his power. His first care was the regulation of the interior economy of the state, and he again regulated the Marzfelder, or annual general state assemblies, which had been for some time neglected or irregularly held, and in which the ancient democracy (the freemen) was now completely overruled by the new aristocracy formed by the clergy and the vassals. The piety of the Bavarian Plectrudis, the wife of Pipin, secured to him the favor of the church. The period had also now arrived for confirming the external security of the state. The Franks, rendered powerful by their union, no longer deigned to tolerate the insolence of their neighbors and that of the rebellious tribes, and the consequent insurrections of the Basques, Goths, and Bretons in France were easily quelled by Pipin. The war on the frontier of Austrasia proved more difficult; particularly that carried on in Friesland against Rathod, the pagan king, who was vainly besieged in his impregnable peninsulas and islands, the capital of which was Heligoland, at that time a large island, now reduced by the encroaching waves to a sea-girt rock. At the close of the sixth century, St. Faro and the two Ewalds, and in the seventh century, Suibert, vainly endeavored to convert the Saxons. The Thuringians also obstinately resisted the introduction of Christianity by the Franks. Hetan, the son of Radulf, had married St. Bilihilda, but his son, Gozbert, was induced to apostatize by Gailana, his brother's widow, whom by the ecclesiastical law he was prohibited to marry. This circumstance occasioned the martyrdom of St. Kilian, who was then preaching in Thuringia. An insurrection, secretly incited by Pipin, broke out against Gozbert, who was killed and his whole race exterminated.

Bavaria had been Christianized by Regintrudis, the Frankish wife of the duke, Theodo, and by the saints, Rupert and Emmeram, the former of whom destroyed the heathen altars at Altötting, where the seven deities or planets were worshiped, and founded the celebrated bishopric of Salzburg. At first the wild mountaineers would not listen to him, and said that the God of the Christians was poor, or he would not let his worshipers suffer so much from want, and jealous, as he would not tolerate any other god besides himself; but they speedily altered their opinion when they saw the mines and salt-works progressing under the direction of the saint. It is related of St. Emmeram, who founded the bishopric of Ratisbon, that, being accused by Uta, the daughter of Theodo, as her seducer, in order to save the life of the real criminal, he meekly suffered the punishment from motives of Christian charity, and that his innocence was proved by a miracle after his death.

To these legendary times belong St. Ottilia and St. Goar; the former of whom was the daughter of Eticho, count of Alsace, who, being born blind, received sight at her baptism, and lived as a saint on the mountain near Strassburg, called after her, the Ottilienberg. St. Goar, toward the close of the sixth century, built a hut beneath the frightful rocks of the Lurlei, in the narrowest part of the Rhine, in order to save the shipwrecked, and to feed the starving wanderer.[1] Pipin's eventful life closed in 714, and in the same year his son, Grimoald, was murdered in a church at Liege, at the instigation of some of the jealous nobles.

C. *Charles Martell*

THE deaths of Pipin and of Grimoald occasioned fresh confusion in France. Plectrudis, the widow of Pipin, who had found means to usurp the chief authority, being anxious to retain the mayoralty for her grandson, Theudoald, the son of Grimoald, kept Charles, a natural son of Pipin, in prison, fearing lest he might prove a dangerous opponent to her designs. The Neustrians, who had unwillingly brooked the authority of Pipin, now seized the favorable moment.

Theodorich the Third was succeeded by Chlodwig the Third, Childebert, and Dagobert the Third, A.D. 715, who was succeeded by Chilperich the Second in Neustria, where the nobles elected, in his name, Raganfried, as their mayor, and instantly attacked Austrasia. The youthful Theudoald was defeated, and shortly afterward died; and the Neustrians, the better to secure their victory, entered into an alliance with Rathod of Friesland. The harassed Austrasians now bethought themselves of the imprisoned Charles, who was no sooner set at liberty than he marched at their head against the Frisii, but owing to the numerical insufficiency of his troops suffered a defeat, A.D. 716. The winter was spent by him in inspiriting the Austrasians, and in collecting a fresh and powerful army, with which in the ensuing spring he defeated the Neustrians at Cambray, by mak-

---

[1] The little town of St. Goar retained, in memory of the hospitality of this saint, even to our times, the custom of placing a brass necklace around the neck of the passing stranger, with the inquiry "whether he would be baptized with water or with wine?" If with water, he was well besprinkled; if with wine, he was offered a full golden goblet, which he emptied to the health of the emperor, and in return placed his alms in the poor-box.

ing use of a curious stratagem. A single Austrasian rushing into the enemy's camp, ran straight through it calling them to arms, and while the astonished Neustrians were engaged in running after him, Charles fell unexpectedly on their rear. After the battle he hastened to Cologne, where, after depriving his proud stepmother of his father's treasure, he sent her back to Bavaria, her native country. Having secured the country to the rear, he now returned to Neustria, where he set Chlotar the Fourth, a descendant of a side-branch of the Merovingian family, up as king. Chilperich fled to Eudo, duke of Aquitania, whose Basques and Goths, stimulated by their ancient and hereditary enmity, marched in great numbers against the Franks, A.D. 719, but, being completely beaten at Soissons, concluded peace with Charles, to whom Eudo delivered Chilperich, whose life speedily drew to its close when in the power of his victor. Charles, nevertheless, remained true to the policy of his family, and deprived the jealous nobles of every pretext for revolt, by placing Theodorich the Fourth, a son of Dagobert the Third, on the throne. Thus were the hapless Merovingians raised and deposed at will.—The Bavarians revolted against Charles, who was again victorious, and married the beautiful Sunichilda, the daughter of Grimoald, their duke, who, being killed by his own people, he made her brother, Huebert, duke. Freising was at this period founded by St. Corbinian.

An immense army of the fanatical and hitherto invincible Moors, led by the brave Abderrahman, after destroying the Visigothic kingdom in Spain, poured across the Pyrenees into France; a far more dangerous foe than Etzel and his Huns, who, merely greedy of conquest, sought not to enslave minds, like the enthusiastic children of the South, who, the sword in one hand, the Koran in the other, Allah and Mahomet their war-cry, their aim the reduction of Europe and the extirpation of Christianity, marched beneath the Crescent, the standard of their prophet, against the hardy sons of the North.

The frontiers of Spain were, at that time, guarded by

Eudo, duke of Aquitania, who had long aspired to independence. Neustria and Austrasia were at feud. France, torn by internal dissensions, seemed on the point of sharing the fate of Spain, when the destruction with which Europe and Christianity were threatened was warded off by the intrepid Charles. Eudo, who had at first hoped to make use of the Moors in forwarding his designs against him, had given his daughter in marriage to Munuz, one of their princes. Abderrahman, struck with her beauty, indignantly asked Munuz, "how he had presumed to keep such a treasure for himself, instead of sending her to the caliph," struck off his head for having ventured to profane such beauty, and sent the noble lady to the caliph's harem at Damascus. Eudo attempted to revenge this insult, but was defeated on the Garonne, and compelled to fly for protection to Charles, beneath whose standard the whole arrier-ban of Austrasia, the Netherlands, the Rhine, Thuringia, Swabia, and Bavaria had assembled, while Luitprand, at the head of his Lombards, crossed the Alps to aid in the defense of endangered Christendom. A battle took place between Tours and Poitiers, A.D. 732, in which the true-born German Austrasians, the flower of the North, who by their weight bore down the impetuous Moors, distinguished themselves by their unyielding valor. Abderrahman was slain, and 375,000 of his followers were left on the field. Europe was saved, and the Crescent driven beyond the Pyrenees. Charles, who at the head of his Austrasians had slain numbers of the enemy, striking them on the head like an iron hammer, was henceforward revered as the hero and defender of Christianity, and received the surname of Martell, or hammer, in memory of his prowess. Six years after this event the ruinous contest was recommenced by the jealous Neustrians. Gothic Provence attempted to assert its independence under Maurontius, who called the Arabs to his aid against Martell, by whom their power was again, and so completely, crushed at Narbonne, A.D. 738, that they never again ventured across the fatal Pyrenees, and Charles secured that frontier by incorporating the remaining Visigoths into his kingdom. While he was thus engaged in the South, the heathen Frisii and Saxons invaded the northern frontier, but were defeated, and Rathod was at length reduced to submission and compelled to embrace Christianity. Not long before this event, he had caused St. Wigbert to be put to death for having slaughtered some sacred oxen. Charles Martell now sent to him St. Wolfram, by whom he was at length persuaded to undergo the ceremony of baptism. A bath was accordingly prepared, and Rathod, plunging one foot into the water, was about to immerse his whole body, when, turning to the saint, he inquired whether his ancestors were in heaven, and being answered, "No, in hell, for they were heathens," withdrew his foot and declared that he preferred remaining with them. It is related of another of the Frisii that he had himself several times baptized for the sake of the gift bestowed, on the occasion, by the clergy on the convert. Religion must be ever and unavoidably desecrated when used as a political engine. Poppo, the successor of Rathod, fell opposing the Christians; all attempts to extirpate paganism in Friesland proved, nevertheless, unavailing.

Charles Martell, although the savior of Christendom, was by no means remarkable for piety. The contempt to which his illegitimate birth had subjected him during his youth, ever inclined him, as if from a spirit of defiance, to side with bastards and younger sons, against rightful heirs and elder brothers. He formed them into a bodyguard, made them his boon companions, and enriched them not only with temporal feofs, but also with gifts of bishoprics and abbeys. Before the commencement of the great war with the Moors, he had forced the clergy, under pain of forfeiting their possessions, to appear in person in the field (in those times every man without distinction of rank or profession was bound to carry arms), so that the clergy, enrolled in his service, were already habituated to the license of a camp, and to the pleasures of the chase. The feudal vassals and the clergy consequently intermingled and formed one body. To these rough times belongs the touching legend of St. Genoveva of Brabant, the wife of Graf Siegfried, the lord of Andernach, who, when marching against the invading Moors, intrusted her to the care of Golo, his favorite. Inflamed by her beauty, and enraged at the failure of his attempts upon her virtue, Golo accused her of infidelity, and she was condemned to death. The executioners, moved to compassion, spared her life and that of her child, and she lived for a long time concealed in a forest, in nakedness and solitude. The child was suckled by a doe, and her life was miraculously sustained, until Siegfried, one day, when following the chase, discovered her in her grotto, and her innocence was proved. She is still honored as a saint at Andernach.

CI. *Pipin the Little*

CHARLES MARTELL died in 741, leaving two sons, Carlmann and Pipin, and a daughter, Chiltruda, by his first wife; and by his second, the Bavarian Sunichilda, a son named Grippo, who was deprived of his share in the inheritance and imprisoned by his elder brothers. Sunichilda took refuge in a convent, and Chiltruda, influenced by affection for her stepmother, escaped from her brothers to Bavaria, where she married Odilo, the duke of that country, who, with Hunoald of Aquitania, the Alemanni under Theudewald, and the Saxons under Theodorich, simultaneously attacked the brave sons of Martell. They were defeated both collectively and separately, Hunoald in 742, Odilo on the Lech, by the Franks, who crossed the river and attacked him during the night, in 743, the Saxons in 745, and the Alemanni in 746. Their duke, Theudewald, and many other prisoners of note were executed by order of Carlmann, who passed sentence upon them at Cannstadt, but was subsequently haunted by such deep remorse for his cruelty that, withdrawing to a monastery, he resigned the whole authority to his younger brother, Pipin, surnamed the Little, on account of the shortness of his stature. His strength was so prodigious that on one occasion he cut off a lion's head with a single stroke of his sword. His first act, on the attainment of undivided power, was the liberation of Grippo, who, taking refuge among the Saxons and Frisii, induced them to take up arms against his brother. Finding himself unable to keep the field, he sought the protection of Thassilo, the son of Odilo, who was then reigning in Bavaria, under the tutelage of his mother, Chiltruda. Lanfried, duke of Alemannia, and Suitzo, another powerful Alemannian, lent him their aid, but they were all defeated and taken prisoners by Pipin, who again pardoned his brother. Grippo, discontented and restless, fled anew to Waisar, the son of Hunoald, of Aquitania, who refused to receive him, and he attempted to escape into Lombardy, but was intercepted in the Alps by Frederick, the Graf of the French frontier, and striving to force his way, fell, after a desperate struggle, with the whole of his followers, A.D. 750. Pipin was, at the time of this occurrence, engaged in a second campaign against the Saxons, on whom he again imposed an annual tribute of three hundred horses.

No less prudent in his policy than fortunate in the field, Pipin now saw that the time had at length arrived for putting the long-cherished projects of his ancestors into execution. Four generations of the Merovingians, degraded by sloth, despised, neglected, and almost forgotten, had passed away, while the Carlovingians possessed the real authority and the popular esteem, and it became daily more evident which of the two families was the more fitted for the throne. Pipin, whose ancestors had consolidated their power by making common cause with the vassals, now secured success by gaining over the pope and the clergy. The pope, Zacharias, at that time hard pressed by Aistulf, king of Lombardy, willingly countenanced plans that favored his own interest, while Pipin, in order the more deeply to impress upon him the value of his support, designedly delayed his much wished-for assistance, and, sending an embassador to Rome, proposed this question to the pontiff, "Whether he was king who sat carelessly at home, or he who bore the burden of government?" The pope instantly replied, "that the latter alone merited the crown." Upon this, Pipin called a general state assembly at Soissons, and the whole nation assenting to the pope's verdict, Childerich, the last of the Merovingians, was torn from the throne of his fathers, consigned, with shaven head, to the cloister, and Pipin was unanimously proclaimed king. St. Bonifacius placed the crown on his head, and anointed him, according to ancient custom, like his predecessor Chlodwig, with the sacred oil. At the same time the general state assembly, held in March, was transferred to May, A.D. 752, a change by which Bonifacius hoped to obliterate every remembrance of paganism, and Pipin, that of the Merovingians.

After the death of Zacharias, Pipin still retarded the promised aid against the Lombards, in order to render Stephen, the new pontiff, as tractable as his predecessor. The pope at length, urged by necessity, crossed the Alps in person, and prostrating himself at the feet of the French monarch, humbly solicited his protection. Pipin, satisfied with this act of humility, marched, accompanied by the pope, into Italy, and forced Aistulf to accept the most disgraceful terms of peace, A.D. 754. The Lombards, however, fully alive to the danger with which they were threatened by the increasing power of the pope, and by his alliance with France, resolved to struggle to the last, and Aistulf, breaking the treaty, again besieged Rome. Pipin again marched to the relief of the city, A.D. 756, and the Lombards, after suffering a complete defeat, were reduced to submission. Aistulf was killed by the falling of his horse. Desiderius, a court official, became king of Lombardy through French influence. His son Adelgis married a French princess, and his daughter Desiderata was wedded to the youthful Charles, afterward Charlemagne. Pipin, anxious to erect a strong power, in opposition to that of the Lombards, in Italy itself, gave the then existing exarchate or great territory of Ravenna and Rome in fief to the pope, who, in return, named him patrician and guardian of Rome.

Thus commenced the temporal power of the pope, whose spiritual authority was, at the same time, subservient to that of the monarch; an alliance whose influence could not be long resisted by any of the states independent of the empire, or by any power still possessed by the people. Pipin was also successful in his wars against the Saxons, whom he again rendered tributary, and in that undertaken against Waisar, duke of Aquitania, whom he pursued so long and unremittingly in the Pyrenees that his subjects, the Basques, at length put him to death for the sake of peace. Thassilo, the youthful duke of Bavaria, impatient of the yoke imposed by Pipin, refused to render feudal service in the field against Waisar; a conduct which Pipin prudently overlooked. Pipin died, shortly afterward, in 768.

CII. *St. Bonifacius*

THE co-operative policy of the Frankish rulers and the Roman bishops laid the foundation to what may be termed the body of the church, while her spirituality was solely fostered by the independent, free, and pure zeal of the Anglo-Saxon and Irish monks. In the British isles, far beyond the influence of the Roman hierarchy and of the feudal aristocracy of France, Christianity had taken a democratic form, and, unpolluted by the new spirit of political conquest and of feudal tyranny, had blended with the ancient spirit of popular freedom. Here were no imperious and covetous feudal churchmen, too fully occupied with the pastime of the chase, with war and politics, to be interested in the promulgation of the gospel, but humble, pious teachers of brotherly love, who, instead of shutting themselves within their abbey walls, instead of accumulating wealth or seeking to extend their temporal power, went forth, like the first apostles, to guide their erring brethren, and to enlighten the yet unconverted heathen, to whom, far from imposing

Christianity upon them with the bigoted zeal of conquering despots, they preached the doctrine of eternal peace, compelling no one to embrace the mild religion of Jesus, but gently persuading them by precept and example of its truth and beauty. The first Anglo-Saxon apostles strongly reprobated the political corruption of the Frankish church, and the arrogant pretensions of the pope, against which St. Columban wrote, and consequently fell into disgrace with the Frankish court. The mayors of the palace, however, perceived at length that the pious, disinterested Anglo-Saxons were calculated, far better than the Franks, to succeed in converting the heathen inhabitants of eastern Germany, on account of their enthusiastic zeal and superior religious knowledge, added to the circumstance of their being, in their character of foreigners, less obnoxious to the Frisii, Saxons, Thuringians, Alemanni, and Bavarians, who regarded the Franks in the light of oppressors and deceivers; they therefore countenanced the foreign monks, and repeatedly invited them into the country.

During the seventh century, St. Fridolin founded the monastery of Seckingen on the Upper Rhine;[1] St. Columban destroyed the pagan images at Bregenz on the Bodensee; St. Gallus founded a hermitage, afterward the celebrated monastery of St. Gall, in the depths of the forests, where he was served by a bear; St. Amandus destroyed the image of Odin at Ghent; St. Eligius converted the Saxon prisoners; the saints, Wigbert, Wolfram, Willebrand (the first bishop of Utrecht, A.D. 799), preached among the Frisii; the saints, Suidbert and Sturmio (a Bavarian by birth, and first abbot of the great monastery of Fulda), among the Hessians; St. Magnoald founded Füssen in Swabia; St. Theodore, Kempten; St. Offo, Offonszell; St. Landolin (who, for cutting down a sacred fir tree and forming a cross out of it, was murdered by the heathen Alemanni), Ettenheimmünster;

---

[1] The people of Glarus made pilgrimages and paid contributions to it at an early period, and the arms of that canton still retain the figure of Fridolin, in the dress of a wandering hermit.

and St. Pirmin, Reichenau. Besides these, in Thuringian East Franconia and in Bavaria, St. Kilian suffered martyrdom at Würzburg; St. Sebaldus (according to tradition, a Danish prince who fled on his wedding night and abandoned earthly for heavenly love), died at Nüremberg; St. Corbinian founded Freising; St. Emmeram, Ratisbon; and St. Rupert, Salzburg. The foundation of the celebrated monasteries in Alsace, Altaich, Benedictbeuren, Tegernsee, Prüm, and Lorsch also date during the eighth century.

Winfried, an Anglo-Saxon, better known by his monkish surname of St. Bonifacius, distinguished himself above all these apostles, by his energy, zeal, and success. Zealously imagining that the temporal and spiritual rule of the church ought to be universal, and that the power of the Romish-Frankish church might consistently blend with the Christian zeal and brotherly love of the Anglo-Saxon monks, he no longer contented himself, like his predecessors, with converting the heathen and with founding hermitages in the forest solitudes, but aiming at the reformation of the existing Frankish church, intermeddled with the proceedings of the bishops and with the policy of the state. Pipin, who had just concluded his alliance with the pope, A.D. 755, with the intention of placing the Carlovingian dynasty on the throne of Merowig, found a strenuous supporter in Bonifacius, the enemy of schism under whatever form. The unity of the kingdom of God upon earth, the fraternization of all mankind gathered beneath the care of one shepherd, the pope, Christ's vicar upon earth, was his visionary scheme, and, in his enthusiasm, entirely overlooking the diversity of nations and languages, he sought to obviate that difficulty by rendering the Latin tongue the only one authorized by the church. This new and unnatural tyranny met with vehement opposition. Virgilius, bishop of Salzburg, the most enlightened man of the age, who had gained great and merited fame by the peaceable conversion of the Slavi, in the mountains of Carinthia and Carniola, and who on account of his scientific and astronomical knowledge was denounced as a sorcerer [1] by the pope and his confederate, Bonifacius, A.D. 742, inquired mockingly of the latter, "whether the senseless form made use of in baptism by a German priest ignorant of the Latin tongue, 'Baptizo te in nomine Patria et Filia et Spiritus Sancti,' was efficacious?" and was answered, "Yes, because faith ought to be blind!" In Thuringia, Dortwin, Berthar, Tanbrecht, and Hunred, and in Bavaria, Ariowulf, Adelbert, and Clemens, distinguished themselves in opposition to Bonifacius, who condemned them as heretics, and, supported by Pipin and the pope, succeeded in his hierarchical schemes.

Bonifacius, moreover, zealously applied himself to the conversion of the heathen, which was formally organized by a synod, held at Lestines, A.D. 742, and a form of abjuration [2] was drawn up, by which the German pagan renounced his former religion and the specified superstitious customs. He went personally among the heathen, preaching and converting with the energy and zeal that rendered him so famous. He it was who cut down the great Donnereiche (oak of thunder) at Geismar, in Hesse. Zealously upholding the institutions of his predecessors, he sent fresh preachers to the flocks abandoned by their pastors. With the intent of especially promoting the conversion of the women, he sent for pious nuns from England; among others, St. Thecla, the foundress of Kitzingen; St. Lioba, that of Bischofsheim; and St. Walpurgis, that of Heidenheim. The bishoprics of Wurzburg, Freising, Eichstadt, Salzburg, and Ratisbon, were organized under his direction, he being, as archbishop of Mayence, the head of the German church. In his seventieth year, being anxious to convert the pagans of Friesland, he visited that country, where the Frisii, who viewed him as a deceitful Frank, put him to death, A.D. 755.

---

[1] The fame of Virgilius the sorcerer spread into Lombardy, and at a later period, the Italians, ignorant of the existence of a bishop of Salzburg, made Virgil, the Roman poet, the hero of the legend.

[2] Ek forsacho diabole end allum diabol gelde end allum diaboles werkum end wordum, Thunaer ende Woden ende Saxnote, end allum them unholdum, the hira genotas sint.

CIII. Charlemagne

PIPIN left two sons, Carloman and Charles, the former of whom inherited Neustria, the latter Austrasia. Charles had already distinguished himself in the last wars of Pipin, and the legends record the most extraordinary proofs of his wonderful strength of mind and body when still a child. Pipin, unwilling to allow the pope the supremacy in Italy, upheld the now powerless Lombards, and gave the daughter of Desiderius in marriage to Charles, in defiance of the anger of Pope Stephen, who had said, "That the noble Frank should not defile himself with the unclean Lombard." Charles, not finding Desiderata to his taste, divorced her. His brother Carloman being accidentally killed, he seized Neustria, and Gilberga, the widow of Carloman, and her two sons sought refuge at the court of Desiderius, who was highly offended at the treatment of his daughter. By this act of treachery to his nephews, Charles became in 771 master of the whole of France. Urged by uncontrollable ambition, he burst through every barrier that opposed his entrance into the great and brilliant course he was destined to run; his fame, like the sun at early morn, obscured by rolling clouds, shone forth again with undimmed luster. His energetic and creative intellect, ever actively and simultaneously employed in conducting his wars abroad and in improving the internal condition of his empire, changed, during the forty-three years of his reign, the aspect of affairs, not only throughout Germany, but throughout the whole of Europe, and laid the foundation, as will be seen in the course of this history, to a new and important era. With him the history of ancient Germany closes. All the ancient free German states and kingdoms were united within the limits of his immense empire, whose erection impressed a new character on the different nations of Germany. Antiquity sank into oblivion, and the middle age commenced with the grand and brilliant reign of Charlemagne, by which, however, we must not allow ourselves to be blinded to the fault he committed in failing to secure the national freedom as well as the external grandeur of Germany. True to his father's policy, he rooted the imperial power in the feudal system, and increased the privileges of the nobility and clergy at the expense of those of the people. His policy might possibly have taken an opposite bias had he met with firm support from the people, but at that period the nations of Germany were still at enmity with each other; the Goths, Lombards, Alemanni, Bavarians, and Thuringians, hated the French as their tyrants, and the pagan Saxons were struggling, as if for life, against French dominion and the imposition of Christianity. The unity of the empire could therefore only be achieved in despite of the people, and Charles found his sole support in the vassals, attracted by his victories and largesses, and in the bishops and monks, who by representing the unity of the empire, to the refractory nations, as a necessary consequence of the unity of the church, and as one of the intentions of the Christian religion, rendered themselves indispensable. Had the people been more advanced in knowledge, had they been able to comprehend the idea of unity, Charles probably would not have given so great a preponderance to the vassal lords and clergy, a preponderance which was only too soon and too severely felt by his successors on the imperial throne. Without having recourse to violent measures, he could never have succeeded in uniting the nations of Germany, in guaranteeing the empire from the attacks of its foreign foes, the Moors, Slavi, Norsemen, Avari, and Hungarians, or in extirpating the barbarous customs of heathen antiquity. The different German nations, at feud with one another, partly pagan, partly Christian, would in course of time have exterminated each other, while the Hungarians, aided by the pagan Saxons, would probably have renewed the savage times of Attila. The unity of the empire was a boon required by the exigency of the times, and that by means of it Charlemagne preserved Christendom from the encroachments of paganism at that time still prevailing in the East, and from those of Mohammedanism equally powerful in the South, besides refining the barbarous manners of the age by the introduction of the arts of civilization and of scholastic learning, forms his great and all-sufficing exculpation. The Anglo-Saxons in England certainly attained to a considerable degree of cultivation without sacrificing their freedom, but, inclosed within the narrow limits of their fortunate island, they had fewer difficulties to encounter than Charles, who, placed in the midst of the broad continent, was surrounded by open enemies and doubtful friends.

CIV. *Fall of the Kingdom of Lombardy*

THE attempt made by Desiderius to force the pope to anoint the two sons of Carloman kings of France, served as a pretext for Charles to cross the Alps and to annex the whole of Italy to the empire. He accordingly crossed by Mount Cenis, and his uncle, Bernard, by Mons Jovis, which, from this circumstance, received the name of the great St. Bernard; Desiderius, meanwhile, closely guarded the Alpine passes, and checked the advance of the invading army: at length a secret path that led into Lombardy was discovered to Charles by a traitor, who, it is recorded, was permitted, in reward, to sound a horn, and to each passer-by who replied in the affirmative to his demand of whether he had heard it, to give a box on the ear, in sign of vassalage. The mountain passes were no sooner forced than opposition ceased. Charlemagne's presence insured victory. The common herd, awed by the greatness of his fame, were rendered powerless, before the contest commenced, by their belief in his invincible prowess, which worked more wonders in favor of his cause than that prowess itself. The Lombards trembled at the mere aspect of the hero, whose achievements lay yet concealed within the bosom of futurity. Numbers deserted to the Franks, and Desiderius, shut up in Pavia, his capital, was driven by famine to capitulate, after a siege of seven months' duration. An ancient chronicle relates that

Desiderius, when gazing from the battlements upon the French squadrons, in expectation of perceiving Charles as each advanced, and at length beholding him ride forward armed cap-à-pie, conspicuous by his stature amid the surrounding multitude, and mounted on an iron-clad charger, was struck with such amazement at his awful aspect that he mournfully exclaimed to those around him, "Let us descend and hide ourselves beneath the earth from the angry glance of such a powerful enemy," and forthwith yielded the city to his opponent, who, judging him unworthy of a throne he was unable to defend, secluded him in the monastery of Corvey. His son, Adalgis, a brave man worthy of a better fate, fled to Constantinople, and Charles placed the ancient iron crown of Lombardy himself on his own head. The people were permitted to retain their national privileges. The same year, A.D. 774, he visited the pope at Rome, confirmed him in the possession of the gifts of Pipin, received like him the title of patrician, and renewed the alliance that had already been formed by his father with the pontifical chair. Meanwhile the free-spirited Lombards revolted against the severe yoke imposed upon them, and Adalgis, returning, made another but fruitless attempt to regain his throne, A.D. 775. Paul Warnefried (Paulus Diaconus), the celebrated historian of Lombardy, labored zealously in his cause, and having on that account been sentenced to lose his eyes and hands, Charles indignantly exclaimed, "Where shall we again find hands able to record the events of history so beautifully as his?" A.D. 776.

Two subsequent insurrections in Lombardy, A.D. 786, excited by the dukes of Friuli and of Benevento, were successively quelled by Charles, who, although engaged in a winter campaign in Saxony, suddenly quitted that country and fell upon Radogund, duke of Friuli, in the high mountains at Tarvis, where he was celebrating the Easter festival. Aregis, duke of Benevento, Charles's brother-in-law (his wife, Amalberga, being daughter to Desiderius), was compelled to deliver up his sons as hostages. The only article in the treaty of peace that he insisted upon was, "that he should not be forced to see his hated relative." On his death Charles sent his son, Grimoald, back to his native country, and gave him the dukedom of Benevento to hold in fee. Grimoald opposed the Greeks in Lower Italy. The empire extended to the south as far as the island of Sardinia, which had been conquered by Graf Burkhard. Pipin, the son of Charlemagne, A.D. 807, was compelled to relinquish his attempts upon Venice, and the island city proudly maintained her liberty.

CV. *The Saxon Wars*

IN earlier times the Romans had incessantly attempted the subjugation of their free neighbors, the Germans, by whom their empire was threatened from without, while it was at the same time endangered within by the contrast between their free constitution and the despotism of the Roman government. The Franks, equally despotic with their ancient masters, were also ceaseless in their endeavors to crush the Saxons, who still retained their ancestral independence, and the breach was still further widened by the national hatred, which from time immemorial had been cherished between Frank and Saxon, and which in later times had been strengthened by difference of religion, the Frank in his proselyting zeal attempting to enforce the conversion of the Saxon to Christianity, while the Saxon, who naturally regarded the new religion as subversive of freedom, remained the more obstinately attached to that of his fathers. Continual feuds had deluged the banks of the Rhine with the blood of the contending nations under the Merovingians. A short peace took place under Dagobert, but the war was kindled afresh, and its extinction baffled the most strenuous exertions of Bonifacius. The physical strength, great endurance, and enthusiastic valor of the Saxons, who were inspirited by the love of their liberty, their country, and their religion, aided by the dissensions that convulsed France, had up to this period rendered the issue of their ancient struggle doubtful.

The Saxons, although often constrained by the warlike mayors of the palace to pay a dishonorable tribute, had never been more than temporarily subdued. Affairs bore this aspect on the accession of Charles, who speedily turned his chief attention to the subjection of his warlike neighbors, the first necessary step in the furtherance of his plans for the future protection of France against their aggressions, for the union of all the nations of Germany, for checking the progress of the Slavi in the East, and for the erection of one vast empire in the heart of Europe, whence civilization and Christianity were to radiate as from one bright center, and, calling the whole physical strength of his kingdom to the aid of his genius, undeterred by the obstinacy with which he was opposed, by the dread of obscuring his fame by the commission of monstrous acts of cruelty, by the numerous wars in which he was constantly engaged, or by his paternal concern for the internal welfare of the state, he was at length rewarded, in his old age, with success, after a murderous and unremitting war of two and thirty years, in which his perseverance, power, exalted genius, and noble aim cast into shade the heroic fortitude of the Saxons, who, worthy of their ancestral fame, valiantly struggled, during more than a quarter of a century, in defense of their ancient liberty and religion, and crowned their very fall with glory. Wittekind, duke of Westphalia, the brave Saxon leader, may not unfelicitously be compared with Armin. Animated by a kindred spirit, he fought on the same ground for a similar object and with equal glory. His followers, inspirited by his enthusiasm, were ever ready for fresh revolt, after each bloody defeat and each extorted treaty; success attended their attempts for freedom during the absence of Charles, whose return ever reimposed a yet more galling chain, until at length, humbled by the protracted struggle, they voluntarily submitted and embraced Christianity.

CVI. The Progress of the Saxon Wars

IN 772, Charles convoked a general state assembly at Worms, in which the war with Saxony was unanimously voted. Religion served as a pretext. The urbanity and eloquence of St. Lebuin, who had previously been commissioned to preach to the Saxons during their great national festival at Marklo, having proved ineffectual, fire and sword were the next means resorted to for their conversion. This decision had been purposely committed to the nation by Charles, who sought, by giving the war a national and religious character, to render it popular. At the head of the great arrier-ban of the French, Charles crossed the Rhine and marched victoriously as far as the Weser. His greatest achievement, during this campaign, was the capture of the Eresburg, where he destroyed the sacred column of Irmin.[1]

Charles's absence in Italy, necessitated by the revolt of Rotgaudus, the Lombard duke of Friuli, whom he reduced to obedience, was instantly turned to advantage by the Saxons, who broke into open insurrection, headed by Wittekind of Westphalia, the soul of the war, whose activity was emulated by that of Alboin, duke of Eastphalia, A.D. 773. A second invasion of Saxony ensued, and the triple alliance of the two Phalias and of Enger was successively defeated by Charles. The coasts alone remained unsubdued. No sooner, however, was his presence again required in Italy by a fresh revolt of the duke of Friuli, than Wittekind recommenced the struggle; a general levy took place, whole forests were

---

[1] An old rhythm is still extant in Westphalia, which, by some, is ascribed to the period of this invasion, by others, to the more ancient one of the wars of Armin against the Roman emperors.

>Hermen, sla dermen,
>Sla pipen, sla trummen.
>De kaiser will kummen
>Mit hamer und stangen,
>Will Hermen uphangen.

The Eresburg occupied the present site of Stadtbergen on the Diemel, in the district of Paderborn.

thrown down in order to form abatis throughout the country, and every man stood to arms. Charles reappeared, and all again yielded before him. He remained encamped in the heart of the country until a royal residence was erected at Paderborn, whither he summoned the vassals of the crown and the embassadors from foreign states, among whom appeared a number of Moorish princes from Spain, who had thrown off their allegiance to their mother-country, and came to implore the aid of the mighty sovereign of France. The Saxons also sent delegates to Paderborn, promised peace and submission, and resigned their Allods and their freedom to their conqueror. Wittekind alone, despising the favor of the monarch, fled to Denmark, where, protected by Siegfried, the pagan king, he awaited an opportunity to recommence the struggle for liberty; accordingly, Charles had no sooner led his arrier-ban across the Pyrenees in order to awe the Moors than Wittekind returned, and the Saxons, forgetful of their newly-imposed allegiance, again rebelled and laid the country waste up to the walls of Duits and Cologne, A.D. 778. Charles returned, and the following year directed his whole force against them. Two great battles took place on the Eller and in the Buchholz, in which the Saxons were worsted, and Charles, fixing himself in the country, erected numerous fortresses on the Elbe, in which he placed strong garrisons of the French, and endeavored at the same time to gain over the people, more especially the nobility, by kindness, affability, and promises. The hostages taken from the Saxons during his previous campaigns had been purposely educated in monasteries, and, on their return to their native country, they peaceably forwarded the work of conversion. Affairs seemed to prosper, and Charles deemed himself as securely master of Saxony as Varus had formerly done in the same country and under precisely similar circumstances. But he was equally deceived. Enforced subjection ever produces dissimulation, and the Saxon, still mindful of his ancient freedom, beheld with secret rage the fortresses he had been compelled to aid in erecting, and which he merely awaited an opportunity to destroy. Taught hypocrisy by necessity and injured pride, he lulled his conqueror to repose, in order to take a surer and more deadly aim. Whoever conscientiously embraced Christianity was secretly branded as a traitor, and destruction to the Frank was vowed in the silent depths of the forest, in the name of the ancient deities of Germany. The form of oath ran thus:

Hilli kroti Woudana ilp osk un osken Pana Uitikin ok Kelta of ten oiskena Karleui ten slaktenera. Ik tif ti in our un ton scapa un tat Rofe. Ik slacte ti all tranca up tinen iliken Artis beka.

Charles, far from suspecting the true state of affairs, again quitted Saxony, and, with perfect confidence, commissioned his generals, Geil and Adalgis, to strengthen the army under their command by an immense levy of Saxon troops destined for the invasion of the territory of the Slavi on the other side of the Elbe and Saal, who then threatened France. The Saxons obeyed the call with great alacrity, and soon outnumbered the French troops, who, in the commencement of the campaign, A.D. 782, while carelessly crossing the Sundel Mountain on the Weser (Hausberg between Minden and Rinteln), were unexpectedly attacked by their companions, by whom the slaughter in the Teutoburg forest was renewed—Geil and Adalgis, with the greater part of their troops, being left on the field.

When the news of this terrible catastrophe, by which his plans upon Slavonia and Saxony were at once rendered null, reached Charles, he vowed to wreak a fearful revenge on the rebels, and to regain by cruelty and severity the kingdom his mildness had lost. Crossing the Rhine, he laid waste the country by fire and sword, and exterminated all who refused to embrace Christianity. Thousands were driven into the rivers to be baptized or drowned. On the Eller at Verden 4,500 Saxons, taken in arms, were beheaded. Destruction marched in the van. Desolation, carnage and flames marked the path of the conqueror. Undismayed by the danger, the Saxons rose to a man in defense of their national liberties.

Every deed of cruelty was doubly repaid, and victory began to waver. At Detmold, Wittekind headed the enthusiastic patriots against Charles's superior forces, and a dreadful battle was fought, in which the victory remained undecided. In petty warfare, the Saxons proved invincible, and it was not until they again hazarded a general engagement on the Hase that Charles's superior tactics prevailed against them. When at length he was once more securely fixed in the interior of the country, prudence counseled milder measures, and while he still devastated the northern districts, his subjects in the Binnenland were treated with a gentleness which, seconded by the exhaustion consequent on their numerous defeats, at length induced a general submission. Wittekind and Alboin, the stanch defenders of their country's rights, with implicit confidence in the honor of their conqueror, came to Attigny in France, and were there voluntarily baptized, A.D. 785. According to the legendary account, Wittekind went, disguised as a beggar, into the church at Wolmirstadt (so called from Charles's once exclaiming, "Wohl mir!" Good luck to me! when victorious there over the Saxons), where a shining white child appeared to him in the host, and convinced him of the truth of Christianity.

CVII. *Termination of the Saxon Wars*

EVEN this peace proved but of short duration; and that nation must be justly deemed worthy of admiration which, after such experience in suffering, still retained sufficient courage and pride to persevere in the struggle for the preservation of their ancient liberties and honor, and to prefer misery, nay, annihilation, to the stain of subserviency. Charles, deeming the North submissive, turned his attention southward, and while he was engaged in forcing the powerful Avari to retreat into Hungary, and in preserving a communication between the Adriatic and the Danube, his fertile genius conceived the project of bringing the whole of southern and northern Germany into yet more direct communication, by cutting through the country lying between the Rednitz, whose waters flow through the Maine into the Rhine, and the Altmühl, which falls into the Danube. Had this canal been completed, a communication by water would have been opened throughout Germany, which must not only have greatly facilitated the internal traffic of the different provinces, but also have given a powerful impulse to general commerce, by opening a line of communication between the Black Sea and the Baltic. A canal 300 feet broad had already been carried some distance, when the work was destroyed by violent storms of rain, and the war with Saxony again breaking out caused it to be entirely abandoned; nor was it undertaken again until our times, a thousand years later. The Saxons, in the hope of receiving support from the Avari, suddenly rose in arms in every part of the country, but, hearing of Charles's approach at the head of a formidable army, and the Avari remaining quiet, they as suddenly disbanded, and Charles, on his arrival, finding the country tranquil and being unable to discover the authors of the revolt, contented himself with taking hostages from them, and with establishing his seat of government at Aix-la-Chapelle, A.D. 794. For the future, however, he kept a vigilant watch over their movements, and caused the country to be continually patrolled by his troops. The Nord-Albinger, northward of the Elbe (modern Holstein), alone obstinately refused to submit, and incessantly harassed the troops sent to inspect the country. Many thousand Saxons were torn from their homes and transplanted into Brabant and Flanders as well as to Sachsenhausen, now a suburb of Frankfort on the Maine. The remainder still defended themselves in their fastnesses on the coast, and again roused the anger of the emperor, by putting his embassadors to the Danish court to death, when passing through their country. Anxious to insure their complete subjection, Charles entered into alliance with the Slavian Obotrites, a Vendian race, at Mecklenburg, whose prince, Thrasico, aided by the Franks, attacked the northern Saxons, four thousand of whom were slain at Suintana, A.D. 798. Submission was now inevitable, and Charles, in order to confirm his conquest, made use of the nobles, whose Wergeld he trebled, and whom he loaded with favors, against the Frilings and Lazzi; by which means he created an aristocracy similar to that of the grand feudatories of France, which acted as a sure check upon the people. In commemoration of this victory, a magnificent palace was erected at Paderborn, A.D. 799, whither flocked all the great vassals of the crown and many a ladye fayre. The beautiful daughters of Charlemagne daily graced the chase. Pope Leo came from Rome to supplicate for aid against his rival Hadrian and the Antifrank party. The pope and the emperor embraced each other near a spring once sacred to a heathen deity, in the sight of the astonished and enraged Saxons. A monk from Jerusalem brought holy relics. The great caliph of the East, Haroun-al-Raschid, Charlemagne's worthy contemporary, whom dislike of the petty Moorish usurpers of Spain had rendered his ally, presented him with a costly tent, a curious clock, fine cloth the produce of the Eastern loom, spices, and an elephant. Four years later, after Charles's coronation at Rome, he revisited Saxony, and finally regulated the affairs of that country by the treaty of Selz (Konigshofen on the Saal), A.D. 803, by which he ratified the ancient laws, the privileges of the nobles, and declared the Saxons on an equality with the Franks.

Wittekind was killed in a border fray by Count Gerold of Swabia, A.D. 807, a proof of the insincerity of the conciliation. The murder might, possibly, have been politically designed, Charles's aim being to deprive Saxony of her temporal rulers, and to place her beneath the pastoral staff of the church.[1]

---

[1] Geroldus dux Sueviæ percussit Witekindum Angrarorum regem, cujus terram Carolus divisit in 8 episcopatus.—*Corneri Chron.*

CVIII. The Wars in Spain

DISSENSION was rife among the Moors in Spain. The last descendant of the caliphs of the house of the Omaijades fled from Africa to that country, where the Moors still adhered to him, and there founded the kingdom of Cordova. Some of the emirs, however, who aimed at asserting their own independence, refused their allegiance, and, uniting with Ibnalarabi, lord of Saragossa, opposed his authority and implored the assistance of Charlemagne, who, finding the opportunity favorable for another display of the superiority of France, for annihilating the power of the Mahometans by dissolving their union, for irremeably averting the danger with which the empire might be threatened from that quarter, and for extending the boundary of his dominions, speedily led his arrier-ban across the Pyrenees, A.D. 778. The legends that refer to this war are replete with strange adventure, and recount the glorious deeds of the famous Roland, who was first in command under Charlemagne. The emperor had reinstated Ibnalarabi at Saragossa, had erected Catalonia, with its metropolis, Barcelona, into a dukedom (that province being included within the French boundary), and had received the oath of fealty from Alonzo, a petty Gothic king, who dwelt in the mountains of Galicia and Asturia, when the revolt in Saxony again required his presence in Germany, and compelled him to relinquish his projects upon Spain. While recrossing the Pyrenees, the Basques, faithful to their ancient enmity against the Franks, fell upon his rear, and a great slaughter took place in the narrow mountain passes near Ronceval, where Roland the Brave was slain; his death was avenged by that of Lupus, the Basque duke, who was executed by order of Charlemagne. Roland has been celebrated by the poets of both olden and modern times, and appears to have been the favorite hero of the Franks, who long retained the custom of singing the famous song of Roland, now unfortunately lost, when marching to battle. The so-called pillars of Roland seen in different towns are falsely supposed to refer to him.

In 799, Charlemagne undertook a naval expedition against the Moors and deprived them of the Balearic Islands, Majorca and Minorca. He might possibly have succeeded in driving them out of Spain, had he not been called away by the affairs of Saxony.

CIX. *Thassilo*

THE ancient Agilofingian dynasty enjoyed considerable eminence, and retained the ducal dignity in Bavaria until the reign of Thassilo, who, cowardly, false, and base, justly incurred the contempt of his subjects, and caused the downfall of his house, by his unworthy conduct. Although the husband of Luitberga, a daughter of Desiderius, and, even in the time of Pipin, the avowed enemy of the Carlovingians, he deserted the Lombards at the most critical moment, and only ventured to attack Charles when he had suffered defeat in Saxony. After refusing to perform feudal service in the field, he declared himself independent and slew the French count, Chrodbert, who was sent to oppose him. Charles, upon this, taking advantage of the first moment of tranquillity in Saxony, marched into Bavaria and surrounded him in the valley of the Lech. The cowardly duke, instead of defending himself with spirit, basely took a false oath of fealty to the conqueror, and expressly recommended to his subjects beforehand, "while they were swearing allegiance to *think* the contrary." Charles pardoned his treachery, took one of his sons as a hostage, and permitted him to retain the ducal throne, A.D. 787. The following year he plotted with the Avari, aided by whom he hoped to surprise Charles, but having delayed openly to declare hostilities, on account of the emperor being then at peace and holding a great diet at Ingelheim, at which he had the audacity to appear, his plans were detected, and he was tried in full court and condemned to death. The sentence was commuted by Charles to imprisonment in a monastery. His fate was shared by his son, and Bavaria was subsequently governed by French counts, to whom the Bavarians, who had not even pretended to take part with the ruler they despised, and who had remained firm in their allegiance to the emperor, quietly submitted.

CX. *The Wars with the Slavi*

THE country eastward of the Elbe and Saal, abandoned by the Gothic tribes, had been repeopled by the Slavi, one of whose most noted tribes, the Wendi, took possession of northern Germany, where they first endured a severe struggle with the Saxons, and afterward with the Franks. This tribe comprised the Obotrites, who lay generally to the west in Mecklenburg, and the Wilzi, who lay generally to the east on the coasts of Pomerania. The latter already possessed large commercial towns, one of which, on the mouth of the Oder, the wealthy Wineta, the Venice of the North, was destroyed as early as the eighth century, partly by the ravages of the Norsemen, partly by those of the sea, and was replaced by Julin (Wollin). The sacred towns of Arcona on Rügen and Rhetra on the Priegnitz were celebrated among these northern nations.

South of the Wendi, on the Saal and the Upper Elbe, dwelt the Sorbi, of which the Daleminzii were the chief tribe. The name coincides with that of the Serbii, who dwelt in the vicinity of the Bulgarians, in the north of Greece. Yet the Slavi in the Austrian mountains were known from Trient to Venice as Wendi; hence Venice or the Windian boundary. The names of Croatia and Carinthia were merely provincial. The ancient name of the Vindelicii possibly reappears in that of these southern Wendi, in the same manner that the Bohemians took their name from the ancient Boii (Bojenheim), although they are named in their own language Tschechen. To the rear of the Wendi and the Sorbi dwelt the Lechen (Poles), and Tschechen (Bohemians), two kindred tribes. In the eighth century Crocus reigned in Bohemia. His daughter, Libussa, a prophetess, having, as the legends relate, to make choice of a husband, commanded search to be made for a man eating off an iron table, and Przmisl, a peasant, being found eating bread on a plow, became her husband and king of Bohemia. He founded the city of Prague. After Libussa's death, her maid-servants, instigated by Wlasta, rebelled, built the city of Diewin (Magdeburg), and put every man who fell into their hands to death. After a desperate struggle they were finally subdued by Przmisl. This war of the Bohemian maidens is detailed at greater length in some of the finest of the ancient legends. History is silent on the subject, and merely records that the wars, commenced at an earlier period against the Slavi who dwelt to the east of Germany, were continued by Charlemagne and increased in animosity after the subjection of Saxony, which brought the whole eastern frontier of the French empire everywhere in close contact with the confines of the Slavian territory, where the want of union among the Slavian tribes rendered their numbers powerless against the collective force of the whole German empire, wielded by a single arm.

The Saxon war for some time delayed the execution of the emperor's projects against the Slavi, and it was not until A.D. 789 that he invaded their territory and defeated the Obotrites and Wilzi, who, being only momentarily intimidated, did not long remain in a state of submission. Their destruction, however, was speedily caused by their disunion. The Obotrites, who lay nearest to the frontier, were disliked by the other tribes, and Charles, sensible of the advantages offered by their position for the furtherance of his designs, entered into close alliance with them, and loaded them with favors. He also made use of them against Saxony, and rewarded their services with its eastern districts, the ancient country of the Angli, now Mecklenburg. In 805 and 806, he marched against the Sorbi, defeated their kings, Samela and Misito, rendered them tributary, and laid the first stones of the towns of Halle and Magdeburg, which latter place is supposed to have received its name from the circumstance of his having there destroyed the images of the goddess of love and her attendant nymphs. At this period, he also subdued the Bohemians, on whom he imposed a tribute of one hundred and twenty fatted oxen, and the Poles, whose king, Lecho, is said to have fallen in battle.

CXI. *The Wars with the Avari*

THE Avari, a wild Tartar race, had followed the Longobardi, and had settled in Hungary and Austria as far as the Enns. They were incessantly at war with the Slavian Bohemians and with the dukes of Friuli. Thassilo, uniting with them against France, invaded and laid waste that country, A.D. 789. In 791, the emperor descended the Danube with a fleet and a powerful army, defeated them, drowned ten thousand men in the river, and devastated their country as far as the Raab. At the same time, his son, Pipin, made a successful inroad from Friuli into Hungary. Charlemagne, not venturing to advance, now merely sought to retain his newly-acquired domain, and, true to his maxim of ever watching over a dubious possession in person, besides anxious to impress the people with awe by a display of his power and magnificence, held a synod at Ratisbon, A.D. 792, in which he caused the doctrine of Felix, the Spanish bishop, to be condemned as heretical. Close upon the frontier of Bohemia, and not far from that of Hungary, was he thus pleased to show himself as the defender of Christianity, in order to impose upon his dangerous enemies by the united pomp of church and state.

Soon after this, the war with the Avari broke out anew. Dissensions arose between their princes or khans. Tudun, one of their number, visited Charlemagne at Aix-la-Chapelle, and there received baptism. The rest bade him defiance, but were, in the midst of their broils, attacked by young Pipin and by Erich, the brave duke of Friuli, assisted by the Slavi. In Hungary, the Avari had erected circular fortifications, one within the other, which they deemed impregnable, but which after a long and indecisive struggle were, at length, carried by storm by Duke Erich, A.D. 796. The enormous booty found by the Franks, heaped up within them, was carried to Aix-la-Chapelle by order of Charlemagne, who presented a moiety of it to the pope. In this war, Graf Gerold and his Swabians distinguished themselves so greatly as to gain from the emperor the honorable distinction of marching first in order in every war for the future undertaken by the state. Among these Swabians was a man from Thurgau, who spitted seven Avari at once on his enormous lance, and who, on account of his gigantic strength, was named Einheer, one of the Einherier or companions of Odin in Walhalla, according to the yet unforgotten pagan belief. The Avari, however, remained still unsubdued, and vigorously carried on the war. Tudun deserted the imperial cause. Gerold was killed in battle, and Tudun was captured and put to death. At length, weakened by continual disaster, the Avari submitted, A.D. 799, some of them to the Germans, the rest to their neighbors the Slavi.

Had Charlemagne been less continually occupied with Saxony, he would have extended his dominions by the conquest of the Avari beyond the Raab, and might possibly have reached Constantinople. A communication between the West and the East, by the already-mentioned union of the Maine with the Danube, might then have been carried into execution. For the present, he contented himself with making Croatia, the country recently torn from the Slavi, the eastern boundary of the empire, and with settling several Swabian and Bavarian colonies in modern Austria, whence the name, Bavarian frontier, or Astarrichi. The inhabitants of these boundaries were in an extremely peculiar position in regard to each other; the Slavi had long found themselves perplexed between Avari and Bavarians, heathens and Christians; at length the nobles sided with the former, and the people with the latter; the war carried on with their enemies abroad was consequently accompanied by revolutions at home. The peaceful conversion of the Slavian peasantry was at first due to the humane exertions of Virgilius, bishop of Salzburg, in the eighth century. Graf Gerold, already mentioned as one of the ablest servants of Charlemagne, afterward undertook the regulation of these mountainous districts, aided the peasants in exterminating the pagan nobility, granted them great privileges, and planted fresh German colonies among them. Only one, probably a Gothic tribe, the Gotscheer, had preserved its independence among the Slavi, in the mountains of Croatia.

The celebrated ceremony which attended the election of the duke in Carinthia, and was observed for centuries, dates from this period. The Furstenstein, or prince's stone, is still to be seen at Karnburg near Clagenfurt. A peasant, seating himself upon this stone, commanded the newly-elected duke to be brought before him: "Who is he that so proudly prances along?" asked the peasant, and the people shouted in reply, "Our country's prince." "Is he also a righteous judge, an increaser of the land, a defender of Christianity, of widows, and orphans?" again asked the peasant, and the people replied, "He is and will be!" The peasant then bade the duke assume his dignity, and giving him a box on the ear yielded his seat to him. This privilege was obtained by the peasantry, when they first embraced Christianity, and, after driving away their own nobility, accepted German rulers.

CXII. *The Wars with the Norsemen*

NORSEMEN, or men of the North, was the general term for all Scandinavians who quitted their native country to seek for adventure, or to plunder by sea or by land. In ancient times all the German nations had migrated for these purposes. Christianity put an end to the migrations in the South, and the Scandinavians, the last of the pagan German tribes, alone retained this ancient custom. Until now, Saxony had proved a sufficient bulwark against the Norsemen, but that country was no sooner conquered by Charlemagne than the robbers and warriors of the North threatened France herself. The Danes, the allies of the Saxons, afforded Wittekind both shelter and support. Their king, Gottfried, attacked the Obotrites, and was, with difficulty, repulsed by the Franks. As a security against invasion, he separated the Danish peninsula from Germany by a great wall and moat, called the Danewirk, that had only one outlet. In 810, he sailed with 200 ships to Friesland, where he landed and threatened Aix-la-Chapelle, the capital of the empire. The arrier-ban was instantly summoned, and the emperor took the field against the invading horde, but learning, on his march, that they had slain their king for his arrogance and tyranny, and had retreated to Denmark, he concluded peace with Hemming, Gottfried's successor, and made the Eyder the northern boundary of the empire. Graf Odo, in Itzehoe or Hamburg, and the Waldgraf Liderich, in Flanders, guarded the northern coasts, but Charlemagne, being unpossessed of a fleet, was unable to keep the bold Norsemen in check at sea—probably from his unwillingness to trust the Saxons with so much power—and these northern pirates even infested the Mediterranean. The sight of their vessels, as they crossed on the ocean, is said to have drawn tears from the eyes of this great emperor, as he sat watching their movements from his castle at Narbonne, in the south of France, and foretold their future devastation of his empire.

CXIII. Charlemagne the First of the German Cæsars

SUCH were the warlike achievements of the greatest of the Frankish monarchs, whose empire extended from the Ebro to the Raab, from Benevento to the Eyder. Every German race, except the English and the Scandinavians, were, for the first time, united under one sovereign; all the western Romans, with part of the Slavi and Avari, owned the same allegiance. The discordant component parts of this gigantic empire, held together by a social compact whose strength was doubled by the pressure from without, were scarcely influenced by the distinction that certainly still existed between the Romans and the Germans, the conquered and the conqueror, the adherents of royalty and the advocates for the ancient democracy. The exclusive sway of the Catholic religion, now that of the state, the enthusiasm of its votaries, its spiritual power, its character, well adapted to impress the minds of the illiterate, and its well-regulated papal government, all tended to promote concord, while the danger with which Mohammedanism threatened Christendom from the South, united Romans and Germans in one common cause, nay, even caused the ancient hereditary feuds among the latter to be forgotten amid the general enthusiasm, which rendered them equally zealous, whether arrayed in opposition to the Grecian empire or to the pagan Slavi and Norsemen. England, naturally and politically insulated, alone stood aloof, but manifested her sympathy by sending forth her missionaries to aid in the work of conversion carried on by the Franks in the East.

The distinctive peculiarities of the different tribes of Germany, who were thus suddenly and for the first time united, became gradually and naturally less prominent, while a similarity in their national characters began to develop. Their common hatred of the Moors, the Greeks, and the Slavi, added another link to their bond of union. A state exclusively German was also by no means the idea of the times, the Romans having kept pace with the Germans, and the church, far from being satisfied to rule within the narrow limits of a German empire, aspired to universal dominion; still it must be conceded that the spirit of fraternization that at this period prevailed throughout Germany, chiefly conduced to the internal harmony of the state, the extension of whose limits, the wars and conquests, naturally recalled the ancient Roman empire to remembrance, whose still unforgotten splendor kindled anew a desire for pomp and pageantry, and swelled alike the heart of the ruler and the subject with the proud consciousness of power. The resemblance of the new empire with that which had passed away, and the ancient reverence attached to the name of Rome, facilitated their connection, and the new empire received the name of Roman. This combination of circumstances produced the idea of an empire whose temporal power and mode of formation should be a vivid image of that of ancient Rome, and whose spiritual power should extend over the whole world, and fraternize all nations, by uniting them in one faith and under one sovereign. Thus originated the Holy Roman Empire, which contained within itself two separate powers, the church and the state, each of which owned a visible head, the representative of God upon earth; the spiritual head being the pope, and the temporal head the emperor. "God," it was said, "had given two swords wherewith to govern the world, the one to the pope, the other to the emperor." The spirit of the times favored this transformation in the affairs of Europe. Charlemagne was in fact but the outward and visible instrument destined to carry into effect the gradual and hidden work of centuries. His greatness solely consisted in his having comprehended and acted up to the spirit of the times, by forcibly producing a union whence sprang a new spirit, a new life, to which he gave free scope. For the sake of unity, he certainly sacrificed the ancient liberties of the people, which, until his time, had been upheld by the independence of the several petty tribes and states. He gave them unity, but deprived them of freedom; but Germany was not then fitted for the simultaneous enjoyment of these two great advantages.

Charlemagne, while engaged in these bloody wars, preserved a strict friendship with the pope, Hadrian, whom he supported in his measures for the government of the church, and who, in return, assisted his schemes by converting the heathen, and by placing his wild followers under spiritual subjection. When the threats of the sovereign were disregarded, the eloquence of the churchman often prevailed. Hadrian di d, and his relatives, conspiring against his successor, Leo the Third, ill-treated him in a tumult, upon which he fled to Paderborn to sue the emperor for aid, A.D. 799. The restoration of the Roman empire was there concerted between them, and, in the ensuing year, Charlemagne appeared with a numerous retinue in Rome, where, on Christmas eve, the crown, which for one thousand and six years after represented the union and supremacy of Germany, was placed upon his head by the pope, while the assembled multitude shouted, "Charles Augustus, crowned by God, great and pacific Cæsar! Life and victory to the Roman emperor!" A.D. 800.

Charlemagne's ambition soared still higher. In the hope of gaining possession of the imperial throne of Greece, he sent the bishops, Hatto of Basle and Hugo of Tours, to Constantinople, to sue for the hand of Irene, the empress widow, who, meanwhile, was deprived of the throne by Nicephorus. This usurper, enraged at the ill-timed embassy, ill-treated the bishops, a disgrace that was repaid by the contempt with which his embassadors were treated at Selz, where Charlemagne finally concluded peace with Saxony; at least so says the loquacious monk of St. Gall.

CXIV. *The Empire under Charlemagne*

THE feudal system, which was first planned by Chlodwig, who raised the armed adherents, immediately attached to his person, above the freeborn Franks, was perfected by Charlemagne, whose whole power rested upon it. The authority of the mayors of the palace of the Carlovingian dynasty was founded on the favor of the vassals, and their policy chiefly consisted in converting freehold property into fiefs and in rendering the fiefs heritable. The feudal system had by this means already become so general as materially to lessen the numbers and weaken the influence of the Frilings, and Charlemagne was consequently enabled without difficulty to bring it to full maturity, and, after his coronation as emperor, to exact from every subject within his empire, without distinction, an oath of allegiance, similar to that by which the vassal (*homo, Leut, vasall,* servitor) bound himself to his lord. By this step, he declared himself universal sovereign, whom every vassal of the empire was bound to serve in person, and also possessor of the land and universal liege. Whoever still remained free and retained possession of an Allod was at least bound to appertain, both person and property, to the empire, to be subject to the supremacy of the emperor and to the authority of the counts (Grafen), whose election now rested with the crown instead of with the people, and who were now exclusively termed *comites*, or royal followers. The Frilings became Frilings of the empire, over whom the protection of the emperor was as compulsory as his feudal right over his vassal. The treatment these Frilings received was, however, such as to lead them to prefer feudality to freedom; they were, in fact, so arbitrarily oppressed by the Grafs, and the already powerful vassals of the crown, that Louis the Pious, Charlemagne's successor, visited the different parts of his empire for the especial purpose of checking this injustice, but in vain. Many of the Frilings were compelled to convert their Allods into fiefs, while others did so voluntarily, in order to free themselves from the arrier-ban, in which they were obliged to serve as long as they retained their freedom. According to the old custom, the Frilings were forced to join the arrier-ban whenever war broke out, and as Charlemagne was perpetually in the field, those who remained at the conclusion of the war were ruined by the neglect into which their property had fallen, while the vassals in the personal service of some great lord, or in that of the church, were either not summoned, or were indemnified for their service by their spiritual or temporal lieges; such oppressive freedom was naturally often gladly exchanged for the more agreeable species of servitude. Still, in the interior of Germany, many of the Frilings proudly maintained their independence, and in Saxony and among the Alemanni there were whole districts or tithings of free peasants of the empire. These Frilings refused to serve in the field under the customary Graf, on account of his ever attempting to usurp feudal power in his district, and demanded a Sendgraf, a Graf specially commissioned on extraordinary occasions for a short period, immediately from the emperor. Partly in order to replace the deficiency in the arrier-ban, and partly to provide for the better security of his person by the formation of a body-guard, Charlemagne raised the Scaren, so called from *Schaaren*, troops, bands of mercenaries, paid from his private revenues, and clothed in red, whence the word "scarlet"—*Schar*, a troop, and *Lach* or *Laken*, cloth.

The new method of administering justice was an additional fetter upon ancient popular freedom. The Germans were no longer permitted to appear armed before the tribunal; and the judiciary power, formerly exercised by the assembled community, now rested solely with the Grafs elected by the crown. The numerous new laws, or Capitularies of Charlemagne, compiled in Latin, being, independent of the unknown language in which they were written, of too circumstantial a nature for the people to be able to retain them, like their ancient laws, in their memories, rendered necessary the formation, in each community, of a species of guild, composed of men who had made the law their chief study, and who, under the title of aldermen (*scabini*), were always present, and sat next to the Graf, during the administration of justice. Charlemagne had permitted the Franks, Goths, Longobardi, Burgundians, Alemanni, Thuringians, Bavarians, Saxons, and Frisii, to retain part of their national laws, after expunging those that referred to their ancient liberties, and adding new feudal and ecclesiastical ordonnances, which also contained the separate contracts, donations, and privileges of each bishopric, monastery, and temporal fief, and thereby produced a mass and a perplexing variety of laws, which being too intricate for the comprehensions of the commonalty, consequently caused their total exclusion from the administration of justice. Popular freedom, nevertheless, received its death-blow from Catholicism, more especially in the interior of Germany, where the new religion had taken firm root before the introduction of the feudal system, which the Frankish lords did not venture to enforce among the Swabians and Saxons, among whom monasteries and bishoprics had met with an easy reception. Never did the Germans voluntarily bend the knee to any save to their God, in their zeal for whose service they bound themselves as vassals to, and held their lands in fief from, the church; ere long, richly-endowed houses of God inthralled the free community, and even the Frilings, who refused vassalage to the church, were by law compelled, under pain of death, to pay tithes.

The ancient liberties of the people and the insolence of the nobles, who like Thassilo aspired to independence, were equally suppressed by Charlemagne, who, putting an end to the dukedoms, governed the empire by means of Grafs, who, being less powerful, less endangered its unity, and by Sendgrafs (*missi dominici*), traveling envoys, who were charged with the inspection of the provinces. Foreseeing that the assemblies of the nobles might frustrate his projects, he separated that body, by holding especial ecclesiastical synods and special assemblies of the vassals (*Hoflager—placita*), by which aristocratic two-chamber system the third class or commoners were totally excluded from any share in the government, and it was only at the Field of May, or great original assembly of the states, that the Frilings were admitted, when their votes merely confirmed decisions already determined upon. He also took the precautionary measure of holding any extraordinary meeting of the bishops and vassals at different places and seasons, by which means he was apparently ever present, and hindered conspiracies being laid in unguarded parts of the country. His Capitularies frequently mention the conjurations, conspiracies, or fraternities, and their severe punishment; among them, the secret confederacies of the Saxons are most particularly pointed out, whose prevention, requiring his presence in the country or in its vicinity, caused him generally to convoke thither the assemblies of the vassals.

CXV. *The Church under Charlemagne*

CHARLEMAGNE, habituated to command, was no less absolute in ecclesiastical than in temporal matters, and never again has the church, since her assumption of authority, been so completely under the control of a temporal sovereign. In order to guard equally against the convocation of general ecclesiastical assemblies independent of the laity, and the union of the clergy and the people against the crown, he presided as a layman at all ecclesiastical meetings, which he convoked separately from the Fields of May and the Placita. He consequently arbitrarily governed their decisions, in which the voice of the people was necessarily unheard. In the ecclesiastical assemblies, held in 792, at Ratisbon, in 794, at Frankfurt, and in 815, at Mayence, he laid down new regulations for the internal management of the church. His word was law. Pope and clergy bent submissively before him, and his rules of moral discipline were strictly enforced among the monks and secular priests. As a check upon the disorder introduced by Charles Martell, and left unremedied by Bonifacius, he forbade the clergy to carry arms, to keep falcons, dogs, or fools, but, aware of their invincible predilection for the chase, permitted them to retain this amusement on condition of their converting the skins of the animals they killed into binding for books, which he hoped by these means to render more general. Moderation, decency, and gravity of demeanor were enjoined upon all priests, and the monks were obliged to find employment in the fields and schools. He also interfered in doctrinal matters. It was not the pope, but the emperor, who condemned Bishop Felix and his sect of Adoptians, A.D. 792, who simply confessed the existence of two natures in the Godhead, and regarded Christ as a man adopted by God as his son. It was the emperor who, in opposition to the pope, condemned the worship of images and pictures, A.D. 794, and interdicted, throughout his empire, the adoration of the saints.

The interest of the church, moreover, induced her to submit to the decisions of the crown. Charlemagne, although in name merely a layman, acting in reality as if he were himself pope, and only intent upon her welfare, immeasurably added to the power of that dignitary and to her unity. The dangerous influence of the Lombards was forever destroyed; the donations of Pipin were confirmed, and secured to the pope by the power of the empire, while the esteem in which he was held by the emperor, the closeness of their alliance, his influence over the numerous clergy spread throughout the empire, and the recognition of his sanctity, which empowered him to bestow the crown and a new title, in the name of God, on the emperor, at once raised him next in rank to that sovereign, to whose temporal power his spiritual power alone ceded, nay, his authority ere long rose so high, as, during succeeding centuries, to render it questionable whether precedence was not his due. Charlemagne also widely extended the influence of the church, by the conversion of several million heathen to Christianity, and by the erection of powerful bishoprics in the interior of Germany; among others, that of Paderborn, one of his favorite places of residence, and Bremen, distinguished as the outpost by which Christendom was guarded against the pagan North.

The jealousy that existed between the conquered Saxons, Thuringians, Hessians, Bavarians, and Swabians, and, in fact, between all the Germans and the Franks, cautioned Charlemagne against placing Frankish Grafs over these provinces, and he, accordingly, set over them bishops, whose spiritual and apparently gentle rule bound them in fetters stronger than those imposed by force. Upon these spiritual lords he conferred the greatest possible temporal prerogatives and power, in order to render their authority equal to that of the Grafs, and to enable them to act as a check upon the native Grafs, whose allegiance appeared doubtful. Penal judicature, the power of life or death within their dioceses, was, for these reasons, one of their prerogatives; it was even exercised by abbots, as, for instance, those of Fulda and St. Gall, who thus united in their persons not only the authority of the ancient judges of peace, but, in their capacity of feudatory lords over their armed vassals, that of the ancient dukes. These measures, calculated to meet the exigency of the times, at a later period greatly endangered the empire, by giving a preponderance of wealth, prerogative and power to the church.

Alcuin, an Anglo-Saxon monk, Charlemagne's spiritual guide, a man of comprehensive intellect and deep learning, was his agent in the most important ecclesiastical affairs, and particularly in the management of the academies, whose foundation gave a fresh impulse to German civilization.

CXVI. *The State of Learning under Charlemagne*

THE academies founded beneath the despotic rule of Charlemagne in aid of the church were the means of raising Germany from her ancient barbarous state. A kind of academy, composed of the most learned and talented men of the age, was established at the imperial court; among the number were: Alcuin, the Anglo-Saxon, whose numerous letters and other writings are still extant; Paul Warnefried, the celebrated historian of Lombardy; Angilbert, Peter of Pisa, Paulinus of Aquileia, Theodolfus, the pious bishop Turpin, and young Eginhart, the two biographers of Charlemagne, Riculf, Theodulf, Adelhard, Wala, Wigo, Arno, Sigulf, Fredegis, and Richbod. Alcuin generally resided at Tours, where he founded a classical academy, which produced most of the above-mentioned scholars, and, at a later period, many more. The society of these men was the favorite relaxation of the emperor, whenever a pause occurred in war. Each branch of science became, in turn, the theme of conversation; etiquette was thrown aside, and each of the academicians was distinguished by a name taken from the

Bible or from the Greek and Roman classics, which at that time were carefully collected and diligently studied. Charlemagne was named King David; Wala, Jeremiah; Fredegis, Nathaniel; Alcuin, Horace; Angilbert, Homer; Theodulf, Pindar; Eginhart, Calliopius, etc. Refinement and learning long distinguished the family of the emperor, one of whose grandsons, Nithard, became celebrated as a historian. Charlemagne was also the patron of poetry. By his direction, a number of the ancient legends and ballads of Germany were collected and committed to writing, some of which were probably retouched at a later period, and are those that have reached our times—in fact, are all that remain of ancient legendary lore; the Gothic legends, for instance, particularly those of Dietrich, and those of the Burgundians, of Etzel and Gonthachar, which, in the Nibelungenlied, were connected with those of the Franks and of the North. The deeds of Charlemagne became the theme of many later German and French poets.

Charlemagne also founded several monastic schools for the diffusion of useful knowledge among the commonalty, and more especially among the clergy. The most celebrated were those of Fulda, Mayence, St. Gall, Reichenau, and Weissenburg, which produced a crowd of distinguished scholars. The emperor sometimes assisted in person at these academies, and one day, perceiving the superior intelligence and industry of the commoners over the nobles, vehemently expostulated with the latter, possibly foreseeing in this circumstance the future downfall of the class for whose establishment he had so zealously labored. Masters for writing, arithmetic, singing, and music, were brought from Italy, where Latinity and art had been preserved by the clergy. At Paris, a concert was given by the emperor, which decided the superiority of the Italian over the French singers. A grammar of the German language was composed. The first bell was cast at St. Gall by a monk named Tancho, who is said to have received a hundredweight of silver from the emperor, for the purpose of founding a second one, but who kept the silver for his own use, and made a bell of common metal, at whose first peal, by the decree of Heaven, he fell dead.

Charlemagne, besides being a distinguished patron of learning, was, for the times in which he lived, a great promoter of agriculture, trade, and commerce. He improved the calendar, and his Capitularies contained separate regulations for each class. Notwithstanding the disinclination of the Germans for commercial pursuits, he attempted to encourage them by granting extraordinary privileges to merchants. The Jews, who, after the destruction of Jerusalem, had been carried away captive by the Romans, and scattered over the face of the earth, had, since Rome had fallen under the dominion of Germany, busied themselves exclusively with commerce, and Charlemagne, uninfluenced by the prejudices of the Christians, rewarded their skill and industry by granting them every privilege demanded by humanity and consistent with the advantage of the state. Roads were built, and traveling merchants were protected by severe laws. An alliance was formed with the commercial towns of the Slavi on the Baltic, and with the Greeks, the former of which carried on a traffic in slaves and furs, the latter in precious stones, rich stuffs, and fruits. New markets, open to foreign merchants, were erected in the interior of Germany, at Bardewyk, Magdeburg, Erfurt, Forchheim, Ratisbon, and Lorch. The imperial palaces, more particularly Aix-la-Chapelle, Heristal, Nimwegen, Diedenhofen, Rense, Andernach, Prüm, Ingelheim, Worms, Tribur, Paderborn, and Salzburg, whose gardens, fields, vineyards, arable lands, and forests were cultivated and managed by the emperor's servants under his own superintendence, afforded proof of his acquaintance with husbandry, by serving as models to the whole empire for economy and good management. It was here that he carried into practice the knowledge he had acquired from the Romans and the Slavi, who were far in advance of the Germans in the arts of husbandry, that he cultivated the fruits and reared the animals of foreign countries, and made experiments for the improvement of agriculture. To the inhabitants of these demesnes he gave a particular law, the Capitulare de Villis, which contained a complete set of rules for the agriculturist, and served as a manual for the rest of his subjects.

The only artificers at this period were women and servants. The daughters of Charlemagne and the daughters of the peasants were equally engaged in weaving, embroidery and housekeeping. The Capitularies prescribed rules to the artisans, and were an evidence of the zeal with which Charlemagne endeavored to introduce the refinements of the South into Germany, and the variety of trades, from that of the jeweler to that of the shoemaker, mentioned in them, prove how greatly he had already contributed to the comfort and elegance of domestic life. The use of richly-worked and embroidered dresses, gay coats and flags, devices, carved wainscoting, ornamental furniture in gold and silver, sculptured drinking cups, splendid arms and coats of mail, glass windows and musical instruments, ere long gave indication of a love of splendor and of a higher degree of civilization and social intercourse. Architecture was still neglected, owing to the dislike of the Germans to the erection of cities or even castles. The emperor's palaces at Aix-la-Chapelle were considered so wonderful in the North that the people compared them to the papal residence, and named them "Little Rome." At Ingelheim, on the Rhine, stood another palace, the remains of whose ruins fell not many years ago. Some of the elegant columns that once formed part of it may still be seen near the old well in the court of the castle of Heidelberg. Among other treasures, Charlemagne is said to have possessed one golden and three silver tables, the latter of which bore representations of ancient Rome, modern Rome, and the globe.

CXVII. Charlemagne

CHARLEMAGNE is said to have been seven feet in height. His crown, preserved at Vienna, is of gigantic size. Strong and active in his person, he was a perfect adept in the tournament and in the use of weapons. His arm was as irresistible as his commanding genius. The ponderous iron lance was wielded like a toy in his powerful grasp. In swimming he was unequaled. By never indulging in excess or luxury, his strength, maintained by daily exercise, endured to extreme old age. Warlike and majestic in his deportment, every heart throbbed higher, every head bent with deference and awe, at his presence. Wisdom and nobility sat enthroned on his broad, open brow; every eye sank beneath his piercing and commanding glance. His dress, generally simple and warlike, consisted of a doublet composed of the fur of the otter. When his courtiers first began to wear sumptuous silken dresses, he led them one day mockingly into the heavy rain, which quickly spoiled their gay attire. On public and solemn occasions, he wore a short golden gown, fastened with a girdle; gay-colored ribbons placed crosswise over his trousers and stockings, uncut diamonds on his shoes, and a mantle, generally either white or green. The handle of his enormous sword bore his seal, and he was wont to say, "With my sword I maintain all, to which I affix my seal."

He was married five times, and had five concubines. Beauty and virtue guided his choice of a wife more than high birth. It is related of Hildegarde, the Swabian, whom he wedded shortly after his divorce from the Lombard princess, that a servant, named Taland, enraged at the contempt with which she treated his criminal advances, accused her of infidelity to the emperor, who divorced her also; upon which she retired to Rome, where for some time she led a life of great sanctity, and devoted herself to the care of the sick, until happening to meet with Taland, wandering about blind, she restored him to sight, and the wretched man, struck with remorse, confessed his crime and led her back to her husband. The legends also mention the beautiful daughters of Charlemagne, who sometimes accompanied him to the field of battle. His secretary, young Eginhart, became deeply enamored of his daughter Emma, and the youthful lovers, fearing his anger should he discover their affection, only met at night. It happened that one night, while Eginhart was in the princess's apartment, a fall of snow took place. To return across the palace court must lead to inevitable discovery by the traces of his footsteps. The moment called for resolution; woman's wit came to the assistance of the perplexed lover, and the faithful and prudent Emma, taking her lover on her back, bore him across the court. The emperor, who chanced to be gazing from his window, beheld this strange sight by the clear moonlight, and the next morning sent for the young couple, who stood before him in expectation of being sentenced to death, when the generous father bestowed upon Eginhart his daughter's hand, and the Odenwald in fief. The tomb of Eginhart and Emma is still to be seen at Erbach. The counts of Erbach claim from them their descent. Eginhart became a celebrated historian, and it was chiefly through the medium of his pen that the deeds of his great father-in-law were handed down to posterity. Bertha, the second daughter, carried on a similar intrigue with young Engelbert, and, without being formally married, became the mother of Nithart, who distinguished himself as a historian. Odoin the brave is named as the lover of the third daughter. Louis, Charlemagne's successor, no sooner mounted the throne, than he imprisoned his sisters in a convent and persecuted their lovers. Odoin, too proud to flee, stood firm and fought bravely to the last against his assassins. The lenity with which Charlemagne treated his daughters and their lovers unquestionably arose from a political motive. Had he wedded them to men of distinction belonging to the old ducal families, the empire must ere long have been partitioned between his sons-in-law. In order to avoid this, and to preserve the unity of the state, by rendering rivalry impossible, he consequently refused his daughters any share in the heritage or legal marriages.

Charlemagne had three sons: Charles, who died early. Pipin, a young man of talent, who, after serving in several campaigns, particularly in those against the Avari and the Lombards, rebelled against his father and died in prison. His history is extremely obscure. Louis, the third son, unfortunately of weaker parts than his brethren, was the only one who survived him.

This great emperor died in 814. He lies, or, more properly speaking, sits, buried at Aix-la-Chapelle, where, on his tomb being opened by the emperor Otto the Third, he was found sitting upright as on a throne, attired in his imperial robes. So great was his renown, so great were the love and veneration he inspired, that he was canonized, and pilgrimages were made to his grave. The effect of his genius, far from ceasing with his life, shed a luster over succeeding centuries. Radiant with majesty and sanctity, the founder of the new empire stood, as it were, on the threshold of that great and brilliant era, his creation, the middle age, then opening on the world. His fame, unsurpassed and unequaled by that of succeeding emperors, dazzled posterity, and the memory of his glory bestowed imperishable dignity on the imperial crown, though subsequently placed on such unworthy brows. Hence the great emperor, his warriors, his sages, and their mighty exploits, naturally formed the inexhaustible subject of the poetry of the Middle Ages, and his reign has been immortalized by German, French and Spanish poets, in whose productions the great events of later times, and the results of more modern civilization, are ascribed to it as the concentrating point of all that is sublime, glorious, great, and beautiful. The Capitularies and letters of Charlemagne himself, the numerous writings of Alcuin, the historical work of Eginhart, a manuscript chronicle at Paris, and the romantic account of the monk of St. Gall, are the only sources of information concerning this emperor now extant. The romance of Turpin and the Weaver are mere fables.

PART VII

THE HISTORY OF THE NORTH

CXVIII. *Odin*

THE North, or Scandinavia, separated from Germany by the Baltic, stretched far into the frigid zone. Denmark lay to its extreme south. From time immemorial the fertile lowlands were cultivated by a hardy population. Steep Alps separate Sweden from Norway. Ages ago, along the extensive rocky coasts, called the Scheeren, and along the streams flowing through the valleys, dwelt tribes of Fins, who, at an unknown period, were driven into Finland, and amid the eternal snows of Lapland, which they still inhabit, by Germans, who crossed the Baltic and took possession of the countries lying to the North.

The most ancient sources of Northern history are the legendary accounts of celebrated royal dynasties, which, as is usually the case in these sort of legends, drew their origin, in the fabulous ages, from the supreme deity, and became the first rulers over the people. Thus the Swedish, Norwegian, Danish, and Anglo-Saxon kings claim as their common ancestor the great god, Odin, who is said to have subdued the whole of Northern Germany and Scandinavia, which he divided between his sons, giving Eastern Saxony to Vegdeg, Western Saxony to Balldr, Franconia to Sigge, Denmark to Skiold, Norway to Säming, and Sweden to Yngwi-Freyr. With his own hands he raised the great temple at Upsala in Sweden, where he was represented under the figure of a warrior standing before an enormous flaming sun. Here was his earthly throne, whence he gave laws to the whole North, and to him are ascribed the invention of religious ceremonies, magic, the Runic letters, poetry, the institution of the popular assembly or Thing, and of the administration of justice, heroism, the regulations of the warriors or warlike retinue, which he composed of Berserkers, and every important popular institution. For some time after the death of Odin, his sons appear to have shared his divine attributes. They were called Drottar or lords, a word, in its full meaning, signifying God-kings, who possessed power equaling that of Odin. The whole of Sweden was under the jurisdiction of the temple-court at Upsala, the seat of government of the Ynglinger (from Yngwi-Freyr); the whole of Norway under that of the sacred city of Thrandheim, where the Säminger sat enthroned; and Denmark, under that of the great temple of Lethra, which was guarded by the Skioldunger. So far extend the ancient traditions of the gods, which soon after assume a more worldly tone, and treat of men. The laws and institutions of ancient Germany appear to have spread over the North as well as the South. The Swedish legends record that Dygwe, the seventh Ynglinger after Yngwi-Freyr, was the first who exchanged the title of Drottar for that of king.

CXIX. *The Kings*

THE lineal descendants of Odin maintained their authority at Upsala, Thrandheim, and Lethra, and even after the extinction of their race, the ancient veneration for these sacred cities gave to the districts to which they belonged, and to their kings, a sort of pre-eminence over the other districts and their kings, which usually simply consisted in the honor of presiding at the national festivals, except in cases when this dignity chanced to be attained by some great warrior, who made use of the superstition of his countrymen to increase his authority. Besides these sacred monarchs, there arose numerous petty Fylker-kings, so named from the independent Fylker or districts over which they reigned. These kings were, at first, side-branches of the race of Odin, and united in their persons the offices of Lagmenn or guardians of the laws, of Höfdingiar, presidents of the popular assembly and administrators of justice (chiefs of the Thing), and of Blotmenn, high priests of the altar; they were also Heerkönige, or kings of the army by land, and sea-kings by water.

The people consisted of free peasants or Bonden, who possessed a heritable and inalienable Allod or Odol, freehold. They had the right of electing the king, and of holding their public councils or Things under his presidency. Wealthy Bonden had their vassals or feudal tenants (Lendirmenn), and servants or slaves (Trälle). Individual warriors, who assembled followers and practiced piracy, received the title of sea-kings, or, when they fixed their abode on a small island or rock (*Naes*), that of Naes-kings. Other warriors formed a republic of pirates, each of whom enjoyed equal privileges and was subject to the same regulations, which were often extremely severe. War and piracy were the daily occupation of the people. The kings were ever at feud. Sometimes a king was murdered for attempting to tyrannize over the people; or some mighty warrior was, for a short time, successful in his attacks upon neighboring kings; or part of the people migrated to the South.

The state of the North, about the middle of the first century after Christ, is thus described in numerous legends, in which, in the midst of the universal confusion, its three great causes, the love of war, the attempts of the Trälle to escape from thralldom, and the sturdy opposition of the Bonden to the arbitrary rule of the kings, may ever be traced. This continual struggle necessarily produced a new order of things; war was preferred to peace, the military ruled the civil power, and the warriors tyrannized over the Bonden, whose Allods were alienated by the kings, and the feudal system was introduced. Superstition gave the sacred kings the upper hand over the minor rulers, and, finally, the introduction of Christianity tended to bring the people into subjection and to fix the throne on a firmer basis.

It is remarkable that the change in the government of the three kingdoms proceeded from totally different causes. In Denmark, where war was the ruling passion, the people crowded beneath the banner of their kings, who easily extended the authority they thus acquired. In Sweden, the people were inthralled by superstition, and the kings, unaided by the sword, exercised supreme power in Odin's sacred temple. In Norway, the authority rested with the people, and the Bonden, whose warlike deeds surpassed those of their monarchs, held royalty in check; and it was only after a long and cruel struggle, which, like a pestilence, swept away half the population, that they at length fell beneath the arbitrary rule of one warrior king.

CXX. *The Danes*

THE Danes bear a prominent part in the history of ancient Germany. As early as a century before Christ, they appeared on the other side of the Pyrenees and Alps, under the denomination of Cimbri, and, at a later date, sent forth the hardy Longobardi. Invincible in their own country, they spread their conquering arms, at different periods, over the whole of the North, where their power for some time equaled that attained by the Franks in the South. Frotho, the second king after Skiold, is said to have subdued upward of a hundred of the minor kings who dwelt along the shores of the Northern Ocean and the Baltic. He is described in the legends as a great lawgiver, and as so beloved by his subjects, that, despairing to find his equal, they bore his body about the country for three years; at length they resolved to elect as his successor on the throne whoever composed the best poem in his honor, and one Hiarne obtained the prize. The sixth king after him was Dan Mykelati, who gave his name to the country. Several new regulations are ascribed to him, among others, the abolition of the burning

of the dead and the introduction of tumuli. in which the
dead bodies were placed unconsumed, and which gave name
to the subsequent age, that anterior to this king being known
as the Brandalter, or age of burning. The power of the race
of Odin appears to have ceased with him. His tenth successor was Hrolf, surnamed the Dwarf, on account of his diminutive stature. His commanding intellect insured the respect of his subjects. At his decease the state was divided
among several minor kings, who preserved their independence until their subjection by Ivar Widfadmi (the far-spread-
ing) and his warriors, who also conquered many other countries. This king drove the Ynglinger out of Sweden, and
placed his brother on the throne of Upsala. After his death,
the kingdom became a prey to faction, and brethren and
sons strove for dominion. In the eighth century Gorm the
Old seized the supreme authority. During his reign the first
attempt to convert the Danes to Christianity was made by a
traveler, named Thorkill, who had embraced that religion
during his stay in France, and who, on his return to Denmark, produced such an effect by his preaching on the mind
of the aged king that he died of remorse for having spent
his long life in error and idolatry. The new doctrine was
rejected by the people. Gottrik, or Gottfried, the son of
Gorm, aided Wittekind and the pagan Saxons, and was on
the point of attacking Aix-la-Chapelle, when he was murdered by his subjects. Hemming, his successor, made peace
with the emperor. After fresh disturbances, Regnar Lod-
brok came to the throne. He was one of the greatest of the
Danish warriors, and his fame formed the theme of numerous legends. His prowess was celebrated throughout the
whole of the North. His expedition against Ella, the Saxon
king in England, proved fatal to him. He was captured by
that prince, to whom he was unknown, and imprisoned in a
towei full of snakes, where with undaunted courage he re-
counted his deeds in song until life was extinct. He was a
zealous heathen, and expelled his brother, Harald Klak, for
his attachment to the new doctrine. Harald fled to the em-

peror of Germany, Louis the Pious, the son of Charlemagne, and was baptized at Ingelheim. In the same year, A.D. 826, St. Anscar, a pious monk, afterward known as the apostle of the North, visited Denmark, and soon afterward Sweden, where he preached the gospel at the peril of his life. In 834 the bishopric of Hamburg was founded as a means of accelerating the conversion of the North.

The history of this period is very obscure. The kings strove for supremacy, some of them favoring Christianity from interested motives, while the rest defended their ancient gods. Christianity, cruelly persecuted, spread but slowly, and the German priests, in order to curry favor with the people, either omitted part of the Catholic doctrine or assimilated it with paganism. Thus the conversion was always commenced with the *primsignung*, or first mark with a cross. Whoever was marked in this manner could live as he chose, either as a Christian or a heathen. The majority of the people and their rulers still adhered to the worship of Odin, and Hamburg was again destroyed during their destructive inroads into the German empire.

In 931, Gorm the Grim ruled Denmark, and persecuted the Christians. His son Harald Blaatand (blue tooth) favored them, but, making himself hated by his despotism, was murdered by a peasant.[1] His successor, the pagan Svend, carried on extensive wars, particularly against the Iomsburger, a republic of warriors and pirates on the island of Wollin near Pomerania, and against the Wendi. In his reign, another piratical horde, the Ascomanni or Schachtelmänner (box-men), assembled and greatly endangered Saxony. They were so numerous that the Saxons killed 20,000 of them in one battle.

Canute the Great, the most celebrated of the kings of the North, the conqueror of Norway and England, was the pro-

---

[1] Named Toki. The circumstances of this murder correspond minutely with those of the murder of Gessler, the Swiss governor, by Tell. Even the name is the same; Toki and Tell signifying, like the Latin Brutus, a simpleton.— *Saxo Grammaticus*.

moter of Christianity, which took firm root in Denmark. He left new laws, extended the royal prerogative, and was the founder of a new era, that of the middle ages, in the North. Toward the close of the twelfth century, the history of Denmark was written in Latin by an erudite Dane, named Saxo Grammaticus.

CXXI. *The Swedes*

DYGWE, the seventh Ynglinger, first assumed the title of king. During the reign of his tenth successor, Eigill, a civil war broke out; the Trälle, headed by Tunni, one of their class, revolted, and were in eight bloody battles victorious over the Bonden, whom they completely expelled, together with their king, and Tunni became sole sovereign. Eigill fled to the court of Frotho, the great king of Denmark, and the conqueror of the North, who, lending him his aid, overran Sweden at the head of his veteran warriors, and, after nine battles, in the last of which Tunni and the majority of the brave Trälle were left dead on the field, restored Eigill to the throne.

The petty Fylker-kings subsequently asserted their independence. Eigill's sixth successor, Ingialldr, desiring to regain the supreme authority, invited six of these kings to a banquet, and, after inducing them to carouse deeply, set fire to the house in which they slept. His punishment did not tarry long. Ivar Widfadmi, the Dane, marched victoriously through the North and arrived in Sweden. Ingialldr, sensible of the futility of opposition, but too proud to yield, invited all his followers to a great banquet, and when they were helpless from inebriety, set fire to the palace in which they sat, and was destroyed with them. His son, Olaf, meanwhile, accompanied by numbers of the people, took refuge in the northern mountains, and discovering a fertile and uninhabited country, settled there, and named it Wermeland. Soon after their settlement, a famine, occasioned by the bad cultivation of the ground, broke out among them, and they offered up their king as an expiatory sacrifice to the gods. The descendants of Olaf, by their bravery and by their intermarriages with the noblest families of Norway, rose ere long to great power, and finally seized the monarchy.

Sweden was, meanwhile, long governed by kings of Danish origin, during whose reigns Christianity was first introduced from Denmark. In 829, St. Anscar visited the country, but the new doctrine met with violent opposition. In 865, St. Rimbert made another short but useless attempt, and paganism was not eradicated until 930, when Unno, bishop of Bremen, who was succeeded in his pious mission by other Germans, visited Sweden for that purpose. The last pagan king of Upsala was Eric the Victorious.

About the year 1000, Olaf, surnamed the Schoos, or bosom king, on account of his having been proclaimed and raised in the arms of the people, was the founder of a new era in Sweden. He was unanimously elected by the Fylkerkings as their common sovereign. During his reign, Christianity was firmly established throughout his dominions.

CXXII. *The Norwegians*

NORWAY was subdivided among a crowd of Fylker, army, sea, and Naes kings, who strove with each other by sea and land. The independent spirit of the Bonden was long an invincible obstacle to union; in no other country has the people been possessed of so much power, in no other has it been so difficult for the kings and the military to bring the free peasantry into subjection. In the ninth century, one of the petty kings, Harald Harfagra (with the beautiful locks), who is said to have been a descendant of the expelled Ynglingers, succeeded, after a long and desperate struggle, in usurping dominion over the whole of Norway. His proffered love being treated with contempt by Gyda, the most beautiful and the proudest of the maidens of Norway, who had vowed that she would alone bestow her hand on him who presented her with the whole of her country as a morning-gift, he swore that he would not comb his beautiful hair until he had gained the sole sovereignty, and, assembling a crowd of youthful warriors beneath his standard, unexpectedly attacked and subdued his neighbors, one by one. The fame of his irresistible prowess quickly spread, and some of the provinces voluntarily submitted to him. One of the petty kings, rather than incur disgrace by flight or by defeat, buried himself alive with his dependents and friends. At length, the kings who still remained unsubdued made common cause, and a great battle was fought, in which Harald was victorious. Subsequent rebellions proved vain; Harald's power became gradually more firmly secured, and, after the lapse of a few years, he grasped the scepter of Norway. He now combed his locks and espoused the beauteous Gyda. His throne, raised upon ruin and bloodshed, could alone be supported by treachery and violence, and while he caused the nobler and more resolute of the petty kings to be murdered, he cajoled the more cowardly with rich gifts and high but empty honors. He deprived them of their thrones and their independence, placed them, in the capacity of Stadtholders or Jarls, over the provinces they formerly governed, and by his despotic violence obtained for them far greater power over the Bonden, whom he transformed into vassals, and richer revenues than they had hitherto enjoyed. Popular freedom was annihilated at a blow; every Odol (freehold) was declared crown property, and for the future held in fief by its original possessor. This destruction of the old German Allod and Gau system was unprecedentedly sudden and violent, and the more astonishing from its happening to the German tribe most jealous of its freedom; nor was this revolution in any way aided by the obedience inculcated by the precepts of Christianity, Harald and the Norwegians being still idolaters. Unwearied by the ceaseless warfare, Harald ever pursued his aim with unremitting perseverance. Rebellion was foreseen and crushed in the bud, and flight alone secured the rebel from death; hence it naturally resulted that the continual migrations gradually reduced the population of Norway to half its original number. On the death of Harald, his empire, erected at the cost of so much bloodshed, fell to pieces, but the people were too enfeebled by tyranny to raise themselves entirely from their state of subjection. The Bonden assembled for the purpose of electing a new king, and strife was about to ensue, when Hakon, surnamed the Good, the son of Harald, who had been bred up as a Christian in England, appeared, and peaceably addressing them, promised to revoke the tyrannical impositions of his father, and especially to restore to each man the free tenure of his Odol. Pleased with these promises, the people elected him at Thrandheim, and he was subsequently proclaimed king throughout the Fylker. A new source of contention arose from his attempting to introduce Christianity, which the Bonden successfully resisted, and forced their king to preside at their sacrificial feast, and to eat of the flesh of the sacred horse.

In the latter part of the tenth century, Olaf Tryggvason, who had been a bold pirate in his youth, and had become a convert to Christianity, was elected king, and undertook the work of conversion with a zeal worthy of Charlemagne. At the great Things or assemblies, the Bonden, headed by their Blotmenn, and sometimes by their idols, now confronted the monarch, surrounded by the Christian bishops, and his brilliant train of warriors. The debate upon religion usually lasted several days, and terminated in violence. Olaf finally had recourse to arms, and the most dreadful scenes of slaughter ensued. He would sometimes unexpectedly invade secluded valleys, or isolated tracts, whose inhabitants obstinately rejected Christianity, and lay them waste by fire and sword. The Bonden, meanwhile, were not idle; the arrow, the signal for a general rising, flew through the country, and Hakon, one of the most powerful of the Jarls, who was scarcely inferior to the king in talent and bravery, placed himself at their head; but his success was rendered null by his ambition, arrogance, and licentiousness. The Bonden, deeply injured by his forcible abduction of their wives and daughters, or offended by his haughty demeanor, revolted against and murdered him; an event that proved little favorable to Olaf, who, being defeated by Eiric, the son of Hakon, and by his allies, the Danes and Swedes, in a great sea-fight, threw himself, together with all his followers, into the sea, rather than incur the disgrace of captivity. Norway was partitioned by the victors, but, in the beginning of the eleventh century, was again united under the scepter of Olaf the Holy, who was canonized on account of his zeal in the work of conversion. His first attempts for the conversion of his heathen subjects, by means of instruction, failing, he had recourse to persecution, and emulated his predecessor, Olaf Tryggvason, in cruelty, laying whole villages of unbelievers waste with fire and sword. At length, a casual occurrence was the means of effecting a general conversion. A great Thing was being held at Thrandheim, as usual, by moonlight.

The Bonden stood, in immense numbers, forming a half circle, armed and with threatening aspect, opposite the king and his warriors. Olaf exerted his utmost eloquence in the cause of Christianity, but the Bonden replied to his arguments by saying, "A God whom we can neither see nor touch, is no God," and pointing to a gigantic wooden image of Thor, richly ornamented with gold, called upon the monarch to show them his god. The king mocked the wooden god, which had not the power of motion, and must be carried by his worshipers. At that moment, the rising sun illumined the eastern horizon. "Behold!" exclaimed the enthusiastic monarch, "Behold! our God approaches!" as he uttered these words, one of his followers split the image with one blow of his battle-ax, and snakes and mice, which had nestled inside, came rushing out, and the Bonden, mute with awe, turned from the prostrate idol to bend in adoration to the sun, which that day shone upon a Christian land.

Olaf was the founder of a new era in Norway, but did not escape the punishment he merited for his numerous deeds of cruelty. At that period, Canute the Great undertook the conquest of the North, and some of the Norwegians, thirsting to revenge their slaughtered brethren, some ambitious Jarls, and all, in fact, who hoped to profit by a revolution, invited him into their country. Olaf, after being defeated in a great sea-fight, fell a victim to treachery, and Norway became a Danish province.

Snorri Sturleson, the great Norwegian historian, compiled his work in the Icelandic tongue, in the earlier half of the thirteenth century.

CXXIII. Christianity and the Feudal System in the North

SUBSEQUENTLY to this period, the history of the North presents little worthy of remark until the time of the Reformation, and will for the future be merely referred to in this work when in relation with the affairs of Germany. The three kingdoms, or generally two of them, appear to have been sometimes forcibly united under one sovereign, at others again ruled by independent kings, and a long list of bloody broils between monarchs, and of contentions for the succession to the throne, blacken the page, which is alone rendered interesting by the repeated attempts made by the peasantry, at different periods, in each of the three kingdoms, to rescue their privileges from the deadly grasp of their kings or stadtholders, to abolish the tithes exacted by the clergy, and to check the rising power of the vassals of the crown, and the growing importance of the cities; but, although these revolutions often proved fatal to the monarchs, the authority of the state, the church and the nobility was already too firmly based on the superstitious belief of the Middle Ages to be shaken by the futile attempts of a body of peasants for the restoration of the ancient German system of government, which, however, still pervaded the constitution of the three kingdoms, founded upon that of the Franks.

The divine right of kings was the more easily recognized from its accordance with the legendary superstition anciently attached to the Drottars, the descendants of Odin. A brilliant court, composed of a noble band of scalds or bards, and of a warlike retinue, added splendor to royalty. The monarch nominated his Jarls as stadtholders over the Fylker and subordinate Herses over lesser tracts; the former of whom corresponded to the Grafs, the latter to the Centners, of the Franks. Sometimes it happened that a more powerful Jarl was placed over several others, and eventually received the Frankish title of duke. At the side of the temporal governor or Jarl stood his spiritual colleague, the bishop. The Fylker still retained the privilege of holding popular assemblies, which the king, the Jarl, or the bishop attended in person. At a time when the royal prerogative was still held in check by these assemblies, the Lagmann, or guardian of the national laws and privileges, confronted the monarch at the head of the Bonden, by whom he was chosen as the representative of their class; a dignity at once sacred and formidable.

The formation of a new class of nobility, composed of the vassals of the crown, and the gradual rise of cities and communities, greatly checked the power of the Bonden, and a struggle naturally ensued, in which the peasantry, although vanquished, finally retained, through their brilliant exploits and unwearied perseverance, an honorable position in the state. The great council of state—which in each of the three kingdoms replaced the general popular assemblies and greatly diminished the authority of the sovereign—was composed of deputies, the representatives of the clergy, the nobility, the communities, and the peasantry; a prerogative that was never enjoyed by the peasantry of the German empire.

CXXIV. *Iceland and Greenland*

DURING the reign of Harald Harfagra, A.D. 863, the island of Iceland, with its snow-capped mountains—one of which, Hecla, was at that time vomiting fire—was discovered by a Norwegian vessel, driven northward out of its course, which bore news of the discovery to Norway, where it was hailed with delight by the people, who, oppressed by tyranny, were at that period quitting their homes in thousands to seek elsewhere an asylum for their threatened liberty. The first settler, Ingolf, was speedily followed by such crowds of fugitives that the island, notwithstanding its size, seemed likely to be over-populated, and it was accordingly enacted, A.D. 873, that each new-comer should receive the portion of land covered by the smoke arising from a burning heap of fagots.

At first each tribe was headed by its own chief or elder (Godar), but at a later period they were all included in four provinces (Fiordungen), independent of each other, according to the ancient German system, and answering to the four cardinal points in their position on the island.

The fraudulent plans of Olaf Tryggvason, for the possession of the island, were foiled by the decided refusal returned to his flattering proposals by the national assembly. Christianity was first introduced in 981, by a Saxon priest named Frederich, and in the year 1000 it had already become so widely diffused that the Christian party succeeded in causing their religion to be proclaimed, in the public assembly, that of the state; this led to the dissolution of the Gau system, and to the union of the island into one state, governed by a Lagmann, whose dignity was not hereditary, and who presided over the general assembly or Althing. This simple republican form of government continued until 1261, when the union of the island with Norway was managed by the clergy and the Norwegian kings, with the concurrence of the people, who were allowed to retain their own laws. Since this period the island has sunk into insignificance. The ancient German system of government was maintained for a longer period and in greater purity in Iceland, while she retained her independence, than in any other part of

Europe, and her historical importance now alone consists in her possessing the only records in existence of the language (which is still spoken by the inhabitants), the poetry, religion, and legends of the ancient North, by which the obscurity of its history can be elucidated. The influence and fame of Rome, which spread over Germany, casting into oblivion remote and pagan times, scarce echoed to that distant shore, whose hardy sons and cold ungenial clime alike disdained the culture of the South, and where whose gods, now no longer adored, still live in song.

Shortly after the discovery of Iceland, Greenland, the northeastern part of the continent of America, was discovered by the Norwegians, who thus claim the honor of the discovery of America about five centuries earlier than that of Columbus. Greenland, so named on account of the verdure of the land and forests, must, at that period, have been a fine country. The Norwegians, who had settled there in great numbers, were carrying on a great traffic with Norway, and the Jarls, placed over the new country by the Norwegian monarchs, had become great and powerful,[1] when sudden destruction fell upon the colony; a fearful frost spread from the north pole, and covered the country with snow and ice, as it is to be seen at the present day. The land, deserted by the Norwegians, was soon completely forgotten, and entirely disappeared from history, until the second discovery of America.

The Norwegians also sailed to the southwest of Iceland and Greenland, and landed in a new country, which they named Winland, from the vine which there grew wild. They afterward made several expeditions to this coast, which, doubtless, formed part of that of America, and returned richly laden with its natural productions.

The Shetland, Orkney, and Faro Islands were, in the ninth century, cultivated by the Norwegians, and governed by Jarls. The Faro Islands are said to have been long re-

---

[1] Snorri gives a detailed account of these facts.

tained in paganism, by the cunning of old Trund of Göte, a sorcerer of legendary fame.

The distant expeditions undertaken by the Norwegians prove their naval skill. They were the first who ventured into the open sea. Other nations, until then, were only acquainted with the navigation of the coasts. It is also evident, from their bold and distant voyages, that they possessed a sort of compass. The Northern navigators who penetrated the Mediterranean, and settled in Greece and Italy, taught their art to the Southerns. All the terms made use of in navigation at the present day by all the nations of Europe may also be traced to a German origin.

CXXV. *The Norsemen*

THE daring expeditions and armed fraternities of the ancient Germans were common to all the Northern nations, and ceased only with the ancient system of government. They were continued to a much later period among the Scandinavians, and figure in history as the expeditions of the Norsemen, the general appellation for all the Scandinavian nations among the people of more southern latitudes.

The whole of the North swarmed with sea and Naes kings, and piratical republics, who attacked alike foreign and native ships, and landed indiscriminately on any coast for battle or for plunder; nor was the authority of either the monarch or the Fylker-kings respected by their subjects, until some great and piratical expedition had added luster to their name. These warlike and piratical expeditions received an additional impulse when the monarchical power in each of the three kingdoms became almost despotic and drove the people, wild as the element with which they strove, to seek refuge from tyranny at home on the ocean wave. During the reign of Harald Harfagra, half the population of Norway fled at times for safety to their ships. Immense numbers of these pirates wandered about the Northern Ocean, striking their native shores with terror, while others, as has been already related, colonized the northern islands and Greenland. Others, again, devastated the coasts of Saxony and France, ventured up the rivers, and fought many a hard battle with the Germans and Neustrians. A great multitude of this description, led by Rollo and flying from Harald Schönhaar, took possession of the northern coast of France, hence named Normandy, and voluntarily embraced Christianity. Rollo received the name of Robert, and took the oath of allegiance to the French monarch as first duke of Normandy, A.D. 911, while his followers, a mere armed multitude, naturally adopted the feudal system. Similar hordes and the Danish kings, at the head of immense armies, invaded, and, at different times, took possession of the whole of England, peopled some of the provinces, and, although finally obliged to yield to the ancient Anglo-Saxons, made a deep and lasting impression on the British language, manners, and constitution. At a later period, a duke of Normandy conquered and reigned over England, where he introduced the feudal system, A.D. 1066. Other hordes ventured into the Mediterranean, and opposed the Moors. Adventurers from the North also founded a state in Sicily, and shortly afterward the powerful kingdom of Naples. The expeditions of the Norsemen to the East are equally remarkable. The Danish and Swedish kings waged bloody wars with the Wendi, whom they often subdued and rendered tributary. All the Finnish races, on either side of the Baltic and within the Gulf of Finland, were also subdued by the Swedes. Indications of solitary expeditions having been made into Russia, even in pagan times, for the purpose of discovering ancient Asgard, or Caucasus, still exist; the body-guard of the Greek emperors was also formed from similar wanderers who reached Constantinople, and who, like the Gothic body-guard of earlier times, in the same city, were named Varingians, and were always recruited by fresh adventurers, who traversed Russia or the seas. The Russians, at that period the most barbarous of the Slavonian nations, became, by these means, acquainted with the brave Norsemen; and their history, according to the Chronicle of the monk Nestor, commences with a unanimous resolution, on the part of the people, to elect a Knæs or ruler, but as none of the nation was deemed worthy of the elevation, they invited the Norsemen into the country, and elected a gigantic warrior, named Ruric, a heathen, for their Knæs, who in this manner became the founder of the Russian empire. Like the rest of his countrymen throughout ancient Russia, he was named a Warager, a term synonymous with that of Varingian.

SECOND PERIOD

THE MIDDLE AGES

Zwei swert licz Got in ertriche zu beschirmene dy cristenheit, dem papste das geistliche, dem keiser das werltliche.—SACHSENSPIEGEL.

PART VIII

THE CARLOVINGIANS

CXXVI. *Louis the Pious and his Sons*

THE Middle Ages commenced with the German empire. The struggle between paganism and Christianity ceased, and the church of the new era, which, for seven succeeding centuries, has imposed its mysteries upon the nations of Germany, was triumphantly raised by the newly-acquired power of the emperor and the pope.

The period immediately subsequent to the reign of Charlemagne was troubled and gloomy. The scepter wielded by the Carlovingian monarchs, who had ever proved themselves the greatest men of their times, was now held by the feeble hand of Louis, the youngest, the most incapable, and the only surviving son of the great emperor, who long and deeply deplored the loss of Charles and Pipin. Pipin left a son, named Bernhard, to whom Charlemagne intrusted the government of Italy, and in whose favor, as successor to the imperial crown, a strong party was formed at court by the most influential among the nobility, headed by Wala, a descendant of Charles Martell; but Charlemagne, equally unbiased by their wishes as he was unmoved by his own inclination, declared his son, Louis, his heir. This emperor no sooner mounted the throne than he revenged himself on Bernhard's party, confined Wala in a monastery, caused Odoin the Brave, his sister's lover, to be assassinated, and replaced his father's gay and witty courtiers with devotees, by whom he was led to favor the interests of the pope. The guiltless Bernhard, perceiving the danger with which he was momentarily threatened, at first showed a disposition to rebel, but instantly submitted on receiving through the Empress Irmingarde an assurance of pardon, and a safe conduct from Louis, and came unarmed to Chalons in order to do homage to the faithless emperor, who caused his eyes to be torn from their sockets in so barbarous a manner that he expired within a few days. No sooner, however, had Louis thus glutted his revenge than, struck with remorse for his crime, rendered doubly poignant by grief for the death of Irmingarde, A.D. 818, he evinced a desire to abdicate his throne, and to seclude himself within a cloister, but was dissuaded by the priests. The pope, Stephen, who had instigated him against Bernhard, presented him with a crown, in return for which he thrice humbly prostrated himself at the feet of the pontiff, whose successor, Paschal, encouraged by this act of humility, caused himself to be elected without receiving the ratification of a sovereign before whom both he and the clergy deemed it no longer necessary to cringe, and who, bending deferentially before them, implicitly yielded to their tyranny and imposed penances, from a superstitious belief that the salvation of his soul depended on an unconditional submission, and on unlimited grants to the church. Wala said that the emperor took too deep a concern in spiritual, and the pope, in temporal, matters.

Louis resembled his father in the gigantic size of his person, and in his skill in warlike sports and exercises, but the narrowness of his mind and his pusillanimity contrasted strikingly with the genius of his great progenitor. Hence arose the aversion manifested toward him by the laity, and the arrogance of the clergy. Devoid of intellect, irresolute, and weak, he was ever swayed by passion or prejudice to do the wrong he dreaded, which was ever followed by remorse, whose stings he sought to allay by a mean submission to his spiritual advisers, who, far from favoring his desire for seclusion, surrounded him with the most beautiful of the daughters of the nobility, and at length induced him to wed the Bavarian, Jutta, of the race of the Welfi, A.D. 819, who, by her skill and beauty, gained unbounded influence over him, and whose policy being to render herself universally beloved, conciliated Bernhard's adherents, and recalled Wala, who, meanwhile, had been chosen abbot of Corvey, to court, Louis, on his part, performing a solemn penance at Altigny, A.D. 822, and making a public protestation of repentance for the murder of his relative, before the assembled Diet.

A trait, strongly characteristic of the times, recorded by the Saxon annalist, strikingly demonstrates the objection prevailing among the upholders of ancient German liberty to the imposition of the new feudal system. Ethico, the Alemann, the father of Jutta, forbade his son Henry to hold any lands in fee from the Frankish monarch; but Henry allowing himself to be persuaded by his sister to hold as much land in fee as he could drive over with a golden plow during the emperor's sleep, the old man's ancestral pride and love of the ancient rights of his family were so deeply wounded that he concealed himself for the remainder of his life in the Schwarzwald.

While these events were taking place at court, the rebellious Bretons and Basques, the Norsemen, Obotrites, the Croatian Slavi, and Bulgarians,[1] were successfully driven from the frontiers. Harald, the Danish king, came to the court of Louis and was baptized.[2] He was afterward expelled by his subjects. St. Anscar, regardless of danger and

[1] Balderich, duke of Friuli, was deprived in 827 of his dignity, on account of his incapacity; the dukedom was dissolved, and divided among Gränzgrafen, or governors of the frontier.

[2] Archbishop Ebbo of Rheims was the first and most active of the missionaries in Holstein. His attempts, however, failed. Two of his disciples who were by chance passing Windbergen in the country of the Dithmarsi on Wodan's day were struck by lightning, and the people imagining this occurrence to be a sign of the wrath of their ancient god, Ebbo lost all his followers.

opposition, continued to carry on the work of conversion in the North, and became the first bishop of Hamburg, A.D. 834.

In Spain, the Moors made unopposed an inroad into the French territory; and Graf Bonifacius of Corsica undertook an expedition against Africa, whence, after fighting five battles near Carthage, he returned, crowned with glory.

Louis traveled through the empire, in order to visit the churches. It was on this occasion that he founded the bishopric of Hildesheim.[1] Several new monasteries were also founded during his reign, the most noted of which were those of Corvey, A.D. 822, Hervorden, Murhard, Schwarzach, Hirsau, Gandersheim, Quedlinburg, etc. At a synod held at Paris he also reintroduced the worship of images and pictures, A.D. 825, which had been prohibited by Charlemagne.

Louis had three sons by Irmingarde, Lothar, Pipin, and Louis, between whom he divided his empire, before his second marriage, in the manner they were to possess it after his death. Lothar was to be invested with the imperial dignity, and to possess Italy and the Rhine country as far as the sea, while Pipin was to reign to the westward over France, and Louis to the east over Germany. Jutta, however, bore a fourth son, Charles, surnamed the Bald, who became the favorite of the old emperor, and a new division of the empire, A.D. 829, by which the eldest sons were wronged, was made in his favor. An unnatural spectacle, that of the sons rebelling against their father, was now beheld by the people, who, although horror-struck at the cause of the war, willingly lent their aid against a sovereign they despised. Temporal power decayed, and the popes took advantage of the universal confusion to increase their influence and to extend their dominion over the minds of the people.

Wala, who resided with Lothar in Italy, equally opposed the worthless old emperor and the division of the empire. The union of the empire under one energetic sovereign was

---

[1] According to the legend, Louis found a blooming rose-tree in the midst of the snow, on the spot on which he afterward caused the cathedral of Hildesheim to be erected.

his most ardent wish, and he sought to rouse Lothar to emulate the great deeds of his grandsire; but this prince, although fond of power, was too spiritless for any undertaking demanding intellect and energy, and Wala's grand plan degenerated to wretched intrigues. The three brethren leagued together, took their father prisoner at Compiegne, and accused their stepmother, Jutta, of adultery with the Markgraf Bernhard of Barcelona, and of having blinded the emperor by her magical arts, A.D. 830. Pipin and Louis, however, quickly deserted Lothar, who grasped at sole sovereignty, and leagued with their father against him, A.D. 831. A negotiation took place between the contending parties at Aix-la-Chapelle, at which Lothar had the weakness to sue for pardon, and the perfidy to condemn his friends and his faithful adviser, Wala, to death, with his own mouth. Wala escaped with his life, but was dragged by the emperor, who feared his talents, from one cloistered prison to another. Jutta was solemnly declared innocent, and Graf Bernhard was compelled to quit the court.

No sooner had Jutta gained this victory than she attempted to secure the chief part of the immense inheritance to her son Charles, a project which again induced Pipin and Louis to league with Lothar for the exclusion of their half-brother. The pope, Gregory IV., foreseeing that the life of the emperor was drawing to its close, and that it was to the interest of the church to favor the stronger party, became their ally. Pipin was the first to quarrel with his father, who deprived him of Aquitania, which he bestowed upon Charles, and the three brethren marched against their parent at the head of a powerful army, which encamped on the Sigwaldsberg, near Colmar. The emperor was at Worms. Long negotiations took place, and even the pope hesitated to give the signal for attack, when Wala arrived on the scene of action and decided the affair. The pope was sent to the emperor to demand his submission, while the allegiance of the imperial army was attempted to be shaken; and before Louis had come to a decision, his followers deserted him to a man, during the night of the 29th of June, 833, and he was obliged to yield himself prisoner to his sons. The field where this took place was known until a very late period as the Field of Lies (Lugenfeld). Public opinion condemned both father and sons, but the clergy and the great vassals found (as at an earlier period under the Merovingians) these family dissensions profitable, and on that account encouraged and augmented the discord that prevailed.

The emperor was carried to a monastery at Soissons, where Lothar caused him to do penance, kneeling on a hair cloth, and in that position to read a paper in which he accused himself of perjury, murder, and theft, of having been deceived by Jutta's witchcraft, etc. He was also deprived of his arms, in order to render him unworthy of bearing the imperial dignity, but in spite of every threat he could not be induced to take the vow that separated him from the world, from a secret hope of a second release,[1] which did not long tarry: the jealousy of Pipin and Louis was again roused by Lothar's superior power, and they once more leagued against him, under the pretext that they could not countenance the ill-treatment of their father, whom Lothar was forced to restore to liberty and to the throne, A.D. 834. The released emperor now divided the empire between Pipin, Louis, and Charles, to the exclusion of Lothar. The Normans attacked Friesland with fire and sword,[2] and the Moors crossed the Spanish frontier, while a Moorish fleet landed in Provence and plundered Marseilles; occurrences by which the emperor, whose thoughts were solely occupied in providing an inheritance for his favorite son, by a new division, remained unmoved. For this purpose he attempted to bribe the Germans by a gift, deemed in those times of inestimable

---

[1] Bishop Drogo, of Metz, a natural son of Charlemagne, ever evinced such fidelity to the emperor that he made him his confidant and confessor, and died in his arms.

[2] The exiled Harald had received Rüstringerland from the emperor in fee, but was killed by the Frisii, who believed that he had invited the Danes into their country. Heligoland was also at this period taken by the Danes.

value, the relics of St. Vitus, which he caused to be borne, in 836, in a solemn procession from Paris to the monastery of Corvey, founded by St. Anscar, in 826, in Westphalia.[1] Countless multitudes accompanied the procession in its progress through the empire; the Parisians wept at the departure of the sacred bones, while the Saxons hailed their arrival with festive joy. The sons of Louis, however, were not disturbed in their plans by this occurrence. Lothar, who had withdrawn to Italy, and whose adviser, Wala, was dead, had an interview at Trient with his brother Louis (surnamed the German, or the Bavarian, in order to distinguish him from his father), probably with the design of warning him against Jutta's fresh projects. Jutta instantly accused Louis of conspiring with Lothar, and established an alliance between Pipin and Charles, who agreed to divide the empire into two equal parts, and to force Lothar and Louis to submit. Shortly after this, Pipin died, and Jutta, perceiving her inability to support the claims she had arrogated for her son, entered into a negotiation with Lothar, who, with characteristic perfidy, consented to divide the empire with Charles to the exclusion of Louis, and of his nephew Pipin, the son of his deceased brother. While these wretched intrigues were being carried on, the emperor expired, A.D. 840, on an island in the Rhine, near Ingelheim, shouting with his latest breath, like the huntsmen, "Hutz! Hutz!" in order to scare the devil from his bedside.

Louis was no sooner dead than Charles discovered that Lothar, instead of placing him on an equal footing, would merely tolerate him as an inferior; he accordingly deserted him, and entered into a compact with Louis the German, with whom he thought more easily to divide the empire, as Louis laid no claim to the title of emperor. The new con-

---

[1] This saint, at a still later period, greatly conduced to the conversion of the Slavi, by the same honors being paid to him which were formerly a part of the worship offered to Swantewit, their ancient deity; and so late as a century ago, the peasants in the country around Ratisbon annually offered cocks on the altar of St. Vitus, as had been their custom a thousand years earlier, when pagans, to offer them on that of Swantewit.

federates now took up arms against Lothar and young Pipin, who were defeated in a great battle that took place on the 25th of June, 841, near Fontenay, in Burgundy. One hundred thousand men fell in this worthless cause, and the nobility was so thinned that for long after it was deemed necessary when a freeman wedded a noble lady to raise him to her rank in order to repair the loss.

Lothar fled to Aix-la-Chapelle, turned the great silver tables of Charlemagne into coin, and proclaimed throughout Saxony that all the Edelings should be deprived of their lands, and that the Frilings and Lazzi, who since the time of Charlemagne had been subordinate to them, should be restored to their ancient privileges. The Saxons rose in crowds, formed the Stellinga (restorers) confederacy, and expelled not only the Edelings, but also the priests, paganism being still rife among the commonalty. Victory, nevertheless, still favored the arms of Louis and Charles, who on the 14th of February, 842, took a federative oath at Strassburg, which was loudly repeated by their respective armies; by that of Louis the German, on the right bank of the Rhine, in the German language, and by that of Charles, on the left bank, in the Roman tongue. At the same time, the two confederates had the cunning to call a synod of bishops, before which they accused their brother Lothar of protecting paganism; and, as the Stellinga was naturally held in abomination by all the temporal lords, who feared lest the example of the Saxon peasantry might influence their vassals and endanger the feudal system, they flocked in crowds beneath the standard of the two brothers; and Lothar, finding himself solely upheld by the Saxons, deserted them with his usual perfidy, and made his treacherous betrayal of them a means of reconciliation with his brothers. While he was carrying on this negotiation with them in France, Louis suddenly marched into Saxony, and after defeating the confederates, treated the chiefs of the Stellinga with unexampled cruelty, causing fourteen of them to be hanged, one hundred and forty to be beheaded, and innumerable others to have their hands chopped off. Thus terminated the first great struggle of one class against the others, of the nobility against the peasantry.

The treaty of Verdun, A.D. 843, concluded between the three brethren, rewarded Lothar's treachery with the imperial crown, and an extensive territory, including the Netherlands, the Rhine country, Burgundy, and Italy, which received the name of Lothringia (Lotharingien, Lotharii regnum). Louis the German received, as his portion, all the country lying to the right of the new empire, and the title of a German king; and Charles the Bald was created king of France.

While these negotiations and the war with Saxony were being carried on, the Norsemen reappeared and plundered the coasts of the Baltic; at the same time, the Moors landed in the south and sacked the town of Arles; the Bretons also again rebelled. Bernard, Markgraf of Barcelona, was seized and executed by order of Charles the Bald,[1] under pretext of disloyalty, but more probably on account of his former intercourse with the empress Jutta. Lothar died in 855, and divided Lothringia among his three sons, who did not long survive him. The only one of any importance was the second son, Lothar II., who, by divorcing his wife Thietberga, and wedding the beautiful Walrade, afforded an opportunity to the pope, Nicholas I., to exert his authority. The marriage with Walrade was, by his influence, annulled by the council at Metz, A.D. 863, and Hugo the son of Walrade was declared incapable of succeeding to the crown. Lothar, upon this, divorced Walrade, but shortly afterward remarried her. His brother, Louis II., protected Benevento (which at that time was divided into the three little dukedoms of Benevento, Salerno, and Capua, and had greatly sunk in importance) against the Moors, who had taken possession of Rome, and had converted the church of St. Peter into a stable.

---
[1] According to another account, Charles is said to have stabbed him with his own hand, and to have spurned the corpse with his foot, although they resembled each other so strongly that every one believed them to be father and son.

Louis the German was, meanwhile, fully occupied in repelling the attacks of the Slavi, who took advantage of the internal dissensions in the empire to rise en masse on all sides. The Obotrites set the example in the North. Louis put their prince, Gozzomvil, to death, A.D. 844, and placed an able man, named Tachulf, as Markgraf in Thuringia. This brave man long waged war with the Slavi, and it is related of him that once, although desperately wounded, he gave audience to the Slavian embassadors, seated on his warhorse, without betraying a symptom of the pain he suffered. The Germans, mistrusting him on account of his attempts to conciliate the neighboring Sorbi, A.D. 849, ventured a battle without him, and were defeated. The flying Thuringians are said to have been welcomed by their wives with blows. So intense was the hatred between the two nations that when Chiztibor, the prince of the Sorbi, wished to make terms with the Germans, he was murdered by his subjects, A.D. 858. Tabamzivil, prince of the Obotrites, submitted, 862.

In the South, the Bulgarians attained considerable power after the complete destruction of the kingdom of the Avari, and advanced into the mountains of Croatia. The Markgraf, Berthold, was defeated by them, A.D. 818; the Markgraf, Rathod, succeeded in expelling them, but afterward rebelling, was deprived of his government. The Slavian Maharanen, or Moravians, also rose under their prince, Rastiz, and began to spread over their confines; they and their allies, the Bohemians, were, however, so bravely resisted by the Markgraf Ernst, who completely routed them, that Carlmann, the son of Louis the German, wedded his daughter Luitswinda. In 858, Carlmann had conceived the project of a nearer alliance between the Slavi and the Germans, for which a good foundation had been laid in the mountains by Graf Gerold and the bishop Virgilius, and for this reason attempted to render himself independent of his father, who overcame him, and removed the Markgraf Ernst, A.D. 863; upon this, Carlmann allied himself with Rastiz of Moravia, but was again defeated by his father, who nominated Gunthachar Markgraf of Austria; but this Markgraf making common cause with Rastiz, Carlmann sought to make amends for his former derelictions by marching against them on his father's behalf. He was victorious, killed Gunthachar, and caused Rastiz, who was betrayed into his hands by his nephew, Suatopluk, to be deprived of sight, A.D. 870. Suatopluk was kept in honorable confinement at Ratisbon, where he lived in luxury and appeared to be perfectly resigned to his fate. Meanwhile, the German Markgrafs, Wilhelm and Engelschalk, treated the Moravians so arbitrarily that they rebelled, and Suatopluk, under pretext of appeasing them, went among them, but no sooner found himself once more among his countrymen, than, loading the Germans with imprecations, he caused his escort to be assassinated. Two Bavarian armies, sent into Moravia, were defeated, and Suatopluk not only preserved, but also extended his dominion, A.D. 872.

In the meantime, Louis the Younger, the second son of Louis the German, formed an alliance in Saxony and Thuringia, with Rathulf, the son of Tachulf, similar to that between Carlmann and Ernst, and kept the Sorbi and Bohemians in check on this side of the empire. On one occasion he surprised the Bohemians when engaged in a great wedding procession, and carried off the bride; whence arose the saying, "No one knows who may lead home the bride." The Bohemians again rose, during a fresh incursion of the Norsemen into Germany, but were repulsed by Poppo, Rathulf's successor. Louis the German died in 876, leaving three sons,[1] Carlmann, who inherited Bavaria and Carinthia, Louis the Younger, who succeeded to the throne of Saxony and Thuringia, and Charles the Thick, who reigned over

---

[1] And two daughters, Hildegarde, who in her twenty-first year became abbess of the convent founded by her father at Zurich, and Bertha, who succeeded her in that dignity. According to the legend, they dwelt in the castle of Baldern, whence they were led by a stag bearing lighted candles on his antlers, to the spot where the convent now stands. Their father is also said to have resided at times at Baldern on the Albis.

Swabia. Carlmann died in 880, and left an illegitimate son, named Arnulf, who became Markgraf of Carinthia.

The race of Lothar no sooner became extinct than a quarrel arose for the Lothringian inheritance, between Charles the Bald of France and Louis the Younger of Germany, and a bloody engagement took place near Andernach on the Rhine,[2] which proved disastrous to Charles, who died during the following year, A.D. 876, leaving an only son, Louis the Stammerer, who died in 879, and left three sons, of whom the youngest, Charles the Simple, ere long only remained.

The natural result of these repeated and manifold divisions, was that the Norsemen and Arabians redoubled their daring attacks upon the empire; that in the East a powerful Slavian kingdom, unopposed by Germany, arose; and that, in the interior of the empire, the power of the pope on the one hand, and that of the great vassals on the other, steadily and surely increased, to the detriment of the imperial prerogative.

CXXVII. *The Incursions of the Norsemen*

THE bold Norse pirates continued to disturb the empire; their insolence surpassed all belief, for not content with plundering the coasts, they advanced in their small vessels up the rivers, and suddenly appeared far up the country before an alarm could be given. Their path was marked by heaps of dead and ruins. They unhesitatingly attacked even fortified cities, of which they took and destroyed several in France, and many a hard contest was fought by them against armies greatly their superiors in number. They always fought on foot, and with such extraordinary activity as easily to overcome the heavy cavalry of the French. If defeated, or in danger of being so, they hurried to their ships, which they rowed with such rapidity as to render pursuit impossible.

---

[2] Besides the gateway and other Roman remains, the fine ruins of an ancient castle of the Austrasian kings are still to be seen at this town.

So greatly and universally were they feared that prayers were read in the churches for deliverance from them.

In 841, headed by Ascar, they burned Rouen. In 843 they advanced up the Loire, but were repulsed in their attempt upon Tours. Undeterred by this check, they continued their depredations under their savage leader, Hasting, along the northern coasts of France, after which they ventured up the Garonne in order to plunder the south, and defeated Totila, duke of Gascony, but were surprised at Tarbes by the peasantry of Bigorre, and for the most part slain. Notwithstanding this disaster, a Norse fleet ventured further south in the following year, plundered Lisbon, advanced up the Guadalquivir into Andalusia, took Seville, and returned laden with booty. The Moors believed them to be evil wizards. Emboldened by this success, they reappeared in the Seine, and their leader, Regnar, took possession of Paris, whence Charles the Bald bribed him to depart on payment of seven thousand pounds of silver, A.D. 845. The Norsemen then turned eastward toward Germany, and devastated Friesland. The emperor, Lothar, had the folly again to give up Rustringerland, together with the fortress of Dorstad, to Rorich, a son of Harald, who had formerly held them, on condition of his guarding the country against the inroads of his countrymen. The treaty was speedily broken. Gottfried, Rorich's brother, again plundered Friesland, and advanced up the Loire as far as Tours, followed by the dreaded Hasting, who once more took Paris, marched into Burgundy, laid waste the whole country, and finally took possession of Tours, A.D. 853, where much treasure had been carried for safety, and which had formerly been the aim of those pirate hordes. No energetic opposition was made to his advance, and his departure was purchased by Charles the Bald with 685 pounds of gold, and 3,250 pounds of silver. Rome, ever clothed in fabled splendor by the imaginative pagans, now became the aim of the enterprising Hasting, who sailed with a hundred ships through the Straits of Gibraltar and plundered the coasts of Spain and Africa.

On arriving in the harbor of Lucca, at that period a city of considerable importance and strongly fortified, which he mistook for Rome, he found the inhabitants engaged in the celebration of the Christmas festival, and sending a deputation of his followers into the city, under pretext of demanding an honorable burial-place for their chieftain, whom they asserted to be dead, the unsuspecting Lombards permitted him to be carried in solemn procession to the church, where, springing from his coffin, he stabbed the officiating bishop to the heart, and at the head of his supposed mourners, all well-armed freebooters, sacked the city and retreated to his ships, heavily laden with booty and accompanied by a crowd of prisoners, consisting of the most beautiful of the women and maidens, whom he afterward had the barbarity to throw into the sea, together with the plunder, in order to lighten his vessels during a storm, a loss he repaired shortly after by sailing up the Rhone, and laying the country waste on both sides. Other Norse hordes also continually devastated the north of France, and forced Charles the Bald to purchase their departure with 3,000 pounds of gold, A.D. 860. In the year 860, Hasting consented to be baptized, and to swear allegiance to Charles on condition of receiving the title of Count of Chartres.

Two German warriors who undertook to guard the coasts are particularly remarkable. Baldwin, Count of Flanders, with the iron arm, seduced Judith, the youthful daughter of Charles the Bald, who, nevertheless, was the widow of two of the monarchs of England, of the father of Ethelwolf, and of his son Ethelbold. The discovery of their intercourse at first greatly enraged the French king, who was, however, finally induced to accept him as his son-in-law, and to place all the other minor Grafs in his neighborhood beneath his jurisdiction. Robert, surnamed the Strong, a native of Saxony, who had become Count of Maine, equally distinguished himself against the Norsemen. He was the ancestor of Hugh Capet, who gave a dynasty to France. He fell in a bloody engagement in which the Norsemen were worsted, not far from Anvers, in 866. For some time after this the country remained undisturbed, the pirates having turned their attention to England, where Alfred, the wise king of that island, anxious for their departure from his coasts, at length found means to persuade their leader Hrolf (Rollo) to re-embark for Germany, where, after defeating Count Reinbold of Friesland, and taking Count Reichard of Hennegau prisoner, in 876, he laid the French territory waste, until bribed by Charles to depart with a gift of 5,000 pounds of silver, A.D. 878. Another Norman horde under Gottfried settled at Ghent and took possession of the castle of Haslau. Gottfried formed an alliance with Hugo, the bastard of Lothringen, the son of Walrade, and married his sister Gisela. Hugo had, until now, vainly aspired to the possession of Lothringen, and had dwelt like a robber in the forests. The Slavi appear to have been also drawn into the plot. Some time before this, Ludolf had been nominated Graf of Saxony in order the better to defend the coasts against the Norsemen; his brother, Bruno, the founder of Braunschweig (Bruno's Wyk), Brunswick, marched at the head of the Saxon arrierban against Gottfried, but suffered a bloody defeat near Ebbekesdorf, in which he fell, together with two bishops and twelve Grafs. This battle was followed by several others, in which the Germans were victorious. Adam von Bremen relates that the Frisii, incited by their bishop, Rembert, fell upon the victorious Norsemen and slew upward of 10,000 of them. According to the account of the monk Regino, the German emperor, Louis the Younger, gained a great victory at Thimiun (Thuin on the Sambre), A.D. 879, but did not follow up his advantage, owing to his anxiety if possible to save the life of his illegitimate son, Hugo, whom he believed a prisoner, but who was afterward discovered among the slain. According to other chroniclers, this battle took place in 880, and the victor mentioned is Louis of France, the son of Louis the Stammerer.[1] Both of these monarchs died in 882. The

---

[1] Adam von Bremen clearly distinguishes the German Louis as victor shortly before his death from the French Louis, who was at first victorious, but finally

Slavian nations, the Sorbi, Daleminzii, and Bohemians, who, after the battle of Ebbekesdorf, had risen en masse and had made an inroad into Germany, were successfully repulsed by Poppo, duke of Thuringia. Unable to settle in Germany, the Norsemen, whom tyranny at home, as has already been mentioned, had driven from their native land, visited other countries, where they founded colonies and new kingdoms.

CXXVIII. *Rise of the great Vassals and of the Popes*

CHARLEMAGNE had arbitrarily removed the great dukes from office, while he favored the lower orders of the nobility, but under the weak rule of Louis the Pious, and during the subsequent partition of the empire among his descendants, their favorites took advantage of the discord that prevailed among them to revive the title of Duke, and to arrogate to themselves such exorbitant power that the kings were forced to purchase the fidelity of their vassals by valuable gifts. The dukes and Markgrafs, moreover, who defended the frontiers against the Norsemen, the Moors, and the Slavi, attained considerable power by their military achievements.

The dukes of Lombardy were almost independent of the emperor. The national hatred of the Italians, and the ambition of the popes, supported them against Germany. They had, however, to endure many desperate encounters with the Moors. The dukes of Saxony and Thuringia became powerful and insolent as soon as they had rendered themselves necessary to the emperor by their exploits against the Norsemen and the Slavi. Ludolf,[1] duke of Saxony, pro-

---

defeated. Luthewicus Imperator (the Younger) cum paganis dimicans victor exstitit et paullo post obiit. Luthewicus Franciæ rex (the son of the Stammerer), victor et victus exstitit. In the Annals of Fulda, under the year 881, the latter is merely mentioned. Regis Hludowici nepos Hludovicus cum Nordmannis dimicans nobiliter thriumphavit.

[1] This duke, and his wife Oda, visited Rome, where he was highly favored by the pope; he founded the convent of Gandersheim, of which, in 853, he made his daughter, Hademoda, abbess. These were the first greetings of the newly-rising powers, the hierarchy and the feudal aristocracy, behind the back of the emperor.

nounced his dignity hereditary, and was succeeded in it by his son Otto. Thuringia also retained its dukes, although they were not all of the same race. Not long before this, Count Baldwin, with the iron arm, had firmly rooted his family in Flanders, where, then as now, the language was half Gallic (Walloon, Neustrian) and half German, although the country was a Neustrian or French fief.[1] In Swabia, the house of the Welfs had already attained considerable importance, although they enjoyed no dignity under the empire. In Bavaria, Count Arbo aspired to independence, and entered into an alliance with the Moravian Suatopluk (also named Zwentibold), who, A.D. 884, greatly extended his territory. He was, however, forced to submit. Burgundy, now possessed by the Lothringians, now by the French Carlovingians, asserted her independence after the death of Louis the Stammerer, and raised one of the native Grafs, Boso (who had seduced Irmengarde, the daughter of Louis II., by whom he was invited to aspire to that dignity), at Montaille to the throne. His popularity with his countrymen rendered the attempts of the weak Carlovingians to dispossess him of his crown unavailing, and he was succeeded by his son Louis. He was also upheld by the clergy, whose unity was strengthened by each division of the power of the temporal rulers.

Vice and unbounded insolence already marked the first triumphs of the church. The history of the infamous Pope Joan belongs to this epoch. She is said to have been a German, named Jutta, Gerberta (several other names are also ascribed to her), who was born at Ingelheim, and received

---

[1] The German and French languages are, even at the present day, bounded by a line running between two ranges of cities. Those on the German side are: Gravelingen, Winnoxbergen, Cassel, Belle, Meessene, Meenen, Cortryc, Audenarde, Rense, Gerärdsbergen (Grammont), Edingen (Enghien), Hal, Brussels, Lyons, Thienen (Tirlemont), St. Truyden, Tongern, Maestricht, Aix-la-Chapelle, Eupen, St. Vith, Reuland, Vianden, Diekirch, Arlon, and Luxembourg. Those on the French side are: Calais, St. Omer, Lille, Tournay, Ath, Nivelles, Wawre, Jodoigne, Hannut, Liege, Verviers Limburg, Malmedy, Houffalize, Bastoigne, Etalle, Virton, and Longwy.

an excellent education from her father, a man of deep learning. Becoming enamored of a monk at Fulda, she disguised herself in male attire, took the oath of celibacy, and joined her lover in his monastery. They subsequently traveled together as far as Greece, and Jutta appeared at Athens in the character of a public teacher. Here her lover died. She, however, gradually rose from one dignity to another, and was finally elected pope, when she took another lover. During her pregnancy, according to the legend, an angel promised her forgiveness for her crime if she would consent to publish her shame before the assembled people, and she was accordingly delivered during a great and solemn procession. She was named Pope John VIII.

Nicolas I., who filled the papal chair in 858, greatly extended the already firmly-rooted power of the church. His annulment of the marriage of Lothar II. and Walrade, and his declaration of the illegitimacy of their son, proved the superiority of the authority of the pope over that of the emperor. As a means of placing the papal power on a firmer basis, he either fabricated or sanctioned the fabrication of the false decretals which issued from Mayence, a city which, since the time of St. Bonifacius, had remained in close alliance with Rome. It was one of the principal repositories of theological learning, and it was hence that the German deacon, Benedictus Levita, promulgated a collection of church ordinances or decretals, which declared the pope the absolute sovereign of the church, set him above the councils, made the nomination of all the bishops to depend upon him alone, reserved to him the decision in all clerical matters, and even in all trivial affairs left the appeal open to him. In order to furnish these decretals with a respectable antiquity, and to give them the validity of laws more venerable than the imperial dignity, their original composition was falsely ascribed to St. Isidorus, a Spaniard, who lived in the seventh century, and their authenticity was asserted by Nicolas, who founded upon them the universal dominion of the papal tiara. He died in 867, and was succeeded by

Hadrian, who pursued the policy of his predecessor. The popes, his successors, were weak and licentious.

There were, besides Benedictus Levita and his popish party, several other German theologians, far more distinguished for learning, who were not all subservient to Rome. The school founded by Alcuin had the reputation of being free in its opinions and spirit. His disciples taught at Mayence, Fulda, Corvey, St. Gall, Reichenau, Prüm, Weissenburg, etc., and in the monastic academies, and a dispute arose between those most noted among them, which may be regarded as the germ whence sprang the controversy of later times between Catholicism, Lutherism, and Calvinism. Paschasius Radbert, for instance, a monk of Corvey, an enthusiastic and imaginative man, defended the real presence of Christ in the eucharist, the worship of the Virgin Mary, and that of images and pictures, in a word, all that influenced the senses in the worship of God; his doctrine became the prevailing one in the Middle Ages; he it was who first aroused that romantic enthusiasm which rendered the mother of the Saviour the ideal of beauty, the mystic deity of every heart. Rhabanus Maurus, archbishop of Mayence, the most famous and the most learned of Alcuin's disciples, sought, on the contrary, to develop the minds of his followers instead of exciting their imaginations, and demanded, like Luther, not only free inquiry, and the free use of reason and philosophy, but also the introduction of the German language into the church service. Gottschalk, finally, a monk of Fulda, asserted, like Calvin, the predestination of each individual to salvation or damnation, and completely denied the existence of free-will and of meritorious deeds. Rhabanus opposed both sectarians, but only succeeded in overcoming Gottschalk. This poor monk, a native of Saxony, with an imagination still fired by enthusiastic feelings, roused by his late conversion to Christianity, obstinately adhered to a doctrine for which he pined twenty-one years in prison. Radbert's poetical belief, on the other hand, gained, in union with the false decretals, the victory over the free-spirited efforts of Rhabanus, and although several distinguished disciples of the latter continued to assert the right of free inquiry, and to demand the introduction of the German language into the church service, they were unable to stem the popular current, or to oppose the increasing power of the popes, who alone tolerated a blind belief and the use of the Latin tongue.

Among the last champions of mental freedom, Walafried Strabo, abbot of Reichenau, distinguished himself, like his master, Rhabanus, by a glossary in the German language, and by manuals on general knowledge; Atfried of Weissenburg, by the composition of an evangelical harmony in German, the History of Christ in verse, which however does not possess the poetical merit of "der Heliand," "the Saviour," a poem that not long ago became known; Notker Labeo of St. Gall, by his German Psalms, and Willeram, abbot of Ebersberg, by a Paraphrase of the Song of Solomon. Rhegino, abbot of Prüm, wrote a universal chronicle, and besides Eginhart, who has already been mentioned, an unknown monk from St. Gall, and the so-called Saxon poet (*poeta Saxo*), recorded the deeds of Charlemagne. Theganus, bishop of Treves, was the biographer of Louis the Pious, and the dissensions of his sons were chronicled by Nithard, the grandson of Charlemagne. The Annals of Fulda are also a celebrated German historical work of the ninth century. There are, moreover, several biographies of different saints and churchmen; for instance, that of Wala.

It was at this period that the prophetess, Theoda of Constance, who announced the near coming of Christ, was sentenced by the council of Mayence to be beaten as an impostor with stripes; while the hermit Meinhard, who was murdered by robbers[1] "in the dark forest," was canonized by the church, and the celebrated monastery of Einsiedeln in Switzerland was raised over his tomb.

---

[1] They were betrayed by ravens, as the murderers of Ibycus were by cranes.

CXXIX. Charles the Thick and Arnulf

CHARLES THE THICK, the youngest of the sons of Louis the German, inherited in 882, on the death of his childless brother, Louis the Younger, all the German and Lothringian territory, with the exception of Burgundy; and in 884, also France, properly the inheritance of Charles the Simple, whose two elder brothers were dead, but who, being the issue of a marriage pronounced illegal by the pope, and, on account of his imbecility, being recognized by the French themselves as incapable of succeeding to the throne, Charles the Thick easily took possession of the country, and before long reunited France with Germany, in which he was greatly assisted by the pope, to whom he secretly made great concessions, in order to be acknowledged by him as legitimate heir to the crown.

Charles the Thick was good-natured and indolent. His favorite project, the restoration of the empire as it stood under Charlemagne, he sought to realize by means of bribes and promises, treaties of peace and other transactions, perfectly in conformity with his character, in which he ever unhesitatingly sacrificed honor to interest. The same means that had succeeded with the pope he imagined would prove equally successful in treating with the Norsemen, who, after the death of Louis the Younger, renewed their depredations under Gottfried, and laid the Rhine country waste. The palace of Charlemagne at Aix-la-Chapelle was converted by them into a stable. Bishop Wala fell bravely fighting at the head of an unequal force before the gates of Metz. The cities on the banks of the Rhine were burned to the ground, and the whole country between Liege, Cologne and Mayence laid desolate. At length Siegfried, the brother of Gottfried, was induced to withdraw his ravaging hordes by the gift of 2,000 pounds of gold, and for the additional sum of 12,000 pounds of silver (to defray which Charles the Thick seized all the treasures of the churches) consented to a truce of twelve years. Gottfried was, moreover, formally invested with Friesland as a fief of the empire. The Norsemen, however, notwithstanding these stipulations, continued their depredations, advanced as far as the Moselle, and destroyed the city of Treves, but were suddenly attacked in the forest of Ardennes, by the charcoal men and peasants, and 10,000 of them cut to pieces, A.D. 883. Charles now became anxious to free himself from his troublesome vassal in Friesland, and the Markgraf Henry, who guarded the frontier at Grabfeld against the Sorbi, brother to Poppo, duke of Thuringia, the confidant of the emperor, invited Gottfried to a meeting, at which he caused him to be treacherously murdered. Gottfried's brother-in-law, the bastard Hugo, was also taken prisoner and deprived of sight. These acts of violence and treason were no sooner perpetrated than the Norsemen, glowing with revenge, rushed like a torrent over the country and laid it waste on every side, forcing their way in immense hordes up the Rhine, the Maese, and the Seine. On the Rhine they were opposed by Adalbert, of the race of Babenberg (Bamberg). The horde, meanwhile, that had advanced up the Seine, quickly reached Paris, encamped upon Montmartre, and besieged the city for a year and a half, when Charles at length marched to its relief at the head of a numerous army, but, instead of trying the issue of a battle, agreed to a most shameful treaty of peace, paid the Norsemen a large sum of money, granted to them free entry into Paris and the navigation of the Seine, besides confirming them in the possession of Friesland, A.D. 887. In the east, he also allowed the Slavi to gain ground, and neglected to support his nephew Arnulf, who could with difficulty defend himself against Suatopluk, who continued to extend his dominions; at the same time, the sons of the old Markgrafs Engelschalk and Wilhelm declared war against each other, and Aribo, a son of the former, went over to the Moravians. Suatopluk was victorious on the Danube, and laid the country waste, until Charles appeared in person to beg for peace, which was concluded in 884 on the Tulnerfeld. This monarch proved himself as weak and despicable in his private as in his public character, by carrying on a scandalous suit against his wife Ricardis, whom he accused of an adulterous connection with his chancellor, Bishop Luitward, and who proved her innocence by ordeal, by passing unharmed through fire in a waxen dress.

The great vassals of the empire, some of whom beheld in the fall of a sovereign they justly despised that of the Carlovingian dynasty and their own aggrandizement, while others were influenced by their dislike of the treaties entered into with foreign powers, the pope and the Norsemen, and by an anxiety to make reparation for the loss of their national honor, convoked a great diet at Tribur in the valley of the Rhine, near Oppenheim, and deprived Charles of his crown, A.D. 887, a degradation he survived but one year.

The Anti-Carlovingian party was partly successful. The French made choice of Odo, Count of Paris, as successor to the crown, while the Lower Burgundians in the Nether-Rhone-land (Arelat) elected Baso, the son of Louis, and the Upper Burgundians in the Western Alps, Count Rudolf, a descendant of the Welfs. In Italy the Dukes Guido of Spoleto and Berengar of Friuli made themselves so independent that they even set themselves up as competitors, through the favor of the pope, for the imperial crown. The Germans alone remained faithful to the Carlovingian house, and elected, to the exclusion of Charles the Simple, who was still alive, Arnulf, the young and energetic, but illegitimate son of Carlmann, a brother of Charles the Thick, who had greatly distinguished himself as duke of Bavaria against the Slavi. The consideration in which he was held was so great that Odo came to Worms to do homage to him as emperor, a ceremony with which Arnulf contented himself, the Norsemen and Slavi affording him no opportunity for recalling his rebellious subjects to their allegiance.

Fresh hostilities instantly broke out on the part of the Norsemen, who made an irruption into Lothringia, and after a bloody engagement defeated the Germans near Maestricht, where the archbishop of Mayence, who had marched against them at the head of his vassals, fell. Arnulf now took the field in person, and a dreadful battle ensued near Louvain, where the Normans had encamped, in which Arnulf, perceiving that the German cavalry were unable to cope with the Norman foot-soldiers, who fought with unexampled dexterity, was the first to spring from his saddle; all the nobles of the arrier-ban followed his example, and the contest became a thick fray, in which the combatants strove hand to hand. Victory sided with the Germans. Siegfried and Gottfried fell on the field of battle, with several thousands of their followers, whose bodies also choked up the course of the Dyle, across which they had attempted to escape. Arnulf, in gratitude for this deliverance, made a great pilgrimage, and ordained that this day, St. Gilgentag, the 1st of September, should be kept as an annual festival. The Norsemen, panic-struck by this fearful catastrophe, henceforward avoided the Rhine, but made much more frequent inroads into the west of France.

Arnulf had also fresh struggles to sustain against the Slavi; the Obotrites crossed the frontiers and laid the country waste. The loyalty of Poppo and of the house of Babenberg, who had been in such close alliance with Charles the Thick, and who now found themselves neglected, became more than doubtful,[1] and Arnulf was constrained to remove the former from his government. Engelschalk the Younger also proved faithless, seduced one of Arnulf's daughters, and then took refuge in Moravia. He was subsequently pardoned, and appointed to guard the Austrian frontier.

As a means of securing the eastern frontier of his empire, Arnulf made peace and entered into an alliance with Suatopluk, prince of Moravia, who was a Christian, in the hope that the foundation of a great Christian Slavian kingdom

---

[1] The murder of Arno, bishop of Wurzburg, is perhaps connected with these circumstances. Arno joined Poppo at the head of his vassals against the Slavi, but was, it appears, deserted by him when reading mass in the open air, and cut to pieces with all his followers by the pagan Slavi. Hence arose the deadly feud that so long existed between the Babenbergers and the Wurzburgers.

might eventually prove an effectual bulwark against the irruptions of their heathen brethren in that quarter. The Slavian Maharanen or Moravians had been converted to Christianity by St. Cyril and St. Methodius, who had visited them from Greece. Borzivoi, prince of Bohemia, being also induced to receive baptism by Suatopluk, his pagan subjects drove him from the throne, and he placed himself (with his wife, St. Ludmilla) under the protection of Suatopluk and Arnulf. Arnulf now gave Suatopluk Bohemia to hold in fee, and unlimited command on the eastern frontier. As a proof of their amity, Suatopluk became sponsor to Arnulf's son, to whom he gave his name, Suatopluk, or Zwentibold; their friendship proved, nevertheless, of but short duration. The Moravian, perceiving that he could not retain his authority over the Slavi so long as he preserved his amicable relations with Germany, yielded to the national hatred, while at the same time he gave fresh assurances of amity to the emperor, A.D. 892. He was also supported in his projects by a great conspiracy among the Germans. The thankless Engelschalk again plotted treason, in which he was upheld by Hildegarde, the maiden daughter of Louis the German, the last of the legitimate descendants of Charlemagne, while the Italians, who dreaded Arnulf's threatened presence in their country, were not slow in their endeavors to incite the Moravian to open rebellion. Arnulf, however, discovered the conspiracy, caused Engelschalk to be deprived of sight, and imprisoned Hildegarde at Chiemsee, but afterward restored her to liberty.

An unexpected ally now came to Arnulf's assistance against Suatopluk. At that period there appeared in ancient Pannonia, first peopled by the Longobardi, and at a later date by the Avari, a nation named in their own language Magyars, or Hungarians (strangers), from whom the country derived its name, or Huns, as they were at that time termed by the German, who imagined that they again beheld in them the Huns of former times. They were pagans, wild and savage in their habits, and extraordinary riders.

Leo, the Grecian emperor, had called them to his assistance against the Bulgarians, and they at first settled under seven leaders (among whom the most distinguished was one named Arpad), each of whom erected a fort or Burg, in the country known from that circumstance as Siebenburgen, but not long after turned westward and threatened Moravia. Arnulf formed an alliance with them, but never, as he has been accused, invited them into Germany, and Suatopluk, perceiving himself pressed on both sides, gladly remained at peace, A.D. 894.

In Italy, Guido of Spoleto was victorious over Berengar of Friuli, and in 891 was crowned emperor by the pope, Stephen V. He died in 894, and his son, Lambert, also received the imperial crown from Pope Formosus. Arnulf had been acknowledged emperor throughout the North, but not having been anointed or crowned by the pope, his right was liable to be disputed by Guido, and being entreated by both Berengar and Formosus, the latter of whom was held in derision by the insolent Spoletan, he resolved to march at the head of a powerful force into Italy. He has been blamed for quitting Germany, at that period not entirely tranquilized, and exposing himself and his army to the hot climate and diseases of Italy, and to the treachery of the inhabitants, which might easily have been turned upon themselves, and never could have endangered him on this side of the Alps. Arnulf's visit to Italy, the first so termed pilgrimage to Rome, which was undertaken with the double aim of having the ceremony of an imperial coronation performed and of receiving the oath of fealty from his rebellious vassals, has been regarded as a misfortune, because visits to Rome became from this period customary, and ever proved disastrous to the empire. But judgment ought to be given according to the difference of times and circumstances. The union between the people of Lombardy and of Rome was not so close at that time as it became at a later period; no Italian national interest had as yet sprung up in opposition to that of Germany; the Italians were uninfluenced by a desire of separating themselves from the empire, as in later times, but were rather inclined to assert their right over it. Guido, who was connected with the Carlovingians, attempted to turn the separation that had taken place between the northern nations to advantage, and appropriated to himself the title of emperor; and, as far as these circumstances are concerned, Arnulf's visit to Italy appears to be justified. The visits undertaken at a later period to Rome were, on the other hand, unjustifiable in every respect, by their imposing, as will hereafter be seen, a foreign ruler on Lombardy and Rome, whose union had become gradually stronger, and whose erection into an independent state, to which they were entitled by their geographical position and by their similarity in language and manners, was ever prevented by fresh invasions.

Arnulf crossed the Alps, A.D. 894. Ambrosius, Graf of Lombardy, closing the gates of Bergamo against him, he took the city by storm and hanged his faithless vassal at the gate. His further progress was impeded by the treachery of Odo, the French king, who took advantage of his absence to arm against him, while Rudolf of Upper Burgundy actually marched to the assistance of the Spoletans, and Arnulf was thus reluctantly forced to retrace his steps. He undertook a second expedition across the Alps in 896, and advanced into Tuscany, where he was amicably received by Adalbert, the faithless Markgraf,[1] and by Berengar, who no sooner found themselves deceived in their expectation of making him subservient to their own interest and of easily outwitting him, than they assumed a threatening attitude. Arnulf, undismayed by the dangers with which he was surrounded, instantly marched upon Rome, whose gates were closed against him by the Spoletans, who successfully repelled every attack on the walls, and the emperor was on the point of retreating,

---

[1] Bertha, the wife of Adalbert (who was blindly guided by her), a woman of an intriguing disposition, was the daughter of Lothar II. and of Walrade. Her first husband was Theobald, Count of Arles, by whom she had Hugo, afterward king of Italy. Sigonius relates the manner in which all the intrigues of those times in Italy and Burgundy were conducted by this woman.

when his soldiers, enraged at the sarcasms of the Italians who manned the walls, rushed furiously to the attack, and carried the city by storm. Lambert's adherents fled, and the rescued pope placed the imperial crown on Arnulf's head. A mode of vengeance to which the Italians have in every age had recourse was now but too successfully attempted against the life of the German hero; slow poison was administered, and he expired at Œttingen, on his way back to Germany. He was buried at Ratisbon.

On Arnulf's death, Lambert regained the sovereignty of Italy, and again reduced Berengar and Adalbert to submission.[1] He was assassinated in 898, and his adherents invited Louis, the son of Boso, into Italy. This prince was a Carlovingian, and grandson to Louis II., and at that time reigned over Burgundy. Bertha, the ambitious wife of Adalbert, who was residing at Lucca, and whose pride could not brook the idea that her son Hugo was merely Count of Arles and Louis's vassal, plotted his destruction. In order to lull his suspicions, she gave him a friendly reception, but no sooner beheld him entirely in her power than she betrayed him to Berengar, who caused him to be deprived of sight, A.D. 905. Hugo then made himself master of Lower Burgundy (Arelat), and after the assassination of Berengar, 925, was placed by his mother on the throne of Italy. This country seemed destined to be governed by women; after the death of Bertha, a wealthy Roman, named Theodora, seized the reins of government, revived the ancient spirit of paganism, and drew all in her licentious train. One of her lovers she caused to be elected pope, as John X. Her daughter Marozia, who surpassed her mother in lewdness, married successively two of the sons of Bertha, first Guido, and then King Hugo, with whom she lived in the most profligate manner. She kept lovers, and he a harem of mistresses, to whom he gave the names of different heathen goddesses. Her son, Octavian, who became pope, as John XI., died suddenly, and Hugo

---

[1] He took the latter prisoner in a stable, and said to him, "Your wife would have made of you either a king or an ass, now you have become the latter."

was driven from his throne, A.D. 947, by his stepson, Alberich, the son of Guido and Marozia, who made Rome his seat of government, while a grandson of Berengar, Berengar II., reigned in Upper Italy. Hugo's former inheritance, and the Arelat or Lower Burgundy, were united with Upper Burgundy under Rudolf II., and even his Italian kingdom seemed forever lost to his remaining son, Lothar, whose wife, the beautiful Adelheid, was destined to decide the fate of Italy.

CXXX. *The Babenberg Feud—The Hungarians*

ARNULF had, during his lifetime, placed his son, Zwentibold, on the throne of Lothringia, in order to guard the frontiers of the empire against the Norsemen. This young prince entered into alliance with Odo of Paris, whose daughter he married, and by his insolence drew upon himself the dislike of the clergy. His ill-treatment of Rathod, archbishop of Treves, also rendered him unpopular with the commonalty. A rebellion broke out in Lothringia, and he lost both his crown and his life in a battle that took place on the Maese, A.D. 900. Odo's reign in France was also of short duration. Charles the Simple was replaced on the throne by the bishops and the vassals, who found their advantage in the imbecility of their monarch. Charles created Regingar duke of Lothringia, and was forced to acknowledge Rollo, duke of Normandy.

In Germany, the great vassals, and the bishops also, usurped the direction of affairs. Louis, the second son of Arnulf, surnamed the Child, on account of his being at that time only in his seventh year, was, by the intrigues of Otto, duke of Saxony, and of Hatto, archbishop of Mayence, who sought to reign under his name, placed upon the imperial throne. The power of the bishops had become exorbitant without the aid of the popes, whose licentious conduct threatened at this period to endanger the church. Hatto, a man of daring courage and deep cunning, unprincipled and cruel, bore unlimited sway in France and in southern Germany, in which he was upheld by Otto, who sought to strengthen himself in Saxony, and to aggrandize his house by the aid of the church. Adalbert, the opponent of the Norsemen, Henry and Adelhart, the sons of Henry of Babenberg, finding themselves neglected, and pressed from the north by the Saxons, from the west by the bishops, set themselves up in opposition. Rudolf, bishop of Würzburg, who was supported by Hatto, having obtained a considerable fief for his family by the abuse of his spiritual authority, Adalbert had recourse to arms, upon which Hatto, probably favored by the ancient hatred of the rest of the vassals to the house of Babenberg, succeeded in having him put out of the ban of the empire. Henry was killed, and Adelhart was taken prisoner and executed. Adalbert, meanwhile, made a vigorous resistance, and slew Graf Conrad, Bishop Rudolf's brother, but was, ere long, closely besieged in his fortress of Bamberg. Hatto, finding other means unavailing, treacherously offered his mediation, and promised him a free and safe return to his fortress, if he would present himself before the assembled diet. Trusting to the word of the wily priest, the Graf issued from his fort, at whose foot he was met by Hatto, who, in the most friendly manner, proposed their breakfasting together within the fortress before setting off on their journey. The Graf assented, and returned with him to the fort; he then accompanied him to the diet, where Hatto declared himself exempted from his promise by his having restored the Graf unharmed to his fortress for the purpose of taking his breakfast, and that he now was free to act as he deemed proper. The assembled vassals, upon this, unanimously sentenced Adalbert to death, and he was beheaded. Conrad, Bishop Rudolf's nephew, was created duke of Franconia.[1] This family of the Wurzburg bishop was surnamed the Rotenburgers, from Rotenburg on the Tauber;

---

[1] But simply missus super exercitum, the bishop assuming the civil authority, and afterward arrogating to himself the whole ducal power.

their descendants acquired, at a later period, far greater celebrity under the name of the Saliers.

The treacherous policy of Bishop Hatto, however, made a deep impression upon the minds of the commonalty, among whom loyalty was still held in higher honor than the sacred head of the churchman, and historians relate that, while the dukes overlooked the conduct of the bishop and yielded to the outbreak of the popular dissatisfaction, Hatto's name and the memory of his infamy were execrated and derided in popular ballads throughout Germany. His name represented the idea of hierarchical lust of power and avarice, and hence arose the legend that records his miserable death. It is said that, during a famine, a number of peasants who came to the bishop and begged for bread were by his order shut up in a great barn and burned to death. From the ruins there issued myriads of mice, which ceaselessly pursued the wretched bishop, who vainly attempted to elude them, and who at length, driven to despair, fled for safety to a strong tower standing in the middle of the Rhine near Bingen, but here also the mice continued their pursuit, swam across the water, and devoured him. The tower is still standing, and is known at the present day as the Mäusethurm or mouse-tower.[1] This example is a manifest proof that the popular fictions were founded upon fact, and clearly express the spirit of those times.

Salomon,[2] bishop of Constance, who made a similar attempt to gain possession of an extensive feudal territory, was abbot of twelve rich monasteries, and equaled a prince in the number of his feudal retainers; he fell into a feud with the most powerful of the temporal lords of Swabia, Erchanger and Berthold, who then exercised the ducal authority as

---

[1] Müsshusz is synonymous with Zeughaus (arsenal). Hence also the word musket. This tower may have been an old store-place for weapons, and the legend may merely have given a different interpretation to the original name.

[2] This bishop had a very beautiful and learned daughter (aliquantis per literata), who was educated in the convent at Zurich, and of whom the emperor Arnulf became enamored. She, however, scorned to be an emperor's mistress, and married a nobleman in Thurgau. Salomon was a handsome, dignified man, extremely popular, and eloquent and impressive in the pulpit.—*Church History.*

Kammerboten, or financial officers, which proved as deadly as that carried on by the bishop of Würzburg against the house of Babenberg. In the Netherlands, Graf Baldwin of Flanders being opposed by Falko, the powerful archbishop of Rheims, he caused him to be assassinated.

The wild Magyars maintained possession of Hungary. After the death of Suatopluk, the kingdom of Moravia completely fell; the Bohemians again severed themselves from the German empire and divided the possessions of Suatopluk with the Hungarians, who, although governed after the death of Arpad by a boy thirteen years of age, their king, Zoldan, continually made fresh conquests along the Danube under their numerous and valiant leaders. Suatopluk the Younger fell in battle; his brother Moymir fled for protection to Duke Luitpold, the stanch defender of the German frontiers. Cussal, the leader of the Hungarians, was defeated in two great battles on the Enns and near to Vienna, and was left on the field, A.D. 900. Undismayed by these disasters, the Hungarians attacked the Carinthian Alps, while the Obotrites under Crito made an inroad into Saxony; but being again repulsed, they made an incursion into Italy and laid that country waste, A.D. 902. For a third time they appeared in such force that Luitpold, the son of Ernst, the former Markgraf, and the brother of Aribo, was defeated and killed near Presburg, and Louis, who was present in this battle, narrowly escaped being taken prisoner. They next invaded Thuringia, A.D. 907, where the new Markgraf, Burkhard, after making a valiant defense, also fell. The following year, A.D. 909, they entered Franconia, where the Markgraf Gebhard vainly attempted to stem their progress, and was killed. The death of these leaders at once proves the obstinate resistance made by the Germans, and the numerical superiority of the enemy. The Hungarian was irresistible in the fury of his onset, invincible in battle by his contempt of death, untiring in pursuit, or secured from it by the rapidity of his horse. His bloodthirstiness, his inhuman treatment of the unarmed and helpless, his destructive and predatory habits, astonished and terrified the milder German, who regarded him in the light of an evil spirit, as the Goth had formerly regarded the Hun, until he became habituated to him. The suddenness with which these mounted hordes appeared in the heart of the country and again vanished, greatly strengthened the belief in their supernatural powers. They also acted with a sort of religious fanaticism, from a belief that every enemy they slew would be their vassal in a future state. They were so bloodthirsty, that they would make use of the corpses of their opponents as tables during their savage feasts. They bound the captured women and maidens with their own long hair, and drove them in flocks to Hungary.[1]

Louis the Child, dismayed by these repeated disasters, concluded a treaty of peace with these people, and consented to pay them a ten years' tribute. The Enns was declared the boundary of Hungary, and the wild Arpads erected their royal castle on the beautiful mountain on the Danube on which the splendid monastery of Mölk now stands. The Germans were deeply sensible of the dishonor incurred by this ignominious tribute, of the danger of their internal dissensions, and of the misfortune of being governed by so imbecile a monarch. It was even publicly preached from the pulpit, "Woe to the land, whose king is a child!" The youthful monarch died, A.D. 911, before he had even reigned, and with him ended the race of Charlemagne in Germany.

CXXXI. *Conrad the First*

THE extinction of the Carlovingian line did not sever the bond of union that existed between the different nations of Germany, although a contention arose between them con-

---

[1] One of the touching stories of the times relates that Ulrich, Graf of Linzgau, being taken prisoner by the Hungarians, his beautiful wife, Wendelgarde, believing him to be dead, devoted the remainder of her life to prayers and almsgiving. One day when distributing her daily alms to a crowd of beggars, one of them fell on her neck and kissed her. Her attendants interposed, but the criminal said, smiling, "Forbear; I have endured blows and misery enough during my imprisonment; I am Ulrich, your Lord."

cerning the election of the new emperor, each claiming that privilege for itself; and as the increase of the ducal power had naturally led to a wider distinction between them, the diet convoked for the purpose represented nations instead of classes. There were consequently four nations and four votes: the Franks under Duke Conrad, whose authority nevertheless could not compete with that of the now venerable Hatto, archbishop of Mayence, who may be said to have been, at that period, the pope in Germany; the Saxons, Frieslanders, Thuringians, and some of the subdued Slavi, under Duke Otto; the Swabians, with Switzerland and Elsace, under different Grafs, who, as the immediate officers of the crown, were named Kammerboten, in order to distinguish them from the Grafs nominated by the dukes; the Bavarians, with the Tyrolese and some of the subdued eastern Slavi, under Duke Arnulf the Bad, the son of the brave Duke Luitpold. The Lothringians formed a fifth nation, under their duke Regingar, but were at that period incorporated with France.

The first impulse of the diet was to bestow the crown on the most powerful among the different competitors, and it was accordingly offered to Otto of Saxony, who not only possessed the most extensive territory and the most warlike subjects, but whose authority, having descended to him from his father and grandfather, was also the most firmly secured. But both Otto and his ancient ally, the bishop Hatto, had found the system they had hitherto pursued, of reigning in the name of an imbecile monarch, so greatly conducive to their interest that they were disinclined to abandon it. Otto was a man who mistook the prudence inculcated by private interest for wisdom, and his mind, narrow as the limits of his dukedom, and solely intent upon the interests of his family, was incapable of the comprehensive views requisite in a German emperor, and indifferent to the welfare of the great body of the nation. The examples of Boso, of Odo, of Rudolf of Upper Burgundy, and of Berengar, who, favored by the difference in descent of the people they governed, had all succeeded in severing themselves from the empire, were ever present to his imagination, and he believed that as, on the other side of the Rhine, the Frank, the Burgundian, and the Lombard, severally obeyed an independent sovereign, the East Frank, the Saxon, the Swabian, and the Bavarian, on this side of the Rhine, were also desirous of asserting a similar independence, and that it would be easier and less hazardous to found a hereditary dukedom in a powerful and separate state than to maintain the imperial dignity, undermined as it was by universal hostility.

The influence of Hatto and the consent of Otto placed Conrad, duke of Franconia, on the imperial throne. Sprung from a newly-risen family, a mere creature of the bishop, his nobility as a feudal lord only dating from the period of the Babenberg feud, he was regarded by the church as a pliable tool, and by the dukes as little to be feared. His weakness was quickly demonstrated by his inability to retain the rich allods of the Carlovingian dynasty as heir to the imperial crown, and his being constrained to share them with the rest of the dukes; he was, nevertheless, more fully sensible of the dignity and of the duties of his station than those to whom he owed his election probably expected. His first step was to recall Regingar of Lothringia, who was oppressed by France, to his allegiance as vassal of the empire.

Otto died in 912, and his son Henry, a high-spirited youth, who had greatly distinguished himself against the Slavi, ere long quarreled with the aged Bishop Hatto. According to the legendary account, the bishop sent him a golden chain, so skillfully contrived as to strangle its wearer. The truth is that the ancient family feud between the house of Conrad and that of Otto, which was connected with the Babenbergers, again broke out, and that the emperor attempted again to separate Thuringia, which Otto had governed since the death of Burkhard, from Saxony, in order to hinder the overpreponderance of that ducal house. Hatto, it is probable, counseled this step, as a considerable portion of Thuringia belonged to the diocese of Mayence, and a collision between him and the duke was therefore unavoidable. Henry flew to arms, and expelled the adherents of the bishop from Thuringia, which forced the emperor to take the field in the name of the empire against his haughty vassal. This unfortunate civil war was a signal for a fresh irruption of the Slavi and Hungarians. During this year the Bohemians and Sorbi also made an inroad into Thuringia and Bavaria, and in 913 the Hungarians advanced as far as Swabia, but being surprised near Œtting by the Bavarians under Arnulf, who on this occasion bloodily avenged his father's death, and by the Swabians under the Kammerboten, Erchanger and Berthold, they were all, with the exception of thirty of their number, cut to pieces. Arnulf subsequently embraced a contrary line of policy, married the daughter of Geisa, king of Hungary, and entered into a confederacy with the Hungarian and the Swabian Kammerboten, for the purpose of founding an independent state in the south of Germany, where he had already strengthened himself by the appointment of several Markgrafs, Rudiger of Pechlarn in Austria, Rathold in Carinthia, and Berthold in the Tyrol. He then instigated all the enemies of the empire simultaneously to attack the Franks and Saxons, at that crisis at war with each other, A.D. 915, and while the Danes under Gorm the Old, and the Obotrites, destroyed Hamburg, immense hordes of Hungarians, Bohemians and Sorbi laid the country waste as far as Bremen.

The emperor was, meanwhile, engaged with the Saxons. On one occasion, Henry narrowly escaped being taken prisoner, being merely saved by the stratagem of his faithful servant, Thiatmar, who caused the emperor to retreat by falsely announcing to him the arrival of a body of auxiliaries. At length a pitched battle was fought near Merseburg between Henry and Eberhard, A.D. 915, the emperor's brother, in which the Franks' were defeated, and the superiority of

---

[1] So great a slaughter took place that the Saxons said on the occasion—
" 'Twere difficult to find a hell,
Where so many Franks might dwell!"

the Saxons remained, henceforward, unquestioned for more than a century. The emperor was forced to negotiate with the victor, whom he induced to protect the northern frontiers of the empire while he applied himself in person to the reestablishment of order in the south.

In Swabia, Salomon, bishop of Constance, who was supported by the commonalty, adhered to the imperial cause, while the Kammerboten were unable to palliate their treason, and were gradually driven to extremities. Erchanger, relying upon aid from Arnulf and the Hungarians, usurped the ducal crown and took the bishop prisoner. Salomon's extreme popularity filled him with such rage that he caused the feet of some shepherds,[1] who threw themselves on their knees as the captured prelate passed by, to be chopped off. His wife, Bertha, terror-stricken at the rashness of her husband and foreseeing his destruction, received the prisoner with every demonstration of humility, and secretly aided his escape. He no sooner reappeared than the people flocked in thousands around him: "Heil Herro! Heil Liebo!" ("Hail, master! Hail, beloved one!") they shouted, and in their zeal attacked and defeated the traitors and their adherents. Berthold vainly defended himself in his mountain stronghold of Hohentwiel. The people so urgently demanded the death of these traitors to their country that the emperor convoked a general assembly at Albingen in Swabia, sentenced Erchanger and Berthold to be publicly beheaded and nominated Burkhard, A.D. 917, whose father and uncle had been assassinated by order of Erchanger, as successor to the ducal throne.—Arnulf withdrew to his fortress at Salzburg, and

---

[1] It appears that he aimed, like the bishops of Mayence and Wurzburg, at the possession of great temporal power, and became on that account the hated rival of the Kammerboten, several of whom on one occasion visiting him, he showed them an oven, in which a thousand loaves were baked at once; an oat kiln that contained three hundred curnocks; vessels of gold and silver, and costly glasses, which the Kammerboten in their envious rage cast upon the ground. The bishop then told them, that he had wealthy shepherds in his mountains before whom they should deferentially uncover their heads, and caused a couple of herdsmen to be attired like noblemen, to whom the Kammerboten unwittingly paid the honor demanded by the bishop, a deception that greatly added to the bitterness of their hatred.

quietly awaited more favorable times. His name was branded with infamy by the people, who henceforth affixed to it the epithet of "The Bad," and the Nibelungenlied has perpetuated his detested memory.

Conrad died, in 918, without issue. On his death-bed, mindful only of the welfare of the empire, he proved himself deserving even by his latest act of the crown he had so worthily worn, by charging his brother Eberhard to forget the ancient feud between their houses, and to deliver the crown with his own hands to his enemy, the free-spirited Henry, whom he judged alone capable of meeting all the exigencies of the state. Eberhard obeyed his brother's injunctions, and the princes respected the will of their dying sovereign.

PART IX

THE SAXON EMPERORS

CXXXII. *Henry the Fowler—Origin of the Middle Classes*

THE princes, with the exception of Burkhard and of Arnulf, assembled at Fritzlar, elected the absent Henry king, and dispatched an embassy to inform him of their decision. It is said that the young duke was at the time among the Harz Mountains, and that the embassadors found him in the homely attire of a sportsman in the fowling floor. He obeyed the call of the nation without delay, and without manifesting surprise. The error he had committed in rebelling against the state, it was his firm purpose to atone for by his conduct as emperor. Of a lofty and majestic stature, although slight and youthful in form, powerful and active in person, with a commanding and penetrating glance, his very appearance attracted popular favor; besides these personal advantages, he was prudent and learned, and possessed a mind replete with intelligence. The influence of such a monarch on the progressive development of society in Germany could not fail of producing results fully equaling the improvements introduced by Charlemagne.

The youthful Henry, the first of the Saxon line, was proclaimed king of Germany at Fritzlar, A.D. 919, by the majority of votes, and, according to ancient custom, raised upon the shield.[1] The archbishop of Mayence offered to anoint him according to the usual ceremony, but Henry refused, alleging that he was content to owe his election to the grace of God and to the piety of the German princes, and that he left the ceremony of anointment to those who wished to be still more pious.

Before Henry could pursue his more elevated projects, the assent of the southern Germans, who had not acknowledged the choice of their northern compatriots, had to be gained. Burkhard of Swabia, who had asserted his independence, and who was at that time carrying on a bitter feud with Rudolf,[2] king of Burgundy, whom he had defeated, A.D. 919, in a bloody engagement near Winterthur, was the first against whom he directed the united forces of the empire, in whose name he, at the same time, offered him peace and pardon. Burkhard, seeing himself constrained to yield, took the oath of fealty to the newly-elected king at Worms, but continued to act with almost his former unlimited authority in Swabia, and even undertook an expedition into Italy in favor of Rudolf, with whom he had become reconciled. The Italians, enraged at the wantonness with which he mocked them,

---

[1] This custom appears to have been discontinued at a later period.—*Wittekind Chron.*

[2] His wife, Bertha, was celebrated as a good housewife. Seals of hers are still extant, on which she is represented seated on a throne spinning. She was long regarded among the people as the protectress of domestic economy, and of industrious maidens, and the memory of "the good old times when Bertha span," continued to a late date. In 1818, her coffin was discovered at Peterlingen (Payerne) in Waadtland, and was solemnly borne by young maidens to the town church, where it was entombed.—*Meyer von Knonau.*

assassinated him.¹ Henry bestowed the dukedom of Swabia on Hermann, one of his relations, to whom he gave Burkhard's widow in marriage. He also bestowed a portion of the south of Alemannia on King Rudolf, in order to win him over, and in return received from him the holy lance, with which the side of the Saviour had been pierced as he hung on the cross. Finding it no longer possible to dissolve the dukedoms and great fiefs, Henry, in order to strengthen the unity of the empire, introduced the novel policy of bestowing the dukedoms, as they fell vacant, on his relations and personal adherents, and of allying the rest of the dukes with himself by intermarriage, thus uniting the different powerful houses in the state into one family.

Bavaria still remained in an unsettled state. Arnulf the Bad, leagued with the Hungarians, against whom Henry had great designs, had still much in his power, and Henry, resolved at any price to dissolve this dangerous alliance, not only concluded peace with this traitor on that condition, but also married his son Henry to Judith, Arnulf's daughter, A.D. 921. Arnulf deprived the rich churches of great part of their treasures, and was consequently abhorred by the clergy, the chroniclers of those times, who, chiefly on that account, depicted his character in such unfavorable colors.

In France, Charles the Simple was still the tool and jest of the vassals. His most dangerous enemy was Robert, Count of Paris, brother to Odo, the late king. Both solicited aid from Henry, but in a battle that shortly ensued near Soissons, Count Robert losing his life and Charles being defeated, Rudolf of Burgundy, one of Boso's nephews, set himself up as king of France, and imprisoned Charles the Simple, who craved assistance from the German monarch, to whom he promised to perform homage as his liege lord.²

---

¹ He had said, "If I do not make every Italian, who wears spurs, ride a mare, my name is not Burkhard."—*Sigonius*.

² Se et Franciam Henrico regi submittit, says Vincentius Bellovacensis. In testimony of the sincerity of his promise, he sent the hand of St. Dionysius, the patron saint of France, set in gold and precious stones.

Henry, meanwhile, contented himself with expelling Rudolf from Lothringia, and after taking possession of Metz, bestowed that dukedom upon Gisilbrecht, the son of Regingar, and reincorporated it with the empire. These successes now roused the apprehensions of the Hungarians, who again poured their invading hordes across the frontier. In 926, they plundered St. Gall, but were routed near Seckingen by the peasantry, headed by the country people of Hirminger, who had been roused by alarm-fires; and again in Elsace, by Count Liutfried: another horde was cut to pieces near Bleiburg, in Carinthia, by Eberhard and the Count of Meran. The Hungarian king, probably Zoldan, was, by chance, taken prisoner during an incursion by the Germans, a circumstance turned by Henry to a very judicious use. He restored the captured prince to liberty, and also agreed to pay him a yearly tribute, on condition of his entering into a solemn truce for nine years. The experience of earlier times had taught Henry that a completely new organization was necessary in the management of military affairs in Germany, before this dangerous enemy could be rendered innoxious, and as an undertaking of this nature required time, he prudently resolved to incur a seeming disgrace, by means of which he in fact secured the honor of the state. During this interval of nine years he aimed at bringing the other enemies of the empire, more particularly the Slavi, into subjection, and making preparations for an expedition against Hungary by which her power should receive a fatal blow.

In the meantime, Gisilbrecht, the youthful duke of Lothringia, again rebelled, but was besieged and taken prisoner in Zülpich by Henry, who, struck by his noble appearance, restored to him his dukedom, and bestowed upon him his daughter, Gerberga, in marriage. Rudolf of France also sued for peace, being hard pressed by his powerful rival, Hugo the Great or Wise, the son of Robert. Charles the Simple was, on Henry's demand, restored to liberty, but quickly fell anew into the power of his faithless vassals.

Peace was now established throughout the empire, and

afforded Henry an opportunity for turning his attention to the introduction of measures, in the interior economy of the state, calculated to obviate for the future the dangers that had hitherto threatened it from without. The best expedient against the irruptions of the Hungarians appeared to him to be the circumvallation of the most important districts, the erection of forts and of fortified cities. The most important point, however, was to place the garrisons immediately under him, as citizens of the state, commanded by his immediate officers, instead of their being indirectly governed by the feudal aristocracy, and by the clergy. As these garrisons were intended, not only for the protection of the walls, but also for open warfare, he had them trained to fight in rank and file, and formed them into a body of infantry, whose solid masses were calculated to withstand the furious onset of the Hungarian horse. These garrisons were solely composed of the ancient freemen, and the whole measure was, in fact, merely a reform of the ancient arrier-ban, which no longer sufficed for the protection of the state, and whose deficiency had long been supplied by the addition of vassals under the command of their temporal or spiritual lieges, and by the mercenaries or body-guards of the emperors. The ancient class of freemen, who originally composed the arrier-ban, had been gradually converted into feudal vassals; but they were at that time still so numerous as to enable Henry to give them a completely new military organization, which at once secured to them their freedom, hitherto endangered by the preponderating power of the feudal aristocracy, and rendered them a powerful support to the throne. By collecting them into the cities, he afforded them a secure retreat against the attempts of the Grafs, dukes, abbots, and bishops, and created for himself a body of trusty friends, of whom it would naturally be expected that they would ever side with the emperor against the nobility.

This new regulation appears to have been founded on the ancient mode of division. At first, out of every nine freemen (which recalls the decania) one only was placed within the new fortress, and the remaining eight were bound (perhaps on account of their ancient association into corporations or guilds) to nourish and support him; but the remaining freemen, in the neighborhood of the new cities, appear to have been also gradually collected within their walls, and to have committed the cultivation of their lands in the vicinity to their bondsmen. However that may be, the ancient class of freemen completely disappeared, as the cities increased in importance, and it was only among the wild mountains, where no cities sprang up, that the centen or cantons and whole districts or gauen of free peasantry were to be met with.

Henry's original intention in the introduction of this new system was, it is evident, solely to provide a military force answering to the exigencies of the state; still there is no reason to suppose him blind to the great political advantage to be derived from the formation of an independent class of citizens, and that he had in reality premeditated a civil as well as a military reformation may be concluded from the fact of his having established fairs, markets, and public assemblies, which, of themselves, would be closely connected with civil industry, within the walls of the cities; and, even if these trading warriors were at first merely feudatories of the emperor, they must naturally in the end have formed a class of free citizens, the more so, as, attracted within the cities by the advantages offered to them, their number rapidly and annually increased.

The same military reasons which induced the emperor Henry to enroll the ancient freemen into a regular corps of infantry, and to form them into a civil corporation, caused him also to metamorphose the feudal aristocracy into a regular troop of cavalry and a knightly institution. The wild disorder with which the mounted vassals of the empire, the dukes, grafs, bishops, and abbots, each distinguished by his own banner, rushed to the attack, or vied with each other in the fury of the assault, was now changed by Henry, who was well versed in every knightly art, to the disciplined maneuvers of the line, and to that of fighting in close ranks, so well calculated to withstand the furious onset of their Hungarian foe. The discipline necessary for carrying these new military tactics into practice among a nobility habituated to license could alone be enforced by motives of honor, and Henry accordingly formed a chivalric institution, which gave rise to new manners, and to an enthusiasm that imparted a new character to the age. The tournament, from the ancient verb *turnen*, to wrestle or fight, a public contest in every species of warfare, carried on by the knights in the presence of noble dames and maidens, whose favor they sought to gain by their prowess, and which chiefly consisted of tilting and jousting either singly or in troops, the day concluding with a banquet and a dance, was then instituted. In these tournaments the ancient heroism of the Germans revived; they were in reality founded upon the ancient pagan legends of the heroes who carried on an eternal contest in their Walhalla, in order to win the smiles of the Walkyren, now represented by earth's well-born dames.

The ancient spirit of brotherhood in arms, which had been almost quenched by that of self-interest, by the desire of acquiring feudal possessions, by the slavish subjection of the vassals under their lieges, and by the intrigues of the bishops, who intermeddled with all feudal matters, also reappeared. A great universal society of Christian knights, bound to the observance of peculiar laws, whose highest aim was to fight only for God (before long also for the ladies), and who swore never to make use of dishonorable means for success, but solely to live and to die for honor, was formed; an innovation which, although merely military in its origin, speedily became of political importance, for, by means of his knightly honor, the little vassal of a minor lord was no longer viewed as a mere underling, but as a confederate in the great universal chivalric fraternity. There were also many freemen who sometimes gained their livelihood by offering their services to different courts, or by robbing on the highways, and who were too proud to serve on foot; Henry offered them free pardon, and formed them into a body of light cavalry. In the cities, the free citizens, who were originally intended only to serve as foot soldiery, appear ere long to have formed themselves into mounted troops, and to have created a fresh body of infantry out of their artificers and apprentices. It is certain that every freeman could pretend to knighthood.

Although the chivalric regulations ascribed to the emperor Henry, and to his most distinguished vassals, may not be genuine, they offer nevertheless infallible proofs of the most ancient spirit of knighthood. Henry ordained that no one should be created a knight who either by word or by deed injured the holy church; the Pfalzgraf Conrad added, "no one who either by word or by deed injured the holy German empire"; Hermann of Swabia, "no one who injured a woman or a maiden"; Berthold, the brother of Arnulf of Bavaria, "no one who had ever deceived another or had broken his word"; Conrad of Franconia, "no one who had ever run away from the field of battle." These appear to have been, in fact, the first chivalric laws, for they spring from the spirit of the times, while all the regulations concerning nobility of birth, the number of ancestors, the exclusion of all those who were engaged in trade, etc., are, it is evident from their very nature, of a much later origin.

CXXXIII. *Conquests in the Slavian Northeast—Defeat of the Hungarians*

THE systematic reduction of the Slavian north of Germany beneath his rule was one of the great projects of the emperor; and, when the recollection of the unfortunate Slavian nations, thinned by bloody defeats, deprived of their ancient privileges, forcibly converted to Christianity, and obliged to adopt the German language, strange and unfamiliar to them, recurs, the barbarity of these measures would naturally rouse indignation; still, the inquiry whether they were not induced by necessity or for safety is but just. The Slavi had long made common cause with the Hungarians, whom they assisted in their predatory excursions against the Germans, whom they attacked in the rear, while engaged in defending themselves against their dreaded foe, and the consequent peril in which the empire stood, together with the alternative of destroying or of being destroyed, rendered victory necessary at whatever price. The whole of the empire, as far as Lothringia and Bremen, was laid waste by the repeated invasions of the lawless Hungarians and their Slavian allies. The whole of Austria, as far as the Enns, had been severed from the state by the conquering Hungarians, while the Slavi attempted to spread themselves northward as far as the Weser. Had the emperor spared the Slavi, and neglected to disarm them during his truce with the Hungarians, they would certainly have assisted them in their first irruption, and might possibly have brought the empire to the brink of destruction. The subjection of heathen nations was, moreover, regarded in those times as a meritorious work, inasmuch as they were, by that means, forced to embrace Christianity.

The ancient Obotrites maintained themselves in Mecklenburg, protected by their forests and lakes, and by their oft-tried valor, while the disunited Sorbian tribes, the Hevelli on the Havel, the Daleminzii on the Middle Elbe, and the Redarii on the Priegnitz, whose territory chiefly consisted of open country, and who, in the moment of danger, were abandoned by their fellow tribes, could offer but a feeble resistance. It was, therefore, upon them that Henry first turned his arms. In 926, he marched against the Hevelli, seized their capital, Brannibor (Brandenburg), converted their country into a frontier of the empire, placed it under the jurisdiction of a Saxon Markgraf, colonized it with Christian Germans, and left no means untried in order to Germanize the inhabitants.

In the following year, A.D. 927, he entered Bohemia,

and took possession of Prague, where, after the fall of the Moravian kingdom of the Christian Borziwoi, his son, Spignitew, who had relapsed into paganism, maintained himself with the aid of the Hungarians, whom he assisted on every occasion against the Germans. He was succeeded by his brother Wratislaw, who wedded Drahomira, a pagan Hevellian princess. Drahomira, inspired by her hereditary enmity against the Germans, caused all the Christians, among others her mother-in-law, St. Ludmilla, to be assassinated, and Henry entered the country under pretext of avenging their martyrdom. Drahomira sought safety in flight. Her son, Wenzel, afterward surnamed the Holy, took the oath of allegiance to the emperor, and was enabled, by the successes of the Germans, to make use of peaceable means for the conversion of his terror-stricken subjects.

The subjection of the Hevelli and of the Bohemians now placed the Daleminzii at the mercy of the conqueror. Henry invaded their country, A.D. 928, took Grona, their metropolis, and built the fortress of Meissen on the Elbe. It appears that the Slavian Parathani (inhabitants of Baireuth), who are mentioned in the history of St. Emmeram, had, at an earlier period, been converted by the monks of Ratisbon and Nuremberg. The fortresses of Saalfeld, Orlamünd, Rudolstadt, Leuchtenburg, Lobeda, Dornburg, Naumburg, were erected on the Saal, now become the line of demarcation between the Germans and the Slavi. Weimar also received its name from *Wenden Mark*, or the Wendian frontier.

The Redarii had driven away their chief, Bernhard, who, there is no doubt, had embraced Christianity. This brave warrior was sent by Henry against his countrymen, who, well aware of the fate that awaited them, made such a desperate resistance at Lunkin (Lenzen) that their whole army, with the exception of eight hundred, who were made prisoners, fell on the field of battle, A.D. 930. Numbers flung themselves in despair into a lake. This terrible defeat filled the neighboring Slavian tribes with consternation.

The truce had now, A.D. 933, expired, and embassadors

were sent from Hungary to demand the payment of the ancient tribute. According to the legendary account, Henry caused a mutilated mangy dog to be thrown before them, and declared a deadly war with their nation. The Hungarians instantly crossed the frontier in two enormous hordes, the lesser of which, 50,000 strong, was encountered by the arrier-ban of Saxony and Thuringia near Sondershausen and entirely routed. The other and more numerous body advanced along the Saal in the vicinity of Merseburg against the emperor, and laid siege to the fortress of a certain Wido, who, according to Wittekind's account, had married a natural daughter of the emperor, and possessed immense treasures. Henry, meanwhile, intrenched himself on a mountain, since known as the Keuschberg, or mountain of chastity, owing to the circumstance of no woman being permitted to enter the camp of the Christians, who strengthened themselves for the coming conflict by devotional exercises. The news of the defeat of their countrymen at Sondershausen soon reached the Hungarians, who instantly kindled enormous fires along the banks of the river, as signals of recall to those of their number who were engaged in plundering the country, and the battle commenced with the coming morn. Henry addressed his troops, who unanimously swore to die on the field or to annihilate their foes. The picture of St. Michael, the defender of heaven, was borne in the van, as the banner of the empire. A murderous struggle commenced, the Hungarians shouting, "Hui! Hui!"—the Germans, "Kyrieleison!" Victory long wavered, but was at length decided by the discipline and enthusiastic valor of the Germans. Thirty thousand Hungarians remained on the field of battle; the remainder fled. An immense number of Christian slaves were restored to liberty. After the victory, Henry knelt, at the head of his troops, on the field, and returned thanks to their patron saint. The Hungarians appear to have been everywhere cut down as soon as they were overtaken. Only seven of their most distinguished chieftains were sent back alive to their country, deprived of their hands, noses, and ears, with the injunction for the future to remain peaceably at home. The terror of the Hungarians now equaled that with which they had formerly inspired the Germans. In the belief that the angel Michael, whose gigantic picture they ever beheld borne in the van of the German army, was the god of victory, they made golden wings similar to those with which he was represented for their own idols. Germany remained undisturbed in this quarter during the rest of this reign. An annual festival, held in the village of Keuschberg, still celebrates the memory of this great victory.[1]

Henry now turned his victorious arms against the Danes, who had secretly invaded the empire. He pursued them as far as the Slie, on whose banks he erected the fortress of Schleswig, in which he placed a German garrison, and forced, A.D. 934, Gorm the Old to abolish the horrid national sacrifice, in which ninety-nine men were offered on the altars of the pagan deities.

The following year, A.D. 935, a friendly meeting took place between him and the kings of France and Burgundy on the Char, a tributary of the Maas. Henry afterward planned a visit to Rome, but died without accomplishing that project, A.D. 936, when at the height of his splendor and renown. He was buried at Quedlinburg, his favorite residence.

CXXXIV. *Otto the First*

OTTO, the son of Henry, was unanimously elected as successor to the throne. The feeling of respect which the newly-acquired greatness of the state instilled into the minds of his subjects, conspired with his own love of magnificence and display to render the coronation of this youthful prince a scene of more than ordinary solemnity. The choice of Aix-la-Chapelle as the theater on this grand occasion dem-

---

[1] The hand of the emperor, and, underneath, a horseshoe, are still to be seen there cut in the rock, a sign of victory, as may also be seen in other places, for instance, on the battlefield of Wolfisholz.

onstrated the high expectations universally inspired by this new sovereign, on whom the spirit of Charlemagne seemed to rest. The entire nation, the clergy, and the nobility, vied with each other in surrounding their monarch with a splendor equaling that with which the first emperor had been environed. The gigantic crown of Charlemagne, the scepter, the sword, the cross, the sacred lance, and the golden mantle, now became objects of still deeper devotion. The archbishop of Mayence held precedence, by the ancient respect attached to his dignity, in the ceremony of anointing; the temporal lords performed their various offices in person; Gisilbrecht of Lothringia filled that of chamberlain, Eberhard of Franconia, that of carver, Hermann of Swabia, that of cup-bearer, Arnulf of Bavaria, that of master of the horse. These new and honorable offices were henceforward retained by the dukes. Editha, Otto's wife, the daughter of Edmund, king of England, was also crowned. Although Otto worthily maintained the dignity he inherited from his father, he scarcely merits the title of Great. He was not endowed with the winning frankness with which his more simple-minded father had gained every heart. His manner was cold and haughty; he surrounded himself with etiquette, and, although by no means wanting in personal bravery, owed his success more to his craftiness and good fortune than to his generosity and magnanimity.[1]

The death of Henry was the signal for a general insurrection among the Slavians and Hungarians. The Redarii revolted, A.D. 936, but were again reduced to submission by a Saxon army sent against them by the emperor, under the command of Hermann Billung,[2] a brave and skillful leader. In the following year the Hungarians made an inroad into

---

[1] Wittekind says: "His demeanor was replete with majesty. His white hair waved over his shoulders. His eyes were bright and sparkling, his beard of an extraordinary length, his breast like that of a lion, and covered with hair."

[2] According to the popular legend, Hermann was tending sheep near Stubekeshorn, when the Emperor Otto chanced to cross the field. Hermann stopped the carriage and refused to allow it to be driven over his father's meadow. The emperor, pleased with the gigantic stature and high spirit of the shepherd boy, took him into his service.

Saxony, but were defeated by Otto in an unknown spot, and pursued as far as Metz; the rapidity of their movements during their predatory incursion having led them across the Rhine almost to the French frontier.

These events were followed by disturbances in the interior of the empire, and by family disputes. Henry had, by his first marriage with the princess of Hatburg, a son named Thankmar (or Tammo), to whom the succession rightfully belonged, but, becoming enamored of the beautiful Matilda, he divorced his wife, under pretext of her having been destined for the cloister. He had three sons by Matilda, Otto, Henry, and Bruno, the first of whom he named as his successor on the throne, which Matilda coveted for her handsome and favorite son, Henry. Great family dissensions arose from these circumstances, not dissimilar to, and as odious, although more fortunate in their result to the emperor, as those that disturbed the reign of Louis the Pious.

The fate of the luckless Thankmar excited a feeling of commiseration equaling that with which Bernhard, the grandson of Louis the Pious, had formerly been viewed. Not content with having deprived him of the imperial throne, Otto also seized his large maternal inheritance in Saxony, and bestowed it upon the Markgraf Gero, who, together with Billung, guarded the Slavian frontier. Thankmar rebelled, and was upheld by the Saxons. He was also joined by Eberhard, duke of Franconia, the same who, at the desire of his brother, the Emperor Conrad, transferred the crown to the Saxon Henry. On the death of that emperor, he attempted to assert his claim to the imperial dignity, being partly influenced by the hatred he bore to Otto, by whom he had been injured.[1] The rebels also attempted to gain over Henry, Otto's younger brother, whom Thankmar contrived to carry

---

[1] Bruning, a Saxon vassal of the Franconian duke, was induced by his hereditary and national dislike, to rebel against his liege, who, in revenge, razed his castle of Elmeri to the ground, and put all the inhabitants to the sword. In order to punish this cruelty, Otto laid a heavy fine upon the duke, and condemned the perpetrators of the dreadful deed (Eberhard's most trusty vassals) to carry dogs.

off from his castle of Badliki on the Ruhr. The emperor marched against the insurgents; Thankmar was besieged in the Eresburg, and slain at the foot of the altar, whither he had fled for safety; Eberhard, abandoned by the greater part of his followers, fell at the feet of the imprisoned Henry, whom he besought to intercede in his behalf with the emperor. To his surprise, Henry replied that he was willing to join with him in his designs against Otto, in order to deprive him of the crown, which he coveted for himself. For the present the two confederates dissembled their projects, and Eberhard made his submission to Otto with expressions of the deepest contrition for his guilt.

Henry, meanwhile, strengthened the conspiracy by gaining over to his party the sons of Arnulf of Bavaria,[1] who had died not long before, Eberhard, Arnulf, Hermann, and Louis, the archbishop Frederick of Mayence, who aimed at the attainment of a pre-eminence in the state similar to that formerly enjoyed by Hatto and Gisilbrecht of Lothringia. Louis, surnamed "Over the Sea"—a son of Charles the Simple, who, in his early youth, had taken refuge in England, whence, after the decease of Rudolf of Burgundy, A.D. 936, he had been recalled by Hugo, Count of Paris, surnamed the Great, or the Wise, and placed on the throne of France— was also invited to join the rebels, but refused, and sought to strengthen himself by an alliance with Otto. The conspirators now contrived to draw the emperor to the Rhine, while Gisilbrecht gave the first signal for revolt, by rising in open rebellion, and at the moment when a division of Otto's Saxon army had crossed the Rhine at Zante, Henry,

---

[1] He is said to have despoiled Ulrich, bishop of Augsburg, to whom, when in return he threatened him with the vengeance of heaven, he sent a goblet filled with wine from his table in proof of his welfare. The bishop said to the vassal who bore it, "Return whence you came, your master is dead": and so it proved. According to another popular account, the devil broke his neck and threw his body into the lake at Scheyern. An ancient manuscript preserved at Tegern records:

"This is Arnulf duke of Bavaria,
Who still lies in the lake at Dscheiren,
Whose neck the devil broke
For his evil deeds."

who, under color of aiding his brother, had marched thither at the head of his vassals, suddenly declared in favor of Gisilbrecht, and fell upon them sword in hand. In this extremity, Otto fell upon his knees before the sacred lance, and invoked the aid of heaven. A Saxon, meanwhile, shouted in Italian, "Run, run"; and the Italian mercenaries in the Lothringian army, being seized with a sudden panic at the cry, instantly ran away. A terrible slaughter ensued. Eberhard and the archbishop of Mayence, terrified by this unexpected disaster, did not venture to declare themselves, and Henry, who had been wounded in the melee, fled to Merseburg, whither the emperor was enticed in order to relieve Gisilbrecht in his quarters on the Rhine. At the same time, the Slavi were secretly instigated to revolt. The plot was, however, betrayed to the Markgraf Gero, who invited thirty of the Slavian princes to a banquet, at which he caused them to be assassinated when in a state of intoxication, A.D. 938, and the Slavi attempting to revenge this act of treachery, Otto was forced to raise the siege at Merseburg, and to march to Gero's assistance. He, at the same time, pardoned Henry, in the hope of separating him, by gentle and conciliatory measures, from Eberhard and Gisilbrecht.

The Hungarians, who, at this time, made a fresh irruption into the empire, suffered two bloody defeats in the Harz Mountains, near Stetternburg and in the Drömling, a marshy forest, whence their horses, weary with the heavy rain and the nature of the ground, were unable to extricate them.

While Otto was engaged in opposing the Slavi, who had entirely cut to pieces a Saxon army under Haika, and again succeeded, after several severe engagements, the details of which have not been recorded, in reducing them to submission, Gisilbrecht won over the French monarch. This intelligence no sooner reached the ears of Otto than he hastened to besiege Gisilbrecht in the castle of Chevremont. Gisilbrecht secretly escaped, and Otto, being forced by the state of affairs in Saxony to return to that country, intrusted the defense of the western frontier to Immo, the

Lothringian Graf, and to the duke of Swabia, who had remained firm in his allegiance. Louis crossed the frontier at the head of a numerous army, invaded and wasted Elsace, which was bravely defended by Hermann, who finally compelled him to retreat. Eberhard, meanwhile, seized Breisach. Immo was closely besieged.[1] Eberhard was on the point of being proclaimed and anointed king at Metz. These events quickly recalled Otto from Saxony, in order to lay siege to Breisach, upon which the archbishop of Mayence, who, until now, had pretended to favor his party, and who was in his camp, suddenly threw off the mask, and went over with his numerous adherents to the enemy, whose principal force was assembled near Andernach, and was merely opposed by a small body of troops commanded by the Graf Conrad Kurzbold, and by Udo, brother to Hermann of Swabia, the former of whom, perceiving that his opponents were spread carelessly feasting on the banks of the Rhine, suddenly fell upon them. A fearful slaughter ensued; Eberhard fell after a desperate struggle;[2] Gisilbrecht was drowned in the Rhine; Otto's party triumphed; Breisach surrendered;[3] the archbishop of Mayence was taken prisoner; and Henry, who had infringed the treaty and again joined the rebels, fled into France. The rebellion was no sooner crushed than

---

[1] The legend relates that Immo, being besieged by Gisilbrecht, ordered beehives to be thrown among the besiegers, who were put to flight by the enraged insects.
[2] Eberhard, the monk of St. Gall, says, Conrad, surnamed Kurzbold, on account of his strength and shortness of stature, surprised the two chiefs when engaged in a game of chess; with a single blow with his lance he foundered the boat in which Gisilbrecht sought to escape across the river, and slew Eberhard on the bank. Conrad was a woman-hater. His deeds are recorded in the popular ballads of that period.
[3] The poetical legend of the Eberstein belongs to these times. Otto besieged Graf Eberhard in the castle of Eberstein in the valley of the Murg, and being unable to carry the fortress by force, had recourse to artifice, and invited the Graf to a banquet, secretly intending to surprise the fort during his absence. Eberhard accepted the invitation, but, during the dance, being informed of the plot by Hedwig, the emperor's sister, he stole away from the scene of festivity, and repaired to his castle, where he had again armed himself before the arrival of the emperor's troops. Otto, delighted with this trait of courage, pardoned the Graf, and, as a pledge of his favor, bestowed upon him the hand of the beautiful Hedwig.

Otto carried his plans into effect. Louis of France had found means, before the emperor was able to succor Lothringia, to seduce Gerberga, the widow of Gisilbrecht, whom he married, in order to insure the possession of the country. The emperor, however, set up Graf Otto, who, in his quality of guardian to Henry, the young son of Gisilbrecht, governed Lothringia, in opposition to him. Although Eberhard's nearest of kin, and consequently his heir in Franconia, was his nephew, Conrad the Red,[1] Otto divided the dukedom, and bestowed a part of the land upon his vassal, Graf Udo of Swabia. Berthold, the brother of Arnulf, was also created duke of Bavaria, to the exclusion of his three nephews.

Gero, meanwhile, continued to oppose the Slavi, and again took firm footing in Brandenburg after the assassination of the last prince of the Hevelli by the traitor Tugumin, who had been bribed to commit the deed by Gero, A.D. 940. Otto invaded France in person, drove Louis as far as the Seine, and made a treaty with Burgundy. After the death of Rudolf II., king of that country, his son Conrad, who was still in his minority, was placed in his hands. Henry and the archbishop of Mayence sought and received pardon; nevertheless, when, in 941, Otto again took the field against the Slavi, and his troops mutinied on account of the difficulty of their position, Henry and his coadjutor, the archbishop, placed themselves at the head of a fresh conspiracy against the emperor, whom they intended to assassinate during the celebration of Easter at Quedlinburg. The plot was discovered; Henry fled, but threw himself in penitential garb shortly afterward at the feet of his injured brother, who once more pardoned him.

A short peace ensued. A personal meeting took place, A.D. 942, at Vouzières between Otto and Louis of France, and peace was concluded. In 944, the emperor bestowed Lothringia, on the death of Henry, the son of Gisilbrecht, and that of his guardian, Otto, on Conrad the Red, together

---

[1] Conrad was the son of a Count Werner and of a daughter of the emperor. Conrad I.

with the hand of his daughter Luitgarde; an alliance which united the Franconian party to his family and Lothringia to the empire. The old duke, Hermann of Swabia, expired in the course of the same year, and Ludolf, the emperor's eldest son, who had married Ida, the duke's only child, became duke in his stead. In the following year the death of Berthold of Bavaria also took place, and Henry, who had already wedded Judith, Arnulf's beauteous widow, was named as his successor, to the exclusion of the sons of both Arnulf and Berthold. The emperor was, by these means, himself duke of Saxony; his son, duke of Swabia; his brother, duke of Bavaria; his son-in-law, duke of Franconia and Lothringia; and Conrad, the young king of Burgundy, remained a hostage at his court.

In 944, war again broke out; the Hungarians invaded the empire, but were defeated in Carinthia by Duke Berthold, who died shortly afterward. France was also disturbed by the struggle between the unfortunate Louis and the great Count Hugo of Paris, who was aided by the Normans, for the possession of the crown. Hugo had, up to this period, been on friendly terms with Otto, whose sister Hedwig he had received in marriage. Otto, under pretext of rescuing Louis from the imprisonment in which he was held by Hugo, to whom he had been delivered by the Normans, invaded France,[1] A.D. 947, but was unsuccessful in his attacks against Paris or Rouen, the capital of Normandy. Peace was at length established between the contending parties by Conrad of Franconia. Hugo voluntarily submitted, and Lothar, the son of Louis, succeeded to the throne on the death of his father, A.D. 954. Both of the emperor's sisters had married a competitor for the throne of France; Gerberga, Louis; and Hedwig, Hugo. The son of the latter, Otto's nephew, the celebrated Hugh Capet, was raised to the throne on the extinction of the Carlovingian dynasty.

---

[1] Hugo having said, vauntingly, that he would swallow seven Saxon bolts at a gulp, Otto replied that he would strew the whole of France with the straw hats worn by his soldiers when not in action.

The war with the French Normans was scarcely concluded than a fresh one arose between Otto and their brethren, the Danes, whose king, Harald Blaatand, or Blue Tooth, conquered Schleswig, and restored the Danewirk. A sanguinary battle took place, in which Otto was victorious. He afterward marched in triumph through Jutland as far as the Ottensund, which received its name from him. Harald was forced to submit to the rite of baptism, and to take the oath of allegiance to the emperor, who restored the frontier, and erected Schleswig, Biepen and Aarhus into bishoprics, under the jurisdiction of the archbishopric of Hamburg, A.D. 948. A victory was, during the same year, gained over the Hungarians by Henry of Bavaria, who, A.D. 950, for the first time, invaded their territory, whence he returned laden with immense booty, and with the wives and children of the chiefs. It was about this time that Otto founded new bishoprics as a means of increasing his power in the conquered territory of the Slavi, Havelberg in 946, and Brandenburg in 948, within the march of Gero; in 946, he also founded Oldenburg in Wagria, which country had just been reduced to submission by Hermann Billung, who had taken advantage of the feud that had broken out between Selibur, prince of the Wagrians, and Mistevoi, prince of the Obotrites. The latter was persuaded to embrace Christianity, and wedded the sister of Wago, bishop of Oldenburg. His son, Wislau, relapsed into paganism. After having thus succeeded in extending and securing the frontiers of the empire, Otto turned his attention upon Italy.

CXXXV. *The Reincorporation of Italy with the Empire*

BERENGAR II. had seized the government of Italy. Adelheid, the widow of Lothar, fell into his hands. The pretensions of this princess to the crown, which were upheld by a strong, although, at that period, suppressed party, and her extraordinary wit and beauty, induced Berengar to offer to her the hand of his son, Adalbert, who, being refused, Berengar imprisoned her in a fortress on the lake of Como,[1] whence she contrived to escape to the castle of Canossa, where she concealed herself. Otto had, at this time, not long become a widower; he sought, moreover, to place the imperial power on a firmer basis, by the addition of great feudal possessions, and by family alliances. In pursuance of this policy, he had only set governors, who were chosen from among his trustiest vassals,[2] over Saxony, over which he reigned as hereditary sovereign, and insured the allegiance of Franconia, Swabia, and Bavaria, by the strict connection that subsisted between his family and those of their dukes. An extensive and hereditary feudal tenure in Italy had long been an object of his ambition. The earnest solicitations of Adelheid for assistance met, therefore, with a favorable reception, and, A.D. 951, he hastened across the Alps to the relief of Canossa, at that time closely besieged, and was rewarded with the hand of the lovely Adelheid at Pavia. His son, Ludolf, fearing to share a fate similar to that of the unfortunate Thankmar, quarreled with his unwished-for stepmother,[3] and suddenly quitted his father, accompanied by the archbishop of Mayence, who again plotted treason. Otto, suspecting their designs, and anxious to prevent mischief, returned upon this to Germany, and intrusted the conduct of the war with Berengar to Conrad of Lothringia, who, fully aware of the immense sacrifice necessary for the maintenance of the emperor's prerogative in Italy, offered terms of peace, and promised a full pardon and the possession of his lands to Berengar. These terms offended the pride of the emperor, who refused his compliance, and threatened again to invade Italy in person; but his indignation was speedily mollified by the submissive behavior of Berengar,

---

[1] She is said to have escaped through a hole that was bored through the wall by a priest, and during her flight was so closely pursued as to be compelled to conceal herself in a field of standing corn.

[2] The church bells of Magdeburg having been rung in honor of Hermann Billung, by order of the archbishop, Adalbert, the emperor sentenced him to furnish the imperial stables with as many horses as there had been bells rung on that occasion.

[3] She was nineteen years younger than the emperor.

who repaired to Germany, took the oath of allegiance at Augsburg, and was permitted to retain undisturbed possession of his lands. A fresh and alarming conspiracy was, meanwhile, secretly ripening; Ludolf, whose pride had already been deeply mortified, was now still more aggrieved by the conduct of his uncle, Henry of Bavaria, who had entered into a close connection with Adelheid, through whom he governed the emperor. A dispute that arose between the uncle and nephew concerning the boundaries of their lands was decided in favor of the former, by the emperor, who, in addition to the extensive dukedom of Bavaria, which already comprehended Carinthia, bestowed upon him the meres of Verona and Aquileia.

Ludolf's sister, the wife of Conrad the Red, to whom Adelheid was greatly obnoxious, espoused the cause of her brother, who also found an ally in her husband, whom the emperor had irremediably offended by his invalidation of the promise made by Conrad to Berengar. The scheme of the conspirators, neither of whom, at first, dreamed of open revolt, merely extended to the exclusion of Henry, to whom, as the tool of Adelheid, they ascribed every evil design, from the imperial council. This they openly declared to the emperor at Ingelheim, and threatened to imprison Henry if he came thither. Otto, unable to oppose them on the Rhine, where Conrad and Ludolf ruled in their right as dukes, made no reply, but, on his return to Saxony, gave full vent to his rage, and deposed the ungrateful nobles, A.D. 953. The Lothringians instantly rebelled, and attempted to throw off the German yoke, but were defeated by Conrad on the Maas: the battle lasted a whole day. Flushed by this victory, Conrad turned against the emperor, who had advanced as far as the Rhine, and who, aided by Henry of Bavaria, laid siege to Mayence, whose archbishop favored the rebels, and which was for some time defended by Ludolf and Conrad against the united imperial forces. Terms of reconciliation were at length proposed; the two princes came forth, and threw themselves at the feet of their indignant parent, but refusing to deliver up their adherents, whom Otto wished to bring to execution, not so much from revenge as from political motives, in order to weaken their party, they returned to the city without anything being concluded. Immediately after this, the Bavarians, incited by Arnulf, the son of the late duke, rose tumultuously in the camp against Henry, and declared in favor of Ludolf and Conrad, who again quitted Mayence, and took the field with this new addition to their force, which received a fresh accession of strength by the desertion of a part of the Saxons under the command of Ekbert, a nephew of Hermann Billung. A fresh body of troops, dispatched from Saxony by Hermann Billung, to the assistance of the emperor, was waylaid and defeated by Ludolf and Conrad. Their commander, Wichmann, another of Hermann's nephews, also joined the rebels. Otto, with characteristic prudence, sought to weaken his opponents by separating their forces, and, with that intent, created his brother Bruno, the archbishop of Cologne, duke of Lothringia. Conrad took the bait, and instantly withdrew across the Rhine, in order to dispute the possession of that country. Hermann, meanwhile, drew Ekbert and Wichmann toward Saxony, in order still more to weaken Ludolf and Arnulf, who suffered a defeat before Augsburg, which city was valiantly defended by Bishop Ulrich and his vassals, A.D. 954. The conspirators now invited the Hungarians— who, headed by their king, Pulzko (Bulgio), spoliated both friend and foe—into the country, under pretext of aiding Conrad, who seized and plundered Metz. He was violently opposed by Bruno's adherents, and at length became so obnoxious to the people, for having caused this new inroad of the Hungarians, and so terrified at the cruelties practiced by them, that he voluntarily quitted his unnatural allies, who, after vainly besieging Kammarich, returned to their native country through France and Italy, burning and plundering as they advanced.

The Germans, alarmed by these disasters, and fearful of the event, now abandoned the leaders of the rebellion, and crowded around the emperor, who held a diet at Cinna (Zenn), where Conrad and Frederick, archbishop of Mayence, made their submission. Ludolf and Arnulf, nevertheless, obstinately continued to defend Ratisbon, where, after a desperate resistance, Arnulf was killed when heading a sally against the enemy, and Ludolf, finding it useless to resist, took refuge in Swabia. Ulrich, bishop of Augsburg, attempted to bring about a reconciliation between the emperor and his now penitent son, who, one day, when the former was hunting, suddenly fell at his feet and begged for pardon. He met with a favorable reception, but was deprived of the government of Swabia. He was afterward sent into Italy and intrusted with the command of an army against Berengar, who had again revolted. He there met with an early death. The dukedom of Swabia was bestowed upon Burkhard, the son of the elder Burkhard, and a relative of Bishop Ulrich. The new duke, who had just attained his majority, wedded Hedwig, the daughter of Henry, who was reinstated in the dukedom of Bavaria. Conrad was deprived of Lothringia, which was partitioned between the Grafs Gottfried and Frederick, the former of whom governed the upper, the latter the lower country, but were subordinate to Bruno, the archbishop of Cologne, the first noble who bore the title of archduke. He was also the first churchman who exercised such great temporal authority, so adverse to the spirit by which the first preachers of the gospel were guided; but Bruno was the emperor's brother, and Otto had learned from experience the importance of intrusting the ducal power solely to his nearest relatives and best-tried friends. In 954, Bruno crowned his nephew Lothar, the son of Louis Over-the-Sea, who had just expired, king of France.

A powerful party in Bavaria, headed by the Count Werner, brother to the fallen Arnulf, were induced by the hatred they bore to Henry to have recourse to the Hungarians, whom they invited into the country. Confident of success on account of their enormous numerical strength, the arrogant barbarians boasted that their horses should drain every river in Germany. Augsburg, whose supposed treasures attracted their cupidity, was besieged by them, but made a brave defense under the command of Burkhard of Swabia.[1] Their king, Bulzko, was encamped at Günsburg. Otto instantly assembled the arrier-ban of the entire empire; the Bohemians united their forces with his; the Saxons, at that time engaged in opposing the Slavi, alone failed. The two armies came within sight of each other on the Lech, near Augsburg. Before the battle commenced, Otto addressed his troops, as his father had done on a similar occasion, and vowed, when referring to the victory won by Henry, to found a bishopric at Merseburg, if God granted him success. It was the 10th of August, 955. The sun poured with intense heat upon the plain. The Hungarians rapidly crossed the Lech, fell upon the rear of the German army, dispersed the Bohemians, and were pressing hard upon the Swabians, when the fortune of the day was again turned by Conrad, who, anxious to retrieve his fault and to regain the confidence of his master, performed miracles of valor at the head of the Franconians. The emperor struggled sword in hand in the thickest of the fight. A vast number of the enemy were drowned in attempting to escape across the river. Conrad was mortally wounded in the neck by an arrow aimed at him by one of the fugitives, when in the act of raising his helmet in order to breathe more freely. A hundred thousand Hungarians are said to have fallen on this occasion. Two of their princes, Lehel and Bulcs, were, by the emperor's command, hanged on the gates of Augsburg. According to some writers, King Bulzko and four of the warchiefs were hanged before the gates of Ratisbon.[2] Werner

---

[1] The chiefs drove the people into the trenches with long whips. One, named Lehel, bore an enormous horn, whose note was the signal for the besiegers to assemble. During a sally made by the weavers of Augsburg they gained possession of the shield of the Hungarian king, which has ever since been borne by their guild.

[2] Döllinger, a citizen of Ratisbon, greatly distinguished himself on a former occasion, by overcoming, in single combat, a gigantic Hungarian, whom no one ventured to attack. The memory of his valor has been handed down to our

was killed by the enraged Hungarians, but few of whom escaped to their country, almost the whole of the fugitives being slain or hunted down like wild beasts by the Bavarian peasants. The adherents of the adverse party were mercilessly punished by Henry of Bavaria, who caused them to be buried alive or burned in beds of quicklime. Herold, bishop of Salzburg, was, by his orders, deprived of sight, and the patriarch Lupus of Aquileia met with a still more wretched fate. This was the last inroad attempted by the Hungarians, who, for the future, remained within their frontier, on their side equally undisturbed by the Germans. The booty was so enormous that a peasant is said to have had a silver plow made out of his share. The innumerable Hungarian horses taken on this occasion also gave rise to the establishment of the Keferloher horsefair.

Henry of Bavaria, Otto's brother, died in 955, and was succeeded in the government of Bavaria and Carinthia by his son Henry, surnamed the Wrangler. Burkhard, who had succeeded Ludolf in the command of the Italian army, also expired shortly after, and was succeeded in the dukedom of Swabia by his widow, Hedwig, Otto's niece, who was celebrated for her beauty and learning. This is the first example of an office relating to the empire being filled by a woman. At Hohentwiel, her residence during her widowhood, she passed her days in study, and read Virgil with her chancellor Eckhard, who afterward became chaplain and counselor to the emperor Otto II., and also served the empress Adelheid. Franconia remained partitioned between Otto, the son of Conrad, and his cousin Henry, Markgraf of Sweinfurt, who was also grandson to the emperor Conrad I., through his father Count Bardo, a son of Burkhard of Thuringia, who had wedded one of that emperor's daughters.

times by a monument and by the popular ballads. The city of Lauingen also boasts a similar incident. A shoemaker of Lauingen is said to have killed a gigantic Hungarian, whom the Marshal of Calatin had refused to meet in single combat. For this valiant deed, the Emperor Otto caused the black Moor's head, borne by the family of Calatin, to be inserted in the arms of the city of Lauingen, and merely allowed the Calatins to bear the figure of a female Moor on their shield.

The Slavi were again humbled. Ekbert and Wichmann, Hermann Billung's nephews, had after Ludolf's defeat taken refuge among these people and incited them to open rebellion. In 954, the Uchri were reduced to submission by Graf Gero, but in the following year almost every Slavian tribe in the country revolted under Nakko and Stoinef, descendants of the ancient royal Hevellian dynasty. Hermann Billung was surrounded and besieged at Gartz, and although promised an unmolested retreat, the garrison was cut to pieces,[1] A.D. 955. This event called the emperor from the Lech, and the Slavi were quickly repelled. Stoinef was assassinated while attempting to flee. His head was, by the emperor's order, placed upon a stake, and seventy Wends were beheaded in a circle around it. Nakko was also taken prisoner and beheaded. Gero, meanwhile, zealously labored to confirm Germanic rule and Christianity simultaneously in the Slavian territory, where, besides the tithes, the Grafs exacted the Wogewotinza, the bishops, the Biscowotinza, two oppressive taxes; to which was added socage, the cruel right of the conqueror over the conquered, so contrary to the doctrine of Christian love and equality: hence the hatred with which the clergy were beheld by the Wends. The manner in which these wretched people were treated is best described by Ditmar of Merseburg, who remarks in his Chronicle, "The submissive slave must eat hay like an ox, and be beaten like an ass." In 957, Wichmann again incited the Rhedarii to revolt, but without success.

While these events were taking place in Germany, Berengar remained unmolested in Italy, more particularly since the death of Ludolf, by whom he had been narrowly watched. Berengar aimed at the independent sovereignty of Italy, in which he was upheld by the majority of the people, whose national pride ill-brooked the despotic rule of either the clergy or the Germans. The Lombard bishops, enraged at the restriction imposed upon them by Berengar, sought the protec-

---

[1] Because a Saxon bestowed a box on the ear on a Wend, for attempting to force from him his wife, who was also a Wend.

tion of the pope, who applied for aid to the emperor. The family disputes that had so lately troubled Otto's domestic peace, the struggle with the Hungarians and the Slavi, had at this juncture been brought to a favorable termination, and the reincorporation of Italy with the empire again became the object of his ambition; accordingly, after causing his son, Otto II., to be crowned king of Germany at Aix-la-Chapelle, and intrusting the government of the empire to his brother, Bruno, archbishop of Cologne, and to his illegitimate son, William, who had succeeded Frederick in the archbishopric of Mayence, he crossed the Alps, A.D. 961, expelled Berengar, and for the first time entered Rome, where the pope, John XII. (a son of Alberich), was compelled to crown him emperor, and an oath was imposed upon the Romans rendering it illegal for them to elect a pope without the consent of the emperor, who no sooner quitted the city than the pope declared the oath null and void, and retracted his former professions. Otto upon this returned, convoked a Concilium, and deposed the pope, who was convicted of the most disgraceful vices.[1] A popular commotion was the immediate result, and Otto was alone saved by the intrepidity of his troops. The pope was taken in adultery and struck dead on the spot by the injured husband. The Romans, without referring to the emperor, elected a new pope, Benedict V., whom Otto cited to appear before him, with his own hand broke his crosier, banished him to Hamburg, and raised Leo VIII. in his stead to the papal chair. About the same time, Berengar, after long and valiantly defending the mountain fort of St. Leo, was compelled to surrender. He was exiled to Bamberg, where he died. His son, Adalbert, fled to Corsica.

In 965 Otto returned to Germany, and held Whitsuntide

---

[1] This pope bestowed the sacred vessels, belonging to the church of St. Peter, upon his mistresses, violated the most beautiful of the pilgrims who visited Rome, drank publicly to the health of the devil, and, while gambling, invoked the pagan deities. His granduncle, King Hugo, had the same inclination toward paganism. Marozia and her mother, Theodora, were descended from an ancient Roman family, and, at that period, Rome still possessed countless monuments and relics of antiquity.

at Cologne, where he was attended by all the German princes, among whom appeared Lothar of France. Peace and security reigned throughout the empire. Graf Wichmann, to whom the emperor had extended the pardon granted to his brother Ekbert, alone sought to disturb the general tranquillity, and again joined the pagan Danes, who were attempting to gain a settlement in Pomerania, where, in the time of Harald Blaatand, the infamous pirates' nest, the Jomsburg, near Wollin, had been built. He may possibly have inspired the Wendi with fresh courage. The Lusicri and Selpuli in Lusatia commenced a sanguinary war against Gero, by whom they were reduced to submission. The deep affliction of this Graf, occasioned by the death of his nephew and of his youthful son, both of whom fell in battle, induced him on the termination of this war to resign his office, and to make a pilgrimage to Rome, where he laid his sword, whose notches bore witness to many a fight, at the foot of St. Peter's shrine, and ended his days within the cloister, A.D. 965. He was the founder of the convent of Gernrode.

The emperor pursued his ancient policy in his treatment of this new conquest. The Lausitz was converted into a new frontier, Eastern Saxony, and placed under the jurisdiction of Hermann Billung. The bishoprics of Merseburg and Zeiz were also founded, and, in common with all the other bishoprics, rendered dependent on the great archbishopric of Magdeburg, a city greatly beautified by the emperor, with whom it was a favorite residence. Bishop Bucco (Burkhard) of Halberstadt, imagining himself injured by the erection of this new archbishopric, A.D. 968, rebelled; he was taken prisoner; but seizing the opportunity of pronouncing a sentence of excommunication against the emperor, who chanced to pass his prison window, the latter ordered him to be set at liberty.

Otto preserved amicable relations with Bohemia, where, A.D. 936, St. Wenzel was assassinated by his pagan brother, Boleslaw I., at a baptismal festival, to which he had been insidiously invited. Boleslaw declared war against Germany, and began to build fortified cities, for instance, Bautzen.[1] He was defeated, and compelled to embrace Christianity, by Hermann Billung.[2] Poland, at that time oppressed by the Danes and by Wichmann, also entered into alliance with Germany. Miseko, king of Poland, wedded Dobrowa, A.D. 966, the daughter of Boleslaw of Bohemia, who introduced Christianity among the Poles. Wichmann joined Selibur, the pagan prince of the Obotrites, who was defeated, and Rethel, a great Slavian sanctuary, demolished, with all the heathen deities contained in it, by Hermann Billung. Wichmann was also defeated by the Poles, into whose hands he fell during his flight, completely worn out with fatigue and hunger; he expired amid their insults, after slaying several of his pursuers. His death confirmed the alliance between Poland and Germany, and Miseko founded the bishopric of Posen, which was subordinate to the archbishopric of Magdeburg.

Otto revisited Italy, A.D. 966, where Adalbert, the son of Berengar, had raised an insurrection in Lombardy; he was defeated on the Po by Burkhard of Swabia. Pope Leo VIII. was dead; the new pope, John XIII., the emperor's creature, who had been expelled from Rome by an adverse party, had been reinstated by Pandolf, the valiant prince of Benevento, the last Lombard who preserved his ancestral bravery and fidelity amid the vices of Italy. Otto's first act, on his arrival in Rome, was the infliction of a severe chastisement on the refractory Romans; thirteen of the most distinguished citizens were hanged. A fresh and closer treaty was concluded between the emperor and the pope, to whose dominions the territory of Ravenna, which had been severed from them, was restored, in return for which he solemnly placed the imperial diadem on the head of Otto II., an incident of rare occurrence during the lifetime and in the presence of the father. All opposition to the irresistible power of the

---

[1] The Bohemian nobles showing an unwillingness to assist in building, Boleslaw struck off the head of the first who ventured to refuse.

[2] According to Hageck, he fell at the feet of the emperor and begged for mercy. The punishment awarded to him was to hold the field-kettle, when they encamped, over the fire, and to bear it in his escutcheon.

emperor had now ceased—the whole of Upper and Central Italy lay in silent submission at his feet. His first step was the imposition of a new form of government upon Lombardy. He replaced the great dukes, with the exception of his ally Pandolf, by numerous petty Markgrafs, the majority of whom were Germans by birth. He also settled a considerable number of Germans in the different cities, and thus created a party [1] favorable to the imperial cause that counterpoised the rebellious spirit of the Lombards and Romans. Pandolf of Benevento, surnamed Ironhead, and the petty duke, Gisulf of Salerno, whose imbecility rendered him ever inconstant to his allies, defended the frontiers of Upper and Central Italy, against the Greeks, who still retained possession of Lower Italy, and the Saracens, who had already settled in Sicily. Otto and his empress, Adelheid, visited Pandolf, A.D. 968, who entertained them with great magnificence. During his residence at Benevento, Otto undertook the conquest of Lower Italy. Bari, the strongly-fortified Grecian metropolis, offering a valiant and successful resistance, he had recourse to his favorite policy, and dispatched his confidant, Luitprand, the celebrated historian, to the court of Nicephorus, the Grecian emperor, in order to demand the hand of the beautiful princess, Theuphano, daughter to Romanus the late emperor, for his son Otto II., probably in the hope of receiving Italy as her dowry. His suit being contemptuously refused, Otto undertook a second campaign, during the following year, and chose with great judgment his line of march along the Alps that separate Lower Italy into two parts, and thus command Apulia to the east and Calabria to the west. Having thus opened a path, he returned the same way, leaving the conquest of the low country to Pandolf, who having the misfortune to be taken prisoner before Bovino, and to be sent to Constantinople, the Greeks, under the patrician Eugenius, crossed the frontier, laid waste the country in the neighborhood of Capua and Benevento, and treated the in-

---

[1] In Florence, known as the Schiatte, from the old German word *Schlacht*, race, family.

habitants with great cruelty. Otto, who was at that juncture in Upper Italy, sent the Grafs Gunther and Siegfried to oppose them; a splendid victory was gained, and the victors, animated by a spirit of revenge, deprived the Greek prisoners of their right hands, noses, and ears. In 970, the Sicilian Saracens invaded the country, but were defeated at Chiaramonte by Graf Gunther. At this time, the emperor Johannes, who, after the assassination of Nicephorus, had ascended the throne of Greece, restored Pandolf Ironhead to liberty, concluded peace with Otto, and consented to the alliance of Otto II. with the beautiful Theuphano, who was escorted from Constantinople by the archbishop Gero of Cologne, Bruno's successor, at the head of a numerous body of retainers. She was received in the palace of Pandolf at Benevento by the emperor and the youthful bridegroom. Her extraordinary beauty attracted universal admiration.[1] The marriage ceremony was celebrated with great magnificence at Rome, A.D. 972. This princess created an important change in the manners of Germany by the introduction of Grecian customs, which gradually spreading downward from the court, where her influence was first felt, affected the general habits of the people by the alterations introduced in the monastic academies. The German court adopted much of the pomp and etiquette of that of Greece. The number of retainers increased with increasing luxury, and the plain manners of the true-hearted German were exchanged for the finesse and adulation of the courtier. The emperor also a lopted the Grecian title of Sacred Majesty (*Sacra Majestas*). Lower Italy remained in the hands of the Greeks.

The emperor returned to Germany, A.D. 972, and besides his lovely daughter-in-law, brought with him a vast quantity of relics, with which he adorned the churches, most particularly that at Magdeburg, for which he had a peculiar

---

[1] The trappings of the horse on which she rode were ornamented with feathers and gold, her Grecian dress was resplendent with jewels and pearls, and her hair was confined in a golden net. Yet all this splendor was outshone by the beauty of her features and the brilliancy of her eyes.

predilection, and which he intended to honor with his own remains. He held a great court at Quedlinburg, where he received the homage of the different nations over whom he ruled, and, after beholding in peace the fruits of his long and busy reign, expired, A.D. 973, at Menleben. He was buried, according to his desire, at Magdeburg. He left the affairs of the empire, whose frontiers he had considerably extended, in a most prosperous condition. Christianity was zealously disseminated amid the Scandinavians to the north by the archbishopric of Hamburg, and amid the Slavi to the east by that of Magdeburg. Bohemia was transformed into a German dukedom. Poland and Denmark owed allegiance to the empire. The sovereignty of Lower Italy was in reversion. In the interior of the state, the power of the sovereign was firmly based. The government of the most important provinces, the dukedoms and Margraviates, was intrusted to the trustiest adherents of the reigning house; and by the appointment of Pfalzgrafs, who managed the imperial allods, royal dues and revenues, in every part of the empire, the dukes could, in case of necessity, be watched and kept in awe. The office of Pfalzgraf dates from an earlier period, it merely received additional importance during this reign. The cities had also increased in number and wealth. The discovery of the rich silver mines of the Harz greatly promoted commerce. A nobleman, when riding through the forest, perceived a piece of silver ore that had been uncovered by his horse's hoof: the spot was investigated, and, A.D. 938, the first mine was opened in the interior of Germany.

CXXXVI. *Otto the Second and Otto the Third*

OTTO II. was short of stature, but strong and muscular, and of an extremely ruddy complexion; his temperament was fiery, but modified by the refined and learned education he had received, and for which he was indebted to the care of his mother, Adelheid; his wife, Theuphano, also sympathized in his love of learning. Still, the Italian blood that flowed in his veins estranged him too much from Germany, and excited in him so strong an inclination for the south that it became as impossible for his mind to be completely absorbed by care for the empire, as it was for his rough, but honest German subjects to adopt the pomp and refinement of his court.

Swabia, on the death of the pious Hedwig, was inherited by Otto, the son of Ludolf, between whom and Henry the Wrangler, of Bavaria, the ancient feud that had arisen on account of the extent of their frontiers between their fathers was still carried on. The emperor decided the question in Otto's favor, and the quarrelsome Henry instantly attempted to rouse the ancient national hatred of the Bavarians, and to stir them up to open revolt. He also entered into alliance with Boleslaw of Bohemia, but was anticipated in his designs by Otto, who threw him into prison, bestowed Bavaria on Otto of Swabia, and Carinthia on a Graf, Henry Minor, the son of Berthold, probably a Babenberger; this Graf sided with Henry of Bavaria, revolted, and was deposed, A.D. 974. Carinthia was, consequently, also bestowed upon Otto. In the following year, Harald, king of Denmark, suddenly invaded Saxony, whence he was successfully repulsed. Shortly after this event, Henry escaped from prison, again raised the standard of rebellion, and was joined by the Bohemians,[1] but again suffered defeat, and was retaken prisoner, A.D. 977.

In 978, war again broke out in the west, where Charles, the brother of Lothar, king of France, attempted to gain possession of Lothringia, but was repulsed by Otto, who advanced as far as Paris, and burned the suburbs. The city, nevertheless, withstood his attack;[2] and on his return homeward, being surprised by the treacherous Count of Hennegau, he was compelled to come to terms with his opponents;

---

[1] A number of Bavarians, who were bathing not far from Pilsen, were suddenly attacked, when naked and defenseless, and cut to pieces by the Bohemians.
[2] Otto had vowed that he would cause the Parisians to hear a Te Deum such as never had been heard before, and he, accordingly, assembled all the clergy of the vicinity upon Mont Martre, where he compelled them to sing. He is said to have struck his lance into the city gate.

Charles was permitted to hold Lower Lothringia in fee of the empire, and Upper Lothringia was granted to Frederick, Count of Bar.

Otto, whose natural inclinations led him to Italy, was speedily called there by the affairs of that country. Crescentius had usurped the government in Rome, and attempted to revive the memory of ancient times by causing himself to be created consul. The pope, Benedict VII., was assassinated by his orders, and replaced by a creature of his own, Bonifacius VII., in opposition to whom the Tuscan imperialists raised Benedict VIII. to the papal chair. Otto's presence in Rome, A.D. 980, quickly restored order. Crescentius was pardoned. Otto was visited during his stay in Rome by Hugh Capet, Lothar's secret competitor for the throne of France, whose claim was countenanced by the emperor, on account of the ingratitude displayed by the French monarch for the services formerly rendered to his ancestors by the imperial house of Saxony.

Lower Italy next engaged the attention of the emperor, who attempted to take forcible possession of his wife's portion. The Greeks, until now unceasingly at war with the Arabs, instantly united with them against their common enemy. Naples and Tarentum were taken by Otto, and the allies were defeated near Cotrona, A.D. 981; Abn al Casem, the terror of Lower Italy, and numbers of the Arabs, were left on the field of battle. The following campaign proved disastrous to the emperor, who, while engaged in a conflict with the Greeks on the seashore near Basantello, not far from Tarentum, was suddenly attacked in the rear by the Arabs, and so completely routed that he was compelled to fly for his life, and owed his escape entirely to the rapidity of his horse. When wandering along the shore in momentary expectation of being captured by the enemy, he caught sight of a Grecian vessel, toward which he swam on horseback, in the hope of not being recognized by those on board. He was taken up. A slave recognized him, but instead of betraying him, passed him off as one of the emperor's chamberlains. The Greeks made for Rossano with the intention of taking on board the treasures of the pretended chamberlain, who, the instant the vessel approached the shore, suddenly leaped into the sea and escaped.[1] Lower Italy remained in the hands of the Greeks, and was governed by an exarch. The Arabians also retained possession of Sicily. Otto, duke of Swabia and Bavaria, dying during the campaign in Italy,[2] the emperor bestowed the ducal crown of Swabia on Conrad, the son of Udo, who was the brother of Hermann of Swabia, and to whom Otto 1. had given the Rhinegau and the Wetterau to hold in fee. Bavaria was restored to Henry Minor, and Carinthia was given to Otto of Franconia, the son of Conrad the Red, who had fallen valiantly fighting against the Hungarians. Henry the Wrangler remained a prisoner.

Hermann Billung had been succeeded in Saxony by his son, Bernhard. The Slavian frontiers were, however, divided into several petty Margraviates, that of Zeiz or Northern Thuringia being governed by Gunther, that of Northern Saxony or Brandenburg by Dietrich, that of the Lausitz by

---

[1] This adventure has been variously related. According to one writer, he slew forty Greek boatmen, with the assistance of a soldier named Probus, whom he met with on the shore; another version records that he enticed the Greeks, to whom he was personally known, to the shore, by requesting them to take on board their vessel his wife and treasures, which had been placed for safety in Rossano; that he sent young men disguised as his wife's female attendants on board the vessel, which they speedily seized. Every account, however, agrees that Theuphano jeeringly inquired of the emperor whether her countrymen had not put him into deadly fear; for which the Germans never forgave her. The fable-loving historian, Vincentius, makes a naval engagement, in 983, take place between the emperor and the Greeks, in which they fought with such animosity that the whole sea was stained with blood, and the emperor was victorious, but received a mortal wound. According to other accounts, he died at Rome, not of his wound, but of grief. He is also said to have been whipped to death on Mount Garganus by the angels, among whom he had imprudently ventured while they were there holding a conclave. It is impossible to unravel the meaning of this strange fable. These examples will, however, suffice to give an idea of the inaccuracy of the chronicles of these times.

[2] It is said that, during this campaign, one of the emperor's daughters eloped to Alba in Montserrat with her seneschal, Graf Alram of Saxony, who was afterward pardoned and created the first Markgraf of Montserrat. The celebrated golden altar, an invaluable work of art, that, in 1698, was stolen and melted by the robber Nicolas List, was, during this campaign, taken from the Arabs and sent to Lüneburg.

Ditmar, and that of Misnia by Riddag. Violence and pillage had become so frequent as to be considered legitimate in this country. A certain Graf Dedo assembled a force in Bohemia, surprised and plundered Zeiz, and carried off Oda, the daughter of Dietrich of Brandenburg, the affianced bride of Miseko, king of Poland. Dietrich emulated Gero in the cruelty with which he treated the conquered Slavi.

Mistevoi, the valiant prince of the Obotrites, favored the Christian religion, followed the banner of Otto II., and served under him in Italy; on his return to his native country, he sued for the hand of Mechtildis, the sister of Bernhard of Saxony, and on being insulted by the jealous Dietrich, who called him a dog and unworthy of a Christian or of a German bride, replied, "If we Slavi be dogs, we will prove to you that we can bite." The pagan Slavi, who were ever ripe for revolt, obeyed his call the more readily, on account of the death of Ditmar, who, with many others of their tyrannical rulers, had fallen in the Italian war. An oath of eternal enmity against the Germans and the priests was taken before their idol, Radegast, and suddenly rising in open rebellion, they assassinated all who fell into their hands, A.D. 983, razed all the churches to the ground, and completely destroyed the cities of Hamburg and Oldenburg, besides those of Brandenburg and Havelburg. The lands of Dietrich became one scene of desolation. Sixty priests were flayed alive. The rebels were, nevertheless, completely beaten by Dietrich and Riddag in a pitched battle near Tangermünde. The emperor, however, more just than his father had been, deprived the cruel Dietrich of his government, and bestowed it on Hodo. Riddag and his cousin, the above-mentioned Graf Dedo, remained in Meissen, whence Riddag was afterward expelled by the Bohemians. It was regained by his cousin and successor, the brave Eckhart, whose exploits were equaled by those of Bernhard Billung, who had returned from Italy in order to oppose the Obotrites on the western frontier. The obstinacy with which the Slavi, notwithstanding their terrible defeats, still held out, is proved by the fact of Brandenburg having been first retaken in 994.

The peaceable conversion of the Bohemians and Poles chiefly contributed to the gradual but complete subjection of the Slavi on the frontiers. The independence of Bohemia and Poland was only possible so long as the powerful Slavian pagan states existed to their rear. This support was now lost. Poland was already Christianized, and the bishop of Prague, Adalbert, was a celebrated Bohemian saint. It was also about this period that Christianity took firm footing in Denmark, although not without fierce struggles. Harald Blaatand, whom Otto I. had compelled to receive baptism, was, when past his eightieth year, expelled by his son, Swein Gabelbart, who favored paganism. He died of his wounds, A.D. 986.[1] Swein conquered the mere of Schleswig, and caused the Graf Siegfried of Oldenburg, and several other knights whom he had taken prisoners, to be deprived of their hands and feet. Saxony and Poland, aided by the Christians of Scandinavia, under the guidance of St. Poppo, a zealous preacher, rose in arms against him. Erich, king of Sweden, one of Poppo's disciples, greatly aided them, in the hope of gaining possession of Denmark by means of the Christian party: this project was realized,[2] and Poppo baptized countless numbers of the Danes in the Hilligbek (*heiligen Bach*), sacred fount,[3] between Schleswig and Flensburg. After the

---

[1] Compare Dahlman's History of Denmark. The legendary account relates that Swein of Palnatoke or Toko, the celebrated chief of the Jomsburgian pirates, was the son of Harald, by whom he was not acknowledged, his mother having been a common slave. Toko, imagining himself injured by this conduct, became the monarch's mortal enemy. Harald took him prisoner, and compelled him to show his skill, for which he was celebrated, as a marksman, by shooting at an apple placed on the head of his son. "Why didst thou conceal another arrow about thee?" demanded the king. "In order to have killed thee," replied Toko, "had I struck my child." The king then placed him in chains in his boat, but, during a storm that arose on the lake, unbound him, in order to be saved by his well-known skill as an experienced boatman. Toko steered against a rock, sprang on shore, and pushed the boat back into the lake. He afterward waylaid the king and shot him.—*Saxo Grammaticus*.

[2] Swein is said to have been taken prisoner three times. He twice ransomed himself by paying his weight in gold, and double that weight in silver. On the third occasion, he obtained his liberty by the cession of the Danish crown.

[3] Erich was merely *primsignet*, or provisionally signed with the cross, as was

death of Erich, his son, Olaf Schooskönig, who completed the peaceable conversion of Sweden, deemed it more politic to treat amicably with Swein, and not only bestowed on him the hand of his mother, Sigrida, but also restored him to the Danish throne, and united with him against the great northern hero, Olaf Tryggvason of Norway, whose successes, A.D. 995, over Hakon Jarl and the pagan party had roused the jealousy of his neighbors. His bitterest enemies were the pirates of Jomsburg and their other northern brethren, the Ascomanni (so named from their great boats, or *Aschen*), with whom the kings of Denmark and Sweden entered into alliance, and defeated Olaf Tryggvason in a naval engagement.[1]

Great changes took place also, at this period, in France. Lothar died, A.D. 986, and, in the following year, his only son, Louis V. Charles of Lothringia, Lothar's brother, aspired to the throne, but was excluded by the Capetian party. The disesteem in which he was held on account of his licentious habits, and the refusal of assistance from Germany, where the emperor, dissatisfied with the conduct of Lothar, no longer favored the Carlovingians, rendered him defenseless; he fell into the hands of his rival, Hugh Capet, and died in prison, A.D. 993. His son, Otto, the last of the Carlovingian race, died, neglected and despised, A.D. 1004.

The death of Otto II., which was occasioned by the hardships he had undergone at Basantello, took place in Italy, A.D. 983. His son, Otto III., a child three years of age, was named as his successor, under the joint guardianship of Theuphano and Adelheid, who gave him such a learned education that he received the appellation of the "*Wunderkind*," on account of the precocity of his intellect.

---

then the custom before initiating the converts in the tenets of the church. Erich believed that the God of the Christians resembled all other gods, and was merely somewhat stronger than those of the pagans, whom it was, nevertheless, also necessary to worship. The zealous Poppo, resolving to convert the king by the performance of a miracle, passed unharmed, in a waxen shirt, through a fiery furnace, upon which the terrified people flocked in multitudes to the font.
[1] See Chapter CXXII.

Henry the Wrangler, who aspired to the throne, and seized the person of the young monarch, had already, by his conduct, estranged from himself his countrymen the Saxons; the memory of the cruelties practiced by his father also rendered him unpopular in Bavaria, and he was speedily reduced to submission by the Franconian party, at whose head stood Willigis, the learned archbishop of Mayence. He was the son of a wheelwright, and adopted a wheel for the arms of the archbishopric, with these words, "Willigis, Willigis, remember thy origin." Next in rank to this spiritual head of the empire stood Conrad, duke of Franconia and Swabia, and Henry, duke of Bavaria. Henry the Wrangler was compelled to deliver up the emperor, and to take the oath of allegiance to him, in consideration of which he was restored to the dukedom of Bávaria, on the death of Henry Minor, which was shortly afterward followed by that of Conrad, who was succeeded in Franconia by his son Conrad, and in Swabia by his nephew Hermann. The mere of Austria was granted to Leopold I., grandson to Adalbert of Babenberg, whom Hatto had betrayed. This brave Markgraf displayed so much activity that in 983 he had driven the Hungarians from the Enns, taken their royal castle of Mölk, and compelled them to keep within the limits of modern Hungary. Their king, Geisa, followed the example of the sovereigns of Bohemia and Poland, and received baptism from the hands of Pilgerin, bishop of Passau; he also sought to preserve peaceful relations with the Germanic empire; Christianity, nevertheless, first became the national religion during the reign of his son, St. Stephen, who ascended the throne A.D. 997, and died A.D. 1038. This monarch married Gisela, the daughter of Henry the Wrangler, a union that strengthened his alliance with Germany.

Leopold planted numerous German colonists in Lower Austria, the country regained by him from the Hungarians, which was visited by fresh missionaries, who there left imperishable records of their zeal. In the mountains, St. Wolfgang performed his miracles on the shores of the lake that still bears his name; and a monastery, in which the relics of St. Colomannus, a Scotch missionary, who was murdered by the pagans, were preserved, was raised over the ruins of the royal castle of Mölk.

The scepter of Germany was no sooner again held by a child than the clergy and the great vassals of the empire sought to regain the power of which they had been deprived during the preceding reigns. The youthful emperor, guided by his mother and grandmother, who greatly favored the clergy, bestowed upon them rich lands and benefices. Peace was, certainly, maintained throughout the empire, the dukes contenting themselves with confirming their power in the interior of the state, unopposed by the emperor. War was, however, still carried on on the Slavian frontier, where Otto was occasionally allowed to appear in person, in order to gain his first spurs. Graf Arnold of Holland, at that period, A.D. 993, also attempted the subjugation of the Western Frisii, by whom he was defeated and slain.

Theuphano and Adelheid, whose thoughts were ever directed toward Italy,[1] their native land, had not been idle in their endeavors to rouse the ambition of the youthful Otto, who, on attaining his majority, aspired to the sovereignty of that country, where, after the death of Otto II., the Italian party again rose in opposition to that of the emperor. Crescentius, who had usurped unlimited power in Rome, caused the pope, John XIV., to be assassinated, and expelled his successor, John XV., who convoked an extraordinary council at Rheims, A D. 995. Hugh Capet, the new French monarch, who planned the foundation of a Gallican church, independent of that of Rome, had deposed Arnulf, archbishop of Rheims, a nephew of Charles of Lothringia, for his zealous exertions in favor of his unfortunate Carlovingian relatives. The German bishops and the pope, enraged at this

---

[1] Adelheid fixed her residence in her widowhood at Pavia, where she was visited by Theuphano when returning from a pilgrimage to the holy sepulcher at Jerusalem. They separated after a bitter quarrel, and Theuphano died shortly afterward at Nimwegen.

conduct, unanimously condemned him at the council at Rheims, and he was compelled to yield. The pope expired during the following year, and the emperor marched into Italy for the purpose of regulating the affairs of the church. Crescentius was speedily overcome and pardoned. Otto, fired by youthful enthusiasm, imagined that the future happiness of the world was to be secured by a closer union of the imperial with the papal power, and with his own hand, although himself scarcely out of his boyhood, placed the tiara on the head of Bruno, the son of Otto of Carinthia, who was then in his four-and-twentieth year, and who received the name of Gregory V. Bruno was grandson to Conrad of Franconia, the hero of the Lech, who had married Luitgarde, daughter to Otto I. St. Adalbert, who had come from Prague, A.D. 996, in order to witness the ceremony, was enraptured at the sight of these two noble youths. By his side stood Gerbert, Otto's preceptor, one of the most profound reasoners of the age, and the energetic Bishop Notker of Liege, both of whom earnestly sought to re-establish the fallen power of the church, while the youthful pope, strong in his native purity, caused even the Italians, in despite of their moral depravity, to foresee the height to which the church might attain if governed by German virtue. His first step was to lay France under an interdict until the reinstallment of Arnulf into his archbishopric, which had been purposely delayed by Hugh Capet, whose son Robert, his successor, evinced greater submission to Rome. St. Adalbert visited Prussia, in order to preach the gospel to the heathen inhabitants, by whom he was murdered, A.D. 997. His death was a bad omen, for scarcely had the emperor quitted Rome than Crescentius again raised the banner of insurrection, inflamed all the dark and fiendlike passions of the Roman populace, already indignant at the assumption of the tiara by a stranger, and elected another Italian wretch, John XVI., pope. The emperor instantly returned, and re-entering Rome, where his presence alone sufficed to calm the uproar, caused the pretender to the popedom to be deprived of sight, and to be led through the city mounted on an ass. Crescentius, who had vainly thrown himself into the Castle of St. Angelo, was executed, A.D. 998. The well-founded hopes of the German party were, however, doomed to be frustrated by Italian wiles, and it is only left for us to imagine what Europe might have become, had these two noble-minded youths been intrusted, for a longer period, with her temporal and spiritual welfare. Gregory V. expired suddenly, A.D. 999. His death was, with great justice, ascribed to poison. Gerbert became his successor, under the name of Sylvester II. His deep science and learning caused him to be generally regarded as a wizard. The death of Gregory, the friend of his youth, caused a deep dejection to prey upon the mind of the emperor, which was still more worked upon by the approach of the year 1000, the period popularly fixed for the end of the world, and by the exhortations of two Italian enthusiasts, the saints Romuald and Nilus, who gained great power over him, and who, being the fellow-countrymen of Crescentius, reproved him most particularly for the severity with which he had treated that traitor, which they denounced as a crime, and he was at length induced to do penance for fourteen days in a cavern, sacred to the archangel Michael, on the Monte Gargano, in Apulia, and to perform a pilgrimage to the bones of St. Adalbert at Gnesen, in Poland. He, nevertheless, reappeared here in his character as emperor, by more strongly cementing the amicable relations that already subsisted between Germany and Poland. Besides consecrating there a church to St. Adalbert, and founding the archbishopric of Gnesen, on which the bishoprics of Breslau, Cracau and Colberg (at a later period, Kamin) were rendered dependent, he bestowed the title of king on Boleslaw Chrobry, the son of Miseko and of the Bohemian Dobrowa, and gave his niece, Rixa,[1] to his son Mieslaus, in marriage. He also, during the

---

[1] She was the mother of Casimir, with whom she afterward took refuge in France, where she caused him to be educated as a monk. He was recalled, and placed upon the throne in his monkish garb. The Poles shaved their heads in order to resemble him, a custom that afterward became a sign of rank.

same year, visited Aix-la-Chapelle, where he caused the tomb of Charlemagne to be opened. That monarch was discovered seated on his throne. On his return to Rome, he announced his intention of making her the capital of the modern, as she had been that of the ancient world, but the Romans were incapable of either comprehending his grand projects, or of perceiving the advantage that must have accrued to them had their city once more become an imperial residence. The senseless and brutal populace again rose in open insurrection. On one occasion, Otto, addressing them from a tower, upbraided them for their folly, and induced them to disperse. His death, which took place in 1002, was ascribed to poison,[1] but was more probably caused by smallpox. In the following year, Pope Sylvester also expired, and with him every hope that had been raised for the reformation of the church, which again fell under Italian influence, and the weak-minded successor to the throne of Germany became her slave instead of her protector.

CXXXVII. *Henry the Second, the Holy*

OTTO dying childless, the succession to the throne was again disputed. Henry of Bavaria, the son of Henry the Wrangler, claimed it as the nearest of kin, and was supported by the clergy on account of his piety, and his munificence toward the church. The next competitor was Hermann of Swabia, who, although of Franconian descent, was nearly allied to the imperial house. He was, moreover, the wealthiest and most considerable of the German dukes, and en-

---

[1] Several chronicles relate that Stephania, the beautiful widow of Crescentius, whom Otto had taken for his mistress, caused his death by means of poisoned gloves. But her name was Theodora, and she was, moreover, at that time a grandmother. It is related of this emperor that his wife, Mary of Aragon, was faithless to him, and having vainly attempted to win the affections of a handsome Italian count, falsely accused him to the emperor, who condemned him to death. The widow of the injured count appeared before his throne, and offered to prove the innocence of her husband by undergoing the ordeal. She passed through it unharmed, and the emperor, convinced of his injustice, sentenced his wife to be publicly burned, A.D. 996.

joyed far more popularity among the laity than his rival, Henry. The third claimant was Eckhart of Meissen, who, for the first time, made use of the unlimited power he enjoyed as governor of the Slavian marches, where the population was reduced to complete servitude, while the dukes or governors of the German provinces were ever circumscribed in their authority by the free spirit of the people.

Henry's party was considerably strengthened by the adherence of Willigis, the pious archbishop of Mayence. Eckhart, his most dangerous opponent, lost his life before he could carry his projects into execution. His indecorous treatment of Sophia and Adelheid (the sisters of Otto III., who actively forwarded the interests of his rival, Henry), into whose dining apartment he forced his way, and destroyed their meal, was avenged by the Saxon Grafs of Nordheim, who attacked him during the night at Pölde, A.D. 1002, and succeeded in depriving him of life after a valiant defense. Henry thereupon repaired to Aix-la-Chapelle, where he was crowned. Hermann resigned his pretensions and submitted to the new emperor. He died shortly afterward, leaving Swabia to his son Hermann, who did not long survive him. He was succeeded by Ernst, the son of Leopold of Austria, and husband to Gisela, his sister, the daughter of Gerberga, and granddaughter of Rudolf III. of Burgundy. Ernst was killed when hunting, and left the dukedom to his son Ernst, whose mother, Gisela, married Conrad, Graf of Franconia, who afterward ascended the imperial throne. His cousin, the Markgraf Henry of Schweinfurt, demanded, immediately after the coronation of the emperor, the dukedom of Bavaria, which had become vacant by Henry's accession to the throne, and which was also aspired to by Bruno, the emperor's brother. Both competitors met with a refusal from Henry, who bestowed Bavaria upon his brother-in-law, Henry, Count of Luxemburg, upon which the two rivals entered into a conspiracy against him with Boleslaw II. of Bohemia, who had not inherited the peaceable disposition of his father. They were defeated by the emperor near Creusen, A.D. 1003, and pardoned. Lothringia, on the extinction of the Carlovingian race, fell to Gottfried of Verdun, the nephew of Gisilbrecht, and Brabant to Lambert of Louvain, the husband of Gerberga, the sister of Otto, the last of the Carlovingians.

Affairs also wore a different aspect in the East; Boleslaw Chrobry of Poland, a great conqueror, reduced Kiow in Russia beneath his rule. In Bohemia, Boleslaw had broken his oath of allegiance to the empire. The ancient race of Crocus had degenerated. A rival race, that of the Wrssowez, was at the head of the democratic and pagan party, but could merely offer a weak opposition, by dint of petty stratagems, to the more powerful Christian party. At length the assassination of one of the Wrssowez, by the order of Boleslaw, occasioned the formation of a conspiracy against him; Boleslaw was enticed into Poland, where he fell into the hands of the enraged Wrssowez, who deprived him of sight, and placed Bohemia, Moravia and Silesia in the hands of Boleslaw of Poland. A great reaction ensued. Boleslaw, at the head of the united Poles and Bohemians, invaded the Lausitz and Meissen. After several severe campaigns, the emperor at length succeeded in separating Bohemia from Poland, and in placing Othelrich or Ulrich, the brother of the blind Boleslaw, on the throne of that dukedom. Othelrich was faithless and tyrannical. In order the more firmly to secure the possession of the crown, he deprived his second brother, Jaromir, of sight. Boleslaw of Poland attempted to win him over, and sent his son, Miseko, to negotiate with him. Othelrich delivered him up to the emperor, who instantly restored him to liberty. The war, nevertheless, was still carried on: The emperor suffered a defeat, A.D. 1015, probably on the Bober, the half of his army that had crossed the stream being suddenly attacked by the enemy. Miseko, inspirited by this success, attacked Meissen: the castle was set on fire, but the conflagration was extinguished by the women, who poured mead on the spreading flames. The emperor afterward undertook a fresh expedition into Silesia, where he laid siege to the city of Nimptsch,[1] but without success. Peace was finally concluded with Poland at Bautzen, A.D. 1018. In Meissen, the house of Wettin was raised to the Margravial dignity, in the person of Dedi I., the brave opponent of the Slavi. A war of extermination was also waged against the Obotrites and the Wilzi by Bernhard II. of Saxony, and Bernhard, Markgraf of Brandenburg, the son of the deposed Dietrich. Mistevoi, prince of the Obotrites, whose sway extended over the whole of the Slavian north, weary at length of the havoc of war, and anxious to secure peace for his people, embraced Christianity. He was, in consequence, expelled by his subjects. He died at Bardewik. In order to strengthen himself against the Slavi, the emperor courted the friendship of the Danes, to whom he gave permission to found, for the first time, an independent archbishopric of Lund. Up to this period, A.D. 1004, Denmark had been dependent on the archbishopric of Hamburg, whose prelate, Liemar, had excommunicated King Erich, on account of his cruelty.

The Italians, unwearied in their struggle for independence, had, upon the death of Otto, again raised a king of their own, Harduin, Markgraf of Ivrea, to the throne of Italy. The bishops, who favored the claims of Henry, from the same motive which caused them to be upheld by their brethren in Germany, alone opposed him. Henry marched into Italy, where he overcame every opponent, and was crowned, A.D. 1005, at Pavia. This powerful city rebelled against the foreign invader, and the citizens so closely besieged the imperial palace, that Henry was compelled to spring from a window, and lamed himself for life. A dreadful revenge was taken by his German troops. The emperor,

---

[1] This city was named Nemezi, on account of its having been founded by Germans. It is supposed to have been an ancient German sanctuary prior to the times of the Slavi.—*Mone's Pagan Antiquity.* In the middle of the valley lying in the vicinity is the Zobtenberg, with its pagan monuments. The country round about was called Silensgau, and was, in fact, the heart of Silesia.— *Ditmar of Merseburg.* This chronicler also mentions, at that period, the city of Breslau (Wrozislawa), a name derived from Wratislau or Brzetislaw.

who now beheld Italy with feelings of disgust, was shortly after recalled into Germany by the outbreak of the Slavian war, and Harduin again caused himself to be proclaimed king. The audacity of the pretender once more drew Henry into Italy; the rebels were this time completely reduced to submission, and he visited Rome, A.D. 1013, where the pope confirmed his claim to the empire, and placed the crown on his head, and on that of his wife, the pious Cunigunda. It was on this occasion that the pope bestowed upon the emperor the golden ball, the emblem of the globe, over which he was destined to rule. It was also at this period that Henry created Berthold, Graf of Walbek (who was supposed to be a descendant of the ancient race of Wittekind), Graf of Savoy. Henry revisited Italy, A.D. 1021, for the purpose of reducing the Greeks in Lower Italy to subjection. Melo of Lombardy, who had resisted their tyranny at Bari, was constrained to flee. At the same time, the Arabs attacked Salerno, whose duke, Waimar, was unexpectedly saved by a ship manned by forty Normans, who were returning from the Holy Land. They were sent away laden with costly gifts, and invited to return. Many of their countrymen afterward emigrated to Lower Italy, under the command of Drengot and his four brethren, who joined Melo against the Greeks and Arabs. Drengot fell in battle. His brother, Rainulf, settled at Aversa, between Capua and Naples. Pandulf, duke of Capua, however, leagued with the Greeks, but was taken prisoner by Henry, whose presence alone seemed to insure victory. An epidemic, at length, which broke out in his camp, compelled him to return to Germany, A.D. 1022.

Disturbances had, meanwhile, arisen in the Netherlands. A robbery, committed upon some merchants by the Frisii, had occasioned a feud between Dietrich, Graf of Holland, and Gottfried of Lothringia, the latter of whom suffered a heavy defeat at Merwe, A.D. 1018. Adalbero, a descendant of the house of Luxemburg, which was highly favored by the emperor through the influence of the empress, had, moreover, seized the archbishopric of Treves;[1] he was deposed by the emperor, who, on the other hand, created Henry, the brother of Cunigunda, duke of Bavaria. Another Adalbero, Graf of the Mürzthal, was nominated to the government of Carinthia. Otto, the son of Conrad of Franconia, had inherited both Franconia and Carinthia, which were divided between his sons, Henry and Conrad, each of whom had a son named Conrad, who, displeased with the emperor's verdict, opposed Adalbero and beat him at Ulm out of the field, but found themselves unable to drive him out of his mountain fastnesses. Conrad, the son of Conrad, retained the dukedom of Franconia. Conrad, the son of Henry, who merely enjoyed the title of Graf, wedded Gisela, through whom he had a claim upon Burgundy, whose king, Rudolf, had solemnly sworn that his dominions should be incorporated, on his demise, with the empire, A.D. 1018.

Henry was extremely devout, and was consequently idolized by the clergy.[2] He held five councils in Germany, improved and corrected ecclesiastical discipline, rebuilt the churches that had been destroyed by the Slavi, and raised a magnificent monument to his own memory by the foundation of the bishopric of Bamberg,[3] which he enriched at the expense of the neighboring landowners, among whom was the bishop of Würzburg, who obstinately resisted his innovations, until appeased by numerous gifts. The pope, Benedict VIII., visited Bamberg, A.D. 1020, for the purpose of consecrating the new establishment. The empress, Cunigunda, was equally pious. The imperial pair had mutually

---

[1] The rightful archbishop, Megingod, had, during the usurpation of Adalbero, received the bishopric of Coblentz by way of indemnification. After his restoration, this bishopric still remained attached to Treves.

[2] It is related of him that he even wished to become a monk at Strasburg, but had no sooner taken the oath of implicit obedience than he was commanded by Bishop Werner to resume his crown.

[3] It is supposed that he sought to expiate the criminal action of his ancestors against Adalbert of Babenberg by the consecration of the lands unjustly seized by them to the service of God. An idea in which he was upheld by Cunigunda. It was on this account that the privileges granted to Bamberg were called Cunigunda's silken threads, by which, it was said, the city was defended better than by towers and walls.

taken the vow of chastity, and remained childless. Cunigunda's virtue, however, did not escape slander, and she voluntarily underwent the ordeal by fire, and walked unharmed over glowing iron. Henry, when on his death-bed, named as his successor Graf Conrad, the husband of Gisela, on account of his being the ablest descendant of the most powerful race that remained in Germany after the extinction of that of the Ottos, thus repaying, with equal magnanimity, the generous conduct of Conrad I., when dying, toward the house of Saxony. He expired A.D. 1024, and was interred at Bamberg.[1]

CXXXVIII. *Immunities—Increasing Importance of the Churches and Cities, and Consequent Decrease of the Ducal Power*

CHARTERS and franchises had been lavishly distributed by the Saxon emperors, for the purpose of creating a multitude of minor nobles and corporations, independent of the dukes, against whose power they served as a counterpoise. This political motive had induced Charlemagne to favor the bishops: their power was still more increased by the Ottos, who did not yet foresee the danger to which it might, at some future period, expose the state. The popes were, moreover, too busily engaged with Italy and too powerless to excite the jealousy of the emperors, in whose hands the church was a mere tool. The numerous armed vassals subservient to the bishops and abbots necessarily diminished the number of those who owed allegiance to the dukes and Markgrafs; and the greater the extent of the lands beneath the sway of the crosier, so much the less could, consequently, be under the control of the temporal lords. To these motives may be ascribed the enormous donations to the church, the endowment

---

[1] On his tombstone stands a figure of Justice with a pair of scales, the index of which inclines a little to one side. As soon as the poise shall become equal the world will be at an end.

of churchmen with temporal rights and power, the union of the imperial office of Graf with the ecclesiastical dignity of bishop, and the immunity or affranchisement from the supreme authority of the dukes.

The Sendgrafs, or commissioned officers of the crown, created by Charlemagne, had, under the Ottos, been converted into Pfalzgrafs, or administrators of the crown lands, revenues, etc., in the different dukedoms, who, at the same time, in some measure controlled the dukes. Besides them, Markgrafs, who acted independently of the dukes, were placed in the newly-conquered frontier provinces, and the elevation within the dukedoms of powerful Grafs, who, although nominally subservient to the dukes, equaled them in wealth and influence, and could even compete with them in political power, was also encouraged by the Saxon emperors, who thus blindly laid a mine destined to shake the imperial throne. The dukes, whose power merely arose from the office they held under the crown, and the independent spirit of the nations to which they belonged, far less endangered the power of the emperor than did the great families of later date, who were hereditarily possessed of immensely extensive lands. And while the emperors were thus endeavoring to hasten the decay of the ancient dukedoms, and to consign the very names of the ancient nations to oblivion, they were far from foreseeing that the time might arrive when new names, that owed their origin to some unnoted fort, would lay the whole empire at their feet.

The ancient division of the empire into dukedoms and provinces (*gaue*) gradually gave place to one more complex, caused either by the formation of ecclesiastical and temporal feudal territories within the provinces and dukedoms, or by the encroachment of one enormous feudal territory on several of the provinces and even of the dukedoms, while the ancient uniformity of condition was everywhere destroyed by charters and franchises or immunities.

The last remnants of the ancient freemen, who had not been gathered into the cities, had formed themselves into communities of free peasantry, who, although recognizing a duke or Graf in his judicial capacity as a delegate of the crown, or a bishop as their spiritual guide, retained their ancient privileges in all other respects. The repeated attempts of the nobles to reduce them to a state of vassalage, were, nevertheless, generally successful, and liberty at length sought refuge amid the peasantry of Lower Saxony and Switzerland. In A.D. 922, the western Frisii had already been reduced to vassalage by Dietrich of Holland, who also made a similar attempt upon the liberties of the free eastern Frisii, but met with armed resistance, and was repulsed in several campaigns.

The eastern Frisii consisted of seven petty republics, called the Seelands, united in the ancient German manner; they held their general assemblies at the Upstalesbome (*Obergerichts baum*, tree of justice), and were governed by their own laws, merely recognizing the archbishop of Bremen as their patron, the only bond that united them to the empire. Saxony also still preserved much of her ancient freedom. The Saxon Grafs, who still, as in times of yore, held their provincial courts of justice in the open air, with the elected aldermen or Schöppen, in the presence of all the freemen of the province, were distinguished by the epithet of Freegrafs, their courts of justice were also called free courts, the aldermen, free aldermen or Freischöppen, and the seat of justice, the Freistuhl or free seat. There were also numerous free peasantry in Switzerland and in Swabia, and, under Otto III., a bloody feud arose in the Thurgau, owing to the attempts of the nobility and clergy to reduce the people to a state of vassalage. The peasants, headed by one of their class, Heinz von Stein, rose in open insurrection, and, A.D. 992, a battle was fought near Diessenhofen, which, although the nobles were victorious, taught the Alpine shepherds caution, and was merely a prelude to the great struggle for freedom that arose at a later period. Radbot, the founder of the Habsburg, may be said to have inoculated his race with hatred to freedom by the violent reduction of his free peasantry to a state of vassalage,[1] A.D. 1018.

While territorial wealth and influence were thus usurped by the clergy and the nobility, the ancient freemen, collected within the cities, strained every nerve, not so much, however, in order to protect as in order to extend their privileges, and to manifest their importance as the third power in the state. The emperors, perceiving that the most efficient remedy against the ascendency of the dukes lay in the flourishing state of the cities, greatly aided their endeavors by the grants and charters freely lavished upon them, and a number of new cities consequently sprang up, into which all the freemen, harassed by the feudal lords, quickly thronged. These cities were liberally chartered by the Ottos. For instance, they granted to townships, that had gradually grown into cities, and were situated on the territory and within the jurisdiction of either spiritual or temporal lords, the rights belonging to free imperial towns, and placed them beneath the imperial jurisdiction; they also granted privileges to the larger cities, such as the right of coinage, and that of exacting customs, which were formerly alone conceded to the bishops and the dukes.

The internal government and legislation of the cities were equally favored by the charters granted to them by the Ottos. The governor, nominated by the crown, only nominally held the supreme direction of affairs, and seldom even resided in the town, but was generally one of the neighboring Grafs, who, contenting himself with receiving the gifts of the citizens, and with being entertained by them, left them completely at liberty. Whenever the emperor chanced to visit a town, the citizens vied with each other in paying him honor, in return for which he conferred additional privileges upon them. The imperial governor or *Reichsvogt* (*Waltbot*, *Ge*-

---

[1] Aided by his brother, the influential Bishop Werner of Strasburg, who built the monastery of Muri with the wealth gained by the subjection of the peasantry. Their grandfather Guntram the Rich, had already collected vast treasures.

waltbote, messenger of power, in Latin, *potestas*, in Italian, *podesta—missus regius, Sendgraf*, royal messenger, *Sendschalk* or seneschal), generally called the *Burggraf* or *Burgvogt*, commanded the city troops in war time, and exercised the judicial office in the name of the emperor: these offices were sometimes separate, but usually devolved upon one person. The twelve aldermen or *Schöppen*, elected by the citizens, were next in rank. Their president, the mayor or *Schultheiss*, at first merely took cognizance of petty civil matters, but finally either filled the office of the governor, when absent, or was empowered to replace him by means of an imperial charter. The mayor and aldermen also formed the town council, to which was committed the management of the public affairs. In the great cities each parish had its separate aldermen, who met in a general town council. All the cities that had originally been governed by an imperial officer remained immediately under the crown, and were distinguished as free imperial towns. Other cities, which had sprung up around the imperial palaces, as, for instance, Ulm, finally became imperial towns, although their citizens were originally merely royal bondmen. Ducal and episcopal cities arose by means of vassals who had settled in the vicinity of a bishop's cathedral, or around the castle of a duke. These also became gradually free towns, without being immediately under the crown, and were therefore merely distinguished as free towns.

The citizens everywhere consisted of the proprietors of houses or of land, part of whom were the oldest *Burgenses*, or burgesses, who had divided the ground on which the town or city was to be raised among themselves, and had built their houses on it; or the proprietors of land in the vicinity of the city; or else the free landowners who withdrew into the cities at a later period, and who still retained their landed property. The ancient *Burgenses*, now *cives* or free citizens of the empire, possessed all the power, and formed a class superior to, and distinct from, that of the bondsmen, who either acted as personal servants under the patronage of the different burgher families, or were people who had placed themselves under the protection of the community, such as artificers, journeymen, porters, sailors, etc. The tyranny of the petty landowners drove multitudes into the cities; hence it necessarily happened that the bondsmen were ten or twenty times superior in number to the ancient burghers, who, being the sole proprietors of the privileges and wealth of the city, treated the second class with all the pride attached to free and noble birth, carefully avoided any connection with them, denominated themselves, by way of distinction, houses or people of gentle blood, formed themselves into an aristocratical association united by intermarriage and general commercial undertakings, and also reserved to themselves the right of holding public meetings or *Richerzeche* (corporations of the rich, *Reichen*, or of the free citizens of the empire, *Reichsbürger?*), while they strictly forbade the formation of any kind of association among the lower classes. The earlier the period, the more distinctly are two different classes of city families to be distinguished, in which the ancient distinction that existed between the Edelings and the Frilings is still clearly recognizable. There was also a third class of knights, probably settlers of a later date, whose knighthood conferred upon them nobility and freedom, but who had not as yet intermixed with the old families. The artificers, however, as they increased in numerical strength, and distinguished themselves in the feuds that arose between the different cities, gradually obtained greater privileges. They divided themselves into guilds, and the assembly of the heads of the different guilds, under the presidency of a burgomaster, ere long threatened the burghers and their mayor with civil broils, which, at a later period, actually broke out between them.

The ancient burghers, before taking the entire management of the city affairs into their hands under the direction of their mayor, had formed themselves into a mercantile corporation or guild, endowed with peculiar privileges (under Henry II.). Even in later times, the city government retained its mercantile spirit, and the civil and commercial polity generally remained inseparably united. Even in cases where the burghers appear as landowners distinguished from the merchants, whose wealth merely consisted in their floating capital, their interests were ever united, and the merchants seem to have been the younger sons of the landowners, who sought a respectable employment, or immigrants who settled in the towns, from whom the inhabitants acquired their knowledge of commerce. The emperor and the princes appear often to have been induced to favor the civil liberty of the towns merely on account of commercial advantage. Commerce made a rapid progress in Germany. It is said that the city of Cologne, in the eleventh century, numbered upward of five hundred mercantile men within her walls. Cologne, Hamburg, Schleswig, and Bremen were staple-towns, and as soon as the piracy of the Norsemen, after their conversion to Christianity, ceased, their ships and those of the Frieslanders visited the northern seas. The ships of Friesland touched at Greenland. The cities traded with all the northern countries, most particularly with England. The intermarriage by which the imperial house of Germany was allied with that of Greece had rendered the emperors doubly solicitous to open a line of commerce from the south. In 996, Otto III. gave the Jews, Lombards and French permission to traverse Germany with their wares: the most remarkable among these traders were those of Cahors in Guyenne, the Caorsini or Italian peddlers.

The age in which the Saxon emperors reigned is remarkably devoid of men of science and learning. The schools of Alcuin and of Rhabanus Maurus had disappeared, while the refinement borrowed from Italy and Greece had been only partially adopted. The higher ecclesiastical dignities were always held by the brothers and relatives of the highest and most influential families, so that the elevation of Willigis, a man of low birth, to the archbishopric of Mayence, naturally gave rise to much surprise and discontent. These dignitaries, moreover, merely interested themselves in increasing their possessions, and preferred war and the chase to study and learning. The people were, naturally, still more ignorant than the clergy, and rendered wild and uncivilized by the covetousness of the nobility, who sought to reduce them to a state of vassalage, similar to that imposed upon the conquered Slavi. The natural inclinations of each individual are necessarily stronger whenever the intellect is neglected; the warlike Gero, who laid down his sword and became a monk, is but one example of the manners of the times, when men, the greater portion of whose lives had been one continued scene of violence and bloodshed, were driven by remorse to expiate their crimes in seclusion and by prayer.

The celebrated Gerbert, Pope Sylvester II., exercised but little influence on his times; that of the Grecian princess, Theuphano, was equally limited, although ancient authors were studied in some of the monasteries, and it is probable that, at that time, several manuscripts were brought from the south into Germany. For instance, the nun, Roswitha, of Gandersheim, A.D. 980, discovered a manuscript copy of the comedies of Terence, in which she took such great delight as to translate them elegantly into Latin. She also composed a song in praise of the Ottos. The monk Eckehard of St. Gall sang in Latin verse the adventures of Walther of Aquitania, the first example of heroic poesy. Rather, the Dutchman, who became bishop of Verona, distinguished himself by some writings, in which he decried the ignorance, lewdness, and vice of the monks, for which he was grievously persecuted. Besides these writers, the tenth century could only boast of three great chroniclers: Luitprand, bishop of Cremona, A.D. 946, who, being attached to the embassy sent by Otto I. to Constantinople, recorded its fate, and described the manners of the Grecian court; he also wrote a chronicle and biography of the popes. Wittekind of Corvey, A.D. 973, wrote an excellent history of Saxony. Ditmar, bishop of Merseburg,[1] a descendant of the Salic race, wrote,

---

[1] He thus describes himself with the pious simplicity of the times: "I am but a little man. My left jawbone and the whole side of my face are disfigured

A.D. 1015, an equally famous account of the Saxon emperors, and particularly mentions the Slavi, among whom he dwelt. The alliance of the Ottos with Italy and Greece was more favorable to the development of art than to the progression of science. By their erection of numerous magnificent churches in the Byzantine and Roman style of architecture, they gave an impulse to art which, in the following century, produced the true German or Gothic style, the transition to which is exemplified in the celebrated cathedral at Strasburg, founded in 1015 by Bishop Werner, and afterward finished on more extensive plans. Nor does painting appear to have been unpatronized. Luitprand asserts that the victory won by Henry I. in the vicinity of Merseburg was represented with such truth that the beholder imagined himself present on the field of battle. Kugler, in his History of Art, says that sculpture progressed more rapidly in Saxony than in Italy. Music also was cultivated by Notker and other ecclesiastics.

PART X

THE FRANCONIAN, SALIC EMPERORS

CXXXIX. *Conrad the Second*

ON the death of Henry II., the last of the Ottos, a general assembly of the different nations belonging to the empire was convoked. They gathered from every quarter, and encamped in countless multitudes on the great plain between Worms and Mayence, on either side of the Rhine, A.D. 1024. The dukes appeared in person, their banners followed by the Markgrafs, Grafs, and minor

---

with an incurable fistula. In my childhood I broke the bridge of my nose, which gives me a comical appearance. Nor are my qualities of heart and mind superior. I am a miserable creature, given to anger, obstinate, envious, and, notwithstanding the ridiculousness of my own person, apt to deride others, a glutton, a hypocrite, a miser," etc.

nobles, besides an innumerable throng of vassals. With equal state came the archbishops, bishops, and abbots of the realm, with their haughty retainers; the broad land scarcely sufficed for the number of noble-born Germans, met for the purpose of electing a successor to their deceased monarch. On the right bank of the Rhine were stationed the Saxons under their duke, Bernhard, the Swabians under Duke Ernst, the Bavarians under Duke Henry, the Carinthians under Duke Adalbero, and the Bohemians under Duke Othelrich. On the left bank were seen the Franconians under Duke Conrad, the Upper Lothringians under Duke Frederick, and the Lower Lothringians under Duke Gottfried (Gozilo).

The house of Franconia, which, through the favor of Bishop Hatto, had first enriched itself during the Babenberg feud, and from which the emperor Conrad I. descended, had fallen to the brave Conrad (who lost his life when opposing the Hungarians), by his marriage with a daughter of that emperor. The fidelity he had evinced toward the house of Saxony was repaid to his son Otto, who was created duke of Franconia and Carinthia, and both of whose grandsons now set up a claim to the imperial throne; Graf Conrad, the husband of Gisela, the younger in years, but the son of the elder brother, and moreover the one recommended by Henry II., when on his death-bed, as his successor, and the Duke Conrad, the elder in years, but the son of the younger son, and less distinguished for talent. The family of these two competitors for the crown was so illustrious that a still more ancient origin was, by way of flattery, ascribed to it, and it was deduced from the Merovingians, and named the Salic race.

The election of one of the Conrads was unanimously resolved upon by all the great vassals of the empire, and both of the competitors, on the declaration of this decision in their favor, magnanimously agreed, for the sake of the state, to yield submissively to the verdict about to be pronounced. The Graf, accordingly, held a private conference with the duke, and it was amicably stipulated between them that the excluded one should be the first to swear allegiance to his elected rival. The electors met, and the first vote, that of Aribo, archbishop of Mayence, was given in favor of Conrad the elder; all the bishops added their suffrages, and Conrad the younger was the first among the temporal lords who rose and gave his vote in favor of the Graf, who was with one joyous acclaim elected emperor by the rest of the vassal princes, and the new sovereign, seating himself at the side of his loyal-hearted cousin, was proclaimed emperor by the shouting multitude. Frederick of Lothringia and the archbishop of Cologne, the only malcontents, silently quitted the assembly. Their departure was perceived by the Duke Conrad, who, hurrying after them, led them amicably back. How could they withstand the entreaties of a man who had just sacrificed his ambitious hopes for the weal of the state? Nor were the expectations of the nation in their elected monarch deceived; Conrad of Franconia was one of the noblest sovereigns who ever swayed the scepter of Germany.

By his first decree, still preserved at Aix-la-Chapelle, he rendered the fiefs of the petty vassals (the lesser nobility) hereditary, a deeply calculated measure, by which he aimed at creating a counterpoise in the state to the great vassals.[1] He visited the different provinces of the empire, in order to arrange its internal economy, everywhere dealing impartial justice. He was, however, speedily recalled by affairs relating to the Burgundian succession, King Rudolf having refused to fulfill the promise he had made to Henry, to the newly-elected sovereign, who was fully aware of the importance of reincorporating Burgundy with the empire. His persuasions, and those of Gisela, Conrad's wife and Rudolf's granddaughter, were at length successful, and the aged king renewed his plighted word.

On the decease of Henry II. the Italians asserted that the hereditary right of the emperors to Italy had expired, and

---

[1] Militum animos in hoc multum attraxit, quod antiqua beneficiap arenti nemini posterorum auferri sustinuit. — *Wippo.*

offered the crown to Hugh, the son of Robert, king of France. Robert refused it, and a friendly interview took place between him and the emperor, on the little river Cher, at that time the boundary of the empire. The Italians next made choice of a son of William, duke of Aquitania, who, in reply, upbraided them for their treachery, so greatly did the French still fear to irritate the German emperor. Conrad crossed the Alps, A.D. 1026, and planted the banner of the empire in the valley of Ronceval, near Piacenza. Rainer, Markgraf of Tuscany, refusing to do homage, the emperor bestowed his lands upon Bonifacius, the lord of Mantua, Modena, Ferrara, and Reggio, who thus became the most powerful of the Italian princes. Pavia rebelled and was vainly besieged by Conrad, and riots, which were suppressed and punished, took place in Ravenna and Rome during his presence in those cities. A splendid court was held by him at Rome, where he and his wife Gisela were solemnly crowned. He was also visited here by two kings, Rudolf of Burgundy and Canute the Great, who had succeeded his father Swein on the thrones of Denmark and of England, and had conquered Norway. This powerful monarch[1] had visited Rome in order to see the wonders of the South. He married his daughter, Cunihilda, to Henry, the son of Conrad, who became duke of Bavaria on the extinction of the house of Luxemburg. Canute held Schleswig in fee of the empire. After re-establishing peace in Lower Italy, Conrad extended the lands held by the Normans on condition of their protecting the frontier. He was shortly afterward recalled by a melancholy occurrence to the other side of the Alps.

The whole of Swabia was in an uproar. The Duke Ernst, as the elder son of Gisela by her first marriage, believed himself justified in claiming Burgundy as his inheritance, in opposition to his stepfather Conrad, although Rudolf, instead of bequeathing his kingdom to the Salic family, had merely reincorporated it with the empire. With him were united

---

[1] His usual body-guard was composed of 6,000 men bearing gilt halberds.

two Swabian Grafs of ancient race, Rudolf Welf, or Guelph,[1] the hereditary enemy of the Salic family, and Werner of Kyburg.

During Conrad's absence in Italy, Ernst, Welf, and Werner attacked the adherents and invaded the lands of the Salic family, which they laid waste without opposition, and took possession of Solothurn. These events caused Conrad to hasten his return, and to convoke a great Diet at Ulm, at which Ernst appeared at the head of his armed Swabians. In vain did Gisela entreat him to submit, and to return to his allegiance. His rebellious spirit, however, was not shared by his vassals, who, when the matter came to an issue, unanimously declared that the oath of allegiance which bound them to their duke in no wise released them from that which bound them to the emperor and to the state, and that, if the duke were at feud with the empire, it was their duty to aid the latter; and with one accord they abandoned their rebellious chieftains. Ernst, thus left at the mercy of his opponents, was arrested and imprisoned on a

---

[1] In the fifth century, Edica and Wulfo appear as princes of the Scirri. Under Charlemagne there flourished a Warin, count of Altorf, whose son and successor, Isenbart, caused St. Otmar of St. Gall to be put to death in prison. He saved the life of Charlemagne, who was attacked by a wild ox, when hunting, and was rewarded with the hand of his sister Irmentraut. The legend relates that one day, chancing to meet with an old woman who had given birth to three children, he declared such an occurrence unnatural, and accused her of adultery. The injured woman, in reply, entreated Heaven that the Countess Irmentraut might be delivered of as many children as there were months in the year. Her prayer was heard, and Irmentraut bare twelve boys. Fearing her husband's severity, she ordered a female attendant to cast eleven of them into the river. The maid obeyed, but on her way thither was met by the Graf, who inquired of her what she was carrying in her basket. "*Welfen,*" "puppies," replied the frightened girl. Isenbart then lifted the cloth from off the basket, and seeing that the children were fine and healthy, acknowledged them for his own, and had them secretly brought up. When they were grown up, he presented them to their mother. It was owing to this circumstance that this family received the name of Welf, or Guelph.

Welf I., one of the twelve, was Isenbart's successor; his granddaughter, Jutta or Judith, married the emperor Louis the Pious. Her father, Eticho (see Chap. CXXVI.), succeeded to the family honors. Since his time, the Welfian house dwelt generally in retirement, on the Bodensee, at Altorf. It is probable that the ancient enmity between this house and that of Saxony caused it to side with the Babenbergers. Duke Ernst, the descendant of the ancient house of Babenberg, now stood again opposed to the reigning imperial family.

charge of high treason, in the fortress of Giebichenstein in Saxony. Welf was exiled. Werner of Kyburg, A.D. 1027, valiantly defended his castle for several months against the imperial troops, but finding it at length untenable, contrived to make his escape. Three years later, A.D. 1030, Conrad restored his stepson to liberty, and, in the presence of his mother Gisela, promised to replace him on the ducal throne of Swabia, on condition of his betraying the secret of Werner's retreat. "How can I betray my only true friend!" replied the unfortunate duke. In consequence of this refusal he was declared by his peers guilty of misprision of treason, placed out of the ban of the empire, and reduced to complete beggary. Driven to despair, he took refuge with his friend Werner in the Black Forest, where they led a robber's life, and were aided by Adalbert of Falkenstein, who gave them his castle for a stronghold, whence they laid the whole country under contribution. The Swabians, headed by Graf Mangold of Veringen, besieged the fortress, surrounded the garrison during a sally, and, after an obstinate struggle in which Mangold fell, succeeded in cutting them to pieces. Hermann, Ernst's younger brother, succeeded him as duke of Swabia, A.D. 1037. The valor and wretched fate of Duke Ernst[1] made a deep impression on the imagination of the people, and he became the hero of many a ballad. The emperor was used to say of him, "Mad dogs never increase their race!"

Other cares, meanwhile, divided the attention of the em-

---

[1] In the following century, the adventures of Duke Ernst were ingeniously and poetically intermixed with the Oriental ideas introduced by the Crusades, and were detailed at length in a legend still extant among the popular ballads of those times. The hero is there conducted into the East, where he is opposed by all the most terrific creatures, men and beasts horrible to behold, intended as allegorical representations of his actual misfortunes. Each monster personifies an enemy or a betrayer. He reaches a black mountain, which signifies his prison. He is borne by an old man aloft amid the clouds; thus was he carried away by his ambition. His ship is wrecked on the Magnet mountain; his collision with the emperor. The nails fly out of his ship, and it falls to pieces; his abandonment by his vassals. These legends are not unworthy of note, inasmuch as they prove the interest felt by the people in the fortunes of their chiefs, and in themselves record the popular poetical taste.

peror. Boleslaw had been succeeded on the throne of Poland by his son, Miseko, who again refused to take the oath of allegiance to the empire, and, invading Saxony, laid the country waste and carried off an immense number of women and maidens. The seat of the bishopric of Zeiz, which was most exposed to the inroads of the Poles, was, on that account, at this period removed to Naumburg. Conrad invaded Poland, vainly besieged Bautzen, and wandered fruitlessly in the vast unpeopled forests, A.D. 1029. In the following year, Miseko again invaded the empire and exercised unheard-of cruelties on the Elbe and Saal; his chief victims were the wives of the nobility and other ladies of high birth, whose only refuge was death.[1] Othelrich of Bohemia, and also Stephan of Hungary, invaded the empire, but were successfully repulsed by Conrad, who also drove Adalbero out of Carinthia,[2] and bestowed that dukedom on his cousin and noble-minded rival, Conrad, as his paternal inheritance. The fortress of Enns, on the Hungarian frontier, was intrusted to Graf Ottocar, who erected the fort of Steyer, in the country that afterward took thence the name of Steyermark, or Styria, A.D. 1031. Shortly after these occurrences, Miseko was deposed by the Poles, and, seeking protection from Othelrich, was treacherously seized by his host and delivered up to the emperor, who generously restored him to liberty, saying, "I will not buy an enemy from an enemy." The Poles again accepted him for their king, and, won over by the unexpected generosity with which he had been treated,

---

[1] Matronas religiosas et nobiles armata manu sibi vindicavit. Solum tantorum fuit levamen malorum exoptata mors.—*Annalista Saxo, A.D.* 1030.

[2] To this epoch belongs the legend of St. Hemma, a relative of the emperor Henry II. Her husband, William, Graf of Friesach, being slain by Adalbero, she lived in widowed retirement in the castled fort of Purgstall with her two sons, William and Hartwig. Her castellan became enamored of her, and caused an insurrection of the miners of Zeyringen, by whom her young sons were murdered at his instigation, from an idea that he should be able to get the mother by that means the more easily into his hands. St. Hemma left the castle secretly, in a carriage drawn by oxen, which she allowed to go whither they would. They stood still, at length, on the spot where she afterward caused the convent of Gurk, of which she became abbess, to be erected, A.D. 1042: at a later period, it was converted into a bishopric. The castellan sank, together with the castle of Purgstall, into a morass.—*Hoomayr's Taschenbuch of* 1821.

he concluded a permanent peace with the emperor, A.D. 1034. Othelrich again rebelled, and was again reduced to submission. His son, Brzetislaw, carried off the beautiful Jutta, a relation of the emperor, from a convent at Ratisbon, and made her his wife; an adventure that at first roused the emperor's displeasure, but which afterward produced a reconciliation.

About this time, Udo, the son of Mistevoi, was assassinated by the Saxons. His son, Gottschalk, who had been sent to a German monastery for his education, made his escape, and placing himself at the head of his people, bloodily revenged his father's death. But one day, when passing through the wasted country, he was struck with remorse for the misery he had caused, and voluntarily gave himself up to the Saxons, A.D. 1036. The emperor, convinced of his sincerity and of his anxiety for the confirmation of peace, restored him to liberty; upon which he attempted the conversion of the Slavi, and consequently drew down upon himself their bitterest hatred. While these events were passing, he became the son-in-law of Canute the Great, and the town and fortress of Ratzeburg in western Poland being yielded to the duke of Saxony, he acquired sufficient influence to found the bishoprics of Ratzeburg and Mecklenburg. The Liutizii, the head tribe of the Wilzi, in Pomerania, were alone refractory. It was finally agreed between them and the Saxons to leave the decision of their quarrel and the choice between their different religions to the issue of single combat. Victory sided with the pagan Liutizii; and when the Saxons, regardless of the stipulated terms, continued their system of oppression, their opponents cried shame upon the God of the Christians, and mutilated the figure on a crucifix. This sacrilegious act was speedily avenged by the enraged emperor, who laid their country waste with fire and sword, and mutilated the prisoners, but was unsuccessful in his attempt to penetrate as far as the coasts through their wild forests and deep morasses.

The death of Rudolf, A.D. 1032, was the signal for feudal

strife in Burgundy. Odo, the French count of Champagne, the son of Gisela's elder sister, set up a claim to the throne in right of primogeniture, while Conrad claimed Burgundy, not as a family inheritance, but as a state lapsed to the crown, and caused himself to be crowned king of Burgundy at Geneva, A.D. 1033. The whole of the country lying to the south of Lothringia, along the Saone and the Rhone as far as the sea, belonged to the kingdom of Burgundy: viz., the dukedom of Lower Burgundy (Bourgogne), with its capital Tischaw or Dijon; the county of Upper Burgundy (Franche Comté, free county), with the free imperial city of Bisanz or Besançon; the county of Wälsh-Wien (Vienne) or the Delphinat, so called on account of the surname of Delphin borne by its counts, with its capital Graswalde or Grenoble; the county of Savoy, formerly divided from Alemannia by the river Aar, and, at a later period, by the Reuss, when Humbert the White-handed, count of Savoy, extended his domains, and rendered himself almost an independent sovereign during the reign of the weak Rudolf of Burgundy;[1] further to the south, the county of Provence, with its capital Arles, whence the whole of Lower Burgundy received the name of the Arelat. Besides these were the archbishopric of Wälsch-Leyden (Lyons), and the bishoprics of Wälsch-Aachen (Aix), Parantaise, Valence, Marseille, Avignon, Toulon, Chalons, Orense, Lausanne, Sion, etc. A

---

[1] There is an apparent connection, since the treaty of Verdun, between the frontiers that separate Burgundy from Alemannia, and the line traced by similarity of language. The Burgundians, at that period, had adopted the Italian tongue, while the Alemanni remained faithful to that of their fathers. This latter line (that distinguished by similarity of language) may, at the present day, be traced westward from Solothurn across the Jura to the Bieler Lake, to Thiel and Broy, leaving Mürten, the eastern part of the city of Freiburg, Bürglen, Giffers, Passelb, Jaun, Sauen, to the left, touches the frontiers lying between Berne and Valais, runs into the latter as far as Siders, keeping the valleys of Leuk-Turtmann and of Matter to the left, and mounts the chain of the Rothhorn, that separates Lysthal from Val di Challant. Eastward of this line, the Alemannic and German tongues prevailed and are still in use, although Savoy for some time claimed the country of the Alemanni as far as the Reuss. Westward of this line the Burgundian-Italian still prevails, except in the villages to the south of Monte Rosa, whose inhabitants speak a peculiar German dialect, and are, without doubt, the only remaining descendants of the ancient Burgundians.—*Albert Schott.*

campaign was carried on in the depth of winter by the emperor, and notwithstanding, as Wippo relates, the horses' hoofs were sometimes frozen into the ground, he laid the whole of Champagne waste.

The Italians, discontented with the despotic rule of the emperor, sought to strengthen their cause by an alliance with the rebellious Odo, to whom Heribert, archbishop of Milan, offered the throne of Lombardy. A second expedition into Italy, on the part of the emperor, was the immediate result. During his absence, Odo again invaded Lower Lothringia, but was completely routed in the battle of Bar-le-Duc, by the duke Gottfried (Gozilo), A.D. 1036. In Italy, the emperor had gained fresh adherents in the Valvasors or lower nobility, who were grievously oppressed by the spiritual and temporal lords, and rose, sword in hand, A.D. 1035, to claim the privileges granted by the emperor Conrad to the German vassals at Aix-la-Chapelle. It chanced that Heribert, archbishop of Milan, the most tyrannical of the petty princes of Italy, who, up to the present period, had been the most zealous partisan of the emperor, counted for that reason on his protection; but Conrad, faithful to his system of supporting the lower nobility against the great vassals, threw him, contrary to his expectation, into prison. In 1037, he gave the new feudal code to his Italian vassals, by which the estates of the petty vassals were rendered hereditary, the alienation of a fief by the feudal lord without the consent of the feoffee was forbidden, and the right of being judged by their peers, and of an appeal to the emperor in disputes between them and their lieges, was secured to the petty vassals. The concession of these privileges to the German nobility explains their adherence to his cause, particularly in the affair between him and Duke Ernst. His successors, nevertheless, were ignorant of the art of forming the minor nobility into one great mass, and they, consequently, remained uninfluenced by any common bond, under the rule of the great vassals, who gradually regained the power over them of which they had been deprived by Conrad. The emperor lengthened his stay in Italy, in order to confirm his authority in that country. Parma rebelled, and was, by his order, almost entirely demolished. His most active adherent was the Markgraf Bonifacius, who had wedded Beatrix, the daughter of Frederich of Lothringia. He entertained the emperor sumptuously at Marengo and Vivinaja. Wine was drawn in buckets attached by silver chains from the fountains, etc. These festal scenes were interrupted by the breaking out of the plague, which carried off almost the whole of Conrad's army. Hermann of Swabia, Conrad, duke of Carinthia, the emperor's cousin, Cunihilda, the bride of Henry, the youthful heir to the crown, were among the victims, A.D. 1038.

The feuds carried on between the Grafs and the other great vassals in Burgundy now called the emperor into that country. Reinhold, count of Franche Comté, who was at enmity with him, was reduced to submission by Louis, count of Mümpelgart, the emperor's stanch adherent. The right of private warfare was upheld even more in France and Burgundy than in Germany, and the clergy alone possessed the power of checking the martial spirit that prevailed. An abbot of Clugny, at length, declared himself commissioned by Heaven to announce a universal and holy peace, which was to be kept weekly, from Wednesday evening until Monday morning, and again from Advent Sunday until the eighth day after Epiphany, from Septuagesima until the eighth day after Easter, under pain of excommunication. During these intervals, feuds were thus strictly prohibited. The truth of this pretended mission was gladly recognized by both the temporal and spiritual lords, first in France, A.D. 1027, in Burgundy, A.D. 1032, and on two separate occasions, in A.D. 1038 and 1041, by the emperor, by whom this holy and universal peace was passed into a law,[1] the benefit of

---

[1] Conrad, nevertheless, unlike his predecessor Henry II., was no slave to the church. When the pope, without referring to him, as to his superior, raised the abbot of Reichenau to the episcopal dignity, he prohibited its acceptance, and caused the brief to be burned.

which was ere long felt throughout Germany. Conrad expired at Utrecht, A.D. 1039, during the solemnization of the Whitsuntide festival. He was interred at Spires, where, A.D. 1030, he had laid the foundation-stone of the cathedral. His son and successor, Henry, accompanied the funeral procession, and, while passing through the town, assisted in bearing the coffin.

CXL. *Henry the Third*

EDUCATED by a father as intelligent as he was energetic and warlike, and by a mother whose noble intellect had been strengthened by misfortune, Henry early developed the qualities befitting a statesman and a soldier. The popes even were awed, and the power of the dukes completely reduced, by this emperor, whose iron despotism surpassed that of any of his predecessors.[1] Had his life been lengthened, the ducal dignity, so greatly had he succeeded in depressing it, would probably have been entirely abolished.

He allowed the ducal throne of Swabia to remain for some time unoccupied, and finally bestowed it on Otto, Markgraf of Schweinfurt, in Eastern Franconia, a man of an inert disposition. The nomination of Welf, the son of Welf the elder, to the dukedom of Carinthia, conciliated the feudal animosity of that house. Welf died, A.D. 1055, without issue, and his family was continued, in default of heir male, by Welf, the son of his sister Cunigunda, who had espoused Azzo, an Italian Markgraf. The crown of Bavaria was presented by Henry to his wife, the empress Agnes. At that time Graf Berthold, a nephew of Radbot of Habsburg, distinguishing himself in the Breisgau, Henry promised him the reversion of the ducal crown of Swabia on the death of Otto. Bernhard of Saxony, although the only one who maintained his ancient independence, made himself respected by the emperor, who sought to diminish his power

---

[1] "Omnia Cæsar erat," was the graphic expression of Godellus, the monkish historian of Limoges.

by creating a counterpoise to him in the neighboring states, and accordingly made Thuringia independent, and nominated Louis the Bearded as her Landgraf. He also supported Adalbert, the talented archbishop of Bremen, who had twelve bishoprics under his jurisdiction, and, during his residence in Germany, always fixed his seat of government at Goslar, in the heart of Saxony, in order to keep that dukedom under his own eye. He also humbled the haughty and dreaded archbishop of Mayence, by giving precedence to the archbishop of Cologne, when solemnizing the coronation of his youthful heir.

The Bohemians were the first to rise in open warfare. Brzetislaw again attempted to regain his independence, in which he was supported by Severus, bishop of Prague. After a struggle that lasted for two years, he was finally reduced to submission, A.D. 1042, and compelled to swear fealty to the emperor on his bended knees at Ratisbon. His son Spignitew, on mounting the throne, immediately expelled all the Germans, even his own mother, Jutta, from Bohemia.

In the following year, the discontented Burgundians rose in open insurrection, but were again subdued by Henry, who, by his marriage with Agnes of Poitou, A.D. 1044, who was closely connected with the most powerful of the Burgundian families, at once settled all differences.

This was followed by disturbances in Hungary. Stephan the Holy having died without issue, Gisela, his German queen, placed his nephew, Peter, on the throne. The crimes of this monarch, and the favor in which the Germans were held at court, gave rise to a popular tumult. Peter was deposed, and Aba was elected king in his stead. A battle took place between him and the emperor at Menfew, A.D. 1044. The Germans had already been put to flight, when a storm of wind suddenly arose, and whirling the sand of the plain into the faces of the pursuing Hungarians, caused such confusion that the Germans rallied and gained the victory. Peter was replaced upon his throne at Stuhlweissenburg, and Aba was assassinated. The Hungarians again revolted on Henry's departure, deprived Peter of sight, and raised Andreas to the throne. This induced a second expedition into Hungary on the part of the emperor, whose army was surrounded, when in a dangerous position, by the enemy, and, after suffering dreadfully from famine, was finally enabled, by the dexterity of his maneuvers, to retreat across the frontier, with the loss of all the sick, whom he was compelled to abandon, and who were cut to pieces by the enraged peasantry. He returned, A.D. 1051, at the head of a more numerous army, and although he recognized Andreas as king of Hungary, compelled him to do him homage, and to accept the Bavarian constitution, by which Hungary was, as at the present day, divided into *comitate* or counties. The country between the Calenberg on the Danube, in the vicinity of Vienna, and the Leitha, was also permanently severed from Hungary, and united to the mere of Austria.

The greatest confusion, caused, on the present occasion, by a schism or disunion of the church under several contemporary popes, reigned, meanwhile, in Italy. Benedict IX., who had given way to the most unbridled license, was opposed by an anti-pope, Sylvester VII. Benedict, becoming enamored of a beautiful girl of high birth, abdicated the pontifical chair, in the hope of obtaining her in marriage, but, being disappointed in his purpose, retook his dignity and remained pope, although he had sold his right to the triple crown to a third pope, Gregory VI. These three heads of the church reigned simultaneously in Rome; Benedict in the Lateran, Gregory in the Vatican, and Sylvester in St. Maria Maggiore. In order to terminate this scandal, the emperor visited Rome, A.D. 1046, and held a great ecclesiastical convocation at Sutri, by which he caused the three popes to be deposed, and a German, Suidger of Meyendorf, bishop of Bamberg, to be placed in the pontifical chair, under the name of Clement II. All the imperial prerogatives, by the exercise of this right of election on the part of the emperor, received fresh confirmation. Henry afterward visited

Apulia, and extended the Norman fief, held by the twelve brave sons of Tancred, one of whom, named Drogo, who, A.D. 1039, had defeated a numerous body of Grecian troops, he created duke of Apulia. The revolt of the Lombards against the new rulers of Lower Italy was the immediate result, and Drogo was murdered. His brothers, Hunifrid and Guiscard, nevertheless, maintained their authority in Apulia, and Raimund, a descendant of the earlier Norman settlers, was equally successful in Aversa.

Henry returned to Germany with the three popes in his train. Their German successor, Clement II., died A.D. 1049, probably from poison, and another German, Poppo, bishop of Brixen, who was sent by the emperor to replace him as Pope Damasus II., did not survive his elevation to the pontifical chair three weeks. The emperor next elected one of his own relatives, Bruno of Dachsburg, bishop of Tull, as his successor, who, under the name of Leo IX., distinguished himself by the force of his intellect, and by his comprehensive plans for the reformation of the church, in which he was zealously aided by a young man named Hildebrand, the son of a blacksmith of Siena, who had accompanied Gregory VI. to Germany, and whom the new pope, attracted by his high talents, had taken into his service. It has been asserted that Leo was merely a tool in the hands of this monk; this could not be: the actions of Leo originated in himself, and instead of owing his fame to Hildebrand, the contrary was the fact—it was he who first raised Hildebrand from obscurity. The principal evil in the church, besides the irregular election of the popes in Rome herself, was the simony[1] carried on throughout the provinces. Each ecclesiastical dignity, from the highest to the lowest, had its price, and, consequently, fell into the most unworthy hands; bribery and corruption everywhere prevailed. In order to put a stop to these evils, Leo, besides rendering them liable by law to the severest punishments,

---

[1] Simony, or the purchase of ecclesiastical benefices; so named in reference to Simon the magician, in the Acts of the Apostles, viii.

visited the different countries for the purpose of strictly and personally investigating the conduct of the clergy. The awestruck French clergy yielded implicitly to his commands at a council convoked by him at Rheims. He met alone with opposition from his own countrymen at another held by him at Mayence; and a year later, when he again hastened northward, in order to promote peace between the Hungarians, who had already embraced Christianity, and the Germans, he was mocked in the German camp. Was the emperor jealous of the interference of a pope on whose head he had himself placed the tiara? Heavily was Germany destined to atone for her disrespect toward a German pope! Not long after this Leo fell at variance with Robert Guiscard, on account of his having laid the papal dominions waste; seven hundred Swabians, the pope's body-guard, were slain at Civetella, and the pope quitted the burning city and gave himself up to the Normans, who fell weeping at his feet, A.D. 1053. This excellent pope expired in the following year. He was canonized by the church, and became the guardian saint of the city of Benevento. On his demise, Hildebrand hastened to Germany, in order to entreat the emperor to elect a successor. His choice fell upon Gebhard, Graf of Calw, bishop of Eichstadt, Pope Victor II., who, at a council held at Florence, promised the world that he would continue the reform commenced by Leo.

A petty war for the succession to the dukedom had, in the meantime, broken out in Lothringia. Dietrich, the son of Frederich, duke of Upper Lothringia, died without issue, A.D. 1043. The succession was claimed by Gottfried the Bearded, duke of Lower Lothringia, who, on the donation of the dukedom by the emperor to Adalbert, an Alsatian count, took up arms against him and slew him in battle. Gerhard, Adalbert's nephew, was upon this appointed to succeed him by the emperor, who defeated the contumacious duke, but, struck with admiration of the valor with which he had defended himself, pardoned his aggression, and sent him to Italy, to watch over his interests in that country. Gottfried's allies, Baldwin V. of Flanders, and Dietrich IV. of Holland, who were necessarily sacrificed by this arrangement, contrived to make head against the emperor during the summer months behind their morasses, but were speedily reduced to submission on the setting in of winter, A.D. 1048, when the rivers and canals were frozen over. Baldwin, notwithstanding his having burned down the imperial town of Nimwegen,[1] was freely pardoned, and permitted to hold Ghent, the Ottogau, Œlsterland, Allost, Wars, and Southern Seeland, in fee of the empire. This country was henceforth distinguished as Imperial Flanders from the rest of Flanders, which was a French fief. The emperor hoped, by this clemency, to attach these powerful frontier Grafs to the empire, and to increase the distaste felt by the German Flemings toward their foreign rulers. His system was unfortunately unheeded by his successors on the imperial throne, by whom the Flemings were rarely supported against France. Dietrich of Holland fell, A.D. 1049, in a senseless and sanguinary feud with Cologne,[2] which proved equally fatal to Florens I., his brother and successor. It is remarkable to what an early date the disunion in the German Netherlands may be traced.

Gottfried of Lower Lothringia, unmindful of the clemency with which he had been treated, proved faithless to his trust in Italy, where he joined the malcontents, and after wedding Beatrix, the widow of Bonifacius, made use of the influence and wealth bestowed upon her family by the emperor against their common benefactor. Henry,

---

[1] Dietrich, Graf of Cleve, surnamed the Flyer on account of his extraordinary activity, on one occasion saved the emperor's life during this feud, and received in recompense the city and revenue of Nimwegen, on condition of paying an annual tribute of three pieces of scarlet cloth, each fifty ells in length, to the emperor. This tribute being discontinued by his successors, Frederich Barbarossa deprived them of both the city and its revenue.—*Knapp's History of Cleve.*

[2] This feud was occasioned by the death of a brother of the archbishop of Cologne, who was slain by Dietrich at a tournament. He also cut to pieces four hundred of the Cologne nobility and their allies at Dordrecht, where he was himself slain by a poisoned arrow. Florens was murdered in his sleep during a night attack.

consequently, recrossed the Alps, and after defeating the refractory duke, and taking Beatrix prisoner, returned with her to Germany, where his presence was again required by the renewed pretensions of Henry, king of France, upon Burgundy and Lothringia. His departure was instantly turned to advantage by Gottfried, and his son, Gottfried the younger, who regained their influence in Italy. During an interview between Henry and the French monarch at Ivois, A.D. 1056, the former threw down his glove in token of challenge: it was refused by the French king, who took refuge within his own dominions.

Another and more dangerous enemy now attacked the empire. The Liutizii, notwithstanding the valiant defense made against them by Bernhard of Saxony, William of Brandenburg, son of the elder Bernhard, and Gottschalk, the Christian prince of the Obotrites, succeeded in gaining the upper hand. William fell in a battle near Prizlawa. All the Christians taken prisoners on this occasion being drowned, the Saxon princes, in reprisal, compelled their Slavian prisoners to throw themselves into the river.[1]

During the same year, Germany was visited by earthquakes, plague, and famine, the forerunners of a still worse evil, the death of the emperor, who fell sick and expired at Bothfeld, in the Harz Mountains, in the vigor of life, A.D. 1056. He left the empire in the hands of the empress Agnes, and of his son Henry, a child five years of age. Thus the management of affairs that demanded the utmost energy and sagacity devolved upon a woman and an infant.

A number of monks, who devoted their lives and talents more to the promotion of learning and to the welfare of the state, than to upholding the hierarchical schemes of the pope, had been invited over by Henry from the British Isles, and had founded numerous Scotch monasteries.[2] Agnes, Henry's

---

[1] Alle de so venghen, mosten sich sulven drenken.—*Old Saxon Chronicle.*

[2] The miracle performed by one of those Scottish saints is characteristic of the reaction produced by the contrast of their temperance and sobriety with the luxurious habits of the Roman clergy. Marguard, the first abbot of the Scotch monastery at Wurzburg, is said to have changed the wine of the carousing clergy into water.

learned empress, and his chancellor and historian Wippo, also greatly assisted him in carrying his plans for the reformation of the Romish priesthood into effect. Agnes was regent of the empire during her son's minority. She was a virtuous, pious woman, with a mind highly cultivated indeed, but totally deficient in the energy befitting her station, the possession of which would have rendered her the heroine, instead of the victim, of her times. Gentleness, love, persuasion, and the most disinterested sacrifice of herself, were the means by which she sought to rule the wild and daring spirits of the age. Well aware of the impossibility of bearing despotic sway, like her deceased husband, over the distant and extensive provinces of the empire, without the intermediate aid of dukes, and, moreover, anxious to convert the enmity of those whose pretensions had been neglected into friendship, she raised one after the other, the bitterest enemies of her family, to the vacant ducal thrones. Another aim of her short-sighted policy was by means of the dukes to keep the haughty archbishops in check. Rudolf, the insolent Graf of Rheinfelden, by whom her daughter Matilda had been violated, received not only pardon for his crime, but also Swabia and Burgundy in fee of the empire. The turbulent Swabian nobles, ever at feud with one another, required a master. A Graf of Hohenzollern is at this period, A.D. 1058, for the first time mentioned in history as an actor in one of these feuds. In order to satisfy the just pretensions of Graf Berthold, Agnes bestowed upon him the dukedom of Carinthia, and the county of Verona in Italy, A.D. 1060; besides which he possessed the Breisgau. His descendants received the surname of the Zähringer,[1] from

---

[1] The legendary origin of the Zähringer is thus related in the ancient Freiburgian Chronicle. Their ancestor was a charcoal burner in the Black Forest, who, discovering by chance some silver in the earth with which he covered the smoldering wood, gradually collected an immense treasure. An emperor who had taken refuge on the Kaiserstuhl mountain in the Breisgau, fell into great distress, and promising to bestow his daughter's hand on the person who would come to his aid, the charcoal burner laid his ponderous riches at his feet, wedded the princess, was created duke, and built the castle of Zähringen and the city of Freiburg. Maddened by prosperity, he longed for human flesh, and caused a

Zehring, a province above Judenburg. She also bestowed Bavaria on Otto, the brave Graf of Nordheim, and restored Lothringia to the son of her hereditary enemy Gottfried, Gottfried the Hunchback, a noble-minded man, who was afterward almost the only one who served the Salic family with fidelity. Besides Lothringia, he also possessed the extensive Tuscan margraviate in right of his wife Matilda, the daughter of his own stepmother Beatrix.

The Frieslanders again figure in history during this period. Bernhard of Saxony, and Adalbert, archbishop of Bremen, enraged at the insubordination of these brave peasants, who resisted their attempted imposition of a tax, marched at the head of a numerous army into their country, but were completely put to the rout, and the camp of the nobles was sacked by the victors, A.D. 1060. Henry, the pious bishop of Augsburg, and Guibert, the talented archbishop of Ravenna, were the empress's counselors. The mildness of her government, however, did not shield her character from the imputations which the opponents to the imperial throne cast upon her and her counselors in order to hasten their downfall.

CXLI. *Ecclesiastical Government of the Empire*

VICTOR II. died A.D. 1057, and the Italians placed the tiara on the head of Stephen IX., the brother of Gottfried the Hunchback, who also expired in the following year. Their choice next fell upon Benedict X. This election caused deep displeasure to Hildebrand, who still continued his endeavors to raise the church to her former level by means of the empire. He therefore earnestly petitioned the empress to nominate another pope, and Gerhard of Burgundy, bishop of Florence, was accordingly sent by her to fill the pontifical chair.

This pope entered into Hildebrand's views for the ag-

'boy to be killed and roasted. While feasting on this unnatural food, he was seized with remorse, and, in atonement for his crime, erected the monasteries of St. Ruprecht, and of St. Peter in the Black Forest.

grandizement of the church. The time had arrived for the popedom to rise again from her impotent obscurity, and for the realization of the gigantic idea of universal ecclesiastical rule; so intense was the devotional feeling of the times that the church merely required an energetic head, and the empire a weak ruler, for the temporal power of the latter to pass into the hands of the former. This head appeared in the person of the monk Hildebrand, at a time when the imperial scepter was swayed by a child. The character and virtues of Hildebrand fitted him for the hero of the church and of his age. His irreproachable life and morals, his entire renunciation of all worldly pleasures, rendered him universally venerated. His mind, formed in monastic seclusion, was firm and strong, and, inspired by his deep devotional feelings, he cherished a lofty view of the destinies of the world. Early recommended to the notice of the great and powerful by the superiority of his talents, he was an adept in transacting worldly affairs, had been actively engaged in promoting the interests of the church, and, during his residence in Germany, had taken a just and comprehensive view of the state of Christendom. Worldly knowledge, pliability, and even dissimulation—unholy means for the attainment of a design, the offspring of a pure and lofty mind—were his chief characteristics, in common with the rest of his countrymen. His surpassing eloquence, another of his numerous gifts, did not equal in effect the indomitable sternness which empowered him singly to enter the lists against the whole world. Even during his lifetime, his numerous enemies, created as much by the earnestness of his zealous endeavors as by the harshness with which circumstances often compelled him to act, attempted to lower his fame; and in later times, the despotic rule usurped by a church whose power was due to him has caused him to be reproached as the originator of crimes which, in the purity of his zeal for the reformation of the church, and through her of the reformation and improvement of the universe, he could not have foreseen.

His great work commenced under Nicolas II., whose approbation was the more readily secured, on account of its having originated with the German popes, and on account of the necessity of preserving peace and order, the continuation of which was at this period endangered by the minority of the emperor. Two men, his steady coadjutors, Petrus Damiani, whose religious zeal and strict morality rendered him the idol of monks and devotees, and Lanfranc, the celebrated theologian, his equal in learning, must also not remain unnoticed.

Two important acts passed by a council at Rome, A.D. 1059, were the first-fruits of Hildebrand's long-planned endeavors. By the former, the election of the pope was declared for the future to be independent of the emperor, and to be solely dependent on the votes of the cardinals, or ecclesiastics of the highest rank, whose dignity arose from the number of chapters or canonships attached to their sees. By the latter, the pope was declared, like the emperor, lord paramount over the feudatories in his dominions, and the Normans were accordingly solemnly declared feudatories of the pontifical chair, and freed from their allegiance to the emperor. The independent spirit of Robert Guiscard of Apulia, and of his brother Roger of Sicily, caused them willingly to league with the pope in freeing themselves from the shackles imposed upon them by the emperor. The Greeks, Arabs, and Lombards in Lower Italy were also at that period reduced by them to submission. It is worthy of remark that Nicolas carefully avoided any interference with heretics, in order not to be hindered in his more important operations for the aggrandizement of the church. Berengar, a canon of Tours, although compelled to abjure his heretical doctrine against transubstantiation, that is, against the belief that the wine and bread made use of in the sacrament was the real body and blood of Christ, was treated with great lenity.

Nicolas II. died A.D. 1061. The election of Alexander II. by the cardinals roused Agnes to a sense of her infringed dignity, and declaring the election null and void without her consent, she caused Honorius II. to be elected pope by the German bishops at Basle.

One of the most distinguished men of that period was Anno, archbishop of Cologne (a Graf of Pfullingen), a man of an ambitious mind and stern temper, more fitted to bear the scepter or the sword than the crosier. The precedence given to him by Henry III. over the haughty archbishop of Mayence had only served to inflame his ambition, and, insatiated by the power he possessed, he even grasped at the regency of the empire. He has for that reason been unjustly accused of attempting to separate the German church from that of Rome; the accordance of his views with those of Hildebrand clearly demonstrate the contrary. It is true that he filled several important bishoprics with his adherents. His brother Wezilo (Werner) was created archbishop of Magdeburg; his grandson Cuno (Conrad), archbishop of Treves, and his other grandson, Bucco (Burkhard), bishop of Halberstadt. The adherence of these prelates, however, merely contributed to his temporal power. His principal object, the only one worthy of his powers, but for the attainment of which he had recourse to ignoble and barbarous means, was to snatch the helm from the powerless hand of the weak woman who guided the state. The life of the youthful emperor had been already attempted. Otto, the brother of William of Brandenburg, had been passed over in the succession, and Udo, Graf of Stade, had been created Markgraf in his stead. An insurrection ensued. Numbers of the Saxons, to whom Henry III. had made himself obnoxious, entered into a conspiracy with Otto, whom they intended to raise to the throne, against the emperor's life. A duel that took place between Otto and Ekbert, Graf of Brunswick, a zealous partisan of the imperial family, in which both combatants fell, crushed the hopes of the Saxon conspirators, A.D. 1057. Anno pursued a safer and more certain plan. He hated Agnes and the bishop of Augsburg, and viewed her government with contempt. His project of ruling the empire in the name of the youthful monarch was shared by Otto of Nordheim, the greatest general, and by Ekbert, Markgraf of Meissen, the most valiant knight of the age, who were moreover by their Saxon blood the hereditary foes of the reigning dynasty. These three men formed a plot to gain possession of the person of the emperor. The empress and her son were invited by them to pass the Easter festival at Kaiserswerth, A.D. 1062. After the banquet, under pretense of showing the child a fine boat, he was taken to the Rhine, put on board a vessel, and taken away. The courageous boy no sooner perceived the intention of his conductors to separate him from his mother than he sprang into the water, but was instantly followed by Ekbert, who overtook and bore him back to the vessel. The entreaties of the unfortunate empress for the restoration of her child were unheeded by the treacherous vassals, who, although pursued for some distance on both sides of the river by the country people, succeeded in reaching Cologne with their prisoner. The broken-hearted mother resigned the regency and retired to an Italian convent. Her counselor, Henry, bishop of Augsburg, was tortured to death.[1]

In order to place his undertaking under more favorable colors, Anno caused a decree to be passed by the assembled vassals of the empire, empowering the bishop within whose diocese the young emperor resided to act as regent of the state; a title he instantly assumed on account of the enforced residence of his prisoner at Cologne. He caused him to be strictly educated, compelling him to learn Latin like a chorister, and to undergo the severest discipline.

The dispute between Honorius II. and Alexander II. called Anno, as regent of the empire, into Italy; in this character he, at first, strongly opposed Hildebrand, but the interests of the church ere long reconciled their differences; Anno also rejected the pope nominated by the empress, lent his countenance to the one elected by the cardinals, and Alexander retained the tiara.

---
[1] Coleis ligneo palo pertusis.

During the absence of Anno, Henry had fallen into other hands, and the ambitious primate of Cologne, at a later period, merely guided the affairs of state at two short and different times. The city of Cologne, meanwhile, fully occupied his attention. In 1063, or, according to other accounts, later, a violent feud sprang up between him and the merchants, affording an example of the struggle between rival interests, which speedily broke out in several other episcopal cities. Anno's servants insolently took possession of a merchantman that lay close inshore, heavily laden, and after lightening it of its cargo, laid an embargo upon it as a pleasure-boat for the archbishop. The son of the merchant to whom the vessel belonged hastened with his men to the spot, and compelled the archbishop's servants to retire. Anno ordered peace to be preserved, but harshly refused to pass judgment on the offenders; the people of Cologne, well aware of his despotic temper, resolved to oppose violence by violence, and rising en masse, stormed the episcopal palace, which they utterly destroyed, and laid siege to the church of St. Peter, within whose walls the archbishop had taken refuge. Anno escaped by night, assembled a numerous army, and shortly appeared before the gates of Cologne. The citizens, already struck with remorse for their daring, and unable to contend on equal terms with their old master, now sued for mercy, and Anno, who, with his customary sternness, reserved judgment for himself, was permitted to enter the town. The merchants justly fearing his anger, six hundred of their number left the city during the night, carrying with them all their movable goods. The son of the merchant whose opposition to his tyranny had given rise to the tumult, fell into the hands of the archbishop, who caused him and his adherents to be deprived of sight.

Anno greatly improved the city of Cologne, and adorned it with churches. He was canonized after his death, and a song in his praise, one of the best examples of the versification of the Middle Ages, is still extant: the extreme tenderness and pathos of this poem strikingly contrast with the real character of its hero, whose stern inflexibility seems to have imparted a similar character to Cologne, perceptible even in her glorious attempt for the reformation of the church.

During the absence of Anno in Italy, Henry had fallen into the hands of Adalbert, archbishop of Bremen, Anno's rival for the regency, to which the favor with which he had been beheld by Henry III., and the decree passed by Anno, furnished him with a title; independently of this, he regarded himself as the most polished and learned man of the times, as the only one capable of ruling the empire and of rearing the monarch. A lineal descendant of the noble house of Wettin of Slavonia, handsome and dignified in person, learned and witty, he regarded the gloomy sternness of Anno and the coarse manners of the nobles with the contempt natural to a man of refined taste and high birth, and by the gentleness of his treatment ere long caused the youthful monarch to rejoice at his good fortune in having fallen into his custody. Henry was, however, entirely corrupted by his new guardian. The sudden change from the severity with which he had been treated by Anno, to the unlimited liberty he enjoyed under Adalbert's roof, was of itself pernicious. The gravity and study to which he had been inured were now suddenly exchanged for the thoughtless gayety of a licentious court, where affairs of state were treated as lightly as a jest. The most unbridled simony was practiced by the archbishop, who thus sought to fill the most important benefices with his partisans, and by means of a new toy, or the caresses of beautiful courtesans,[1] or a fresh amusement, the invention of the ready brain of his favorite, the handsome Graf Werner, he easily obtained the letters, signatures, and donations requisite for the success of his plans. The worst result of the influence gained by Adalbert over the mind of the young monarch was the contempt with which he studiously inspired him for the dukes, and more especially for the stupid German people, to whom Adalbert imagined himself to be so superior, as well as a dislike

---

[1] Among whom were abbesses and nuns of high birth.

of the Saxons, which he only too speedily imbibed. During the reign of Henry III. the Saxons and the archbishop had been at feud, and it was therefore of consequence to him to have the monarch on his side, and Henry thus unwittingly acquired an antipathy as unbecoming to him when emperor as it in the sequel proved dangerous.

In 1063, Henry accompanied Adalbert in a campaign against Hungary, where Bela, after rebelling against and assassinating Andreas, had expelled his son Salomo, the affianced bridegroom of Jutta, the emperor's sister. Adalbert restored Salomo to the Hungarian throne, on condition of his holding it in fee of the empire, and bestowed upon him the hand of Henry's sister. Hildebrand's anger was greatly roused by this proceeding; Hungary, according to him, being a papal fief. During the same year, Henry beheld at Goslar the struggle for precedence in church during divine service, between the bishop of Hildesheim and the abbot of Fulda, on which occasion several men lost their lives, so lawless were, at that period, the manners of the clergy, who were equally unchecked by both Adalbert and Anno, the former of whom cherished an ambitious hope of elevating the see of Bremen to the patriarchate of the North, and, in the name of the emperor, of rendering the temporal lords submissive to his authority, an attempt which drew upon him universal hatred.

In 1065, Henry was solemnly declared capable of bearing arms. Scarcely was his sword girded on than he drew it jestingly upon Anno, who was present; an action at once indicative of dislike and levity.

CXLII. *Henry the Fourth*

HENRY IV., ever accompanied by Adalbert and Werner, held his imperial court with his habitual splendor near Goslar, at the Harzburg. The Saxons were treated with the utmost scorn. The country people in the vicinity were oppressed with taxes and enforced labor, and the dislike with which the Saxons were viewed by the monarch ere long became as unbearable to them as his licentious habits, which were, with reason, a scandal and a shame to the whole empire. His mistresses were seen in public adorned with gold and precious stones, taken from the consecrated vessels of the churches, etc. The jealousy with which the vassals of the empire beheld Adalbert was, nevertheless, the chief motive of the conspiracy. Anno again suddenly intermeddled with state affairs, and convoking a general assembly at Tribur, cited Henry to appear before it. On his refusal, the conspirators surrounded the palace, and seized his person; Adalbert narrowly escaped being taken prisoner, and remained for three years in concealment, while the Saxons laid his lands waste. Werner was slain. The courtiers were dispersed, and Henry was compelled to abjure his mode of life, and to wed Bertha, the daughter of the Italian Markgraf of Susa, to whom he had some time earlier been affianced; a noble-spirited woman who alone wanted beauty in order easily to supplant the mistresses of the young emperor, who returned with her in extreme displeasure to Goslar, A.D. 1066.

Anno was again at the head of affairs, but the whole empire still presented a scene of anarchy; the temporal and spiritual lords disputed the possession of feudal territories, and offices of church and state. Cuno, archbishop of Treves, who owed his elevation to the intrigues of Anno, was precipitated down a mountain by the enraged citizens. The dissensions that prevailed throughout the empire, and the freebooting expeditions of the Saxon chiefs into the archbishopric of Bremen, induced a fresh insurrection among the northern Slavi, and the heathen party, headed by Plasso, Gottschalk's brother-in-law, extirpated Christianity. The vain attempts of Ordulf, the son of Bernhard, and, after his death, those of his son Magnus, to oppose the inroads of the Slavi, merely added to the misery of the Saxons, and imbittered their hatred of their inactive and licentious emperor. Hamburg and Mecklenburg were destroyed by the pagans, who sacrificed John, bishop of Mecklenburg, to their deities, stoned St.

Ansverus, the abbot of Ratzeburg, and twenty-eight monks, to death, assassinated the noble Gottschalk at Lenzen, at the foot of the altar, and turned his Danish wife out naked. Plasso was murdered by his own followers, A.D. 1066, but Cruco, prince of the Rugii, who succeeded him in his dominions, attained to considerable power, being entirely unmolested by the Saxons, whose attention was fully occupied by their contests with the emperor.

In this year important changes took place in the North. Canute the Great, king of Denmark, Norway, and England, had espoused Emma, the princess of Normandy, the widow of Ethelred and mother of Edmund Ironside, the last of the Anglo-Saxon dynasty. She became the mother of Hardicanute, who, on the death of Canute, A.D. 1036, succeeded to the thrones of Denmark and Norway; Harold Harefoot, the son of Canute by a former marriage, inheriting that of Britain. On the death of these princes, A.D. 1041, a general revolution took place, and Denmark alone remained in the possession of a nephew of Canute the Great, Suen Estridsen, whose daughter, Siritha, wedded Gottschalk, the pious prince of the Obotrites. Harald Haardrade (the Hard), a half-brother of Magnus the Good, was raised to the throne of Norway. The youth of this soldier of fortune had been spent in search of adventure; he had commanded the Wäringers at Constantinople, had served with great gallantry against the Turks and the Servii, had refused the hand of Zoë, the Greek empress, for which he had been thrown into prison, whence he escaped, married Elisifa, the daughter of Jaroslaw, the Russian czar, and finally returned to the North, to mount the throne of Norway, where his brother Magnus had already made terms with Hardicanute. The throne of England was occupied by Edward the Confessor, a son of Ethelred and of Emma, who was, consequently, half-brother to Hardicanute, whose birth excited in his breast such unnatural hatred toward his mother that he openly accused her of having a bishop for her paramour, and condemned her to undergo the ordeal by fire. She was accordingly compelled to pass over nine red-hot plowshares. Edward was childless. His brother, Edmund Ironside, had left two sons, who had been sent by Canute into Denmark, whence they had escaped to Hungary, where they had been kindly received by the king, Salomo. One of these sons, Edward, had several children born to him in Hungary, among whom was Edgar Atheling, the last scion of the ancient Anglo-Saxon dynasty. Edgar was invited by his great-uncle, Edward the Confessor, to England, but proving incapable of governing, Harold, the son of Goodwin, a powerful Anglo-Saxon noble, was raised to the throne, and Edgar, on the death of Edward the Confessor, sought the protection of William, duke of Normandy, his maternal relative. Harald Haardrade, of Norway, meanwhile took advantage of the disturbances in England to attempt the conquest of that country. Toste, the brother of Harold the Saxon, had, through envy of his brother's accession to the crown, joined Harald Haardrade, who landed in England at the head of a powerful army, and a bloody engagement took place between him and the English near Stamford,[1] in which both Harald Haardrade and Toste were slain, and the Norwegian army was almost annihilated. The losses of the English were also so considerable in this engagement that William of Normandy took advantage of their weakness to make a descent upon England under pretext of reinstating Edgar, but, in reality, with the intention of taking possession of the country for himself.

The independent spirit of the Anglo-Saxon clergy had been long beheld with uneasiness by the pope, who, in the hope of increasing his influence in England, greatly favored the Norman expedition. The emperor also permitted the duke to raise soldiers within his states, and crowds of Germans flocked beneath his standard. He also promised to

---

[1] The Norwegians, who consisted entirely of foot-soldiers, formed into a phalanx on landing from their ships, and with their shields presented an impenetrable front to the attacks of the Saxon horse, who being put to flight, the Norwegians set off in pursuit, and breaking their serried ranks became an easy prey to the English, who turned and cut them to pieces.

make an inroad into France, in the event of an attack upon Normandy during the absence of her duke, by the king of that country, whom William greatly feared. Thus arose the first treaty between England and Germany against France.—William sailed for England at the head of a gallant and numerous army, and was opposed by Harold with more courage than prudence. The celebrated battle of Hastings, A.D. 1066, in which Harold, after an obstinate struggle, was defeated and slain, decided the fate of England. William, with a perfidy equaling that of Harold, consigned the claims of Edgar to oblivion, placed the English crown on his own head, and, after either expelling or assassinating the Anglo-Saxon nobility, replaced them by those among his own followers who had distinguished themselves in the field, among whom were adventurers from almost every nation in Europe.[1] The feudal system, introduced by William the Conqueror and his new nobility, replaced the ancient Anglo-Saxon Germanic commonwealth; the Anglo-Saxon language also became intermixed with numerous French words, which the Normans had learned from their neighbors.

The imbecile Edgar did homage in person to the new sovereign. His sister, Margaret, acted with greater spirit, and, with a vast number of followers, emigrated into Scotland, where she was well received by the king, Malcolm, the son of Duncan, who was murdered by Macbeth. Malcolm made her his queen, and the Saxon tongue and customs introduced by her followers were partially adopted by the wild and hardy Scots. Margaret was canonized. Her daughter, Matilda, wedded the son of her enemy, Henry I. of England, and from her descends, in an unbroken line on the female side, the present queen of England, while from Margaret,

---

[1] Numbers of the Flemings accompanied William of Normandy to England; Gilbert of Ghent, a near relation of Balduin, Graf of Flanders, was endowed with the Barony of Gaunt, so named after him, and of Folkingham; Walter Bec le Flamand, Lord of Eresby; Drogo de Beverer, Lord of Holderness; Cheebod le Flamand, created Earl of Chester, who fell in battle and left no issue; Walcher, Earl of Northumberland, who was murdered by the people, and many others mentioned by Gautrel in his Nouvelles Archiqes Historiques.

upward, the race of the ancient Anglo-Saxon kings is, by the old chroniclers, carried as far back as Odin.

While the North was thus convulsed, the imperial court presented a continued scene of petty dissension. The emperor, still influenced by the prejudices of his youth, was alternately swayed by conflicting passions, but at length, notwithstanding the opposition of Anno and Bertha, recalled Adalbert to court, A.D. 1069. The fidelity and patience of the wretched empress merely contributed to increase the dislike manifested toward her by her husband, and to strengthen his resolution to free himself from the tie that bound him to her. Siegfried, archbishop of Mayence, offered to assist him in procuring a divorce, on condition of receiving in return the tithes of Thuringia, to which he had laid claim, and which had been hitherto steadily refused by the Thuringians; and Henry made a public declaration at a diet held at Worms, of his unconquerable aversion to his unoffending wife, from whom he demanded a separation on the plea of the marriage having remained unconsummated. His plan being frustrated by the arrival of Damiani, the pope's legate, in Germany, whose eloquence even impressed his versatile mind, he attempted to gain his end by still more unjustifiable means, by exposing Bertha to the seductions of his courtiers. He caused the most beautiful women and maidens to be carried from their homes, and imprisoned within his palace, while he surrounded the empress with the companions of his profligacy, to the handsomest of whom he promised large sums of money if successful in insnaring Bertha, who, nevertheless, escaped their wiles, and a chronicler of the times relates that she and her maidens on one occasion, when the emperor and his wicked companion were listening to their conversation in the dusk of the evening, suddenly attacked and beat them with rods; an incident that seems to have instantly given her a place in Henry's affection, and which is far from improbable, for, despite his deep depravity, his heart was made of far too soft materials not to be eventually touched by her invincible fidelity. Bertha bore him several children, and shared his subsequent misfortunes.

Henry belonged to that class of men whom sanguine, lively, generous dispositions render truly amiable, when uninfluenced by misguided passion, but who, unfitted by nature, are ever unsuccessful when required to govern themselves or others. The actions of such men, dependent upon the impulse or caprice of the moment, must necessarily be indifferently good or bad. Impatient of calm thought, or cool judgment, their impetuous nature renders them incapable of following the dictates of their reason or of their conscience. Dispositions of this kind are rarely understood, and are usually attributed to want of character, and yet those who at one moment condemn them for the crimes induced by the abuse of their weaknesses, are, in the next, struck with admiration at traits of the most extraordinary magnanimity, if not of real heroism; royal qualities, indeed, but still unfit for the throne, where justice and equanimity should reign, and where the sudden change in the sovereign from good to bad, and *vice versâ*, is more to be feared than if he remained true to his vices. That the character of Henry IV. was a compound of sensuality, insolence, levity, choler, malice, revenge, treachery, and mean cowardice, strangely intermingled with real piety, generosity, the most devoted affection, the noblest sympathy, bold resolve, and heroic bravery, may be clearly traced, when the insolence of fortune, total abandonment in misfortune, the wickedness or the success of his enemies, roused his evil passions, or when, swayed by remorse for his own crimes, by the consciousness of possessing nobler and better qualities, by compassion for the sufferings of his enemies, or of those whom he had ill-treated, and by the fidelity of his friends, he suddenly inclined to virtue.

The dangerous and extreme severity with which he treated the dukes appears to have arisen more from his youthful propensity, the love of displaying his power, than from the lessons of Adalbert, or his father's example; and this was evidently strengthened by a desire of avenging his abduction from Kaiserswerth and his imprisonment at Tribur, which, as a monarch, and in the consciousness of his guilt, he ought to have consigned to oblivion. Urged by his hatred of the Saxons, he treated the duke Magnus and the Margraves, as well as the bishops who adhered to Anno's party, with the greatest scorn, imposed heavy taxes on the people, encouraged the Wendi in their attacks upon the country, as thereby doing him service, entered into a secret alliance with the Danes under pretense of securing himself against an inroad of the Saxons, and continually threatened to render Thuringia dependent on the archbishopric of Mayence. The Saxons, impatient of being thus treated like a conquered nation, rested their hopes upon Otto of Nordheim, duke of Bavaria, who was suddenly accused, by a man named Egino, of having hired him to assassinate Henry, whose knavery at that time was so well known as to induce a suspicion of his having himself fabricated the plot. The matter was adjudged to be decided by single combat, but Otto, justly fearing treachery, absented himself, upon which Henry declared him guilty, placed him out of the ban of the empire, and taking possession of his dukedom of Bavaria, gave it in fee to the Welf. This Welf, who had been educated in Italy, and was a master in Italian wiles, was the most ignoble of the princes of those times, and proved as great a scandal to Henry's choice as he was ungrateful to him for his favors. With genuine cowardice, ever joining the stronger party, he had the meanness to send back his bride, the daughter of Otto, in disgrace to her father, who went into Saxony, and confederating with Magnus, raised a rebellion. Both were, however, under pretext of arranging terms of peace, seized, and Magnus was thrown into prison. Otto was allowed to remain at liberty by the emperor, either from a feeling of the injustice with which he had treated him or from a political motive.

The death of Adalbert, which, fortunately for the empire, took place during this year, once more threw the reins of government for a short period into the hands of Anno. Henry, emboldened by his late success, now attempted to reduce the rest of the dukes to submission. His first attack was made upon the weakest, Berthold, whom he deprived of the dukedom of Carinthia, in order to bestow it upon Ludolf, the son of the former duke. Rudolf of Swabia was protected from a similar fate by his superior power, and by his being doubly and closely connected with the emperor by his marriage with Matilda, after whose death he had espoused the sister of Bertha; Agnes, who had purposely quitted Italy for Germany, was enabled to bring about a reconciliation between the contending relations.

Great disturbances also broke out in Flanders. The count, Balduin VI., died in 1071, leaving his widow, Richilda, with two infant sons, Arnulf and Balduin. Richilda governed in the name of the former, but, rendering herself hated by her tyranny, she was abandoned by her subjects, who transferred their allegiance to Robert the Friscian, her husband's brother. Richilda now implored the aid of her feudal liege, Philip I. of France, who accordingly entered Flanders at the head of a numerous army, but was completely routed at Castel (Cassel) by Robert, who was backed by the whole of the German population. Richilda was taken prisoner, and her unfortunate son was put to death. Robert, while too hotly pursuing the retreating French, falling into their hands, Gottfried, bishop of Paris, intervened between the contending parties, and peace was concluded. Robert was restored to liberty, and received the ducal crown of Flanders. Richilda was also set at liberty, and Hennegau was bestowed upon her second son, Balduin, A.D. 1072. A second attempt on her part to regain possession of Flanders proved abortive, and her party suffered a bloody defeat at Brogneroy.

Henry, meanwhile, excited the hatred of the Saxons by his insolence and tyranny. The country was kept in awe by the strongly fortified Harzburg, and by numerous minor fortresses, garrisoned with Franks and Swabians, who were supported by the pillage of the neighboring villages. A synod, held by the emperor at Erfurt, in which he imposed the tithes demanded by the archbishop of Mayence on Thuringia, effectually imbittered the minds of the Saxon bishops against him, and, A.D. 1073, a conspiracy, planned by Otto of Nordheim, was entered into by the Saxons. The chiefs in this conspiracy were Graf Hermann, the brother of the captive Duke Magnus, Udo von Stade, Margrave of Brandenburg, Egbert, Margrave of Meissen, and Dedo, Margrave of the Lausitz, the two sons of the Ekbert who had formerly seized the person of the monarch, Louis, Landgrave of Thuringia, the son of Louis the Bearded, Frederick, the Pfalzgraf of Saxony, the Grafs of Holstein, Waldeck, Suplinburg, and numerous others. Among the spiritual lords were, Wezilo, of Magdeburg, Bucco, of Halberstadt, whose pursuits were rather those of a warrior than of a bishop, Anno's nephew and Henry's most violent opponent, and Benno of Meissen, a peaceful missionary, a planter of the fruit-tree and the vine,[1] besides all the other Saxon bishops, with the exception of those of Bremen, Zeiz, and Osnabruck, who sided with the emperor, and were consequently expelled from the country. Adela, the wife of the Margrave Dedo, an ambitious and rancorous woman, was also ceaseless in her endeavors to incite the Saxons, whose complaints against their emperor, although just in the outset, were purposely exaggerated.

The object of the conspiracy of the princes, instead of being the relief of the people, merely aimed at securing their own independence; a project that was, however, defeated by the reciprocal jealousy between the rulers of Northern and Southern Germany. The Saxon league at first laid its complaints before Henry at Goslar, in the form of a petition for redress, and the noble-spirited Otto of Nordheim offered to be imprisoned in the place of his brother Magnus, on condition of his being restored to his dukedom. The deputation,

---

[1] He first introduced the vine into Thuringia. He was also a patron of music, and the author of the melody, "Ein Kindelein so lobelich."—See *Hase's Palæologus.*

after being allowed to remain during a whole day in the anteroom, was at length scornfully dismissed by Henry. The Saxons, provoked to violence by this conduct, were still more excited by Otto of Nordheim, who loudly called upon them to revenge the insult, and suddenly assembling to the number of sixty thousand, they besieged the emperor in the Harzburg. Overcome by fear, Henry sought safety by secret flight, in which he was assisted by Berthold of Zähringen, who accidentally happened to be present. The Harzburg was taken by the Saxons, who, nevertheless, did not venture to destroy it; several other forts also fell into their hands; the rest were gallantly defended by the imperial garrisons. Magnus was set at liberty in exchange for seventy Swabians, who were captured in a fort by his brother Hermann; a circumstance that gave rise to the Saxon proverb, "One Saxon is worth seventy Swabians."

Henry fled to Hersfield, where, finding the Upper Germans, whom he had shortly before summoned for the purpose of invading Poland, assembled, he resolved to make head with them against the Saxons, and called a meeting at Gerstungen, in which, although the Upper German princes declared their unwillingness to enter into a contest with Saxony, the Saxon party attempted to work upon the passions of Rudolf of Swabia, by means of a person named Regingar, whom they caused to make the false assertion of his having been hired by the emperor to assassinate him. Ulric of Cosheim, Henry's true and valiant adherent, challenged the accuser to single combat, which never took place, Regingar being deprived of his senses before the day appointed for the trial. The princes, meanwhile, withdrew their allegiance from Henry, who, seeing himself universally abandoned, took refuge in Worms, where the brave citizens, jealous of their new privileges, had, at that period, just followed the example of their Cologne neighbors, by expelling from their city Adalbero, their bishop, a man of inordinate corpulence. The emperor was received with every demonstration of delight, the cities, as well as the free peasantry, supporting him against the pretensions of the princes and minor nobility; and had Henry understood how to make use of the means thus voluntarily put into his power, the victory would have easily been his: but ignorant of the strength of his new adherents, and influenced by an undue fear of that of the dukes, his cowardly behavior ere long cooled the zeal of the citizens. He again suddenly appeared in the assembly of the Upper German princes at Oppenheim, and throwing himself at their feet, at length drew from them a lukewarm promise of assistance against the Saxons. His troops, however, refusing to attack the enemy on the Werra, he was compelled to sign a treaty of peace at Goslar, in which he granted all the demands of the Saxons. The tithes were abolished; every fortress, even that of the Harz, which Henry vainly entreated might be spared, was razed to the ground. The Saxons had even the barbarity to drag the remains of a brother and of a son of the emperor from the grave, in order to bestow upon them every mark of indignity, A.D. 1073; an act of sacrilege so revolting to the feelings of the times that every prince of the empire, those of the Rhine country, and of Upper Germany, nay, even the Bohemians, joined in a crusade against them, and Henry quickly found himself at the head of an immense army. The contempt with which the Saxons treated their brother nations, and the petty hatred that had ever subsisted between the Upper and Lower Germans, greatly contributed to the universal exasperation. The Saxons, fearing the event, offered to yield to any terms, even to the reconstruction of the Harzburg; but Henry, inspirited by revenge, had sworn their ruin, and suddenly attacked them near Langensalza, on the Unstrutt. A bloody battle ensued, which was decided by the valor of the Swabians, under Rudolf. The Saxon nobles turned their horses and fled; the infantry, deprived of every means of escape, were cut down by thousands, and thus, while the Saxon peasants alone suffered, numbers of the nobility in the imperial army fell on this occasion; among others, Ernst of Babenberg, Margrave of Austria. The ancient privilege.

of the Swabians to head the imperial army was again confirmed to them on the field of battle.

Rudolf, Welf, and Berthold, after this, fearing the rising power of the emperor, withdrew; but notwithstanding the consequent diminution of his forces, Henry succeeded in reducing the Saxons (who had become a prey to internal dissension, the peasantry being unable to forget the late dastardly conduct of the nobility, and who were, moreover, threatened by the Danes and Wends) to submission, A.D. 1076. They laid down their arms at Spira, in Thuringia; all the princes gave themselves up, and were thrown into prison, with the exception of Otto of Nordheim, who, although Henry's bitterest enemy, had ever been viewed by him with more admiration than dislike. He was nominated duke of Saxony.

CXLIII. *Gregory the Seventh*

ALEXANDER II. died, A.D. 1073, and Hildebrand, now advanced in years, deemed it necessary, for the success of his plans, to place the tiara on his own brows, under the name of Gregory VII. The Saxon war favored his projects. At first he sought to gain Henry's friendship, and Agnes offered to use her influence in his favor, but he quickly perceived how little dependence could be placed on the caprices of that monarch, and resolved to act in future for himself alone.

This pope evinced the most extraordinary degree of activity. Although unsuccessful in Germany, he rendered the papal authority respected throughout Spain, France, and Hungary. He then proceeded to carry out his favorite projects for the reformation of the church, by punishing simony, encouraging morality, and depriving the laity of the right of interference in spiritual matters. For this purpose he published two edicts, which will ever be memorable on account of their influence not only on the ensuing century, but also on our own times.

His next step was to decree the celibacy of all the clergy. Up to this period, A.D. 1074, the monks alone had practiced celibacy, the bishops and priests having wives and children. Piety, and the renunciation of worldly joys, had arrived at such a pitch of enthusiasm that chastity seemed to have become a necessary quality in a priest, more especially since the introduction of the worship of the Madonna, whose supposed eternal virginity presented an idea of purity and sanctity which swayed Christian minds the more powerfully on account of the contrast it presented to the tenets of the Mahometan religion, founded alone on license and sensual gratification. The sufferings of Christ and those of the martyrs were eternally cited as proofs that the highest aim of the Christian was to suffer and to practice self-denial; the priests were, consequently, expected to set the first and highest example. They were (during their earthly pilgrimage) to personate the saints and the holy angels. By this means Gregory also hoped to strengthen the unity of the church. As long as the bishops were allowed to marry, their families took hereditary possession of the bishoprics, and sought, like the nobility, to render themselves alike independent of both pope and emperor. Celibacy at once controlled the ambition of the clergy, and dissolving every tie between them, their country, and their kindred, rendered them the servants of the pope and of the church, and formed them into a class distinct from the rest of mankind; but Gregory falsely reckoned when founding this great institution. He expected too much from human nature. Celibacy is at variance with laws both human and divine, and nature vindicated herself by broken vows, hypocrisy, and dark and secret crimes. The priests, particularly those in Germany, strongly opposed this decree, and when Siegfried of Mayence proposed the measure in an assembly of the German bishops at Erfurt, it was opposed with such violence that his life was in danger. Altmann, bishop of Passau, Gregory's most zealous partisan, was expelled by his own chapter.[1] Gregory upon this raised

---

[1] Gregory rewarded him by placing his own miter on his head at Rome. Altmann built the monastery of Gottweich, afterward celebrated for the erudition of the monks, on a lofty rock, as a sign that God is higher than all the potentates of earth.

a popular feeling against the uxorious clergy, by placing them under excommunication, and by forbidding the people to attend mass. His policy proved successful. It was in vain that Otto, bishop of Constance, and Ulrich, of Ratisbon, justified the marriage of the clergy, by the citation of passages from the Epistles of St. Paul, and from other parts of the Bible; it was in vain that they appealed to the laws of nature; the priest, in the opinion of the people, was to be as free from earthly taint as an angel of light; and natural affection was denounced by them as a culpable and sensual weakness. The German clergy were, before long, compelled to obey the decree of their superior.

A second decree of equal importance followed. The pope forbade the election of the bishops by the laity, and by thus rendering the possession of benefices no longer dependent on the caprice of the monarch and his courtiers, effectually prevented simony. This decree further declared the church independent of the state, and the extensive lands, which, up to this period, had been held as feofs of the crown through the monarch's right of election, the property of the church. The clergy alone were invested with the power of electing the bishops, who were confirmed by the pope, the temporal sovereign being without a voice in the matter.

Gregory also confirmed without delay the interdiction formerly pronounced against the doctrines of Rantram and of Berengar of Tours, and laid down as an eternal truth, that the body and blood of Christ were really present in the sacramental bread and wine, and that the priest alone—in fact, every priest indifferently, whether personally worthy or unworthy—was enabled, merely by virtue of his office, to transform the host into the real body of the Saviour (*transubstantiatio*). Moreover, in order to place the church, now powerful and independent, under one head, Gregory bestowed upon himself, and all future popes, unlimited authority over the councils, and declared every assembly of the clergy invalid unless convoked by the pope. Like Charlemagne, who, when he had firmly rooted his power, governed his extensive territory by means of Sendgrafs, Gregory dispatched his legates, who, acting in his name, were infallible like him, to the various European courts. He declared, "the pope is through God and instead of God on earth, therefore all powers, whether temporal or spiritual, are subject to him. The pope is the sun, the emperor the moon that shines with borrowed light."

The Saxons had not failed to lay their complaints against their sovereign before the pope, and Henry, by thoughtlessly complaining to him of his rebellious subjects, gave him an opportunity of setting himself up as umpire. Gregory, well aware of the weak nature of the emperor and of his own power, treated him without reserve, and openly accusing him of simony, haughtily commanded him to come in person to Rome, and excommunicated those among the bishops who had been guilty of a similar crime. Henry, unacquainted with Gregory's character, took the matter lightly, and held a convocation of the German bishops at Worms, A.D. 1076, by which Gregory was deposed. This called forth a still more decisive step on the part of the bold pontiff, who placed the emperor under an interdict, released his subjects from their oath of allegiance, and declared him deprived of his dignity. Henry at first treated the acts of the proud monk with scorn, but was quickly struck with terror on perceiving their instantaneous effect. With the exception of the inhabitants of the cities, whose commercial habits, and the free peasantry, whose ancient Germanic constitution, had ever been opposed to papacy, Henry was deserted to a man by his subjects, who avoided him as one infected with the plague. The Saxons, led by Otto of Nordheim, instantly flew to arms. The foreign garrisons were driven out of the country. Several of the imprisoned princes escaped. The remainder, after a touching appeal from Henry for peace and aid, were restored to liberty: but his evil hour had at length arrived; all his enemies, even Welf, who owed him such a debt of gratitude, found an excuse for their treason, their revenge, or their rapacity, in the papal interdict, and

Henry, abandoned by all, was, notwithstanding his earnest entreaties, declared, in a diet held at Oppenheim, deprived of his dignity, until he had freed himself from the interdict, and the pope was invited to visit Augsburg during the following year, in order to settle the affairs of Germany. The election of Rudolf in Henry's stead was next attempted, and in order to render it impossible for the unfortunate emperor to free himself from the interdict, he was assigned a close residence at Spires, and deprived of any mode of communication with Italy. In this desperate situation he found that his only chance of safety lay in being beforehand with the rebellious princes, by escaping to Italy, and imploring the pope at any price to raise the interdict; and he accordingly secretly set off with that intent, accompanied by Bertha, his infant son, and a solitary knight, who, it is not known upon what grounds, is said by the Swabian chronicler, Crusius, to have been Frederick of Büren, the ancestor of the Hohenstaufen family. The winter of this year, A.D. 1076, happened to be colder than had been known within the memory of man, and the Rhine remained frozen over from St. Martin's day until the April of 1077. It was in this dreadful weather, about Christmas time, that the imperial pilgrims, each moment dreading discovery from Rudolf's spies, crossed the pathless Alps, and reached Vevey on the Lake of Geneva in safety. Here they were forcibly detained by Bertha's mother and by her brother Amadeus, Graf of Savoy, from whom they purchased a free passage by the cession of five Burgundian bishoprics. They crossed the St. Bernard during the depth of winter, and Bertha, whom neither danger nor distress could separate from her husband, was drawn over the ice seated on an ox-hide, while the most Christian emperor climbed like a chamois hunter along the rocky, dangerous paths.

On entering Lombardy he was unexpectedly met by numbers of the Italian princes and bishops, by whom he was deferentially greeted as emperor. Those among the Italians who had at that time fallen under the papal interdict, particularly the bishops of Milan and Ravenna, joined Henry, and exhorted him to place himself at their head for the purpose of dethroning the pope; but, still influenced by his awe of the German princes, the dispirited emperor refused, and resolved to remain faithful to his original intention of imploring Gregory's pardon. The pope, who happened at this moment to be on his way to Augsburg, was not a little alarmed on receiving the news of Henry's arrival in Italy, and for the better security of his person threw himself into the fortress of Canossa, whose gates were opened to him by his ally, the Countess Matilda, who shortly before had become a widow. Gottfried the Hunchback, Henry's most faithful adherent, was secretly assassinated,[1] and Gregory, on account of his intimacy with Matilda, who bestowed her wealth on the church, was accused by his enemies of the crime. The accusation of an improper intercourse between him and Matilda is, there is no doubt, false; Gregory's natural inclinations rendered him no admirer of the sex, nor could any temptation have induced him to cast the slightest stain on his sacred character. Superstitious zeal and piety bound Matilda to his cause, and he fully appreciated the value of so powerful an adherent.

Henry now entreated Matilda to intercede in his behalf, and Gregory, at first surprised at his penitence when backed by a body of armed partisans, quickly understood his position, and assumed the greatest severity, commanding him to come alone and as a penitent to Canossa. Henry obeyed, and was allowed to enter the castle. The gates closed behind him, and for three days and three nights he remained bareheaded and barefoot, without food, exposed in a woolen garment to the severe cold, between the double walls of the fort, until the pope, moved by the earnest supplications of those around him, especially by those of Matilda, called him into his presence, and released him from the interdict, on

---

[1] At Antwerp, A.D. 1076. The young Count Dietrich of Holland has been accused of this murder, because, on the death of Gottfried, he took possession of Holland, of which his uncle had been deprived.

condition of his leaving to him the final settlement of affairs in Germany, and of not resuming the title of emperor until permission was granted so to do. A solemn mass was then performed, and Gregory, taking the holy wafer into his hands, broke it in half, saying, "If the crimes of which you accused me at Worms be true, may the host that I now eat cause me instantly to die." He then swallowed it, and turning to the emperor, said, "Now eat the other half, and make a similar protestation of your innocence of the charges I make against you." Henry refused, and after undergoing every species of humiliation was dismissed by the triumphant pope.

The Italians, indignant at his weak and cowardly conduct, now openly deserted him. Unable to endure their scorn, he resolved to break the oath he had just taken, and shut up Gregory so closely in the castle of Canossa as effectually to put a stop to his further progress to Augsburg or his return to Rome; at the same time the interdicted bishops[1] and Henry's partisans among the German laity, among whom Eberhard, Graf of Nellenburg, may be chiefly distinguished, flocked beneath his standard.

CXLIV. *The Papal Kings*

THE German princes, meanwhile, vainly awaited the arrival of the pope. At length came the news of Henry's unexpected re-establishment, and Rudolf, yielding at once to the press of circumstances, and to his ambition, threw off his allegiance, and caused himself to be proclaimed emperor at Mayence, where he was crowned by the archbishop. The citizens of Mayence, Henry's partisans, viewed the ceremony for some time in enforced silence, but a quarrel breaking out during the tournament that followed, a general rise took

---

[1] Among them, Benno of Osnabruck particularly distinguished himself as Henry's most faithful friend and counselor. He had also done penance at Canossa, but on a different occasion. Vide Moser's *History of Osnabruck*. Another Benno, bishop of Meissen, favored the papal party.

place, and, after a desperate affray between them and the Swabian troops, Rudolf was compelled to quit the city; he then proceeded to Worms, with the intention of securing himself within the fort, but found the city gates closed against him. This was the prelude to a general struggle throughout Germany between his party and that of Henry, which was rendered the more desperate by the refusal of the interdicted bishops of Henry's party to cede their bishoprics to the bishops who had been nominated to supersede them by Gregory. Henry found numerous adherents in the mountains, and although Welf had seized the passes, and laid the country of the Grisons, where the emperor's party was upheld by Dietmar, bishop of Chur, waste, Sieghart, the patriarch of Aglar (Aquileia), opened Carniola to him; Marquardt, the son of the lately expelled duke, Adalbero, drove Berthold of Zähringen out of Carinthia. Henry also found an ally in Wratislaw of Bohemia, and received great accessions to his party from Welf's numerous enemies among the Bavarian nobility. On reaching Ulm, he held a public court, and put Rudolf and his adherents out of the ban of the empire.

The whole of Germany was divided into two parties, that of the emperor and that of St. Peter, which gave rise to the great division in the German nation which, at a later period, attained such melancholy celebrity as the strife between the Welfs and the Waiblinger, or Guelphs and Ghibellines. Swabia, where the people fluctuated between the duke and the emperor, was in uproar. The nobility and the bishops favored both sides; the cities and free cantons all pronounced in favor of the emperor. In Augsburg, Mathias Corsang preached against, and Geroch in favor of, the pope; the latter was driven by the citizens out of the town. Würzburg made a desperate defense against Rudolf, and twelve thousand peasants from the cantons swelled the ranks of the imperial army. Franconia, A.D. 1078, was laid waste, and became the seat of war. A pitched battle was fought between the contending parties near Melrichstadt, in which the victory remained undecided, one wing of the imperial army, commanded by Henry, routing the enemy, while the same part was performed on the other side by Rudolf's Saxon adherents, headed by Otto of Nordheim. Siegfried of Mayence, the wicked bishop of Worms, and the papal legate, fell into Henry's hands; Wezilo of Magdeburg was killed during his flight. The brave Eberhard of Nellenburg and the Swabian peasants, were, on the other hand, cut to pieces by the Saxons; a dreadful fate awaited every peasant who was taken prisoner by the nobles, who had resolved, at whatever price, to crush these dangerous defenders of liberty.

For a while either party rested. Berthold of Zähringen died of grief, A.D. 1078, for the losses he had suffered in this battle, into which he had been driven against his will. His son, Berthold, favored Rudolf, whose daughter, Agnes, he married. Rudolf was, nevertheless, superseded in the dukedom of Swabia by Frederick of Hohenstaufen, a Swabian noble, who had given striking proofs of fidelity to the emperor, and by whom he was further raised by the gift of his daughter Agnes in marriage. Frederick's name was von Büren, until the building of the castle of Staufen (on which the whole glory of the German empire was destined to rest), at the outlet of the Swabian Alp.

Gregory, greatly disconcerted by this turn in affairs, temporized, in order to see on which side victory would declare herself. The Saxons, irritated by this conduct, and, moreover, incited by Gebhard, archbishop of Salzburg, who had been deposed by Henry, addressed three letters to him, which received the nickname of "the cock-crowing," being intended, like the voice of St. Peter's cock, to move his successor to remorse. A whole year passed in fruitless negotiations. In the winter of 1080, Henry again attacked Rudolf, and a second engagement took place near Fladenheim in Thuringia, in which the invincible Otto of Nordheim again proved victorious. This success decided Gregory in Rudolf's favor, and he not only confirmed him in the title he had usurped, but, as the genuine crown jewels of Charlemagne, and of Otto the Great, were in Henry's possession, also presented him with a new diadem, for which he was to hold the empire as a papal fief: the inscription it bore ran thus, "Petra dedit Petro, Petrus diadema Rudolpho." He then again solemnly excommunicated Henry, who, on the other hand, convoked a German concilium at Brixen, by which Gregory was for a second time deposed, and the archbishop of Ravenna was nominated in his stead, as Pope Clement III., A.D. 1080.

During the same year, Henry invaded Saxony, burned Erfurt, and a third engagement took place near Grona on the Elster, in the great plain lying between Merseburg and Leipzig, famous for the victory gained by Henry the Fowler over the Hungarians, and, at a later period, the scene of many a hard-fought battle. Otto of Nordheim was again victorious; Rudolf was mortally wounded, and in the struggle was deprived of his right hand by Gottfried, a cousin of Gottfried the Hunchback, whom he succeeded in the dukedom of Lower Lothringia; he afterward acquired great celebrity under the name of Bouillon, his maternal inheritance. When dying, Rudolf exclaimed as he looked at his mutilated limb, "This is the hand by which I swore allegiance to Henry." He was buried with regal honors at Merseburg. On the capture of this city shortly after by Henry, he was advised to destroy his tomb, to which he replied, "Would to God that all my enemies were as splendidly entombed."

The death of Rudolf left his party without a leader, and rendered their late victory useless. Henry gained daily fresh adherents, and was ere long enabled to leave the conduct of the war in Germany to Frederick of Hohenstaufen, and to visit Italy in person, for the purpose of humbling his old antagonist, Gregory. He quickly crossed the Alps, overthrew Matilda's party near Parma, and pushed on to Rome, to which he laid siege for three years without success; at length, Wiprecht von Groitsch, a Saxon knight, mounted the walls, and took the city by storm, A.D. 1083. Gregory, who had shut himself within the castle of St. Angelo, secretly escaped to Salerno, where he was joyfully received by the Normans. Henry, meanwhile, placed Clement III. in the papal chair, and, after being solemnly crowned emperor, returned to Germany. Gregory instantly returned to Rome at the head of the wild Normans, who took the city, and, deaf to his remonstrances, began the work of pillage. The Romans, rendered desperate, collected in vast multitudes, drove the enemy beyond the walls, and compelled the pope again to seek shelter in Salerno, where he died, A.D. 1085. His last words were worthy of his life: "Because I have loved justice," exclaimed he, "and punished injustice, I die an exile!"

In Germany the Saxons had proclaimed Hermann of Luxemburg their king, at Eisleben. He received the nickname of "the garlic king," on account of the quantity of garlic that grew around Eisleben. He was a man of mean intellect, and completely subservient to Welf, Berthold von Zähringen, and Leopold of Austria. Otto von Nordheim was killed by a fall from his horse. Welf was beaten by Frederick of Swabia at Hochstadt, and Leopold of Austria and Altmann, bishop of Passau, by Wratislaw of Bohemia at Mauerberg. The free peasantry of Friesland, headed by the archbishop of Bremen, fought on Henry's side; they were put to the rout and cut to pieces by the Saxon Count von Mansfeld, and the nobles again betrayed the hatred they bore them by leaving their dead bodies unburied on the field.

In 1085, the emperor returned from his Italian expedition, and, after several fruitless attempts at negotiation, again invaded Saxony, and rapidly reduced his opponents, the newly elected king, Hermann, Hartwig, the new archbishop of Magdeburg, and his oldest and bitterest enemy, Bucco, to submission. The two latter fled into Denmark, and, on Henry's departure from Saxony, instantly returned thither to plot anew against him. In 1086, Hermann marched upon Würzburg, in the design of uniting his forces with those of Welf in Upper Saxony, but being beaten at Pleichfeld by the emperor, he resigned his crown, A.D. 1087, from a conviction of the inutility of opposition. He was despised even by his own menials. He was shortly afterward accidentally killed by a woman, when storming his own castle by night, in order to test the vigilance of his men.

The rebellious Saxons, who were still headed by Ekbert von Meissen, and by Bucco, bishop of Halberstadt, proclaimed the former king. After the death of the brave Otto von Nordheim, Ekbert, the powerful governor of the Slavian frontier, the descendant of the house of Wettin whose wealth and power were founded on rapine and oppression, was Henry's most dangerous opponent; nor did he present a solitary instance of the boundless ambition of the Slavian Markgrafs, whose absolute sovereignty over their enslaved subjects caused them insolently to grasp at the imperial crown. But his attempt proved vain; Welf, actuated by jealousy, abandoned him in order to win for himself a kingdom in the south of Italy. He married his youthful son to the aged Countess Matilda, in the hope of annexing her possessions in Lombardy to Bavaria. On the death of Gregory, his party elected Victor III, and, on his death, Urban II., pope. Clement III. was expelled; Gregory's plans were carried out; and the emperor was continually excommunicated. Henry suffered a fresh defeat at the castle of Gleichen in Thuringia, notwithstanding which fortune favored him. Bucco was surprised and assassinated by the citizens of Goslar, and Ekbert was killed by the servants of the Princess Matilda (Henry's sister, the abbess of Quedlinberg, a woman of great power and influence), who discovered him in a mill, A.D. 1088. Berthold, the son of Rudolf, also died, and Welf, discontented with the Countess Matilda, who had bestowed her rich possessions on the pope, entreating for peace, the empire once more tasted its blessings, A.D. 1093. The contending parties retained their former possessions, Welf remaining duke of Bavaria, Magnus, duke of Saxony, Frederick von Staufen, duke of Swabia, Berthold von Zähringen, duke of Upper Alemannia, or Switzerland,

Ludolf, duke of Carinthia, Gottfried de Bouillon, duke of Lower Lothringia, while the Margrave Udo retained Brandenburg, the Margrave Leopold, Austria, and the Landgrave Louis, Thuringia. Hermann, a nephew of Berthold von Zähringen, was nominated to the Margraviate of Baden, and the important march of Meissen was bestowed upon the gallant Wiprecht von Groitsch, who was, moreover, confirmed in the possession of the Lausitz, which he had seized with the aid of Bohemia. Wratislaw of Bohemia was raised to the dignity of king, and his brother Conrad was created Margrave of Moravia.

Boleslaw of Poland also took the title of king, and made the important acquisition of Pomerania. Cruco, prince of the Rugii, after besieging Buthue (the son of the unfortunate Gottschalk, who had attempted the restoration of the kingdom of the Obotrites), in Plön, and causing him to be murdered, fell himself by the hand of Buthue's brother, the Christian Henry. Cruco's beautiful wife, Slavina, who was deeply enamored of the youthful Henry, entered into the plot, and Cruco was deprived of his head at the banquet table, by a single stroke of his adversary's sword, A.D. 1105. The pagan Slavi united and made a determined resistance against Henry on the one side, who, as the vassal of the Saxon duke Magnus, received his aid, and against the Poles on the other. Henry gained a decisive victory at Smilow, and another at the mouth of the Trave, A.D. 1106. Pomerania was annexed to Poland.—In Denmark, Sueno the Pious had been succeeded by his son, Canute the Holy, who preserved peace with Germany. His opposition to the pretenders to the imperial crown, and his severity toward his subjects, caused them to revolt. He was besieged and assassinated in a church, whither he had fled for refuge, A.D. 1086. He was succeeded by his brother Olaf, and, in 1095, by his second brother, Erich Evegod. Charles, the son of Canute, fled into Germany, and was created Count of Flanders. His virtues caused him, at a later period, to share his father's fate. He was murdered by his faithless vassals. Canute and Charles were canonized as martyrs.

All opposition had now ceased within the empire; the pope, Urban II., alone proved refractory, and Henry, in order to punish his insolence, once more appeared in Italy. Matilda's army was speedily vanquished, and Clement III. reinstated in his dignity. Henry then returned to Germany, leaving his son Conrad at the head of affairs in Italy. This young man was incited to rebel against his parent by the Countess Matilda, the ex-pope Urban, and Roger of Sicily, who bestowed upon him the hand of his daughter, Iolanta. Love, ambition, the dread of being excommunicated, and of forfeiting the imperial crown by fidelity to his father, led to this rash and guilty determination, and, in 1095, he caused himself to be solemnly crowned at Milan. His father, after vainly attempting to win him from his purpose, disinherited him, and he was constrained to limit his ambition to Italy, where he was at the mercy of his adherents, who acted solely with a view to their own aggrandizement. The consciousness of his weakness and his remorse for his guilty conduct brought him early to the grave, A.D. 1101.

CXLV. *The Crusades*

IT was about this period that an immense movement, caused by the agitation of men's minds, took place throughout Europe, and produced a second and enormous migration. Fired by religious enthusiasm, countless multitudes collected from various parts of Europe, in order to combat the infidels, and in these crusades the spirit of the Middle Ages stood fully developed, freed from the petty feuds that marked the times.

As early as the reign of the Ottos, pilgrimages to the holy sepulcher at Jerusalem had become frequent; a black garment, a long staff, a broad-brimmed hat ornamented with the mussel shells found on the coasts of Palestine, and a rosary from Jerusalem, formed the garb worn by the pilgrims. The Arabs, the possessors of the holy city, respected these peaceable wayfarers, and granted them permission to build churches and a hospital[1] in honor of John the Baptist. The Arabian empire was, at that period, on the brink of destruction, and the caliphate was divided. The Ommaijadæ reigned in Spain, the Fatimites in Egypt, and the Abassidæ at Bagdad; the two last dynasties had already fallen beneath the rule of the Turks, who had at first served under them as mercenary troops, whose sultans acted in the same capacity to the caliph as the major-domo to the kings of France. The great affluence of Christian pilgrims roused the jealousy of the Jews, who until now had monopolized the whole of Eastern commerce, which they feared might gradually pass into the hands of the Christians. The suspicion of their having persuaded Hakim, the caliph of Egypt, to destroy the church erected over the holy sepulcher, and to expell all the Christians from Jerusalem in 1010, occasioned a general persecution of the Jews in France. Daher, the son of Hakim, restoring matters to their former state, and insuring the safety of the pilgrims and the freedom of commerce, the holy sepulcher became an object of still deeper interest, and the number of pilgrims greatly increased. St. Colomannus, a Scotch pilgrim, being hanged in company with two robbers, at Stockerau in Austria, the tree on which he hung began to blossom, and the people, recognizing him by that sign as a man of God, carried him to Mölk and treated his remains with the greatest honor. The fame of this pilgrim was henceforward reflected upon all who bore the staff, and before long not only the commonalty, but princes also became humble wanderers. Robert of Normandy was the first who visited Palestine, A.D. 1033. He was followed by Litbert, bishop of Kamerich, A.D. 1054, and by St. Helena of Sweden, A.D. 1060. The first great expedition was undertaken, A.D. 1064, by Siegfried, archbishop of Mayence, and the bishops of Bamberg, Ratisbon, and Utrecht, at the head

---

[1] A hospital for pilgrims was built as early as the ninth century on Mount Cenis, and another during the following century on Mount St. Bernard.

of seven thousand pilgrims, of whom two thousand alone returned. Their path was surrounded with danger. On one occasion they were attacked by a body of twelve thousand Arabs, one of whose sheiks came into the house in which the bishops had taken refuge, and attempted to molest them, upon which Gunther, the gigantic bishop of Bamberg, felled him to the ground with one blow. The Christians, after a valiant defense, were at length rescued from their perilous situation by a tribe of friendly Arabs. Gunther died while on his return to Germany.[1] Altmann performed the pilgrimage on foot, before his elevation to the bishopric of Passau, and Robert the Friscian also, in order to do penance for his sins, A.D. 1082.

On the advance of the Turks upon Jerusalem, of which they took possession, a dreadful persecution commenced, A.D. 1086, which roused the whole of Europe. Rage and consternation filled every bosom, and one idea, that of invading the Holy Land, and of freeing the sepulcher from pollution by dint of arms, pervaded all classes. The spirit infused into the church by Gregory VII. was one great motive of this general enthusiasm, while the example of the Spaniards influenced the whole body of Christian chivalry. The valiant descendants of the Visigoths had, since the commencement of the eighth century, been engaged in ceaseless warfare with the Moors, at first in defense of their liberty and their religion, and at a later period for the recovery of Spain. It was exactly at this conjuncture that Henry, count of Burgundy, the son-in-law of Alfonso, king of Leon, the most powerful of the petty Christian monarchs in Spain, conquered Portugal. The appearance of a remarkable French pilgrim, Peter of Amiens, named the Hermit, however, chiefly contributed to hasten the event. On his return from Palestine with a petition from the persecuted patriarch of Jerusalem, he asserted that he had also been commissioned by Christ himself to save the holy sepulcher. Attired in his

---

[1] Marianus Scotus.

travel-soiled pilgrim's garb, and mounted on an ass, having in one hand the letter, in the other a crucifix, he passed through France and Italy, summoning, with enthusiastic eloquence, people of every class and of every nation to unite against the infidels. Multitudes obeyed. Urban II. placed himself, as pope, at the head of the faithful, and, not venturing to appear in Germany, convoked a great meeting of the clergy, first at Piacenza in Italy, and afterward at Clermont in France, where he addressed the people in a broad green field, graphically depicturing the sufferings of the church in the East, the desecration of the sacred precincts, the temple converted into a Turkish stable, the holy sepulcher of the Saviour defiled by dogs, his followers scorned, tortured, and slain; and concluded by divulging the command from heaven to revenge the cruelties practiced by the infidels, and to rescue the sanctuary. Scarcely had he ceased, than a deafening shout of "It is the will of God! it is the will of God!" arose from the innumerable throng, and numbers dedicated themselves to the service of Christ, in sign of which they wore a red cross on one shoulder.

The lower classes, who in France were suffering from a famine, occasioned by the failure of the crops for several successive years, and who, moreover, may have beheld, in this general arming in honor of God, a means of escaping from the tyranny of the nobility, were first seized by the spirit of religious enthusiasm; and shortly afterward, if not at the same time, every serf who volunteered to serve in the Holy Land was declared free and capable of bearing arms. The first armament, consisting of fifteen thousand men, marched, under the guidance of the knight Walther de Perejo, and his nephew, Walther Sensavehor, or Havenought (who had spent the whole of his fortune on the expedition), from the north of France, A.D. 1096, and solemnized Easter festival at Cologne; on reaching Hungary, disputes arose concerning their supplies, and they were almost entirely cut to pieces in Bulgaria. The elder Walther died; the younger reached Constantinople with the remnant of his followers.

Peter the Hermit followed with forty thousand men, among whom were several Germans, took Semlin by storm, forced his way through the Bulgarians, was attacked and beaten by them at Nissa, and, after losing ten thousand men, appeared before the gates of Constantinople with the remainder of the pilgrims, bearing green palm branches in their hands.

The spirit of religious fanaticism, the seeds of which had been so zealously sown by Peter the Hermit, spread, meanwhile, throughout Germany. Signs were beheld in the heavens, and it was currently reported that Charlemagne had risen from his grave, in order to place himself at the head of the crusaders. Gottschalk, a priest from the Pfalz, marched with fifteen thousand men into Hungary, and, after laying the country waste, had the stupidity to allow himself to be persuaded by Kolmany, the Hungarian king, to deliver up his arms, on condition of receiving a free passage, which was no sooner complied with than the faithless Hungarians attacked and cut to pieces the whole of the defenseless Germans, at Meszburg (Mosony?). This expedition was succeeded by another of still greater magnitude, which, proceeding from France, passed through Germany, like the rude Lawine, gaining strength and volume on its course. Without a leader to guide its movements, this senseless multitude followed in the direction taken by a goose and a goat which were driven in advance. William, surnamed the Carpenter, a French knight, was the only person of any note among the number; but when the Germans began to join them, Volkmar the priest, and the Count Emicho von Leiningen, who was influenced by remorse for the sins of his youth, placed themselves at the head of this fresh body of crusaders, who, acting on the notion that the infidels dwelling in Europe should be exterminated before those in Asia should be attacked, murdered twelve thousand Jews. In Treves, many of these unfortunate men, driven to despair, laid violent hands on their children and on themselves, and multitudes embraced Christianity, from which they lapsed the moment the peril had passed. Two hundred Jews fled from Cologne and took refuge in boats; they were overtaken and slain. In Mayence, the archbishop, Rudhart, took them under his protection, and gave them the great hall of his castle for an asylum; the pilgrims, nevertheless, forced their way in, and murdered seven hundred of them in the archbishop's presence. At Spires the Jews valiantly defended themselves. At Worms they all committed suicide. At Magdeburg the archbishop, Ruprecht, amused himself by attacking them during the celebration of the feast of tabernacles, and by seizing their property. The pilgrim band, which is said to have consisted of two hundred thousand souls, chiefly women, priests, and unarmed rabble, advanced into Hungary, but suddenly, while engaged in the siege of Meszburg, was, without any known cause, seized with a panic, put to the rout, and almost entirely cut to pieces. Emicho fled, covered with shame, to his native country. But, notwithstanding this disaster, part of the pilgrims reached Constantinople by other roads through Italy.

A number of Italians had also set off for the same place by sea; the republics of Pisa, Genoa and Venice favoring the crusade from motives of commercial advantage, as well as from piety; and thus by degrees an army of one hundred thousand pilgrims collected beneath the walls of Constantinople, under the banner of Peter the Hermit. The emperor Alexius, weary of supplying their wants, sent them over to Asia, where Peter intended to have awaited the arrival of the great body of knights, which was to have quickly folowed on his track; but the French, impatient for war, and greedy of booty, made predatory incursions on their own account into the Turkish territory; and the Germans, animated by their example, pillaged the country and garrisoned the fort of Xerigordon, where they were ere long surrounded by the Turks, to whom they were betrayed by their leader, Reinold, and three thousand of them slain. The French and Italian pilgrims were also cut to pieces, with the exception of three thousand, who made such a valiant defense in an ancient fort that the Greeks spared their lives at Peter's earnest request. Peter escaped, but Walther Sensavehor was slain.

This unsuccessful attempt of the lower orders among the people was succeeded by a much more brilliant armament, composed of chivalry, and led by princes. Godfred, duke of Lower Lothringia (Brabant), surnamed Bouillon, from his castle of that name, the ancient ally of the emperor, Henry IV., and the successful antagonist of Rudolf, the pretender to the crown, raised a body of ten thousand horse and seventy thousand infantry. He was accompanied by his brothers, Eustace and Baldwin, his cousin, Baldwin de Bourg, Count Baldwin von Hennegau, etc.; besides being joined by Count Robert of Flanders, the son of the Friscian, afterward known as Robert of Jerusalem; Hugh de Vermandois, the brother of Philip, king of France; Robert Shortshank, duke of Normandy, the son of William the Conqueror; and the aged one-eyed Count Raimund of Toulouse. The Netherlanders under Godfred marched in excellent order and unmolested through Hungary, while the French took the route through Italy, A.D. 1096. The latter were joined en route by the fair-haired Bohemund, the son of Robert Guiscard, a man of gigantic stature, and by his cousin Tancred, the most warlike among the Normans of their times. Ademar, the venerable bishop of Puy, accompanied them as legate from the holy see. The French went by sea, and consequently were the first to reach Greece, where Hugh de Vermandois no sooner landed than he was seized and thrown into prison by the emperor Alexius, who only restored him to liberty on condition of his doing homage to him as his liege lord. Alexius, filled with inquietude for the safety of his own empire, left no means untried to effectuate the conquest of the Holy Land in his own name, in order to reduce it to its former state of dependence as a province of the ancient eastern empire. Godfred, on his arrival, learned with rage and astonishment that the brother of the French monarch had taken the oath of allegiance to the Greek emperor; but quickly perceiving the necessity of gaining him as an ally, he submitted to the same ceremony, and his example was followed by all the other princes. Godfred was in return adopted by the emperor as Cæsar; that is, as his son. The whole of the crusaders (whose numbers, said to have amounted to six hundred thousand men, are probably exaggerated) crossed over to Asia, and found the country around Nicæa covered with the yet unburied remains of their unfortunate predecessors. Nicæa was taken by storm with considerable loss, and given up to the Greeks. Here the Normans separated from the main body, and taking a line to the left, again divided, in order the more conveniently to procure supplies; in this condition they were attacked by the Turks,[1] and with great difficulty rescued by Godfred. Desert tracts, and burning wastes, destructive alike to the warriors and their steeds, now obstructed the advance of the crusaders. The path was strewn with the dying and the dead. Numbers of the pilgrims turned back in despair. Godfred was dreadfully torn by a bear, from whose claws he bravely rescued one of the unarmed pilgrims. His brother Baldwin, who had been joined by a number of Dutch, Frisians, and Flemish pirates, who for eight years had infested the Mediterranean, marched in advance of the main army, and took the important town of Edessa, where he was met by a procession of Armenian Christians, bearing crosses and banners, who, filled with astonishment at his prowess, sank on their knees before him. The main body meanwhile reached the celebrated city of Antioch, of which, thirteen years before, the Greek emperor had been deprived, and which still retained its ancient splendor. Its walls long resisted the untaught valor of the warriors of the West, three hundred thousand of whom are said to have laid siege to it. Hunger and pestilence, however, gradually diminished their number, and, in the beginning of 1098, seven hundred horses were all that

---

[1] A great number of ladies who accompanied this expedition fell with the camp into the hands of the Turks. Albert von Aix observes that they should instantly have adorned themselves, in order to have enslaved their captors by their beauty.

remained within the Christian camp. These were mounted by seven hundred knights, who attacked and overcame a body of the enemy's cavalry, twenty-five thousand strong, and captured one thousand horses. Godfred continued to fight in advance, and is said, on one occasion, to have cut a Turk so completely in half with a downward stroke that, while one half of his body fell to the ground, the other was borne away by his horse. The Mahometans made great preparations in order to raise the siege of Antioch. The means of retreating upon Constantinople were cut off, and the Danish prince Sven and his bride Florina,[1] the daughter of Duke Eudo of Burgundy, with one thousand five hundred Danish knights, were cut to pieces. The great sultan of Bagdad levied the whole force of the Mahometan East, and dispatched his vizier, Kerbugha, at the head of an immense army, to the relief of Antioch, but, before his arrival, the city was betrayed to the Christians, in the June of 1098. The pilgrims were now in their turn suddenly besieged by Kerbugha, whose troops covered the whole country, and rendered it impossible for them to bring supplies into the already famished city. The distress soon became unbearable; and numbers of the pilgrims secretly let themselves down by ropes from the city walls, and fled to the sea-shore, spreading a report that the city was already lost, and inducing the captains of the Genoese ships, the last hope of the crusaders, to return home; upon which the emperor Alexius, who was marching to their relief, in order to take possession of Antioch in his own name, also turned back. The situation of Godfred and the pilgrims now appeared desperate, hunger daily thinned their numbers, and the survivors wandered up and down the city, wan, weak, and spiritless; but, just when they were driven to the last extremity, a priest of Provence, one Peter Barthelemy, announced that the apostle Andrew had appeared to him, and revealed the spot in An-

---

[1] She intended to have married him at Jerusalem. She bravely defended herself to the last, although pierced by seven arrows.

tioch where the real holy lance, with which Christ had been pierced when hanging on the cross, lay buried; that they were to seek for it and to bear it before them to victory. The rusted head of a lance was found in the place indicated, and the confidence of the pilgrims once more returned. Peter the Hermit went into Kerbugha's camp and threatened him with destruction, unless he instantly embraced Christianity. Kerbugha treated him as a mad man, and being, in his contempt of the pilgrims, willing to spare unnecessary bloodshed, resolved, instead of storming the city, to continue the blockade. While he was carelessly engaged in a game of chess, the crusaders planted a black banner on the highest tower in Antioch, and marched in procession out of the gates, headed by the bishop Ademar, bearing on high the holy lance. They advanced in battle array singing hymns, and attacked the Turks with such fury that half of the besiegers were already put to the rout before their comrades became aware of their peril. The starving Christians took the immense camp, killed one hundred thousand of the enemy, flung themselves upon their Turkish horses, and pursued the fugitives to a considerable distance. After a public thanksgiving, Bohemund was created Prince of Antioch, and it was declared to the emperor Alexius that no further conquests should be made in his name, unless he speedily afforded them the promised aid. Hugh of France was sent with this message as embassador to Constantinople; but instead of returning to the camp, proceeded to France, being discontented with the treatment he had received from the rest of the crusaders, by whom he was held in slight esteem. The second embassador, Baldwin, count of Hennegau, was attacked near Nicæa by the Turks, and all traces of him were lost.

The Mahometans, terrified at this unexpected disaster, no longer opposed the advance of the pilgrims, who were joyfully greeted by the Syrian Christians; and the Arabian emirs, who until now had groaned beneath the Turkish yoke, offered to enter into a friendly alliance with them. But dissension broke out among the pilgrims themselves. Raimund of Toulouse envied Bohemund the possession of Antioch, and now, rather ungratefully it must be owned, Peter Barthelemy was accused of having invented the fable of the holy lance (which was now said to be a common bit of iron), in order to answer the exigency of the moment. Peter, in order to prove his innocence and the authenticity of the weapon, underwent the ordeal by fire; with the lance in his hand, he ran between two flaming piles of wood, and, although he came forth again alive, died shortly of the effects. A strong re-enforcement, among which were Alain Fergent, duke of Brittany, and Edgar Atheling, the last scion of the Anglo-Saxon dynasty, here joined the crusaders; a remarkable coincidence, Robert, the son of William the Conqueror, the destroyer of the Saxon race, being in the same camp and fighting in the same cause. The caliph of Egypt sent costly gifts to the crusaders, with an offer of permitting the free exercise of the Christian religion in Jerusalem. He would gladly, with the aid of the crusaders, have driven the dreaded Turks out of Syria; but the crusaders had now almost reached the termination of their long and wearisome pilgrimage, and the conquest and actual possession of the holy sepulcher were regarded by them as indispensable duties. The emir of Tripoli again took up arms and was defeated. The hermits and the ancient Christians descended from Mount Lebanon to welcome the pilgrims. Nicopolis was at length reached, and as every one was anxious to be the first to behold Jerusalem on the following morning, they continued their march during the whole night. It so happened that an eclipse of the moon took place during this night, which caused great joy among the pilgrims, who beheld in it an omen of the fall of the Mahometan empire (whose emblem is the crescent moon). At break of day on the 10th of June, 1099, they reached the heights of Emaus, and suddenly beheld the holy city, the long-wished-for object of their toil, and with one accord sinking on their knees, they kissed the sacred soil, which they only ventured to tread barefoot.

The greatest difficulties had still to be overcome. The number of the crusaders had diminished to one thousand five hundred horse and twenty thousand foot; the country around Jerusalem was an arid waste; the city was strongly garrisoned, and the harbor of Joppa, where a Genoese fleet had just landed troops, was strictly blockaded by the Egyptians. All communication with the sea was consequently cut off; the Genoese, however, abandoned their ships and advanced as far as Jerusalem, where their skill and handicraft materially assisted the knights in their rough attempts at scaling the walls. They manufactured different machines, particularly high towers, consisting of several stories, mounted on wheels, which were pushed close to the walls upon which the warriors were to mount. Most of these machines were destroyed by the inextinguishable "Greek fire." The pilgrims, in their enthusiasm, now recalled the fate of Jericho, and, ranged in solemn procession, chanting hymns, marched around the city, from whose walls they were, meanwhile, treated with every mark of indignity by the garrison. Peter the Hermit preached on the Mount of Olives, and the city had sustained a two days' storm, when a knight, clad in white armor, was beheld standing on the Mount of Olives, like an angel of God, encouraging them to battle in his cause.

The general enthusiasm now rose to fury, and two brethren, Ludolf and Engelbert, closely followed by Duke Godfred, were the first to mount the battlements; and the pilgrims rushing into the city, a deadly struggle took place in the streets, in which seventy thousand of the Mahometans were slain. The Jews were burned alive in their synagogue; no quarter was given. Every infidel, of whatever nation, age, or sex, was mercilessly killed. In the midst of this disorder, Godfred, in penitential garb and with unsandaled feet, threw himself on his knees before the holy sepulcher, and the rest of the crusaders, imitating his example, threw away their blood-stained weapons, and chanting penitential hymns, marched in procession through streams of blood to the grave of the Saviour of mankind. Jerusalem was taken on the 15th of July, 1099.[1]

The joy of united Christendom at this glorious liberation of the holy sepulcher was still further increased by the discovery of the wooden cross on which Christ had suffered. This cross owed its first discovery to St. Helena, the mother of Constantine the Great; it was afterward concealed during times of danger, and ultimately again lost. Godfred, the faithful hero of the church, was unanimously proclaimed king of Jerusalem; but, although he accepted the dignity, he refused to wear the golden diadem that was offered to him, saying, "that it was not for him to wear a crown of gold in the place where the Christ had worn one of thorns." His brother Baldwin became prince of Edessa. His other brother, Eustace, returned to Lothringia. Bohemund was already prince of Antioch; Tancred became count of Galilee. Raimund of Toulouse, who coveted the possession of Antioch, remained in Palestine, and aided the emperor Alexius in his attempts to undermine the power of the rest of the crusaders. Robert of Normandy returned home, and, falling into the hands of his faithless brother, Henry, ended his days in prison. Robert the Friscian also returned to his native country, but, while engaged in a feud, fell from his horse and was trodden to death. Tola, the wife of Baldwin von Hennegau, who had disappeared, made a pilgrimage to Jerusalem, and, after wandering in fruitless search of him over the half of Asia, reached her home in safety.

After giving laws, known as the ordonnances of the sepulcher, to his new kingdom, Godfred marched against his nearest and most threatening opponent, the caliph of Egypt, whom, although his superior in numbers, he defeated near Ascalon, which, but for the treachery of Raimund, would also have fallen into his hands. The city of Arsuf, on the sea-shore,

---

[1] William of Tyre relates in one of his legends that all the spirits of the crusaders who had fallen on the way appeared in the city on this occasion, and fulfilled their vow at the same time with their living comrades.

was shortly afterward taken,[1] and he received a fresh re-enforcement of twenty thousand Italians, who were led thither by Dagobert, archbishop of Pisa, who was probably secretly commissioned by the pope, as he was nominated patriarch of Jerusalem, and before long asserted the supremacy of the church over the throne. Bohemund, too weak to cope with his antagonists in Antioch, and betrayed by Raimund and the Greeks, was imprisoned by the sultan of Iconium; and, shortly after these events, Godfred expired, A.D. 1100. He was succeeded on the throne of Jerusalem by his brother Baldwin, who resigned Edessa to his cousin Baldwin de Bourg. The patriarch wished to place Bohemund, who had just been captured by the sultan of Iconium, on the throne, and Baldwin, opposed by intestinal factions and beset by the Turks,[2] with difficulty retained the scepter in his grasp. The glowing descriptions of the pilgrims who had returned from the Holy Land during the previous year to Germany and France, and the sacred relics they bore, had again roused the enthusiasm of the people to such a pitch that fresh crusades on a still more extensive scale, having for aim the extirpation of Islamism from the earth, were undertaken. Bagdad, the Turkish capital, was marked as the first object of attack.

The first great armament consisted of Lombards under

---

[1] Gerhard d'Avesnes, a Flemish knight, whose descendants reigned in Flanders, was here taken prisoner, and suspended on a cross over the walls, where he was exposed to the bolts of his besieging countrymen, whom he entreated to desist in their attempt; but being exhorted by Godfred to suffer martyrdom in honor of his Lord, who likewise suffered on the cross, he prepared for death, and was pierced by ten arrows. Some time after the conquest of Arsuf, he suddenly reappeared, alive and well. His wounds had not proved mortal, and his life had been saved by some compassionate Arabs.—Some of the wandering Arab tribes, attracted by the report of his extraordinary strength, visited Godfred, who, on one occasion, yielded to their importunity, and deprived some of their camels of their heads with one stroke of his sword; and on their expressing surprise at finding him, although a king, humbly seated on the bare ground, he replied, "The earth will be my tomb when I am dead, why then should it not serve me for a seat while I am alive?"

[2] The conquest of Cæsarea put the Genoese, who were among the crusaders, in possession of the emerald dish, supposed to be the identical one made use of by the Saviour at the last supper, and which, under the name of the Holy *Graal*, plays so important a part in the poetry of the Middle Ages.

Anselmo, archbishop of Milan, of French under Stephen of Blois, and of a little troop of Germans under Conrad, who is mentioned by the historians of the times as master of the horse (*stabularius*) to the emperor, Henry IV. This army reached Asia Minor in safety, and was joined by Raimund of Toulouse, who hoped by their aid to get possession of Antioch, which was defended by Tancred in the name of the imprisoned Bohemund; but Anselmo, impatient to carry out his plans for the reduction of Bagdad and the destruction of the Turkish empire, incautiously led his army, amounting to two hundred and sixty thousand men, into the burning deserts and amid the pathless mountains, where their footsteps were dogged by all the Mahometan princes of Asia Minor, who suddenly, when their numbers and strength were reduced by the heat and by famine, fell upon and cut them to pieces. Raimund, who had been nobly rescued from the Turks by Conrad, fled the moment he beheld his benefactor in danger. His example was followed by the Lombards and the French, who, in order to hinder pursuit, left their camp and women unprotected and at the mercy of the Turks, who thus added upward of a thousand females to their harems.— A second French crusade, under William, count of Nevers, consisting of fifteen thousand men, and an incredible number of women, followed on their footsteps, and, falling into a Turkish ambuscade, shared a similar fate. William of Nevers escaped and returned half-naked to Antioch.—A third and still more numerous body of French followed, commanded by Hugh, the king's brother, who was anxious to retrieve the dishonor of his former flight, and by William of Poitou, duke of Aquitania, a celebrated troubadour (*Minnesinger*) and defender of the sex, who drew in his train immense numbers of women of every rank. This crusade was joined on its passage through Germany by Reinhold, duke of Burgundy, the old Duke Welf of Bavaria, Dietrich (Thiemo), archbishop of Salzburg, the Margravine Ida of Austria, and numerous other Germans, among whom were many noble-born dames and maidens in the Margravine's suite.

This immense but helpless multitude reached Asia Minor, suffered the same hardships as their predecessors, and when about to rush into the river Halys, in order to assuage their thirst, was suddenly assailed by a shower of arrows; a dreadful confusion ensued, which terminated in flight. William of Poitou, the poet and defender of the sex, fled timidly away and abandoned his fair followers to their fate, while Hugh of France fought gallantly until wounded in the knee by an arrow. He escaped only to die of his wound. The archbishop, Thiemo,[1] was taken prisoner and tortured to death for refusing to embrace Islamism. Welf and Reinhold of Burgundy escaped, and the poor Margravine Ida and her women, abandoned by all their knights, were captured by the Turks. It is said that Ida afterward espoused a Turkish prince, and became the mother of the celebrated Zengis, the terror of Christendom,[2] A.D. 1101.—Reinhold of Burgundy died of a pestilence, and the aged Welf expired at Cyprus on his way home. The rest of the crusaders collected under the standard of Raimund of Toulouse, and took the city of Tortosa, where Raimund fixed himself. Conrad was almost the only one among the pilgrims who reached Jerusalem and fulfilled his vow. Thus disastrously terminated this great expedition, intended for the destruction and conquest of Asia.

Baldwin I. of Jerusalem was now, A.D. 1102, thrown upon his own resources. A battle took place between him and the Egyptians, near Rama, in which he was defeated, and the noble-hearted Gerhard d'Avesnes, who had so courageously resigned himself to a martyr's fate, lost his life. The king and the remainder of his army took refuge in

---

[1] He was celebrated as a sculptor and modeler.
[2] Itam comitissam, matrem Leopoldi, marchionis orientalis unus de principibus Saracenorum rapuit et impurissime sibi matrimonia copulavit, ex eaque sanguinem illum sceleratissimum, ut ajunt, progenuit.—*Monachus Weingartensis.* Other chroniclers record a similar legend. Ida, nevertheless, could not have been Leopold's mother, but merely his stepmother, as he was thirty years old at the time of this crusade. It is further certified by Eastern writers that Zengis was seventeen years of age, and his father, Casimeddaulah Acsonker, was dead at this very period.—See *Hormayr, The Bavarians in the East.*

Rama, where they could not long maintain themselves. Baldwin was saved by a grateful Arab, an emir, whose wife had fallen into Baldwin's hands, and, being taken in labor on the march, had been treated with the greatest care and kindness. The rest were either slain or taken prisoners. Conrad, who had prepared for his return home, could not refrain from joining the expedition against Rama; when that city was taken by the Arabs, he performed such prodigies of valor that the infidels, struck with wonder and admiration, offered him their hands in token of peace.[1] He was most honorably treated, and finally restored to liberty. The Egyptians did not follow up the advantage they had gained; fresh misfortunes were, however, in store for the Christians; a fleet, brought by the troubadour, William of Poitou, was shattered by a storm, and Baldwin was dangerously wounded with a lance by a Moorish spy. A quarrel broke out between Bohemund, who had escaped from prison,[2] and the Greeks, who wanted the possession of Antioch; causing a report of his death to be spread, he had himself borne in a coffin through the Grecian fleet that was on the watch, and collected a great army in the West for the conquest of the Grecian empire, in reality the only means of securing that of the Holy Land, but wasting his time and strength before Durazzo, a town he was unable to carry, his army disbanded, and he died broken-hearted, in his native city of Tarentum, A.D. 1105. The enterprising citizens of Genoa and Pisa, who, with the view of getting the whole of the trade of the East in their hands, had assisted the crusaders in the conquest of the maritime cities of Syria (anciently those of Phœnicia), were far more active and successful. In 1104, the Genoese already possessed the important town of Accon (Ptolemais). The siege of Tripolis, which had been commenced by Raimund of Toulouse, lasted for nearly ten years. In 1105, Raimund was besieged by

---

[1] Albertus Aquensis.
[2] By the secret aid of a princess, who had become deeply enamored of him. Another account is that he was exchanged for a princess who had been captured.

the Turks in his castle on the Pilgrim's Mountain, and was suffocated by the smoke of the burning houses. His son, Bertrand, swore to revenge his fate, and, assisted by the Genoese and Pisanese, laid siege to Tripolis, which finally fell into their hands in 1110; and an enormous library contained in this city was barbarously burned by the victors.[1] In the same year Sidon also fell. In this siege the crusaders were assisted by Sigmund Jorsalafar (Jerusalemfahrer, the traveler to Jerusalem), a youth of seventeen, of remarkable beauty, great-grandson of Harald Haardrade (who fell at Stamford), at the head of ten thousand gigantic Norwegians, armed with battle-axes.[2]—The Christians suffered repeated defeats in the interior of the country. The Turks of Bagdad now rose up against them, as the Egyptians had formerly done. Bohemund had scarcely escaped from prison, when Baldwin of Edessa was taken prisoner. Tancred defended Antioch and Edessa with wonderful perseverance and bravery. He died in 1112; on his death-bed he placed the hand of his wife, Cecilia, a daughter of the French king, in that of the youthful Pontius, who had succeeded his father Bertrand in the government of Tripolis. The following year Baldwin suffered a fresh defeat, but was rescued by Roger of Sicily, who governed Antioch in the name of the youthful Bohemund, the son of Bohemund I. Peace, only interrupted by slight disturbances, endured for a while. Baldwin I. died in 1118, and was succeeded by Baldwin de Bourg, his cousin, formerly prince of Edessa, who had not long before

---

[1] The destruction of the great Christian library at Alexandria, by the caliph Omar, caused a great outcry among the Christians, who, on taking Tripoli, finding that the first room in the library merely contained Korans, burned the whole library, which contained three hundred thousand books, without inquiring what the rest of the rooms contained. It is probable that many ancient Greek works lay here concealed.

[2] The Norwegians still retained so strong an impression of their ancient religion that, on entering the hippodrome at Constantinople, they believed that the Grecian statues, with which it was adorned, were intended to represent their Asen and legendary heroes—*Snorri.* Shortly before this, Erich the Good (Evegod) made a pilgrimage to the holy sepulcher; he expired at Cyprus, A.D. 1105. The origin of his pilgrimage was curious: a singer, who had the power of rousing every passion by his art, had excited him to such a pitch of fury (Verserkerwuth) that he slew several people, whose death he afterward resolved to expiate.

been restored to liberty. In 1119, Roger fell, opposing the Turks; in 1123, Baldwin II. was again imprisoned by the Turks; in 1124, a great Venetian fleet arrived, and seized the beautiful harbor and city of Tyre, which the Venetians coveted on account of its commercial advantages. Bohemund II. fell in battle. Baldwin regained his liberty upon certain conditions, but was no sooner free than he broke his oath, and was ceaselessly engaged in petty warfare until his death, in 1131. During his reign, two orders of knighthood were formed in Jerusalem; the Hospitalers of St. John, who at first merely devoted themselves to the care of the sick, and the knights of Solomon's Temple, or Templars, who were bound by the vow of celibacy, exercised a spiritual office, and devoted themselves to unceasing warfare against the infidels, in which they were afterward imitated by the knights of St. John. Both of these orders were filled by Italian knights, the Germans taking but little part in them. Unfortunately for the Holy Land, by far the greater part of the foreign settlers were French, the Germans merely making a crusade thither, and returning to their native country.

The crusades were not without influence in Europe; the power of the pope, the earthly representative of the God before whom all the kings and nations of the West bent in humble adoration, and that of the church founded by Gregory VII., were rendered absolute by their means; while the church was enriched by the immense wealth of those who fell in the East: still, the change they gradually wrought, by the introduction of new plants and animals, new modes of dress, luxuries and manners, the novel and surprising tenets and writings of the Greeks and Arabs, tended so greatly to enlarge and enlighten the ideas of the western nations, as, at a later period, to endanger the authority assumed by the popes.

END OF VOLUME ONE

www.ingramcontent.com/pod-product-compliance
Lightning Source LLC
Chambersburg PA
CBHW051853300426
44117CB00006B/374